T0373186

DUMBARTON OAKS
MEDIEVAL LIBRARY

Jan M. Ziolkowski, General Editor

THE POEMS OF

CHRISTOPHER OF MYTILENE

AND JOHN MAUROPOUS

DOML 50

DUMBARTON OAKS MEDIEVAL LIBRARY

Jan M. Ziolkowski, General Editor
Alice-Mary Talbot, Byzantine Greek Editor

Byzantine Greek Editorial Board
Alexander Alexakis
Maximos Constas
John Duffy
Niels Gaul
Richard Greenfield
Anthony Kaldellis
Derek Krueger
Stratis Papaioannou
Claudia Rapp

Byzantine Greek Advisory Board

Albrecht Berger
Wolfram Brandes
Elizabeth Fisher
Clive Foss
John Haldon
Robert Jordan

Antony Littlewood
Margaret Mullett
Jan Olof Rosenqvist
Jonathan Shepard
Denis Sullivan
John Wortley

The Poems of Christopher of Mytilene and John Mauropous

Edited and Translated by

FLORIS BERNARD

and

CHRISTOPHER LIVANOS

DUMBARTON OAKS
MEDIEVAL LIBRARY

HARVARD UNIVERSITY PRESS
CAMBRIDGE, MASSACHUSETTS
LONDON, ENGLAND
2018

Copyright © 2018 by the President and Fellows of Harvard College
ALL RIGHTS RESERVED
Printed in the United States of America

Library of Congress Cataloging-in-Publication Data
Names: Bernard, Floris, editor, translator. | Livanos, Christopher, editor,
translator. | Container of (expression): Christophoros, ho Mytilēnaios.
Poems. Selections. | Container of (expression): Christophoros, ho
Mytilēnaios. Poems. Selections. English. | Container of (expression):
John, Mauropus, Metropolitan of Euchaita, active 11th century. Poems.
Selections. | Container of (expression): John, Mauropus, Metropolitan of
Euchaita, active 11th century. Poems. Selections. English.
    Title: The poems of Christopher of Mytilene and John Mauropous /
edited and translated by Floris Bernard and Christopher Livanos.
    Other titles: Dumbarton Oaks medieval library ; 50.
    Description: Cambridge, Massachusetts : Harvard University Press,
2018. | Series: Dumbarton Oaks medieval library ; 50 | Texts in Greek with
English translations on facing pages ; introduction and notes in English. |
Includes bibliographical references.
    Identifiers: LCCN 2017036966 | ISBN 9780674736986 (alk. paper)
    Subjects: LCSH: Byzantine poetry—Translations into English. |
Byzantine poetry.
    Classification: LCC PA5189.E5 P64 2018 | DDC 881/.0208 — dc23
LC record available at https://lccn.loc.gov/2017036966

Contents

Introduction

It is a natural choice to place the Byzantine poets Christopher of Mytilene and John Mauropous together in one volume. Although they never explicitly refer to each other, they write about the same time period, the same places, the same persons, also largely sharing the same style, genres, and intellectual profile. Their poems display a sense of wit and a personal voice that is rarely encountered in Byzantine poetry. They bear eminent witness to the eventful times they lived in and provide a vivid image of contemporary court life and of the city of Constantinople.[1]

In the most important manuscripts that transmit their poetry, both collections are entitled "various verses" *(stichoi diaphoroi)*. This points to one of the most obvious and important features of their poetry: its diversity. Both Christopher's and Mauropous's collections reflect the poetic achievements of the entire span of their careers, offering a series of records of successive occasions. As a result, the poems are written for a wide range of addressees, vary greatly in length, and comprise many different genres, such as epigram, epitaph, satire, encomium, didactic, autobiography, and polemics, alongside many poems hard to pinpoint in a generic grid.

Both poets began their careers in the fourth decade of

the eleventh century, attaining the zenith of their social influence and intellectual radiance during the reign of Constantine IX Monomachos (r. 1042–1055). After that, they continued to write, but their works lost their close connection to developments in the capital. An account of these middle decades of the eleventh century will thus facilitate understanding of the historical context of their work.

THE MID-ELEVENTH CENTURY

The mid-eleventh century was a time of instability and change in social hierarchies.[2] While the Macedonian dynasty (867–1056) was nominally still in place, the succession to the throne continued now through marriage rather than filial lineage, and was increasingly dependent on usurpation, intrigues, and informal networks. Romanos III Argyros was an official before he gained the throne in 1028, and Michael IV gained power in 1034 as a result of the intrigues engineered by his family, which in 1042 culminated in the bloody popular revolt that deposed his nephew Michael V. Just like Romanos III and Michael IV, Constantine IX Monomachos, the most important emperor of these decades, ascended the throne by marrying Constantine VIII's daughter Zoe, who was, together with her sister, Theodora, the last scion of the famous Macedonian dynasty. Official imperial communications (among which are the poems in this volume) often represented Constantine together with his two coempresses, as an imperial triad.

Monomachos distributed offices and honors more freely than ever before, coinciding with a period of economic prosperity. This resulted in a remarkable social mobility, which especially benefited a group of nonaristocratic people who based their power on bureaucratic functions, social networks at court, and education. This so-called "civil elite" of Constantinopolitan officials and courtiers, which included our two poets, distinguished itself from more traditional power groups, such as the land-owning aristocracy and the military. Culturally, this class defined itself at least to some degree in opposition to monastic ideals; it valued sociability, elegance, and refined urban culture. Above all, members of this elite venerated a concept called *hoi logoi* (letters), which encompassed everything related to learning and education, including rhetorical skills. Education became a cornerstone of social success. There were several schools in Constantinople, offering primarily (but not exclusively) grammatical and rhetorical education. These schools operated on an independent basis, little influenced by imperial or ecclesiastical structures, although Monomachos was keen to centralize legal studies: he founded a law school and engaged Mauropous to write its foundation document (the *Neara*).

These decades witnessed a renewed interest in secular learning and sophisticated writing, chiefly exemplified by the varied works of Michael Psellos, the dominant intellectual figure of the time.[3] Many fields of knowledge became the subject of study, commentary, and compilation, mostly in the context of education: theology, philosophy, law, exact sciences, history, rhetoric, literary criticism, and so on. Rhetorical writing flourished, with the emperors (especially Constantine IX Monomachos) emerging as the most important patrons. At the same time, some people took other directions than those of the intellectual elite. Niketas Stethatos, promoting the cult of his hero Symeon the New Theologian (d. 1022), defended a very personal strand of religious thinking, valuing mystical experience and denouncing formal theology.[4] The author Kekaumenos (living slightly later than our poets) defended traditional military and familial values and was highly suspicious of the court milieus in the capital.[5] These decades also witnessed the formidable figure of the patriarch Michael I Keroularios (1043–1058), who was supported by a populist faction in the capital, and whose stubborn resistance to papal envoys ultimately resulted in the Great Schism in 1054.

CHRISTOPHER OF MYTILENE

Most information about Christopher has come to us through his own poems.[6] This is supplemented by notices in the manuscripts and one seal, both of which provide information only about his bureaucratic functions. Christopher was born in Constantinople around the year 1000. His surname Mitylenaios (sic; as attested on his personal seals) is a family name and does not refer to his own origin. The designation "of Mytilene" is therefore something of a misnomer but is his standard appellation in modern Anglophone scholarship. The earliest datable reference in his poems is to the death of Romanos III Argyros in 1034. He was connected to the court of Michael IV and his brothers, for whom he wrote an encomium. He was in contact with Constantine IX Monomachos as well, but also composed one rather sympathetic poem (possibly two) on the death of the rebel George Maniakes in 1043. This is the last firmly datable historical reference, although he probably continued to write in subsequent decades, since the reference to Maniakes occurs only one-third of the way through his poetry collection, which is chronologically ordered. Christopher bore the high honorific titles of *patrikios* and *protospatharios* and held the important office of judge of the *velum,* a high tribunal in Constantinople. He was also a *krites* (judge and administrator) in several provinces. When presenting himself in one poem (114), he hinted that people might know him as an imperial secretary.

As far as we are aware, Christopher wrote only metrical texts. Besides his *Various Verses,* he composed four calendars in four different meters (two in hymnographical meters, one in dactylic hexameters, and one, the longest, in dodecasyllables).[7] These calendars, very popular in Byzantine times, enumerate day by day every saint and feast of the year, chiefly describing all the ways in which the saints were martyred. The calendars in dodecasyllables and hexameters were incorporated into the *Menaia,* liturgical books for daily service of the Orthodox Church.

The popularity of Christopher's calendars is in marked contrast to his *Various Verses.* Only one manuscript transmits the collection in its entirety: *Grottaferrata* Z.α.XXIX, which was copied in the thirteenth century, in a milieu of Greek-speaking poets in southern Italy. This manuscript is heavily damaged, because, as Christopher himself seems to have foreseen in poem 103, mice ate away at the book. As often in Byzantine manuscripts, the verse lines were laid out in two columns, to be read from left to right. Since the lacunas often extend over more or less one column, in many poems every other verse is lost. Fortunately, there are some Byzantine poetic anthologies that include dispersed poems of Christopher (mostly not, or wrongly, attributed), which help to reconstruct the complete text. Nevertheless, the poems transmitted only in the Grottaferrata manuscript remain in their sorry state.

This manuscript probably reflects faithfully the way in which Christopher envisioned his collection.[8] The main principle of ordering is chronological, but some cycles of poems cluster around one event, mostly the death of a family member. Also, it appears that Christopher strove to achieve as much variation as possible in the sequence of his poems.

Christopher's poetry shows ample attention to the city of Constantinople.[9] Many epigrams have specific buildings and churches in the capital as their subject. The feverish intellectual life of the city is reflected in poems that address the rivalry between the independent Constantinopolitan schools, a competition in which Christopher favored the school of Saint Theodore of Sphorakiou. He also shows a great attachment to his own neighborhood of Protasiou, mentioning it twice in pamphlets against rivals. He describes in great detail events that take place in the city, such as religious festivals, horse races, and processions. His collection also bears witness to the great historical events of his time, such as the suspicious death of Romanos III Argyros and the violent deposition of Michael V. Numerous poems are devoted to the deaths of family members, expressing personal grief and offering consolation. For his sister and his mother he composed cycles consisting of several poems, each addressing a successive stage of the funeral and consolatory process. Satire and invective receive a prominent place in Christopher's collection.[10] He upbraids presumptuous intellectuals, gluttonous monks, greedy officials, arrogant doctors, illiterate priests, and so forth. On the other hand, he writes many poems dedicated to friends, celebrating their shared devotion to letters. His collection includes (rather uniquely) personal narrative anecdotes. We also find some remarkable poems that describe and praise wondrous works of nature. Finally, Christopher might be the author of a long hexametric poem on the death of Maniakes that is absent from the Grottaferrata collection and not included in this volume.[11]

JOHN MAUROPOUS

Born around the year 1000, John Mauropous came to the capital from Paphlagonia, a remote eastern province on the southern coast of the Black Sea.[12] He seems to have subsequently acquired a reputation as a teacher; Michael Psellos was his most famous pupil. He gained access to the court of Constantine IX Monomachos, probably through Psellos, with whom he maintained a lifelong, if sometimes troubled, friendship, evidenced in many letters.[13] Enjoying the favor of Constantine and the coempresses Zoe and Theodora, Mauropous composed and pronounced orations at important official occasions and wrote the text of the *Neara,* a foundation document for a law school connected to Constantine's foundation of the monastery of Saint George of Mangana.

This blissful period came to an end when Mauropous was appointed as metropolitan of Euchaïta in northern Anatolia. This event, a watershed in his life, likely occurred around 1050. From several sources (notably letters of both Mauropous and Psellos), we know that this appointment, technically a promotion, was in fact experienced by Mauropous as a forced exile. We can only guess at the exact reasons for Mauropous's removal from the capital. Euchaïta was a fairly insignificant city in Pontos, mainly known as a pilgrimage site of the military saint Theodore Teron.[14] Mauropous continued to write for official and liturgical occasions there, while lobbying for a return to the capital. This eventually succeeded around 1075, and Mauropous spent the last years of his life at the monastery of Saint John Prodromos tes Petras in Constantinople. Mauropous's name is also connected to the institution of the Feast of the Three Hierarchs.[15] The date of his death is unknown.

Mauropous's various verses, as well as his letters and orations, are transmitted in the manuscript *Vaticanus graecus* 676. This extraordinary manuscript is now believed to be the copy authorized and sanctioned by Mauropous himself, his so-called master copy (but probably not his autograph).[16] Impeccably written and carefully arranged, this book faithfully reflects the way Mauropous wanted his "collected works" to appear. Presenting a selection of texts that Mauropous wrote through the course of his life, it represents his literary and intellectual legacy. This aspect is emphasized by several poetic prefaces and a poem written by his secretary at the end of the manuscript. All later manuscripts are dependent on the Vaticanus, which is also the sole basis of Lagarde's standard modern edition.

Mauropous's prose orations include homilies for the Virgin Mary and several saints. He also wrote victory speeches when Monomachos defeated the rebel Leo Tornikios and the Pechenegs, as well as orations in the imperial presence on other important occasions. These speeches emphasize the pacific character of Monomachos's reign. The orations from Euchaïta are written for important liturgical feasts, including the feast of Saint Theodore. Mauropous's seventy-seven letters reflect his teaching activities and his powerful position at court, but also his imminent departure from the capital. The latter part of the collection of his correspondence are letters of exile written from Euchaïta, deploring the conditions there and pleading for his recall.[17]

Besides the works transmitted in the *Vaticanus graecus* 676, Mauropous composed numerous liturgical hymns (so-called *kanones*), most of them for the Virgin Mary and Christ, but also for a series of saints.[18] Mauropous's name is also connected to a long didactic poem about etymology.

The *Various Verses* of Mauropous are arranged according to a carefully premeditated plan. The collection achieves a symmetrical effect because certain recognizable genres mirror each other. A poetic preface with dedication is followed by a cycle of religious epigrams on Christian feasts, prophets, and saints, corresponding to the complete iconographical program of a church (poems 2–26). The next section consists of polemical works, prefaces to his own works, funeral elegies for friends, and a notable pair of autobiographical pieces (47–48) on the forced abandonment, and then the recovery, of his house.[19] Throughout this section, the presence of the emperor makes itself more and more felt, culminating in the longest poem of the collection (54), addressed to Monomachos upon Mauropous's entrance at court. This is followed by another long imperial encomium, this time for the two coempresses, and a series of poems dedicated to several imperial patronage projects, for books, icons, gifts to monasteries, and so on. Then the reader encounters some more miscellaneous poems, in which Mauropous clearly shows himself to be a self-conscious and authoritative intellectual figure. Mauropous next returns to the funeral genre, this time for the emperor, very probably Constantine Monomachos, who shows his repentance in the face of death. Poems 89 to 93 form a series of autobiographical pieces, related to the genre of poems *eis heauton* (to himself), introspective dialogues between reason and soul. These poems treat the theme of the tension between worldly ambition and the desire for seclusion from the world, as well as the moral status of intellectual pursuits, a recurring theme through many of Mauropous's works. The threat against his desire for tranquility is gradually identified as Mauropous's appointment as a metropolitan, which is represented as taking place between the writing of poems 92 and 93 (the latter being a recantation of the former). The collection closes with some shorter pieces justifying the works he wrote or abandoned writing.

Formal Features of the Poems

The linguistic register of Christopher and Mauropous is learned Greek, but not overly sophisticated or archaizing. It did not deviate significantly from codified grammatical rules of ancient (Attic) Greek, nor did it allow too much novel vocabulary, although some traits and words from vernacular Greek are recognizable. Its rather straightforward syntax (especially compared to contemporary prose) ensured that it was readily understandable to any educated Byzantine.

The dodecasyllable was the meter of choice for both Christopher and Mauropous. This meter had developed from the iambic trimeter, and had by now achieved its standard Byzantine form. It combined two metrical principles. First, it inherited the prosodic structure of the ancient iambic trimeter, based on the alternation between long and short syllables. Although this had no relevance anymore to the medieval ear, poets of some intellectual prestige (including Christopher and Mauropous), maintained the pretense that they were writing "iambs" as of old and kept the prosodic structure intact (with some concessions). Second, in line with general evolutions in European meter from early medieval times, the dodecasyllable had a fixed number of syllables (twelve) and a rhythmical pattern, of which the most striking feature is the obligatory stress on the penultimate syllable. Their dodecasyllables are thus a remarkable mix of intellectual artificiality and living aural reality.

Unlike Mauropous, who uses dodecasyllables exclusively, Christopher occasionally dabbles in the archaizing meters of Homeric poetry and much postclassical and early Byzantine poetry: dactylic hexameters, elegiac distichs, and, in one case (poem 75), anacreontics. In these poems, he uses a highly artificial language that attempts to imitate Homeric diction, complete with Ionic morphology and obsolete words. These poems are riddled with many literal quotations from the Homeric poems. This does not exclude, however, the intrusion of many later words and expressions.

This poetry rests upon nearly two thousand years of Greek literary tradition. Both poets are familiar with classical sources without being derivative, apart perhaps from instances in Christopher's Homeric imitations. The major sources of classical allusions in Mauropous are Pindar and Euripides. Gregory of Nazianzos was a great model for John Mauropous, especially for his ideas on meter and self-introspection. The majority of quotations and other references comes from the Bible, especially the psalms and gospels. Christopher in particular also often quotes popular proverbs. The poetry of Christopher and Mauropous presupposes acquaintance with ancient mythology and history, and a thorough familiarity with biblical stories, alongside the spiritual lore of saints and their lives and attributes.

Genres and Occasions

The *Various Verses* of both our poets appear to be composed for specific occasions that are firmly embedded in real-life situations. This holds true especially for the epigrams. Mostly, these are so-called religious epigrams, having as their subject an important Christian feast, a saint, or a biblical scene. In nearly every case, the epigrams deal in fact with an image and not primarily with the religious subject *in abstracto:* they are intended to be inscribed on representations of religious subjects, such as icons, frescoes, or miniatures in manuscripts (although none of Christopher's or Mauropous's *Various Verses* has survived in inscriptional form).[20] In some cases, the lemma specifies the form, material, or physical location of the representation. The epigrams themselves often address the viewer, admire the skills of the artist, abound with expressions such as "is represented as," and contain concrete physical references to the representation, such as "here," "this image," and the like. These religious epigrams reflect devotion to a wide range of saints, the angels, and the Virgin Mary. They conform to the standard theological views of the time. In many cases (especially Mauropous), the epigrams are connected to imperial patronage. Both poetry collections also pay special attention to relics, although one remarkable poem by Christopher (poem 114) shows itself critical of overly credulous use of them. A special case are book epigrams, present in both collections: these are epigrams meant to be written in a manuscript, but distinct from the main text it contains. They are mostly closely connected to the production and patronage of a specific manuscript. Both poets also wrote epigrams (or prefaces) for their own works.

Both Christopher and Mauropous are themselves emphatically present in their own works. Their self-assertive voices come especially to the fore in the polemical and invective poems. On repeated occasions, our poets show themselves prepared to defend the value of their poetic achievements and their status as prominent intellectuals. They also attack people who, in their opinion, make improper use of their poems. Mauropous in particular carefully crafted a persona that earned him sympathy also in modern times.

Their poems are often witty, displaying a tendency for satire and ridicule. Wordplay is ubiquitous. Christopher's puns are often intended for humorous effect, whereas Mauropous brings into play the double meanings of highly charged terms such as *logos* and *metron*.

Both poets lavish praise on reigning emperors, showing themselves loyal to the imperial regime and faithfully echoing official imperial propaganda. Yet, there may be some hints of criticism in a few of Christopher's poems (notably poem 8, also critical of the ruling elite in general). Curiously,

Christopher and Mauropous seem not to have known each other; in any case, they do not refer to each other in their poems.

THE TRANSLATION

This is the first English translation of these two collections. The only existing complete translations are in Italian, in publications now difficult to access.[21] Our main goal was to provide a readable and understandable text for the modern reader. Technical terms (especially names of offices) are often translated instead of transliterated, which admittedly sometimes results in slightly anachronistic terminology (thus, χαρτοφύλαξ becomes "master of archives" instead of *chartophylax*). Classical names have been rendered in a Latinized form, and Late Antique and Byzantine names are strictly transliterated from the Greek, with the exception of common names like John and Michael. We have attempted to reflect the fluent, sometimes almost colloquial style of the original. It was not always possible to reflect the many puns and wordplays in Greek, so we often had to resort to an indication in the notes. These notes are primarily meant to help the reader to understand the text, not as a learned commentary. As a result, most bibliographic references relate to the standard reference works and do not exhaustively list all existing scholarship. Psalm texts are referenced with Septuagint numbering first (using the Rahlfs edition); between parentheses the reader will find the numbering as common in Western tradition. Classical texts are cited in the edition of the Loeb Classical Library.

The lacunas in Christopher's Greek text required some

exceptional interventions (see also Notes to the Texts). Ellipses in the Greek text indicate a lacuna in the manuscript, for which no plausible reconstruction is possible. In the translation, words between angle brackets < > are added to clarify the approximate meaning, but there is no extant Greek equivalent, neither in the manuscript nor in editorial conjectures.

Even the most profuse acknowledgments cannot do justice to the enormous amount of time, acumen, and erudition that Alice-Mary Talbot and Stratis Papaioannou invested in this project. Both of them intervened in the many successive stages of preparation. They kept us from making silly errors, offered ideas on interpretations of specific poems (to some of which we agreed only after futile reluctance), and polished the final translation. Moreover, Alice-Mary Talbot repeatedly revitalized this project when it seemed to have bogged down, so we should thank her for her patience and unwavering confidence. Thanks are due also to John Zaleski and Jake Ransohoff, Tyler Fellows at Dumbarton Oaks from 2016 to 2018, who helped to prepare this volume for the press. Finally, we are grateful to Dumbarton Oaks Library and Research Collection for granting us a DOML Short Residency Research Stay.

NOTES

1 For their poetry in a wider literary and historical context, see Paul Magdalino, "Cultural Change? The Context of Byzantine Poetry from Geometres to Prodromos," in *Poetry and Its Contexts,* ed. Bernard and Demoen, 19–36, and Bernard, *Writing and Reading.*

2 See Michael Angold, *The Byzantine Empire, 1025–1204. A Political History* (London/New York, 1997); Alexander Kazhdan and Ann Wharton Epstein, *Change in Byzantine Culture from the Eleventh to the Twelfth Centuries* (Berkeley, 1985). On education and intellectual culture, see also Lemerle, *Cinq études.*

3 Stratis Papaioannou, *Michael Psellos: Rhetoric and Authorship in Byzantium* (Cambridge/New York, 2013).

4 Richard Greenfield, trans., *Niketas Stethatos. The Life of Saint Symeon the New Theologian,* Dumbarton Oaks Medieval Library 20 (Cambridge, Mass., 2013).

5 Paolo Odorico, *Conseils et récits d'un gentilhomme byzantin: Kékaumenos* (Toulouse, 2015).

6 For Christopher, see the introduction in De Groote, *Christophori Mitylenaii Versuum variorum collectio.*

7 See Follieri, *I calendari.*

8 On the arrangement of Christopher's collection, see Demoen, "Phrasis poikilê."

9 See Nikolaos Oikonomides, "Life and Society in Eleventh Century Constantinople," *Südost-Forschungen* 49 (1990): 1–19.

10 See Livanos, "Justice, Equality and Dirt."

11 Matteo Broggini, "Il carme Εἰς τὸν Μανιάκην περὶ τοῦ μούλτου attribuito al Cristoforo Mitileneo," *Porphyra* 15 (2011): 14–34.

12 On Mauropous, see Karpozilos, Συμβολή, and somewhat more succinctly the introduction in Karpozilos, *Letters.*

13 Lauxtermann, "Intertwined Lives."

14 John Haldon, *A Tale of Two Saints: The Martyrdoms and Miracles of Saints Theodore 'the Recruit' and 'the General'* (Liverpool, 2016).

15 See notes to his poem 17.

16 Bianconi, "Piccolo assaggio."

17 Karpozilos, *Letters.*

18 Francesco D'Aiuto, *Tre canoni di Giovanni Mauropode in onore di santi militari* (Rome, 1994).

19 Livanos, "Exile and Return."

20 See Andreas Rhoby, *Byzantinische Epigramme in inschriftlicher Überlieferung* (Vienna, 2009–), of which three volumes have been published.

21 Crimi, *Cristoforo di Mitilene. Canzoniere,* and Anastasi, *Giovanni Mauropode, Canzoniere.* See also Crimi, "Recuperi cristoforei," 231–42.

THE POEMS OF
CHRISTOPHER
OF MYTILENE

I

Εἰς τὴν ἑορτὴν τοῦ ἁγίου Θωμᾶ, παρόντος καὶ τοῦ
... δόντος αὐτήν

Ὦ θαῦμα, Θωμᾶ, θαύματος παντὸς πέρα·
πανήγυρις σὴ τὴν φύσιν τῶν ἀπτέρων
δίχα πτερῶν ἔδειξεν ἐπτερωμένην,
νικῶσαν ὄντως καὶ πτερωτὰ τῷ δρόμῳ.
5 Τὸ πρᾶγμα θροῦς ἦν, οὐχ ἑορτῆς ἡμέρα,
πάντων τρεχόντων ἐν μέσῳ τῶν ἐμβόλων,
πάντων τρεχόντων ἐν μέσῳ τῶν διαύλων,
περισκοπούντων εἰς σκέπην τὰς γωνίας,
πληγαῖς τε πολλαῖς τραυματισθέντων σφόδρα
10 καὶ πρὸς τὸ καινὸν ἐκπεπληγμένων ἅμα.
Τούτων ὁ μὲν προύκειτο τῆς λεωφόρου,
ὁ δὲ τρέχων ἔπιπτε προσπταίων πέτραις·
ἦν ἄλλος ἡμίφλεκτος ἐκ τῶν λαμπάδων,
κηροσταλακτόκαυτος ἄλλος τὰς τρίχας,
15 ἄλλων κατεφλέχθησαν αἱ γενειάδες·
καί τις βαδίζων καὶ προΐσχων λαμπάδα
τυφθεὶς βαρείαις χερσὶν ὀμφαλοῦ μέσον

I

On the feast of Saint Thomas,
in the presence of also the person who
. . . the feast

A wonder, Thomas, a wonder beyond wonders!
Your feast has shown the nature of the wingless
as winged, and without any wings at that!
In their run, men outstripped even birds.
The thing was more a brawl than a festival: 5
everyone running in the midst of the porticoes,
everyone running in the midst of the passages,
looking around for cover in the corners,
or gravely wounded with many injuries,
taken aback by the unusual events.   10
One of them lay in front of the avenue,
another ran, stumbled over the stones and fell,
another one was half burned by the torches,
another's hair was scorched by dripping candles,
and others got their beards consumed by fire.   15
Somebody else walked by, holding a torch,
and, hit by heavy hands right in the navel,

ῥίψας ἐκείνην ἐκράτει τὴν γαστέρα·
ἄλλος δὲ χεῖρα συντριβεὶς ἐδυσφόρει,
20 "ὦ θεῖε Θωμᾶ," τῷ Θεοῦ μύστῃ λέγων,
"πίστευσον· ἀλγῶ καὶ σιωπᾶν οὐκ ἔχω·
ἂν οὖν ἀπιστῇς, καὶ τὸ τοῦ Χριστοῦ λέγω·
'τὸν σὸν νοητῶς ὧδε δάκτυλον φέρε
καὶ χεῖρα βλέψας τὴν ἐμὴν πιστὸς γίνου.'"
25 Ὑπῆρξε τοίνυν πᾶσιν ἡ ψαλμῳδία,
εἰ χρή τι λέξαι πρόσφορον, ῥαβδῳδία,
ὡς πάντας αὐτοὺς τὴν Ἰὼβ φωνὴν λέγειν·
"εἰς κλαυθμὸν ἡμῖν ψαλμὸς ἡμῶν ἐξέβη."
Ἀγράμματος δὲ πανθεώτης τις γέρων
30 ῥαβδοῦχος ἦν ὄπισθεν ἐκβοῶν μέγα,
καὶ πεζολεκτῶν ὡς ἄπειρος γραμμάτων
ἔφασκεν αὐτοῖς· "ὡς κελεύετε, ψίχα."
Οὗτοι δὲ τοῦτο συχνὸν ἠνωτισμένοι
ἔφευγον εὐθὺς τοῦ μέλους λελησμένοι
35 καὶ συντριβὴν κλαίουσι τῶν μελῶν ἔτι.

2

Εἰς τὸν χαρτουλάριον Σολομῶντα

"Εἰ μὴ γένησθε," φησίν, "ὡς τὰ παιδία,
οὐ μὴ τύχητε τῆς ἄνω κληρουχίας,"

he threw the torch away to clutch his belly.
Another, whose hand was crushed, in agony
spoke out to God's disciple: "Divine Thomas,   20
believe me: I am in pain and I can't be silent.
And if you doubt me, I say what Christ said:
'*Put your finger here,* in a spiritual way,
behold my hand, and become a believer.'"
On the lips of all was a psalmody,   25
or should I say bludgeon-ody,
so that they all exclaimed Job's words:
"Our song has been turned into weeping."
And then, a certain old illiterate guardsman,
holding a staff behind them, loudly yelled,   30
and pedestrianly, as one unacquainted with letters,
kept saying to them: "Please, a crumb for me!"
The people, after hearing this go on,
immediately took flight. They forgot the song,
but still mourn the battering of their limbs.   35

2

On the archivist Solomon

"*Unless,*" he said, "*you become like little children,*
you will not inherit the kingdom of heaven."

ὁ Χριστὸς εἶπεν ἐν λόγοις εὐαγγέλοις.
Θάρσει, Σολομῶν, ἐν Κρίσει ταύτης τύχης·
5 φρονεῖς γὰρ ἧττον καὶ βρεφῶν καὶ παιδίων,
κἂν κλῆσιν αὐχῇς τοῦ φρονοῦντος εἰς ἄκρον.

3

Εἰς τὴν Βάπτισιν τοῦ Χριστοῦ· ἡρωϊκά

Μίγνυται ὧδε ἄμικτα, φύσις φλογόεσσα καὶ ὑγρά,
πῦρ θεότητος ἄϋλον Ἰορδάνου τε ῥέεθρα.

4

Εἰς τὸν μοναχὸν τὸν Μουρζοὺλ σιωπῶντα

Σιγᾷς, πάτερ βέλτιστε, μηδέν μοι γράφων;
Εὖ δρᾷς, σιώπα· καὶ γὰρ ἐξ ἐπωνύμου
ἄφωνος ἰχθὺς καὶ δοκεῖς καὶ τυγχάνεις.

6

These are the words that Christ spoke in the gospels.
So fear not, Solomon; at Judgment, that will be your lot.
For you are less wise than even infants and children,   5
although you boast of the name of the eminently wise man.

3

On the Baptism of Christ; hexameters

What cannot be mingled is mingled here: the fiery with the
    fluid natures,
the immaterial fire of divinity with the streams of the
    Jordan.

4

On the monk Mourzoul, who kept silent

You keep silent, my good father, and write me nothing?
You do the right thing. Keep silent. For also by your surname
you seem to be, and are, a voiceless fish.

5

Εἰς τὸν ἅγιον Συμεὼν τὸν Στυλίτην

Παρ' ἀγγέλους τὶ μικρόν, ὦ Θεοῦ Λόγε,
ἄνθρωπον ἠλάττωσας, ὡς Δαυὶδ λέγει·
ὁ Συμεὼν ἤλεγξεν ἐκ τῶν πραγμάτων,
δείξας ἑαυτὸν βελτίω τῶν ἀγγέλων.

6

Εἰς τὸν ἡνίοχον Ἰεφθάε,
πεσόντα εἰς τὸν Χρυσόν

Σὸν ἅρμα χάρμα καὶ γέλως, Ἰεφθάε,
κεῖται πρὸ χρυσῶν ὀργάνων ἐρριμμένον,
ἃ θαυμάσαιμ' ἂν Ὀρφικῆς λύρας πλέον·
καὶ γὰρ σιγῶντα καὶ μέλους πεπαυμένα
5 ἵππους δύνανται καὶ τροχοὺς ἕλκειν ἅμα,
ναὶ μὴν σὺν αὐτοῖς καὶ τὸν ἁρματηλάτην.
Οὐ ταῦτα κρείττω καὶ λύρας τῆς Ὀρφέως;
Ἡ μὲν γὰρ εἷλκε πάντα κρούμασι ξένοις,
τῶν δ' ὀργάνων νῦν ἡ δυὰς τῶν χρυσέων

8

5

On Saint Symeon the Stylite

A little *lower than angels,* O Word of God,
you have created man, as David says.
Symeon has refuted this by his deeds,
showing himself to be better than the angels.

6

On Jephtha the charioteer,
who crashed in the Golden Hippodrome

Your chariot causes laughter and amusement, Jephtha,
as it lies toppled over before the golden organs,
which I could admire more than Orpheus's lyre;
for, though silent and having ceased their tune,
they have the power to attract horses and wheels,   5
and yes, together with them, the charioteer.
Are these not better than Orpheus's lyre?
While it attracted all things with wondrous sounds,
now this pair of golden organs

10 τέθριππον ἕλκει τοῦτο κρουμάτων δίχα.
    Πλὴν εἴ τι πείθῃ τοῖς ἐμοῖς αὐτὸς λόγοις,
    τοὺς σοὺς χαλινοὺς τοῖς στρέφουσιν εὖ πάρες,
    σαυτῷ δὲ τέχνην εἰς ἀφορμὴν τοῦ βίου
    ζήτησον ἄλλην, ἱππικῷ χαίρειν φράσας·
15 κἂν τέσσαρας γὰρ Πηγάσους ζεύξῃς ἅμα,
    ὁποῖος ἵππος ἦν ὁ Βελλεροφόντου,
    πρὸς τοὺς Πρασίνων ἁρματοτροχηλάτας,
    πεζὸς παρ' ἅρμα Λύδιον, φασί, δράμῃς.

7

Εἰς τὸ ἀνακαθαρθὲν πηγάδιον τῆς
Μονῆς τῆς Θεοτόκου· λέγονται δὲ πρὸς
τὴν Θεοτόκον ὡς ἀπὸ προσώπου τοῦ
ἀνακαθάραντος

Τοῖς σοῖς μονασταῖς ἐκκαθαίρων τὸ φρέαρ,
ἐκλιπαρῶ σε, ζῶντος ὕδατος φρέαρ·
εἰς τὸ φρέαρ πεσόντα τῆς ἁμαρτίας
ἀνέλκυσον θᾶττόν με τὸν σὸν οἰκέτην.

soundlessly attracts this four-horse chariot.   10
As for you, if you believe my words,
leave your reins to those who know how to drive,
and seek another trade to make your living,
bidding the track farewell.
For even if you yoked four Pegasuses   15
(that was the horse of Bellerophon)
against the racers of the Greens, you'd run
on foot beside the Lydian chariot, as they say.

7

On the cleansed well of the monastery of the Mother of God; verses spoken to the Mother of God as if by the person responsible for the cleansing

Having cleansed the well for your monks,
I beg of you, *well of living water,*
to draw me, your servant who has fallen
into the well of sin, quickly to the surface.

8

Εἰς τὸν βασιλέα Ῥωμανόν·
ἐπιτάφια ἡρωϊκά

Ἦ μάλα καὶ βασιλῆες ἀμέρσκονται βιότοιο,
πικρὰ δὲ μὴν καὶ τοῖσι Μόρου κιρνῶνται ἄλεισα.
Ῥωμανέ, ποῦ τοι σκῆπτρον ἐπίφθονον ἠδέ τε κῦδος;
Ποῦ θρόνος, ἔνθα κάθησο, μέγ᾽ ἔξοχε κοίρανε λαῶν;
5   Ποῦ τοι δὲ στεφάνη χρυσήλατος, ἣν φορέεσκες,
κοκκοβαφῆ τε πέδιλα ἐΰστροφα, θαῦμα ἰδέσθαι;
Ὤ μοι ἅπαντα ἄφνω θάνατος μέλας ἀμφεκάλυψεν·
ἀλλ᾽ υἷες μερόπων, στοναχήσατε εἵνεκα κείνου,
αὐτὸς δ᾽ ἐξερέω πικρὸν μόρον, ὅνπερ ὑπέστη.
10 Ἦν ὅτ᾽ ἄναξ ἔνεμε χρυσὸν Μεγάλην κατὰ Πέμπτην·
αὐτὰρ ἐπειδὴ νεῖμε καὶ ἐκ θώκοιο ἀνέστη,
αὐτίκ᾽ ἔβη κατὰ λουτρόν· σὺν δὲ κίον θεράποντες·
λούσατο δ᾽ ὕστατα λουτρὰ καὶ ὕστατον ἐσπάσαθ᾽ ὕπνον.
Ἦμος δ᾽ ἠελίου καταδῦναι δίσκος ἔμελλε,
15 δύσετο καὶ βασιλῆος Ῥωμανοῦ ὄσσε φαεινώ.
Καί τις ἀνὴρ ἐλεεινὸν ἀνοιμώξας λίπε λουτρά,
βῆ δ᾽ ἰέναι περίδακρυς ἀνακτορίοις ἐνὶ λαμπροῖς,
δεσποίνῃ ἐρέων πόσιος μόρον, ὅνπερ ὑπέστη.
Ἀγχοῦ στὰς κλαίεσκε καὶ ἔστενε καὶ τάδε ηὔδα·
20 "Κεῖται αὐτοκράτωρ, ὦ ἐπαγγελίης μάλα λυγρῆς."
Ἦ καὶ ἑὰς παλάμας μέγα ἀλλήλαισι πατάξας

8

On the emperor Romanos: funeral verses, in hexameter

Verily even kings are deprived of life
and for them too the bitter cups of Fate are mixed.
Romanos, where now is your envied scepter and your glory?
Where the throne on which you sat, most eminent *ruler of
men?*
Where the crown of beaten gold you used to wear,   5
the well-plaited crimson sandals, *a wonder to behold?*
Alas—*black death has* abruptly *engulfed* all this.
But you, sons of mortals, lament on his account,
and *I will tell* the bitter fate *he has endured.*
It happened when the emperor distributed gold on Holy   10
Thursday.
When he finished the allotments and rose from his throne,
straightway to the bath he went, together with his servants.
He had his final bath and drew his final sleep.
When the sun's disk was about to set,
the *shining eyes* of Emperor Romanos set too.   15
One man, lamenting pitiably, left the bath,
and in tears went to the lustrous palace,
to tell the empress the fate *her husband* had endured.
He stood beside her, and wept, and sighed, and spoke:
"The emperor lies dead, oh what mournful tidings!"   20
Thus he spoke, and smote his hands together,

πολλὰς ἐκ κεφαλῆς προθελύμνους τίλλεν ἐθείρας·
θρῆνον δ᾽ ἐς μέγαν ὦρσε δάμαρτα ἄνακτος, ἄνασσαν.
Αὐτίκα δ᾽ ἀμφὶ θύρας βασιλείων ᾤχετο ἤδε,
25 κλεῖε δὲ ἀσφαλέως καὶ ἀφῄρει κλεῖδας ἁπάσας.
Ἡ μὲν ἄρ᾽ ὧδε ἔρεξεν· ἄναξ δὲ κλίνην περὶ λαμπράν
κεῖτο μέγας μεγαλωστὶ λελασμένος ἧς ἔχε δόξης.
Λαοὶ δ᾽ ἠγερέθοντο, κλίνη δὲ νεκροῖο ἐπῆρτο·
προύπεμπον δὲ ἄνακτα κατὰ πόλιν οἵπερ ἄριστοι·
30 αὐτὰρ ἐπεὶ ῥ᾽ ἵκανόν γε Περιβλέπτου ἐνὶ νηῷ,
ἐνθάδε ταρχύσαντο νέκυν βασιλῆος ἀγαυοῦ,
βὰν δ᾽ ἐπ᾽ ἄνακτα νέον καὶ Ῥωμανοῦ ἐξελάθοντο.

9

Εἰς τὸ σχολεῖον τοῦ ἁγίου Θεοδώρου
τῶν Σφωρακίου

Σχολὴ μεγίστου μάρτυρος Θεοδώρου
πτωθῇ μὲν οὐκ ἄν, πρώξιμον κεκτημένη
τὸν Στυλιανόν, ἀρραγῆ τινα στύλον·
ἧτταν δὲ δεινὴν οὔποτε σχέδους ἴδῃ,
5 ἕως μαΐστωρ ἐστὶ γεννάδας Λέων·
οὗτος γὰρ ἤδη καὶ στομώσας τοὺς νέους

and tore out many hairs from his head by the roots.
He moved the emperor's spouse, the empress, to great
     lament.
At once she went to the palace doors,
and shut them firmly, and took away all the keys.   25
Thus she acted. The *great* ruler *lay* on his bright bier
in his mightiness, forgetful of the glory he once enjoyed.
The people assembled; the bier with the corpse was lifted;
all the eminent men escorted the emperor through the city.
But when they arrived at the church of Peribleptos,   30
they buried the corpse of their valiant emperor there;
then they rushed to a new emperor and forgot about
     Romanos.

9

On the school of Saint Theodore in Sphorakiou

The school of the great martyr Theodore,
having now acquired a sturdy pillar,
the assistant Stylianos, will never falter
or know of dread defeat in dictation's art
as long as noble Leo is headmaster.   5
He has honed the youths for eloquence

καὶ τοὺς ἀγῶνας ἐκδιδάξας τῶν λόγων
ἔξεισι θαρρῶν τοῖς μαθηταῖς ὡς ὅπλοις.
Εἴ τις πέποιθε τῶν διδασκόντων νέους,
10 λαβὼν μαθητὴν τῇ πάλῃ προσελθέτω·
εἰ δ' εὐλαβεῖται τὴν σοφὴν παροιμίαν,
μὴ πρὸς λέοντα δορκὰς ἅψηται μάχης,
συχνὸν τὸ λεῖπον καὶ πάλιν διδασκέτω.

10

Εἰς τὸ αὐτὸ σχολεῖον· ἡρωϊκά

Δείματο οὐρανίη Σοφίη δόμον, ὃν στύλοι ἑπτά
ἀσφαλέως ἀνέχουσιν ἐφεσταότες κατὰ κόσμον·
δείματο καὶ Σοφίη ἐγκύκλιος οἶκον ἑαυτῇ
ἄστεος ἀμφὶ τόπον, τὸν Σφορακίου καλέουσι·
5 στήσατο δὲ στύλον ἔνδον κείνου ἔμμεναι εἶλαρ,
Στυλιανὸν μουσόφρονα, εἰδότα πολλὰ καὶ ἐσθλά·
ἡδυεπῆ δὲ Λέοντα πρόμον ποίησεν ἀγητόν,
ἡλικίην μέσον, οὔτε πελώριον οὔτε δὲ βαιόν,
εὔθετον, εἶδος ἄριστον, ἐπίρρινα, οὐλοκάρηνον,
10 ὀφθαλμοὺς χαρίεντα, μελάγχροον, ἠϋγένειον,
ὀξύτατον νοέειν, λιγύφωνον, καρτερόθυμον,
ὅς ῥα ἐὸν στόμα βάψας Μουσῶν εἰς νόον ἄκρον

and trained them to do battle with their words;
and now he marches out, trusting in his students as his
    weapons.
If any teacher of youths should be so bold,
then let him lead his student to the arena.   10
But if he first gives heed to the wise proverb
that says *no deer should wage battle with a lion,*
he'd best keep training them where they are lacking.

10

On the same school; hexameters

Heavenly Wisdom has built a house, which *seven pillars*
hold up safely, standing in order;
the Wisdom of education has also built herself a house,
in the quarter of the city called Sphorakiou.
She, too, has erected a pillar for support of that house: 5
the muse-minded Stylianos, of vast and wondrous
    knowledge—
and she made the sweet-tongued Leo its admirable leader.
He's of average height, not too tall and not too small,
well disposed, handsome, with stately nose and curly hair,
agreeable eyes and dark skin, well-bearded,   10
quick-minded, clear-voiced, and of tenacious character.
Having dipped his mouth in the Muses' deepest mind,

ῥοῦν ἐμέει σοφίης κούρων αἰεὶ περὶ ὦτα,
οἳ λιπαινόμενοί τε καὶ εὐλογίην ξυνάγοντες
15 τῶν πάντων κρατέουσι νέων σχεδέων ἐν ἀγῶσιν,
οὕνεκα τοῖσι Λέων γε διδάσκαλός ἐστιν ἄριστος·
οὗ δὴ καὶ κλέος ἔσται ἀγήραον ἤματα πάντα·
ὡς δὲ ζώων τετραπόδων κρατέουσι λέοντες
κάρτεϊ, ἠνορέῃ καὶ ὀξυτάτοισιν ὄνυξιν,
20 ὣς ὁ Λέων κρατέει μαΐστόρων ἐνὶ πᾶσιν,
ἔν τ᾽ ἀρετῇ τε κυδρῇ καὶ ἐν σοφίῃ ἐρατεινῇ.

II

Εἰς τὸν μαΐστορα τῆς σχολῆς τῶν Χαλκοπρατείων

Τῶν ὧδε πᾶς τάχιστα φευγέτω τρέχων,
διατριβῇ δὲ τῇδε μὴ προσελθέτω·
ὁ γὰρ Μίδας ζῇ καὶ τὸ φῶς πάλιν βλέπει
καὶ τῆς Πανάγνου τὴν σχολὴν διευθύνει.
5 Τί πολλὰ φημί; Φευγέτω πᾶς, φευγέτω,
μή πως ἀμειφθῇ δυστυχῶς εἰς χρυσίον,
ἅρπαξι χερσὶ συσχεθεὶς ταῖς τοῦ Μίδα,
ὃς νῦν κάθηται καὶ προτείνει τὰς δύο,
πωλῶν ταλάντου τοῖς μαθηταῖς τὰ σχέδη·

he now spews forth a stream of wisdom around the ears of
    the young,
who, nourishing themselves on it and gathering eloquence,
defeat all the other youths in the dictation contests,   15
because Leo is their most excellent teacher.
His fame will be imperishable for all the days to come.
Just as lions are preeminent among the quadrupeds,
in strength, prowess, and the sharpness of their claws,
just so Leo is the best among all schoolmasters,   20
in renowned virtue and delightful wisdom.

II

On the headmaster of the school in the quarter of the Bronze Shops

Flee from this place! Let everyone run his fastest!
Let no one come anywhere near this school!
For Midas lives and sees the light again,
and directs the All-pure Virgin's school.
Why talk so much? Flee, everybody, flee,   5
before you are turned miserably into gold,
seized by the rapacious hands of Midas,
who sits there now and stretches them both out,
selling dictations to his pupils for money.

10 τῷ μὲν λέγει· "δός," τῷ δέ· "πρόσθες τι πλέον,"
ἄλλῳ δὲ καὶ γράφοντι νεύει λανθάνων,
σχεδοπρατεῖον οὐ πρεπόντως, ὦ Δίκη,
Χαλκοπρατείων τὴν σχολὴν δεικνὺς τάλας·
ἀπεμπολεῖ πλὴν οὐχὶ χαλκοῦ τὰ σχέδη
15 ὁμωνύμως πὼς τῇ σχολῇ τῆς Παρθένου,
χρυσοῦ δὲ μᾶλλον, ὧν φιλόχρυσος φύσει
καὶ πρὸς τάλαντα χρυσίου χαίνων μέγα,
καθώς περ εἰς ἄγκιστρον ἰχθύς τις λίχνος.

12

Εἰς τὴν ἐκκλησίαν, ἣν ἀνεκαίνισεν ὁ ζυγοστάτης Εὐστάθιος· ἡρωϊκά

Τόνδε ἑῇ δαπάνῃ περικαλλέα καίνισε νηόν
Εὐστάθιος, χρυσοῖο τάλαντα ὃς εὖ σταθμίζει,
εἰς χαρτουλαρίων μεγάλων ἠδ᾽ ἰλλουστρίων.

To one he says, "Pay," to another, "Pay some more,"   10
to yet another, who is still writing, he slyly nods.
In unseemly manner the wretch turns the school
of the Bronze Shops quarter into a dictation shop. O
    Justice!
Only he does not sell the dictations for bronze
(which would fit in a way the name of the Virgin's school)   15
but rather for gold, loving gold by nature,
and gapes wide before talents of gold,
just like a greedy fish before a hook.

12

On the church restored by the money-weigher Eustathios; hexameters

This wonderful church has been restored, at his own
    expense,
by Eustathios, one of the illustrious and grand archivists,
who well weighs out talents of gold.

13

Εἰς τὴν τοῦ βίου ἀνισότητα

Δίκαια ταῦτα, Δημιουργέ μου Λόγε,
πηλὸν μὲν εἶναι πάντας ἀνθρώπους ἕνα
καὶ χοῦν τὸν αὐτόν, ἀλλὰ καὶ φύσιν μίαν,
τελεῖν δέ πως ἄνισον αὐτοῖς τὸν βίον;
5 Ναὶ ναὶ στάσιν τὰ πάντα πάντως οὐκ ἔχει,
ἐναλλαγὴν πλὴν πραγμάτων, πῶς καὶ πότε;
Κἄν γὰρ δεήσῃ συστραφέντα τὸν βίον
κύκλους ἑλίττειν Βακχικῆς ἀταξίας,
ἐν μὲν χιλίοις πλουσίοις ἢ μυρίοις
10 εἷς δυστυχήσας συγκάτεισι τοῖς κάτω,
ἐν δ' αὖ πένησιν ἀθλίοις τρισμυρίοις
τρεῖς εὐπραγοῦσι καὶ γίνονται τῶν ἄνω.
Τῷ τοῦ δικαίου τήκομαι ζήλῳ, Λόγε,
καὶ ταῦτα πρὸς σὲ φθέγγομαι τὸν Δεσπότην,
15 σὺ δ' ἀλλ' ἀνάσχου μακροθυμῶν, ὡς ἔθος,
καὶ τῶν ἐμῶν ἄκουε νῦν γογγυσμάτων.
Μὴ τὸν μὲν αὐτὸς ἔπλασας ταῖς χερσί σου,
τούτου δὲ πλάστης ἄλλος; Ἢ τί λεκτέον;
Οὐκ ἔργα τῶν σῶν πάντες εἰσὶ δακτύλων;
20 Ἀλλ' οἱ μὲν αὐτῶν οὐκ ἀναγκαίων μόνον
κατατρυφῶσιν, ἀλλὰ καὶ πολλῷ πλέον
καὶ τοῖς περιττοῖς ἐντρυφῶσι τοῦ βίου,

13

On the inequality of life

Are these things just, my Creator, Word of God,
that though all men are from a single clay
and the same dust, sharing all a single nature,
they somehow get unequal livelihoods?
Yes, yes, all things lack all stability,   5
but how do they change and when?
So, what if you command life to revolve
and spin in circles of Bacchic disarray?
Among a thousand rich men, myriads even,
just one unfortunate joins the lowly,   10
while of all the countless wretched poor,
just three prosper and join a higher rank.
O Word, I melt with zeal for what is just,
and therefore, Master, I cry these words out to you.
Be patient and bear with me, as is your way;   15
and listen now to these grumblings of mine.
Perhaps you made one man with your own hands,
while some other creator made another?
Or what should I say? Aren't all men your handiwork?
Yet some not only have their every need   20
sumptuously met, but more than this,
they revel in the excesses of life,

οἱ δὲ γλίχονται καὶ μονοβλώμου τρύφους,
ἢ μᾶλλον εἰπεῖν καὶ τραπέζης ψιχίων.
25 Δίκαιε, ποῦ δίκαια ταῦτα τυγχάνει;
Ἕως πότε στήσειας ἡμῖν τὴν κτίσιν;
Σύσσεισον αὐτὴν ἢ κατάκλυσον πάλιν·
μηδεὶς κιβωτοῦ δευτέρας αὖθις τύχοι,
μὴ Νῶέ τις γένοιτο καὶ πάλιν νέος·
30 οἴχοιντο πάντες· λείψανον μὴ μεινάτω.
Εἰ δ', ὡς ὑπέσχου, μακρόθυμε Χριστέ μου,
τὴν γῆν ἐς αὖθις οὐ κατακλύζειν θέλεις
(καὶ γὰρ φυλάττεις οἶδα τὰς ὑποσχέσεις),
Ἄτλαντα χειρὶ σῇ βαλὼν ἐκ τῶν ἄνω
35 τὴν πᾶσαν αὐτῷ συγκατάστρεψον κτίσιν,
μιγνὺς πόλον γῇ καὶ τὰ πάντα συμφύρων·
οὕτω γὰρ ἂν γένοιτο πάντων ἰσότης.

14

Εἰς τὸ "Χαῖρε, κεχαριτωμένη" καὶ τὸ
"Ἰδοὺ ἡ δούλη Κυρίου"·
ἡρωϊκά

Γήθεο, ὦ χαρίεσσα, Θεὸς Κύριος μετὰ σεῖο.
Ἰδοὺ τοῦ θεράπαινα· γένοιτό μοι ὡς σὺ ἔειπας.

while others struggle for scraps of broken bread —
or, to put it better, for *crumbs off the table.*
How is it, Just One, that such things are just?   25
How long will you preserve creation for us?
Shake it apart, or flood it once more,
but make sure no one gets a second ark;
do not let some new Noah come again.
Let everybody vanish without a trace.   30
But if, as you promised, my magnanimous Christ,
you do not wish to flood your earth again
(I know, of course, you keep your promises),
then cast down Atlas from on high with your hand,
turn all creation upside down with him,   35
mixing heaven and earth and confounding it all;
that would bring equality to everyone.

14

On "Hail, woman full of grace," and "Behold here the Lord's maidservant"; hexameters

"Rejoice, O graceful one, the Lord God is with you."
"Behold here his attendant; may it befall me as you have
     said."

15

Εἰς τὸν πατρίκιον Μελίαν καὶ παραθαλασσίτην

Ἦν ἀλμυρίζων ῥοῦς θαλάττιος πάλαι,
νῦν δὲ γλυκάζων· ἀλλὰ μηδὲν θαυμάσῃς·
κριτὴν γὰρ αὐχεῖ, πικρίας ἀναιρέτην,
ἐπώνυμον μέλιτος, ἡδὺν Μελίαν.

16

Εἰς τὸν τάφον τοῦ αὐτοῦ Μελίου, ἱστορηθέντος ἐν αὐτῷ καὶ ὡς κοσμικοῦ καὶ ὡς μοναχοῦ

Καὶ τῶν φθασάντων μνηνονεύειν σφαλμάτων
καὶ πρὸς τὸ μέλλον σώφρονα ζῆν τὸν βίον
ὁ πατρίκιος Μελίας ὁμοῦ θέλων,
ἤγειρεν αὐτῷ τὸν τάφον, καὶ ζῶν ἔτι.
5 Ὁρᾶτε πάντες, ποῦ τελευτᾷ τὸ κλέος,
ποῦ πλοῦτος αὐτός, ποῦ τὰ τερπνὰ τοῦ βίου,

15

On the patrician and *parathalassites* Melias

In the past the streams of the sea used to be salty;
now they are sweet. But do not be surprised;
for the sea boasts a judge who removes all bitterness,
with a mellifluous name, the sweet Melias.

16

On the grave of the same Melias, being depicted there both as a layman and as a monk

To be mindful of wrongs done in the past,
and to lead a temperate life with the future in mind,
wishing both these things, the patrician Melias
built for himself this grave while still alive.
Look, everyone, where glory meets its end,   5
and where wealth ends, the pleasures of life,

ποῦ καὶ τὰ λαμπρὰ καὶ περίβλεπτα σφόδρα.
Ματαιότης τὰ πάντα, Σολομῶν λέγει,
ματαιοτήτων ἄντικρυς ματαιότης·
10 ἦν γὰρ πάλαι μέγιστος οὗτος Μελίας
ἐν ἀνθυπάτοις, ἐν πατρικίοις ἅμα,
ἐν πᾶσι βέσταις, ἐν κριταῖς Ἱπποδρόμου,
ὁποῖον αὐτὸν ὁ γραφεὺς ὧδε γράφει,
δεικνύντα πᾶσι δωρεὰς Θεοῦ Λόγου.
15 Καὶ ταῦτα πάντα, φεῦ, τελευτὴ σβεννύει.
Οὐ μὴν τελευτᾷ καὶ πόθος Θεῷ φίλος,
ὃν ἔτρεφε ζῶν Μελίας πρὶν ἐν βίῳ·
ἐρῶν γὰρ οὗτος ὁ τρισευδαίμων γέρων
τυχεῖν μοναστῶν σχήματός τε καὶ βίου,
20 ἑαυτὸν ὧδε καὶ πάλιν καταγράφει
πρὸ τοῦ θανεῖν τε καὶ παρελθεῖν τὸν βίον
μελαμφοροῦντα καὶ τρίχας κεκαρμένον,
ὃν εἶχε τὸ πρὶν εὐσεβέστατον πόθον
διὰ γραφῆς ἄριστα καὶ νῦν δεικνύων.
25 Πλὴν σῇ θελήσει, Δημιουργὲ τῶν ὅλων,
ἄρχων ἐδείχθη τῆς θαλάσσης Μελίας,
ἄρχων δὲ καὶ γῆς ὡς κρατήσας τειχέων·
νῦν οὖν μεταστὰς πρὸς σὲ τὸν Θεὸν Λόγον,
ἄρχων γένοιτο καὶ παρ' αὐτῷ τῷ πόλῳ.

and all splendid things men value highly.
Everything is vanity, says Solomon,
vanity, indeed, *of vanities.*
Formerly this Melias was the greatest   10
among proconsuls, among patricians too,
among all *vestai,* and judges of the Hippodrome,
exactly as the painter here depicts him,
showing to all the gifts of the Word of God.
And all of this, alas, death snuffs out.   15
The longing dear to God, though, does not die;
also in life, Melias used to nurture it.
Therefore, this thrice-blessed old man who yearned
to be like monks in habit and in life
depicts himself here for a second time,   20
before his death, and before departing life,
with black clothes and a tonsured head.
With this image, he now shows most finely
the devout desire he had before.
Through your will, Creator of all things,   25
Melias was made ruler of the sea
and ruler of earth, as protector of the walls.
Having now departed for you, God the Word,
may he become a ruler in heaven too.

17

Εἰς τοὺς τέσσαρας τοῦ χρόνου καιρούς· ἡρωϊκά

Οἵδε φθινομένης ἔασι τρεῖς μῆνες ὀπώρης·
πρώτατος οἰνοφόρος Σεπτέμβριος ἀγλαόβοτρυς,
δεύτερος αὖτ' ἐπὶ τούτῳ μὴν Ὀκτώβριός ἐστιν,
εἶτα τρίτος μετὰ τούσδε, Νοέμβριε, αὐτὸς ἂν εἴης.
5   Μῆνες χειμερίης ἔασι τρεῖς ἄγριοι ὥρης·
ὧν τὸν μὲν καλέουσι Δεκέμβριον, ἐστὶ δὲ πρῶτος,
τὸν δ' αὖ Ἰαννουάριον, ὃς μετὰ πρῶτον ἐλαύνει,
οὔνομα δὲ τριτάτῳ Φεβρουάριος μετὰ τούσδε.
Ὥρης εἰαρινῆς ἔασι τρεῖς οἴδ' ἄρα μῆνες·
10   Μάρτιος, ἑξείης δὲ Ἀπρίλλιος, εἶτα Μάϊος
. . . φέρων, ἐνιαυτοῦ ἀμείνονες ἐννέα μηνῶν·
ἡδὺ γὰρ ἥλιος μάλα ἐν τούτοισιν ἀνίσχει.
Τρεῖς θέρεος μῆνας καματώδεος εὕρετο ὥρη·
ὧν τὸν μὲν καλέουσιν Ἰούνιον, ἐν τρισὶ πρῶτον,
15   τὸν δ' ἕτερον μετὰ πρῶτον Ἰούλιον, ὁ τρίτατος δέ
Αὔγουστος μετὰ τούς, μηνῶν ἰνδίκτου ὁ λοῖσθος.

17

On the four seasons of the year;
hexameters

These are the three months of decaying autumn:
the first, wine-bringing September, with splendid bunches,
second, following this one, is the month of October,
and after these the third month—that will be you,
　　November.
Three are the harsh months of the winter season:　　　　5
the first of which is called December,
the next, January, comes after the first.
The name of the third, after these, is February.
These are then the three months of spring season:
March, followed by April, and then May,　　　　10
bringing . . . , superior to the year's other nine months;
for the sun ascends sweetly in those months.
Three months can be found in wearisome summer's season:
of which one is called June, the first of the three;
the second, after the first, July; the third, after these,　　　　15
August, the last month of the administrative year.

18

Εἰς τὸν βασιλέα Μιχαὴλ καὶ τοὺς τρεῖς ἀδελφοὺς αὐτοῦ

Ἡ τῶν ἀδελφῶν τετρὰς ἠγλαϊσμένη
σταυροῦ διαυγοῦς σχηματίζει τὸν τύπον·
οἱ τέσσαρες γὰρ τέσσαρα σταυροῦ μέρη,
κέντρων κρατοῦντα τεσσάρων οἰκουμένης.
5 Καὶ Μιχαὴλ μὲν εἰκονίζει τὴν ἔω,
λαμπρῶς ἀνίσχων, ὡς ὁ λαμπρὸς φωσφόρος,
λίθων τε λαμπρότητι καὶ τῶν μαργάρων
ἢ κρεῖττον εἰπεῖν ἀρετῶν εὐκοσμίᾳ.
Ἰωάννης δὲ σχηματίζει τὴν δύσιν·
10 κἂν τὸν τρόπον γὰρ λευκὸν ὡς τὸ φῶς ἔχῃ
καὶ φωτὸς υἱὸς χρηματίζῃ τῷ βίῳ,
μελαμφορεῖ γε καὶ τυποῖ τὴν ἑσπέραν.
Κωνσταντῖνος δὲ τῆς μεσημβρίας τύπος·
ὡς ἡλίου γὰρ δίσκος ἐν μεσημβρίᾳ
15 μάλιστα λάμπει φωτὶ πλουσιωτάτῳ,
οὕτως ἐκεῖνος, ἔνθα καὶ διατρίβει,
αὐγαῖς ἀπείροις τοὺς ὁρῶντας φαιδρύνει.
Τυποῖ δὲ Γεώργιος ἀρκτῷον μέρος,
Ἀρκτοῦρος ἀστὴρ τὸ πρόσωπον τυγχάνων.
20 Ἀλλ’, ὦ κραταιὲ σταυρέ, τῶν πιστῶν φύλαξ,
ἀνωτέραν φύλαττε παντοίας βλάβης
τὴν σταυροειδῆ τῶν ἀδελφῶν τετράδα.

18

On the emperor Michael and his three brothers

The radiant foursome of the brothers
forms the sign of the shining cross,
because the four men are the four parts of the cross
that rule the four directions of the world.
So Michael is the image of the east,   5
arising like the brilliant bearer of light,
with the brilliance of his gems and pearls,
or rather by the beauty of his virtues.
John, in turn, represents the west.
Though his character is white as light,   10
and in his life he is a son of light,
he wears black and thus portrays the evening.
Constantine, meanwhile, stands for the south,
for just as the disk of the sun at midday
shines most brightly with abundant light,   15
so does this man, wherever he walks about,
brighten the onlookers with countless beams.
Finally, George embodies the northern side,
with a face resembling the Arcturus star.
O mighty cross, protector of the faithful,   20
preserve on high from every harm
this cross-shaped foursome of brothers.

19

Εἰς τὸν αὐτόν· <ἡρωϊκά>

Ἄλλῳ μὲν βασιλήων ἔργα μόθοιο μέμηλεν,
ἄλλῳ δ' ὠκέες ἵππ<οι ὑφ' ἅρμασι κολλητοῖσιν>,
ἄλλῳ δ' αὖ σοφίη καὶ ἱμερόεσσά τε μοῦσα·
σοὶ δ' ἐλεημοσύνη τι<μᾶται ἔξοχα πάντων>·
5   μειλιχίῃ γὰρ ἅπαντα βρότεια γένη ἐλεαίρεις·
οὓς ὀλοῆς πενίης δὲ βέλος δάμα<σεν πολύπικρον>,
τοῖσιν ἄφαρ παρέχεις ἄλκαρ, σκηπτοῦχε, ἀρήγων.
Ὅς σέ γ' ἀπεχθαίρει κρατερό<ν περ ἐόντα ἄνακτα>,
μὴ φιλέει δέ σε πάμπαν καὶ ποθέει περὶ κῆρι,
10 μήποτε οὐρανίοιο Θεοῖο πρόσω<πον ὀρῴη>,
ἀλλὰ οἷ ἄψεα πάντα κόραξ καταδαρδάψειε,
τούτου δ' ὀστέα λευκὰ κύνες σὺν γυ<ψὶν ἔδοιεν>,
ἐς κεφαλὴν δ' αὐτοῖο τριακοσίων δέκα ὀκτὼ
Νικαέων πατέρων θείων ἡ ἀρὴ καταβα<ίη>.
15 Σοὶ δὲ ἔτη βιότοιο γενοίατο τρὶς τριάκοντα·
εἰ δὲ θάνῃς καὶ μοῖραν ἀνατλήσεις ποτὲ π<ικράν>,
εὕροις καὶ βασιλείης οὐρανίης κλέος εὐρύ.

34

19

On the same; hexameters

One ruler attends to the deeds of battle,
another to swift horses with fastened chariots,
another to knowledge and the graceful muse,
but, as for you, you venerate charity most of all,
and with kindness you pity all of mankind.   5
Those whom fierce poverty's bitter arrow strikes,
you, scepter-bearer, swiftly shield with your aid.
Should anyone detest you, mighty ruler that you are,
and not love you, not desire you in his heart,
may he never see the face of God in heaven,   10
but may a raven devour all his limbs,
may dogs and vultures gnaw at his barren bones,
and may the curse of the three hundred eighteen
Nicene fathers descend upon his head.
But you, may you attain thrice thirty years of life,   15
and, should you die and endure a bitter fate,
may you find the broad glory of the heavenly kingdom.

20

Εἰς τὸν πρωτοσπαθάριον Βασίλειον καὶ κριτὴν τὸν <Ξηρόν>

Καλῶν θάλασσαν, τοῦτο δὴ τὸ τοῦ λόγου,
ὁ Ξηρὸς εὑρὼν ὁ κριτὴς τὴν Ἑλλάδα,
ξηρὰν ἀφῆκε, μὴ λιπὼν μηδ' ἰκμάδα.

21

Αἴνιγμα εἰς τὸν ζυγὸν ἤτοι τὸ ζύγιον

Δίκαιος εἰμὶ καὶ δικαίων ἀκρότης·
ἓξ τὰ σκέλη μου, κἄνπερ οἱ πόδες δύο.

20

On the *protospatharios* and judge Basil Xeros

A sea of goods, to use the common phrase—
that was how Xeros the judge found Greece;
but he left it dry, not leaving a single drop behind.

21

Riddle on the balance scale

I am just—the summit of justice.
Six legs I have, but only two feet.

22

Εἰς τὸν μητροπολίτην Κυζίκου Δημήτριον διὰ τὴν ποδάγραν

Τί μακρὸν οὕτω καὶ συχνὸν τὸ πᾶ<ν στένεις>;
Πόδες τὸ πάσχον καὶ ποδάγρα τὸ τρύχον.
Ἀντεξέταζε τοῖς πόνοις καὶ <τὰ στέφη>,
ἅ σοι πλέκουσιν αἱ μακρόχρονοι νόσοι,
5 ἀνθ᾽ ὧνπερ αὐτῶν καρτε<ρεῖς τὰς πικρίας>,
Ἰὼβ μαθητὴς τοῦ πολύτλα τυγχάνων.
Καὶ σαῖνε σαυτὸν τῶν <ἐπάθλων ἐλπίσι>
καὶ μὴ φανείης μὴ πρὸς αὐτῆς Τριάδος
ὁ πάντα νικῶν τῶν μ<ικρῶν ἥττων πόνων>·
10 ὁ ψυχικοῦ γὰρ βελτίων ὀφθεὶς πάθους
ἀρχάς τε τρέψας καὶ <σκότους ἐξουσίας>
στήσας τε τὸ τρόπαιον ἐν βίῳ μέγα
φ. . .
καὶ ποῦ τὸ πυκνὸν τῶν φρενῶν Δημητρίου;
15 . . .
ἡ πίστις ἔστω τμητικωτάτη σπά<θη>
. . .
ἡ δ᾽ ἐλπὶς ἀσπίς, ἔγχος ἡ θεία σ<κέπη>
. . .
20 . . .
ἡ παγκακίστη προσβαλοῦσά σοι νόσος

22

To Demetrios, the metropolitan of Kyzikos, on his gout

Why do you moan about everything so long and so often?
It is your feet that suffer, gout that consumes you.
Up against these pains, hold the garlands
woven for you by the long-lasting diseases,
whose bitter afflictions you endure —   5
a disciple of Job, the long-suffering.
Raise your spirits with hopes of trophies,
and do not, do not appear, by the very Trinity,
to be lesser than petty sufferings, you winner of all!
The man proven greater than any passion of the soul,   10
who has overpowered the principalities and powers of
    darkness,
and erected a great victory monument in his life,
that man . . .
And where is the sharp mind of Demetrios?
. . .   15
Let faith be the razor-sharp blade
. . .
let hope be the shield, and divine protection the spear
. . .
. . .   20
the malicious disease that has attacked you

. . .

καὶ τοὺς ὀϊστοὺς ἀλλεπαλλήλους φέρῃ

. . . ας

25 πατοῦντας αὐτὸν οὐκ ἐνεγκὼν ὁ πλάνος

. . . τ. . .

ἀλλ' αὐτὸς αὐτὸν καὶ πάλιν στερρῶς πάτει

. . . τόας

καὶ θλάττε τοῦτον· κἂν πάλιν δάκνῃ φέρων,

30 . . . να

εἰ καρτερήσεις τὰς ἀμυχὰς εἰς τέλος

. . . <εἰς εὐ>φημίας,

βλέπων τὸ μέλλον καὶ τὸ νῦν παραβλέπων.

23

Εἰς τὸν γραμματικὸν Γεώργιον,
γράψαντα βουστροφηδὸν ἐσφαλμένως

Ὡς κρεῖττον ἦν σοι *βοῦν ἐπὶ γλώττης φέρειν*
ἢ *βουστροφηδόν*, οἷάπερ γράφεις, γράφειν.

. . .

and shoots its arrows one after the other

. . .

the vile one, not tolerating those who trample upon him,   25

. . .

but you should firmly trample on him once more.

. . .

and shatter him; and even if he bites again.

. . .

       30

if you endure the scratches until the end

                       . . . for praise,

looking at the future and ignoring the present.

23

To the grammarian George, who wrote a failed *boustrophedon*

Better to *bear an ox upon* your *tongue*
than write such ox-turned verses as you write.

24

Εἰς τὴν προέλευσιν τοῦ βασιλέως Μιχαήλ

Ὅταν προέλθῃς τῶν ἀνακτόρων, ἄναξ,
καὶ τὴν σεαυτοῦ τῇ πόλει δείξῃς θέαν,
ἄπειρον ἐγχεῖς ἡδονὴν ταῖς καρδίαις
τῶν σε βλεπόντων, κἂν βλέπωσι μακρόθεν·
5   ὅλος γὰρ εἶ σὺ τερπνότης, ὅλος χάρις,
ὅλος γλυκασμός, καὶ πέλας καὶ μακρόθεν.

25

Εἰς τὴν Μεταμόρφωσιν

Ἐοίκασι ξένον τι δηλοῦν ἐνθάδε
οἱ τρεῖς μαθηταὶ καὶ προφητῶν οἱ δύο.
Δηλοῦσι τοίνυν οἱ μαθηταὶ μέν, Λόγε,
τρεῖς τῆς τριλαμποῦς οὐσίας ὑποστάσεις·
5   οἱ δὲ προφῆται τὰς φύσεις διττὰς ἅμα,
θνητὴν ὁ Μωσῆς, ζῶσαν ὁ ζῶν Ἠλίας,

24

On the procession of the emperor Michael

When you go forth out of your palace, lord,
revealing to the city your countenance,
you pour the utmost bliss into the hearts
of those who see you, even from afar,
because you are all delightfulness, all grace,   5
all sweetness, from close by and from afar.

25

On the Transfiguration

How strange a thing they seem to depict here,
the three disciples and the pair of prophets.
The disciples here exemplify, O Word,
the three persons of the triple-bright essence,
while the two prophets show the two natures,   5
Moses the mortal nature, the living Elijah the living—

ἃς καὶ φυλάττεις, οὐ διαιρῶν, οὐ τρέπων·
κἂν ἐν Θαβὼρ γὰρ φῶς καθωράθης ξένον,
ἀλλ᾽ εἶχες ἄμφω τὰς φύσεις ἀσυγχύτους,
10   μορφῆς ἀμείψει μὴ φύρων τὰς οὐσίας.

26

\<Εἰς\> τὸν Ἐζεκίαν περὶ τῆς προσθήκης τῆς ζωῆς αὐτοῦ

Θήκατο προσθήκην δήλην βιότοιο προφήτης
\<Ἐζε\>κίᾳ Βασιλῆϊ ὑποστροφῇ ἠελίοιο.

27

Εἰς τὸν μοναχὸν Νικήταν τὸν Συνάδων

Ἡ ζῶσα πολλοῖς ἐν πόλει γνῶσις πάλαι
ἐν σοὶ μόνῳ ζῇ καὶ σαλεύει, Νικήτα·
κἂν εἰς στενὸν γὰρ ἤλασαν νῦν οἱ λόγοι,
ἀλλ᾽ οὐκ ἐνεκρώθησαν οὔμενουν ὅλως,

the natures you preserve without division or change.
Though on Tabor you were seen as a strange light,
still you maintained both natures unconfounded,
not mixing essences, although your appearance was   10
    transformed.

26

On Hezekiah, about the lengthening
of his life

Through the sun's regression, the prophet revealed
to King Hezekiah that his life would be extended.

27

On the monk Niketas of Synada

Knowledge, once alive in many in the city,
now lives and pulsates in you alone, Niketas.
Though learning is now backed into a corner,
it has by no means died off altogether.

5 λιπόντος αὐτοῖς ζώπυρον τοῦ Δεσπότου
σέ, ζωτικὸν πνέοντα πνεῦμα τῆς τέχνης.
Ἅρμοττε τοίνυν τὴν σοφὴν σύριγγά σου
καὶ πάντας ἕλκε τοῖς λόγοις, λόγων φίλε,
ὡς ἄλλος Ὀρφεὺς τῇ λύρᾳ τὰ θηρία.
10 Ἄνοιγε Μούσης τοὺς καταρράκτας, πάτερ,
ἄνοιγε τούτους καὶ κατάρδευε κτίσιν,
βροντῶν φρενῶν ἔσωθεν ὥσπερ ἐκ πόλου,
λάλων τε πέμπων ἀστραπὰς ἐκ χειλέων
καὶ γνώσεως τὸ μάννα ῥαγδαίως ὕων.
15 Τίς γὰρ σοφῶν ἄριστος ἢ σὺ καὶ μόνος;
Τίνος τὸ λαμπρὸν ἐν λόγοις ἢ σοῦ μόνου;
Τίς πατριάρχαις τίμιος; Τίς πατράσιν;
Ἢ τίς ποθεινὸς τοῖς κρατοῦσι δεσπόταις
συγκλητικοῖς τε πᾶσι καὶ τοῖς ἐν πόλει;
20 Εὐπατριδῶν δὲ τίς κορωνὶς τυγχάνει;
Τίς πᾶν λόγων ἤθροισε κάλλος ἐκ νέου;
Τίς ἀρετὴν ἔσπευσε συζεῦξαι λόγοις;
Καὶ τίς κατ' ἄμφω πάντας ἥττησε ξένως,
ἐν ἀρετῇ μὲν ἀρετῆς τοὺς ἐργάτας,
25 ἐν τοῖς λόγοις δὲ τοὺς ἐραστὰς τῶν λόγων;
Τίνος σεβαστὴ καὶ μόνη μόνον θέα;
Ἢ τίς καθέδρας ἀξιοῦται τῆς ἄνω
ἐν συλλόγοις μάλιστα καὶ συνεδρίοις;
Τίνος γέμουσιν αἱ πόλεις συγγραμμάτων;
30 Τίνος στίχους φέρουσιν οἱ θεῖοι δόμοι;
Τίνος δὲ πάντες καὶ νέοι καὶ πρεσβύται
ἐπικροτοῦσι συγγραφαῖς ἢ σοῦ μόνου;

For the Lord has left for it a vital spark—   5
you, who breathe the art's living spirit.
Bring now your wise shepherd's pipe into tune;
lure everyone with words, O friend of words,
like another Orpheus luring beasts with his lyre.
Open the cascades of the Muse, father,   10
open them, and irrigate creation,
thundering from within your mind as from the sky,
sending lightning from your eloquent lips, and
letting the manna of knowledge fall in torrents.
For who is foremost of the wise but you alone?   15
Whose but yours alone is brilliance in words?
Who is honored by patriarchs, by the fathers?
For whom do the sovereign rulers long,
and all the senators too, and the city's people?
And who happens to be the crown of the nobility?   20
Who gathered anew all the beauty of words?
Who labored to join virtue with words?
And who wondrously beats everyone at both:
virtue's laborers at virtue,
and lovers of words at words?   25
Whose countenance alone is venerable?
And who has merited the highest seat
in every assembly and every gathering?
With whose writings are the cities filled?
Whose verses do the divine dwellings bear?   30
Whose writings do the young and old alike
applaud, if not yours and yours alone?

Τίνος δὲ φήμη μέχρις αἰθέρος φθάνει,
ζητοῦσα χωρεῖν καὶ παρ' αὐτὸν τὸν πόλον
35 καὶ τοῖς ἀΰλοις ἀγγέλοις, ἀρχαγγέλοις
χοροῖς τε λοιποῖς πᾶσι τοῖς ἀνωτέροις
τὸ τοῦ Συνάδων ἐκδιηγεῖσθαι κλέος;
Τίς χρηστὸς οὕτω; Τίς σοφός; Τίς ἀγχίνους;
Καὶ τίς δὲ ῥήτωρ καὶ μένος πυρὸς πνέων;
40 Τῆς γνώσεως τίς εὐφυὴς ὑπηρέτης;
Ἀγροικίας τίς εὐσθενὴς καθαιρέτης;
Τὸ μεῖζον αὐτό, τίς παθῶν ἀναιρέτης;
Ὁ Συνάδων τὰ πάντα συλλαβὼν ἔχει.
Ὦ θρέμμα Μουσῶν, ἀλλὰ καὶ σὺ γνησίως
45 φθέγξαι βραχὺν μὲν ἀλλ' ἐμοὶ φίλον λόγον,
καὶ γλῶτταν εὔρουν μηδαμῶς κλείσῃς, πάτερ,
γλῶτταν γλυκὺ βλύζουσαν ἄντικρυς μέλι,
ἐν ᾗ κατοικεῖ πᾶσα Μουσῶν κομψότης.
Ταύτης μετασχεῖν εὔχομαι τῶν ῥημάτων
50 ἢ τῶν ταλάντων τοῦ Κροίσου καὶ τοῦ Μίδα·
φανήσομαι γὰρ Σαρδανάπαλος νέος,
οὐ θρυπτικῶς ζῶν ὡς ἐκεῖνος ἐν βίῳ,
ζῶσαν τρυφὴν δὲ σοὺς σοφοὺς τρυφῶν λόγους.

Whose reputation reaches the ether
and seeks to get as far as heaven,
to tell the immaterial angels and archangels   35
and all the other choirs on high
about the glory of the man of Synada?
Who is so righteous, so wise, so sharp-witted?
Which orator *breathes such fiery force?*
Who is the naturally gifted servant of knowledge?   40
The staunch annihilator of boorishness?
And more than this, the annihilator of passions?
The man of Synada has all things together in one.
O nursling of the Muses, most sincerely
speak for me a word, still dear if brief,   45
and do not hold your eloquent tongue, father,
your tongue gushing with nothing but sweet honey,
where all the Muses' refinement resides.
I yearn for a share in its utterances
more than for the talents of Croesus and Midas.   50
For I will appear as a new Sardanapalus,
not by leading a degenerate life as that man did,
but by relishing your wise words as a living luxury.

28

Εἰς τὸ ἐγχείριον τῆς Θεοτόκου· ἡρωϊκά

Εἰρήνη τόδε ἔργον χερσὶν ἑῇσιν ὕφηνε
Μητέρι, εἰρήνης συνεχούσης πείρατε γαίης.

29

Εἰς τὸν πτωχὸν Λέοντα

Ἄχαλκος ὤν, ἄραβδος, ἐμβάδων δίχα,
σὺν πᾶσι τούτοις οὐ στολὰς ἔχων δύο,
ἀποστόλου ζῆς μὴ θέλων βίον, Λέον.

28

On the veil of the Mother of God;
hexameters

Eirene wove this work with her own hands
for the Mother, as peace reigned throughout the earth.

29

On the poor man Leo

You have no bronze, and neither staff nor shoes,
and, what is more, you do not have two robes.
Without wishing it, Leo, you lead an apostolic life.

30

Εἰς τὸν ἔπαρχον Ἰωάννην τὸν Ἀμούδας

Ἐπαρχικὴ στολή σ<ε>, ...
τὸν ἀρετῆς χιτῶσιν ἐστολισμένον,
ἔδειξε νῦν ἔπαρχ<ον ἁπάσῃ πόλει>,
στολὴ δὲ πάντως, ᾗ μένεις ἐσταλμένος,
5 ἔνδειγμα τῶν σῶν πράξεων, Ἰω<άννη>.
Ὁ λευκὸς οὗτος καὶ μέλας χιτὼν ἅμα
ψήφων τὸ διττὸν εὐφυῶς ὑ<πογράφει>,
ψήφων ἐκείνων, αἷς δικῶν τὰς πλεκτάνας
τέμνεις δικαίως, ἡ δικαστῶν ἀξ<ίνη>,
10 ἡττωμένοις μὲν τὴν μέλαιναν ἐξάγων,
τοῖς δ' ἐκ νόμου κρατοῦσι τὴν λευκ<ὴν φέρων>.
Τὸ τοῦ τραχήλου σιμικίνθιον δέ σοι
τί βούλεται, βέλτιστε, καὶ τί μηνύει;
Ἔοικε σειρὰ τῶν πόνων σου τυγχάνειν,
15 δι' ἧς κατάγχεις καὶ δαμάζεις πᾶν πά<θος>.
Πέδιλα κιρρά, σφόδρα λαμπρὰ τὴν χρόαν,
ὡραῖον ὄντα τοὺς πόδας σε δεικν<ύει>,
ὡς πρὸς τρίβους κινοῦντα τούτους ἐνθέους.
Ὁ λευκὸς ἵππος, ὅς σε τοῖς νώτοις φέ<ρει>,
20 τῆς ἀρετῆς τὸ κοῦφον ἐμφαίνει τάχα
ἢ καὶ τὸ λαμπρὸν καὶ διαυγὲς ἐκτ<όπως>,
ἐφ' ἧς ὀχῇ σὺ καὶ τρέχεις θεῖον δρόμον.

30

On the urban prefect John of Amouda

You were already clothed in virtue's garb
but now the prefect's robe . . .
shows the entire city that you are its prefect.
The garment in which you are still adorned
is a sign of your actions, John.   5
That robe, at once both black and white,
shows fittingly the two types of votes:
those votes with which you justly cleave
the entanglements of legal suits, O ax of judges,
as you hold out the black one for the condemned,   10
and the white for those who lawfully prevail.
The scarf around your neck,
what does it mean, your excellence, what is its message?
It seems to be the string of toils
by which you choke and stifle every passion.   15
Your orange sandals, so brightly hued,
show that you have beautiful feet
as you move them toward godly paths.
The white horse carrying you upon its back
indicates, perhaps, the agility of your virtue,   20
or even radiance and extreme splendor,
on which you ride as you run the divine course.

Φάλαρα χαλκᾶ χρυσίῳ κεχρ<ωσμένα>
τὴν σὴν φίλοικτον ζωγραφοῦσι καρδίαν·
25 χαλκοῦ σε καὶ γὰρ μηνύει <καὶ χρυσίου>
χορηγὸν ὄντα τοῖς πένησιν εἰς κόρον.
Τὸ δ' αὖ χιαστὸν σχῆμα τῆς . . .
ἐγκαρσίως τὶς εἰ θελήσειε βλέπειν,
ὁ σταυρός ἐστίν, ὅς σε τη<ρεῖ> . . .
30 καὶ τῶν ὄπισθεν ἐξάγει τιθεὶς πρόσω.
Τί δ', ἂν στ<ερηθῆς> . . .
Μόνων στερηθῆς συμβόλων, οὐ πραγμάτων,
καὶ συμ. . .
αὐτὴν ἐκείνην τὴν Ἀλήθειαν φέρεις.

31

Εἰς <τὸν Μόσχον>

Πάλαι σὺ μόσχος, Μόσχε, μικρὸς ὢν ἔτι·
φύσας δὲ νῦν κέρατα, ταῦρος εἶ μέγας.

The bronze cheek-pieces tinged in gold
depict your merciful heart;
for their message is that you are the donor   25
of ample bronze and gold to the poor.
Your cross-shaped . . . , in turn,
should someone look obliquely at this,
it is the cross, which preserves you . . . ,
and takes you from behind and puts you in front.   30
What would happen if you were robbed of <all this attire>?
You would only be robbed of symbols, not of real things,
and those symbols . . .
you carry Truth itself.

31

On <Moschos>

Once, Moschos, as a child, you were a calf,
but now, with horns, how great a bull you are!

32

Εἰς τὰς ἐν τῇ ἐκκλησίᾳ ῥαινομένας δάφνας κατὰ τὰς ἑορτάς

Τεκμήριον πρὶν οὖσα μαντικῆς δάφνη
θείας ἑορτῆς σύμβολον νῦν τυγχάνει,
κοσμοῦσα φύλλοις, ὡς ὁρᾷς, ἡδυπνόοις
Χριστοῦ τὸν οἶκον ἀντὶ τῶν χρηστηρίων.

33

<Εἰς τὸν Σωτῆρα>

Αἰτεῖσθε καὶ λήψεσθε· σὸς λόγος, Λόγε,
αἰτοῦντί μοι γοῦν δὸς παθῶν <θᾶττον> λύσιν.

32

On the laurel leaves that are strewn around in the church on feast days

The laurel, which was once the sign of seers,
is now the symbol of a holy feast,
adorning, as you see, with fragrant leaves,
the house of Christ instead of oracles.

33

On the Savior

"Ask and you will receive." These, Word, are your words.
So I ask you, swiftly grant me deliverance from passions.

34

Εἰς τὸν Σωτῆρα ἕτεροι

Ἐκ τῆς ἄγαν μου τῶν φρενῶν ἐλαφρίας
βαρὺν συνῆξα, Χριστέ, φόρτον πταισμάτων,
αἴρειν ἐλαφρὸν οὐ θέλων σὸν φορτίον.
Πλὴν πρῶτος αὐτὸς τὰς ἁμαρτίας λέγω,
5 σπεύδων γενέσθαι πρῶτος ἐκ τῶν ἐσχάτων·
ὃ σφόδρα κοῦφον, σοῦ θελήσαντος μόνον.

35

Αἴνιγμα εἰς τὴν ἐν τῷ οὐρανῷ Ἶριν ἤτοι τὸ τόξον

Στοὰ ξύλων ἄμοιρος εἰμὶ καὶ λίθων
ὕλης τε λοιπῆς γηΐνης πάσης ἅμα·
οὐδεὶς καταστρέφει με καὶ παρατρέχω·
οὐδεὶς ἐγείρει καὶ συνίσταμαι πάλιν.

34

More verses on the Savior

Out of too much levity of mind,
I gathered, Christ, a heavy burden of sins,
unwilling to take that *light burden* of yours.
But I first tell my sins to you myself,
hurrying to become first among the last,   5
and this is light indeed if you are but willing.

35

Riddle on the Iris in the sky, that is, the rainbow

I am a gallery without wood or stones,
or any other form of earthly matter;
no one destroys me, yet I disappear;
no one erects me, yet I rise again.

36

Εἴς τινα ὑπερλαλήσαντα φίλου ἕνεκα τῶν ... κατ᾽ αὐτοῦ, ἐννοούμενον δέ

Τέμνων κάρας πρὶν Ἡρακλῆς τὰς τῆς Ὕδρας
βοηθὸν Ἰόλαον εἶχε τὸν φίλον,
καὶ Μελέαγρος συγκροτῶν κάπρῳ μάχην
ἄριστον εἶχε σύμμαχον τὸν Θησέα·
5 αὐτὸς δ᾽ ἐγὼ νῦν εἷς συνάπτων πρὸς δύο,
ὁμοῦ τε πρὸς σὲ καὶ πρὸς αὐτὸν σὸν φίλον,
ἄνωθεν ἕλκω τὴν ῥοπὴν καὶ τὴν χάριν·
καὶ φευγέτω πᾶς, ἀλλὰ καὶ φεύγων ἅμα
χάρτην, μέλαν, κάλαμον εἰς γῆν ῥιπτέτω·
10 αὐτὸς δὲ φεῦγε καὶ πρὸ τῶν ἄλλων ὅλων·
πληγὴν ἐμοῦ γὰρ οὐχ ὑποίσεις καλάμου·
τοίνυν μακράν που φεῦγε τῶν Προτασίου.
Ἤδη δὲ φεύγεις καὶ καλῶς ποιεῖς ἄρα
καὶ λειποτακτεῖς δειλὸς ὢν πρὸς τὰς μάχας,
15 καὶ δειλὸς οἷος—σύγκρισιν γὰρ οὐ δέχῃ·
ὃς ἐμφανῶς βάλλειν με μηδαμῶς σθένων,
ἐξασθενῶν δὲ καὶ πρὸς ἄρσεις τῶν ὅπλων,
ἄπειρος ὥσπερ προσβολῶν ἐνωπίων,
λόχους καθίζεις καὶ κρυφῇ πέμπεις βέλη,
20 κἄνπερ βέλη σὰ νηπίων ἐμοὶ βέλη·

36

On somebody who had spoken in defense of a friend because of the . . . against him, but was still recognized

When Hercules once severed Hydra's heads,
he had his friend Iolaus as a helper.
When Meleager waged combat with the boar,
he had his noble ally Theseus.
But I now wage battle one against two,   5
against you and that friend of yours as well,
so I draw support and favor from above.
Flee, everyone, and as you flee
let paper, ink, and pen fall to the ground!
And you, take flight before all the others,   10
for you will not bear the wound my pen inflicts.
So, flee somewhere far from Protasiou!
You flee already, and well you do so,
deserting like a coward before the battle,
a peerless paragon of cowardice   15
without the strength to strike me in the open,
too impotent to take up arms against me,
and inexperienced in frontal assault.
You sit in ambush, shooting secret arrows,
that are to me *the arrows of a baby*.   20

ζητεῖς δὲ βάλλειν ἀλλὰ καὶ φεύγειν ἅμα·
τί καὶ φοβῇ σὺ καὶ φοβεῖς, τὸ τοῦ λόγου;
Τῆς γωνίας πρόελθε καὶ φάνηθί μοι·
οὕτω γὰρ ἄν σε καὶ κατακλύσω λόγοις
25 ἢ μᾶλλον εἰπεῖν καὶ κατακτείνω, τάλα.
Χολᾷς γινώσκω καὶ μέμηνας ἀσχέτως
καὶ κάπρος οἷα πῦρ ὁρᾷς καὶ πῦρ πνέεις,
χλούνης δὲ μᾶλλον ἢ μονιὸς τὸ πλέον·
θήγεις δὲ τοὺς ὀδόντας ὡς ὁ θὴρ ὅδε·
30 φρίσσεις δὲ χαίτην καὶ παταγεῖς μακρόθεν,
ἀφροῦ παραπτύοντα χείλη δεικνύων.
Καὶ ταῦτα μὲν δρᾷς ἐκφοβεῖν ὥσπερ θέλων,
λόχμῃ δὲ κρύπτῃ καὶ σκέπην ζητεῖς ἕλους.
Ἀλλ᾽ εἰ βαλῶ σε ῥημάτων ἀκοντίῳ,
35 λόχμης ὑπερκύψαντα μικρὸν ἐκ μέσου
ἀντικρύ μου τὲ πρὸς βραχὺν στάντα χρόνον,
καί σου κατοίσω καιρίαν μίαν μάλα,
βολὴν ὑποστῇς οὐδὲ τὴν πρώτην ὅλως,
καὶ νεκρὸς ὀφθῇς, οὐ δεηθεὶς δευτέρας.

37

Εἰς τὸν ῥήτορα Μηνᾶν φιλοπότην ὄντα

Ῥήτωρ ὁ Μηνᾶς, ἀντὶ τοῦ πείθειν πίνων.

You try to hit me while you run away;
why are you terrified and terrifying, as they say?
Stop hiding in corners! Come out and face me!
Allow me, then, to drown you in words,
or, better said, to end your sorry life.   25
I know your bile rises, you rage unbridled,
your eyes blaze and you breathe out flames, like a boar—
or shall we say a hog? A swine, let's say.
Anyway, you sharpen your teeth like that beast,
you bristle your mane and gnash your teeth from afar,   30
showing your lips foaming at the corners.
All this you do as if to frighten me, while
holed up in your den and seeking a hideout in the swamp.
But, if I should hit you with my word spear
when you peep out a little from your den   35
and stand before me for a little while,
and when I bring you down with one fatal blow,
one hit alone will be too much for you;
you'll be dead before the next one lands.

37

On the rhetor Menas, who loves to drink

Menas is a rhetor, but he likes his booze more than his Muse.

38

\<Εἰς τὸν στρατ>ιώτην Ἰωάννην, τὰ τῶν συστρατιωτῶν διαρπάζοντα· ἡρωϊκά

... πολεμιστοῦ
οὐκ ἔναρα βροτόεντα ὑπὲκ πολέμοιο φέρουσα
... ἄνευ πολέμοιο.

39

Εἰς τὸν σπανὸν Εὐγένιον

... \<ἐξερυγγά>νεις,
ὦ κλῆσιν Εὐγένιε τὴν ἀπὸ βρέφους
...
ἐν τοῖς λόγοις δίφθογγος ἔστω πρὸς χάριν
5 ...
κενὴ δὲ πάντως μέμψιν οὐχ ἕξει χάρις
...
\<καὶ> μὴ γράφω δίφθογγον ἐκ τῶν γραμμάτων.

38

On the soldier John, who had stolen the belongings of his comrades; hexameters

... of a warrior,
not by bringing back *the gory spoils* from war,
... without a war.

39

On the beardless Eugenios

... you utter,
O Eugenios, having this name from childhood on.
...
in speech let there be a diphthong, to please you,
...
an empty favor cannot be blamed at all,
...
but I will surely not write a diphthong on paper.

5

40

\<Εἰς τὸν\> ... τοῦ Πόθου, ἰδιώτην ὄντα καὶ τοὺς τῶν σοφῶν λόγους συγκρίνοντα

...

...ας καὶ κρίνεις καὶ συγκρίνεις.

...

ἀπασχολῇ νῦν εἰς λόγων τὰς συγκρίσεις

5 ...

αὐτὸς γὰρ ὡς δεῖ μὴ μαθὼν πρῶτον γράφειν

...

ἀντίθρονός τις οἷον ἐν θρόνῳ κάθῃ

...

10 γενοῦ τὸ πρῶτον σκευαγωγὸς ἐν λόγοις

...

εἶτα στρατηγός, εἶτα καὶ στρατηλάτης

...

κώπης ἀπ' αὐτῆς πρὸς τὸ βῆμα μὴ τρέχε

15 ...

καὶ τὸν νόμον, φεῦ, συγκυκῶν καὶ συστρέφων

...

Ἀτὰρ τίς οἶδε; Πτηνός ἐστι τὴν φύσιν

το...

20 τὸ "κάρτα" φάσκει· "τί πρὸς αὐτὸν ὁ Πλάτων;"

40

On the . . . of Pothos, who is an uneducated man and compares the works of the wise

. . .

. . . you judge and compare.

. . .

you now occupy yourself with the comparisons of texts

. . .

for you yourself have not first learned to write, as you
    should have.

. . .

like a usurper you sit on your throne

. . .

become first a baggage carrier in letters

. . .

then a commander, and thereafter a general

. . .

do not run *from the oars to the platform*

. . .

confounding and overturning the rules, alas!

. . .

However, who knows? It is winged by nature

. . .

"Evidently," he says. "What is Plato worth compared with
    him?"

με...
ὑψηλὸς οἷος καὶ διηρμένος θρόνος
καὶ δὴ τ...
ὁ πάντα λαμπρὸς οὗτος ἐν σοφωτάτοις
25 λαλῶν μὲν ο...
οὕτω γὰρ ἂν δόξειεν εἶναί τις μέγας
καὶ προσκυνείσ<θω>...
καὶ δεικνυέσθω παντὶ δήμῳ δακτύλοις.
Φεῦ τῆς ἀγνοίας...
30 ὡς ἠφρονεύσω, δυστυχεστάτη πόλις,
ἐπάλξεων σῶν καὶ πο...
ἔνδον περικλείσασα τὴν ἀγροικίαν,
ἢ καὶ χορεύει καὶ κροτεῖ, φεῦ <τοῦ θράσους>,
κατηγοροῦσα γνώσεως καὶ τῶν λόγων
35 ὡς χρηστὸν οὐδὲν οὐδαμῶς <πεφυκότων>.
Τὸν Ἰσραὴλ ἔκλαυσας, Ἱερεμία,
ἔκλαυσας, ἐθρήνησας αὐτὸν ὀ<ξέως>·
θρήνησον αὖθις καὶ πόλιν Κωνσταντίνου,
θρήνων ἀπείρων τυγχάνουσαν ἀξ<ίαν>,
40 ζητῶν θαλάσσας, οὐχὶ πηγὰς δακρύων·
οὕτω γὰρ ἂν πως πρὸς τὸ θρῆνος ἀρ<κέσεις>·
ἄλγει, προφῆτα, καὶ πάλιν τὴν κοιλίαν·
ἄλγει, προφῆτα, καὶ πάλιν καθὼς <πάρος>,
ἀλγοῦντας ἡμᾶς τοὺς λόγων φίλους βλέπων,
45 ἀνθ᾽ ὧν καθυβρίσθησαν οἱ λόγ<ων φίλοι>,
ἀνθ᾽ ὧν συνέσχε τοὺς σοφοὺς ἀτιμία,
ἀνθ᾽ ὧν κατωρχήσαντο τούτων οἱ <πλάνοι>.
Σὺ μέν, προφῆτα, ταῦτα καὶ μηδὲν πλέον.

. . .
What a high and lofty throne
and indeed, . . .
the one there who is brilliant among the most wise,
speaking . . .   25
for this way he could appear to be someone great,
and he should be revered . . .
and all people should point him out with their finger.
Alas, the ignorance! . . .
You have lost your mind, most wretched city,   30
enclosing the boorishness
inside your fortifications and . . . ,
the boorishness which dances and applauds—ah the
        audacity!—,
accusing learning and letters
of being of no good at all.   35
Jeremiah, you bewailed Israel,
you bewailed and lamented it keenly.
Now, lament again also the city of Constantine,
worthy of countless laments,
searching for oceans, not *springs of tears;*   40
only thus could you worthily join the lament.
Feel pain, prophet, again in your belly;
feel pain, prophet, again, as before,
when you see that we, the friends of letters, feel such pain,
because the friends of letters have been scorned,   45
because contempt has afflicted the wise men,
because the fools have derided them.
As for you, prophet, to this point and no further.

Αὐτὸς δέ μοι λάλησον, εἴπερ οὐ<ν δύνῃ>,
50 εἴπερ διαρθροῖς, οὐχὶ παππάζεις ἔτι,
ὁ σεμνὸς εἶναι τῶν λόγων κρ<ιτὴς θέλων>·
λάλησον, εἰπέ, πῶς γέμων ἀγνωσίας
χωρεῖς ἀπείρως ὡς τυ...
Εἰ δ' οὐ λαλεῖς, ἄκουε τῶν ἐμῶν λόγων
55 καὶ κέρδος ἕξεις, εἴ γ<ε πείθεσθαι θέλεις>,
τὸ σοὶ συνοῖσον ἐκδιδαχθεὶς αὐτίκα.
Τὸν συγκ<ρίνειν θέλοντα τῶν σοφῶν λόγους>
ἔχειν πρὸ πάντων εὐφυῆ φύσιν δέον,
ἔ<πειτα>...
60 τρίτον σὺν αὐτοῖς ἐντελῆ γνῶσιν φέρειν
...
ἄντικρυς ἐστὶ βουκόλος πρὸς συγκρίσεις
...
ἐξημμένον μάλιστα πολλὰ πυκτία
65 ...
καὶ κέρδος ἕξεις ὥσπερ εἶπόν σοι μέ<γα>
...
ἄπελθε, κλαῦσον ἣν ἔχεις ἀγ<νωσίαν>
...
70 ...
ἄπελθε καὶ στέναξον ἐν ταῖς ἀνίαις
...
πρὸς τὸ γραφὰς γὰρ συγκρίνειν ὀρθῇ κρίσει
...
75 χρεία χρόνου σοὶ καὶ κόπου καὶ λυχνίας
...μόσου.

But you, speak to me, if you can,
if you can articulate and have stopped prattling,   50
you who want to be the respectable judge of letters;
speak, tell us, how you, full of ignorance,
proceed without experience toward . . . .
If you do not speak, hear my words, and
you will profit from them (at least, if you heed them),   55
and at once learn something that is expedient for you.
Whoever wants to compare the works of the wise
must possess, above all, a talented nature,
and then . . . ;
third, combined with the first two, he must have perfect   60
    knowledge.
. . .
he is no more than a cowherd on the subject of
    comparisons,
. . .
above all clinging to many books
. . .   65
and you will reap profit from it, as I told you, great profit.
. . .
go away, deplore your ignorance
. . .
. . .   70
go away and moan in your grief
. . .
for to compare writings with a correct judgment
. . .
you need time, effort, and an oil lamp   75
. . .

41

Εἰς τὴν Ὑπαπαντήν

Ἰδὼν τὸν υἱὸν μητρικαῖς ἐν ὠλέναις,
φθαρτοῦ λυθεὶς ἄπελθε συνδέσμου, γέρον,
ὡς ἄν, φθάσας ἄφθαρτον εἰς κατοικίαν,
ἐν Πατρὶ τοῦτον καὶ Παρακλήτῳ βλέποις·
5 κἀκεῖ γὰρ οὗτος Πατρὸς Υἱὸς καὶ Λόγος,
κἂν ὧδε μητρὸς υἱός ἐστι καὶ βρέφος.

42

. . . ον κύκλῳ διὰ ζύμης τὸν ζῳδιακὸν κύκλον, πρὸς τὴν αὐτοῦ ἐξαδέλφην

Τοὺς οὐρανοὺς σῶν εἶδον ἔργα δακτύλων·
ἐκ γὰρ βραχείας ἀλλὰ καὶ λείας ζύμης
ὡς δέρριν ἐξέτεινας ἡμῖν τὸν πόλον,
ἐποίκιλάς τε τοῦτον οἴκοις ἀστέρων,
5 οἴκοις δὲ φημὶ ζῳδίων δὶς ἑξάδι,
τῶν ἀρετῶν τε καὶ παθῶν τινας τύπους

41

On the Presentation in the Temple

After seeing the son in his mother's embrace,
free yourself from perishable bonds, old man, and go away,
so that, when you come to your permanent abode,
you can see him in the Father and Paraclete.
For there too he is the Father's Son and Word,   5
although here he is his mother's infant child.

42

... with dough the zodiac cycle, in a circle; to his cousin

I have seen the heavens in the work of your hands:
from a small but supple bit of dough
you stretched out the sky before us *like a curtain,*
and decorated it with constellations —
I mean to say the zodiac's twelve signs,   5
examples of the virtues and the vices,

προθεῖσα πᾶσιν ἐμφανεστάτως ἄγαν,
τοῖς ἀνδρικοῖς Λέοντα, Ταῦρον ἀγρίοις,
πόρνοις Διδύμους, σωφρονοῦσι Παρθένον,
10 στρεβλοῖς δὲ τὸν Καρκίνον εἰκότως ἄγαν,
Ζυγὸν δικαίοις, βασκάνοις δὲ Τοξότην,
τὸν Αἰγόκερων οἷς διύβρισται λέχη,
ἀγνωμονοῦσι τὸν Κριὸν σοφῶς μάλα,
ὑδρωπιῶσι προσφόρως Ὑδροχόον,
15 Ἰχθῦς ἀφώνους πᾶσι τοῖς φιλησύχοις,
καὶ κεντρογλώσσοις λοιδόροις τὸν Σκορπίον.
Οἶκοι μὲν οὗτοι τῶν πλανητῶν ἀστέρων,
νήσσεια δ᾽ ᾠὰ δὶς πεφυκότα τρία
τῆς Πλειάδος σῴζουσιν ἀκριβῆ τύπον,
20 τὰ δ᾽ ὀρνίθεια τοὺς πλανήτας μοι νόει,
Ἑρμῆν, Σελήνην, Ἥλιόν τε καὶ Δία,
Ἀφροδίτην, Ἄρην τε, πρὸς δὲ καὶ Κρόνον·
κἂν ἀπλανῆ γὰρ ὦσι καὶ βεβηκότα,
ἀλλ᾽ ἑπτὰ τυγχάνουσιν ἠριθμημένα.
25 Ὠιῶν δὲ πέντε μειζόνων τὸ μὲν μέσον
εἰς Ὠρίωνα ληπτέον τὸν ἀστέρα·
ὁρᾷ γὰρ αὐτοῦ καὶ κατευθὺ Σκορπίος,
δηλῶν τὸ συμβὰν ὡσανεὶ πάλαι πάθος·
τὰ δ᾽ ἄλλα τὴν δήλωσιν εὕρηκε ξένην·
30 ἕδραι γὰρ ᾠῶν τέσσαρες τῶν τεσσάρων
κέντρων τετραπλῆ πῆξις ἀκριβεστάτη
ὡροσκοποῦντος, δῆλον αὐτῆς τῆς ἔω,
δύνοντος ἤγουν τῆς ζοφώδους ἑσπέρας,
μεσουρανοῦντος, δηλαδὴ μεσημβρίας,

displaying them vividly for everyone to view:
Leo for the brave, Taurus for the savage,
Gemini for the lewd, Virgo for the chaste,
Cancer the fitting symbol for the crooked,   10
Libra for the just, Sagittarius for the jealous,
Capricorn for those whose beds are defiled,
Aries, wisely, for the inconsiderate,
Aquarius, rightly, for those suffering from dropsy,
speechless Pisces for all lovers of silence,   15
and Scorpio for sharp-tongued slanderers.
These are the houses of the wandering stars.
Twice three is the number of the duck eggs
sustaining the precise outline of the Pleiades.
We must, in turn, see the hen eggs as planets: 20
Mercury, the Moon, the Sun, and Jupiter,
Venus, Mars, and Saturn too.
Even if these eggs are fixed, unmoving,
seven is their number nonetheless.
Of the five larger eggs, the middle one   25
should be taken as the star Orion,
for Scorpio stares directly at his face,
showing the affliction just as it happened in the past.
The other eggs have a curious explanation:
the four eggs' four positions are a precise   30
quadruple fixture of the cardinal points.
The one in the ascendant is obviously the east;
the descending one is the dark side of the west;
the one that is at its zenith is the south;

35 ἀντιμεσουρανοῦντος, ἀρκτῴου μέρους.
    Τὰ δ' ᾠὰ δηλοῖ πνευμάτων τὴν τετράδα,
    κέντρων πνέουσαν ἐκ πόλου τῶν τεσσάρων·
    ἔξεισι γὰρ Ζέφυρος ἐκ τῆς ἑσπέρας,
    Ἀπηλιώτης ἐκ μερῶν τῶν τῆς ἔω,
40 ὁ δ' αὖ Νότος πρόεισιν ἐκ μεσημβρίας,
    Ἀπαρκτίας δέ, κἂν σιωπήσῃ λόγος,
    ἡ κλῆσις αὐτὴ δεικνύει, πόθεν πνέει.
    Τί δ' ἡ τετρακτὺς τῶν ἄκρων κεφαλίδων
    τέσσαρσιν ᾠοῖς ἐκ ζύμης ἐγκειμένων;
45 Ὡρῶν τετρακτύς ἐστι τῶν ἐν τῷ πόλῳ·
    ὡς ἡ σοφὴ γὰρ μαρτυρεῖ ῥαψῳδία,
    ἐν ταῖς πύλαις οἰκοῦσιν ὧραι τοῦ πόλου·
    εἶδον δ' ἂν ἔνδον οὖσαν ὧδε τοῦ πόλου
    καὶ τὴν ἄναστρον σφαῖραν, οἷα τυγχάνει,
50 εἰ μὴ βροτοῖς ἦν οὐδαμῶς ὁρωμένη·
    καὶ γὰρ πέπλασται καὶ πάρεστιν ἐνθάδε,
    ἀλλ' οὐχ ὁρᾶται· τοῦτο γὰρ ταύτης φύσις.
    Οὕτω σοφή τις τὰς φρένας καὶ ποικίλη
    ἡ δημιουργὸς τοῦδε τοῦ νέου πόλου.
55 Ὦ πάνσοφε πρόνοια τοῦ Θεοῦ Λόγου,
    ὅσας χαρίζῃ καὶ γυναιξὶ τὰς τέχνας,
    οἵας δὲ ταύταις ἐντίθης καὶ τὰς φρένας.
    Ἄλλοι δέ μοι λέγουσιν ἄνδρας Φειδίας
    καὶ Ζεύξιδας μάλιστα καὶ Παρρασίους
60 καὶ τοὺς ἀγνώστους ἄντικρυς Πολυγνώτους
    καὶ τοὺς ἀδόξους ἔμπαλιν Πολυκλείτους,
    καὶ νοῦν σκοτεινοὺς αὖθις Ἀγλαοφῶντας

the one at its nadir is the northern side.   35
The eggs themselves symbolize the four winds
that blow from heaven's four cardinal directions.
For Zephyros proceeds out of the west,
the Apeliotes from regions of the east,
while Notos, in turn, comes out of the south;   40
and as for the Arctic wind, even if explanation should fall
    silent,
the name itself reveals whence it blows.
But what are the four extremities at the edge
made of dough, which cap the four eggs?
These are the four seasons found in the sky;   45
for as the wise rhapsody bears witness,
the *seasons* dwell at the *gates* of the sky.
I would have seen inside this heaven
even how the starless sphere looks,
if it were not invisible to mortals;   50
for it has been created, and it is present here,
but it is unseen, according to its nature.
So wise, so versatile in mind is she,
the creatress of this new heaven.
O, wisest foresight of God the Word,   55
how many arts have you bestowed also upon women,
and what minds have you instilled in them!
Let others speak to me of men like Phidias
or like Zeuxis indeed and Parrasius,
or like the wholly unknown Polygnotus   60
or Polyclites, with no renown at all,
or Aglaophon, the one with murky mind,

καὶ ποικιλουργοὺς χεῖρας αὐτὰς Δαιδάλου·
λῆρος τὰ πάντα, κόμπος, οὐδὲν δὲ πλέον.
65 Πλὴν ἡ Γραφὴ μὲν καὶ πάλιν θαυμαζέτω
πασῶν γυναικῶν ἔργα καινὰ καὶ τέχνας,
λέγουσα· "τίς δέδωκε θηλειῶν φύσει
ὑφασμάτων μὲν γνῶσιν ἀκριβεστάτην,
ποικιλτικῆς δὲ πᾶν ἐπιστήμης μέρος;"
70 Ἐγὼ δὲ χωρεῖν εἰς τὸ πλῆθος οὐ θέλων,
μιᾶς γυναικὸς θαυμάσαιμ' ἂν τὴν τέχνην,
τοσοῦτον ἔργον εὐφυῶς δούσης βλέπειν.
Ἀλλ' ὦ γυναικῶν παρθένων σὺ σεμνότης,
ποθῶ τι μικρὸν καὶ πρὸς αὐτὴν σὲ φράσαι·
75 εἰ ταῦτα ποιεῖς ἐξ ἀλεύρου καὶ ζύμης,
ἐκ στήμονος τί καὶ κρόκης, γνῶναι θέλω·
ἀλλ' ὡς μαθεῖν πάρεστιν ἐξ ὧν εἰργάσω,
κἂν τῇ τέχνῃ μάλιστα τῆς ἱστουργίας
πάσας παρέρχῃ Πηνελόπας, Ἑλένας,
80 ἀμὴν λέγω σοί, καὶ γυναῖκας Λεσβίας.

or the crafty-handed artist Daedalus.
It is all nonsense—bragging, nothing more!
Rather, let the Scriptures marvel again   65
at the novel works and arts of womankind,
saying: "*Who has given* to the race of women
the surest knowledge of *weaving,*
and every aspect of *the science of embroidery?*"
But I, not wishing to make a long list,   70
would rather admire the work of just one woman
who has given such beautiful work to gaze upon.
O, majesty of women's maidenhood,
I wish to address some words to you yourself as well:
if you fashion such things from flour and leaven,   75
I would like to know what you could do with warp and
        woof.
But since I can learn this from what you have wrought,
I say that also in the art of weaving you surpass
every Penelope and every Helen,
and even, I tell you truly, the women of Lesbos.   80

43

Εἰς τὸν μοναχὸν Νικήταν τὸν Συνάδων περὶ τῶν ποδοπανίων

Τηρῶν ὁ δεινὸς τ<ὴν ἐμὴν πτέρναν ὄφις>
δάκνειν με τὸν δύστηνον ἠπείλει πάλαι,
ἐσταλμένους δὲ τοὺς <πόδας καλῶς βλέπων>
ὑφ' ὧν δέδωκας σηρικῶν ὑφασμάτων,
5 φεύγει μακράν που μ...
οὕτω δύνανται καὶ δόσεις, ἅσπερ δίδως.

44

Εἰς τὸν ἀδελφὸν Ἰωά<ννην>

Ἀδελφέ, κεῖσαι, σβέννυσαι δὲ καὶ τάφῳ,
ἀλλ' ἐξανάπτεις θλίψεως ἐ<μοὶ φλόγα>,
σφοδρῶς ὑπεισδύνουσαν εἰς τὴν καρδίαν
καὶ μυελοὺς τήκουσαν αὐτοῖς ὀ<στέοις>.
5 Ὄλοιτο λύπη καὶ μεταρθείη βίου,
ἧς, ὥσπερ οὐ πρίν, οὐδὲ νῦν ἂν ἦσ<θόμην>,

43

To the monk Niketas of Synada, about the foot wrappers

The fearsome snake, spying on my heel,
was long threatening to bite poor me.
Now, seeing that my feet are well fitted out,
thanks to the silken cloths you've given me,
he flees somewhere far . . .   5
such is the power of the gifts you give me.

44

On his brother John

Brother, you lie down, smothered in the grave,
but you kindle in me a flame of sorrow
that violently pierces my heart,
and melts the marrow in my very bones.
May the pain depart and vanish from my life,   5
which I would not feel now, just as I did not feel it before,

εἴπερ σὲ καὶ νῦν εἶχον ὡς τὸ πρὶν βλέπειν,
τὸν πάντα μοι βέλτιστον ἐν τοί<ῳ βίῳ>,
οὗ τὴν τελευτὴν σφόδρα δακρύω, σφόδρα·
10 ταύτην γὰρ ἀρχὴν συμφορῶν εἶδον <τότε>·
κἂν σοὶ δὲ πρώτῳ θλίψεως ἐπῃσθόμην
καὶ πένθος ἔγνων καὶ στεναγμὸν καὶ γ<όον>,
οὔπω τὸ πρῶτον γνοὺς τὰ πένθους, οὐδ' ὄναρ,
οὐδ' εἴπερ ἔστι θλίψις εἰδὼ<ς ἐν βίῳ>.
15 Πλὴν ἀλλὰ πενθεῖν ἐξαφεὶς ἕως τέλους,
γλώττης τὸν αὐλὸν εἰς ἐπαί<νους νῦν τρέπω>,
φάσκων μὲν οὐδὲν ὡς ἀδελφὸς πρὸς χάριν,
αὐτὴν δὲ γυμνὴν τὴν ἀλήθεια<ν λέγων>.
Ποῖαι πλοκαὶ γοῦν ἐκφράσουσι ῥητόρων,
20 ὅπως μὲν εἶχες δεξιῶς πρὸς <τὴν φύσιν>,
ὅπως δὲ καὶ σύμπασαν ἐπλούτεις χάριν,
ὅπως δ' ἐπήνθεις οἰονεὶ . . . ,
κἂν νῦν ἀπανθῇς ὡς μαρανθεῖσα χλόη;
Ποῖαι δὲ γλῶτται καὶ . . .
25 ὦ γλῶτταν αὐτὴν ἡδίων ὑπὲρ μέλι,
τὴν σὴν ἐφυμ<νήσουσι> . . .
ἧς ταῦτα πάντως ἦσαν ἐν τούτῳ βίῳ
. . .
ἀστειότης ἔχουσα τὴν εὐκοσμίαν
30 . . .
σπουδῆς λόγοι φέροντες Ἀττικὴν χάριν
. . .
ῥητῶν ἀπείρων ἀστεϊσμοὶ ποικίλο<ι>
. . .

if only I could see you now as I did before—
you who are the best that I had in this life,
you whose end I mourn so heavily.
I thought this was the start of my misfortunes;   10
it was for you that first I tasted sorrow, and
came to know grief and moaning and wailing,
while formerly I knew no shade of grief, not even in dreams,
and had no hint of sorrow in life.
But I will avoid grieving till the end,   15
and turn my tongue's flute now to praise,
not saying anything just to please you as a brother,
but telling nothing but the naked truth.
What clever tricks of orators can then express
how talented you were by nature,   20
how you abounded in all kinds of charm,
how you blossomed like . . . ,
even if now you are withered like faded grass?
Which tongues and . . . ,
O tongue that was itself sweeter than honey,   25
will praise your . . . ?
Of which there were in your life the following signs:
. . .
an urbanity that preserved its decorum
. . .   30
words that show the Attic grace of study
. . .
varied witticisms in countless utterances
. . .

35 χεῖρες τεχνουργοί, Δαιδάλειοι τὴν φύσιν

   . . .

πᾶν εἴ τι φήσεις, εὐφυῶς ἠσκ<ημένον>

   . . .

οἷς ἦν τι καὶ βάδισμα γ. . .

40   . . .

   . . .

ὡς καὶ δοκεῖν ἔμψυχα ταῦτα τυγχάνειν

   . . .

τίς δ᾽ ἂν φράσειε καὶ τῶν μ. . . ων πρὸς μέρος

45   . . .

πρέπουσαν αἰδῶ, μετριωσύνην τρόπου

       . . .μα

καὶ πᾶν καλὸν σόν, ὦ καλῶν σὺ χωρίον,

       . . .ειν

50 ἐκεῖνα λέξω σὺν στεναγμῷ καρ<δίας>

       . . .ων

ὁ χρηστὸς ἔργοις καὶ λόγοις Ἰωάννης

       . . .έων,

ἡμεῖς δὲ πάντες πένθος ἤγομεν μέγα

55   . . .σου

μήτηρ δὲ μᾶλλον, δυστυχὴς πρῶτον τότε

       . . .<προσεῖ>πέ σε

βλέπουσα πυκνὰ καὶ περιτρύζουσά πως

<καὶ τοῖς ἑαυτῆς δακρύοις τέ>γγουσά σε

60 καὶ σοῦ σοβεῖν θέλουσα τὴν δεινὴν νόσον,

<εἰ καί σε μεῖναι θάνατον> πάντως ἔδει,

skillful hands, of a Daedalic character,   35
. . .
whatever you were going to say, it was admirably elaborated
. . .
they also had a gait . . .
. . .   40
. . .
so that they seemed to be alive
. . .
Who could describe also the . . . in detail?
. . .   45
a fitting reverence, and moderate manners
. . .
and every virtue you have, O focal point of virtues,
. . .
this I will say with a moaning of the heart   50
. . .
John, upright in deeds and words,
. . .
We all bore a great grief,
. . .   55
our mother yet more, unhappy for the first time at that
        moment,
                                        . . . she addressed you,
frequently looking up and walking around murmuring,
washing you in her own tears and
wanting to scare that fearsome disease away from you,   60
even if death surely awaited you anyway,

ἄνθρωπον ὄντα· καὶ τί γὰρ φήσω πλέον;
.... <ψ>υχὴ φίλη,
τῶν ζωοποιῶν ὡς ἐχρῆν μυστηρίων,
65   < "οἴκτειρ', Ἰησοῦ Χριστέ> μου," κράξας τρίτον·
τοῦτον γὰρ οἶδα σοῦ τελευταῖον λόγον
.... ν μὲ καὶ παραυτίκα
γλῶτταν πεδηθεὶς τὸν περὶ ψυχῆς ἔθεις.
.... τοιγαροῦν, Ἰωάννη,
70   καὶ χερσὶ θείαις ἐκπνέεις τῶν ἀγγέλων
.... <τούτ>ῳ τῷ τελευταίῳ λόγῳ
τῷ Χριστὸν εἰς τὸν οἶκτον ἐκκαλουμένῳ
<συνεκ>δραμών τε καὶ συνεκπτὰς ἐκ βίου.
Ἀλλ' ὦ κραταιὸν Πατρὸς ὑψίστου σθένος,
75   <ὃς ἐξ>ετάζεις καὶ νεφροὺς καὶ καρδίας,
ὃς οἶδας ἡμῶν πᾶν ἀπόκρυφον μόνος,
<ὃς σ>ῇ θελήσει πάντα ποιεῖς καὶ μόνη,
Ἰωάννου μνήσθητι σοῦ δούλου, Λόγε,
<μνήσ>θητι καὶ δὸς σφαλμάτων αὐτῷ λύσιν,
80   τάττων τὸ τούτου πνεῦμα σὺν σεσωσμένοις.

since you were human; and what can I add to that?
                    . . . beloved soul,
as was needed, of the life-bringing mysteries,
you cried out for the third time: "Have pity on me, Jesus   65
    Christ."
I know that these were your last words
                    . . . immediately,
when your tongue was bound, you ran the contest for your
    soul.
                    . . . therefore, John,
you breathed your last in the divine hands of the angels   70
                    . . . together with that last word,
calling out to Christ for mercy,
you ran away and flew from life.
O powerful strength of the Father on high,
you who *scrutinize the heart and mind,*   75
who alone know all of our secrets,
and who can do all things by your will alone,
remember your servant John, Word of God,
remember him and give him remission of sins,
assigning his soul a place among the saved.   80

45

Εἰς τὰ πεμφθέντα τῷ φίλῳ ἄνθιμα
ἐψυχρισμένα κουτρούβια

Δέξαι ψυχρόν τι δῶρον ἐν καιρῷ θέρους,
ἐκ σφόδρα θερμοῦ πρὸς σὲ πεμφθὲν τοῦ πόθου·
σὺν ἡδονῇ δὲ τοῦτο δέξαι καρδίας·
οὐκ εὐτελὲς γὰρ οὐδ' ἀπόβλητον κρίνῃς,
5 ὅπου γε κεῖται καὶ ψυχροῦ ποτηρίου
μισθὸς παρ' αὐτῷ τῷ Θεῷ καὶ Δεσπότῃ.

46

<Εἰς> τὸν Ἰώβ· ἡρωελεγεῖα

Ὄλβιά σοι τὰ πρῶτα, τὰ δ' αὖ μέσα, φεῦ, ὀδυνηρά,
   <ὕστα>τα δ' εὐλογίην ἔσχον ἀγωνοθέτου·
ἐσθλὰ δ' ἅπαντα μάλιστα, ἐπεί γε τὰ ὕστατα ἐσθλά,
   <ἔμπνοε κ>αρτερίης στήλη, Ἰὼβ πολύτλα.

45

On the jars with cooled aromatic drinks
sent to his friend

Receive a cool gift in the summer season,
sent to you because of a burning desire.
Receive it with pleasure in your heart,
for you will not consider it cheap or worthless,
since also our Lord and Sovereign himself   5
gives a reward for a cup of cold water.

46

On Job; elegiac couplets

Happy was the beginning for you; the middle, alas, was
     painful,
   but the ending received the Judge's blessing.
All is well, since it ended well—
   living monument of patience, much-enduring Job.

47

Αἴνιγμα εἰς τὴν χιόνα

<Κρατεῖς μ>ε καὶ φεύγω σε κεκρατημένη·
φεύγουσαν ἀθρεῖς καὶ κατασχεῖν οὐ σθένεις·
<κἂν γοῦν μέσ>ης σφίγγῃς με παλάμης ἔσω,
κενὴν λιποῦσα φεύξομαι σὴν παλάμην.

48

<Εἰς τοὺς ἐπὶ τοῦ ... κ>αθεζομένους στρουθοὺς καὶ τερετίζοντας

...
ἔμψυχον αὐλὸν ἔμπνοον τὰ στρουθία
...
μέλους ἅμιλλαν συγκροτοῦσιν ἠρέμα
5 ...
κατακτυποῦσι καὶ νάπας καὶ κοιλάδας
...
νικῶσι νήτην, ὑπάτην, παρυπάτην

47

Riddle on the snow

While yet you hold me, I escape your grasp;
you watch me flee and cannot keep me back;
however hard you squeeze me in your palm,
I will escape your hand and leave it empty.

48

On the sparrows that are sitting on the . . . and chirping

. . .
the sparrows <play> a living and breathing flute
. . .
quietly convoking a song contest
. . .
resounding through the glens and valleys
. . .
they defeat the lowest, the highest, and the next-highest
      string

5

...

10 κατὰ πτερωτὰς ἡ φύσις πλάττει λύρας

...

<ἐχούσας ἔν>δον ἀντὶ μὲν χορδῶν φλέβας

...

<καὶ φυσικ>ὴν σύζευξιν ἀντὶ κολλάβων,

15   ... <ἀποθλ>ίβοντες ἡδονῆς μέλος

...

49

<Εἰς τὸν βασιλέα> Μιχαήλ, ὅτε ἀπεκάρη

...

... <π>εδίλοις κοκκίνοις συνεκδύη

...

<τὸ στέμ>μα ῥίψας, Μιχαήλ, καὶ πορφύραν

5 ...

... γὰρ καταγνοὺς ἡδέων ὡς ἀστάτων

τε ...

τιμὴν ἀληθῆ προκρίνων ἐψευσμένης.

. . .

Nature forms them like winged lyres   10

. . .

having veins inside instead of strings

. . .

and <using> natural joints instead of pegs,
they squeeze out a tune of pleasure . . .   15

. . .

49

On the emperor Michael,
when he was tonsured

. . .

you have put off your . . . together with your red sandals

. . .

throwing away the crown, Michael, and the purple,

. . .   5

having realized now that all pleasures are insecure,

. . .

preferring real honor above false honor.

50

Εἰς τὸν χαλκοῦν ἵππον, τὸν ἐν τῷ
Ἱπποδρόμῳ τὸν πρόσθιον πόδα ἠρμένον
ἔχοντα

Ἔμπνους ὁ χαλκοῦς ἵππος οὗτος, ὃν βλέπεις,
ἔμπνους ἀληθῶς καὶ φριμάξεται τάχα·
τὸν πρόσθιον δὲ τοῦτον ἐξαίρων πόδα
βαλεῖ σε καὶ λάξ, εἰ παρέλθῃς πλησίον.
5 Δραμεῖν καθορμᾷ· στῆθι, μὴ προσεγγίσῃς,
μᾶλλον δὲ φεῦγε, μὴ λάβῃς, τὸ τοῦ λόγου.

51

Εἰς τὴν εἰκόνα τῆς ἁγίας Θέκλης,
λελατομημένην ἐκ πέτρας

Κρύπτει <γε> πέτρα, νῦν δ' ὑπεκφέρει Θέκλαν.

50

On the bronze horse in the Hippodrome which has its forefoot raised

That horse of bronze you see there truly breathes.
Yes, it breathes, perhaps it will leap out snorting.
It is lifting up that forward leg,
and will trample you if you come close.
It is getting ready to race! Stop, do not go near!   5
You'd better run or, as they say, you'll catch it.

51

On the image of Saint Thekla, carved from stone

A stone once concealed, but now reveals Thekla.

52

Εἰς τὸν ἀποβασιλέα Μιχαὴλ τὸν
Καλαφάτην, ὅτε διὰ τὸ τὴν δέσποιναν
Ζωὴν ἐξορίσαι τῆς βασιλείας
κατενεχθεὶς ἐτυφλώθη· ἡρωϊκά

Μέλλεν ἄρα τριτάλαινα πόλις Βύζαντος ἰδέσθαι
ὁλκαδοπιττωτοῦ τε καὶ ἀστῶν φύλοπιν αἰνήν·
μέλλε καὶ ἥλιος θεάσασθαι οὐλαμὸν ἄλλον,
ὃν τέκεν ἐξορίη βασιλίσσης εἶδος ἀρίστης,
5 Ζωῆς εὐγενετείρας, ἣν ἁπαλὴν ἔτ᾽ ἐοῦσαν
δέξατο πορφύρα ἠδέ θρέψατο μασθὸς ἀνάσσης,
κουριδίην δ᾽ ἄλοχον λάχε Ῥωμανὸς μετέπειτα,
ἀνὴρ εὐγενέτης, κάλεον δέ μιν Ἀργυρόπωλον,
ὃς καὶ παρθενίην ζώνην ὑπελύσατο τῆσδε.
10 Ταύτης ἐξορίη κακὰ γείνατο ἄστεϊ πολλά,
παισὶ μὲν ὀρφανίην, χηρείην δ᾽ αὖ γε γυναιξίν,
αἵματα ὠτειλάς τε μάχας τ᾽ ἀνδροκτασίας τε,
λευγαλέους θανάτους, πόλλ᾽ ἄλγεά τε στοναχάς τε,
νηπιόεντι νόῳ τέκνοιο θετοῖο ἐκείνης·
15 ὅς ῥα κακῇ αἴσῃ μεγάλης πόλιος βασίλευσεν,
αἴσυλα δὲ φρονέων ταχὺ λάθετο συνθεσιάων,
ᾗσι δ᾽ ἀτασθαλίῃσι κακὴν συμφράσσατο μῆτιν·
ἀμφὶ πόλιν δὲ μέσην μάλα ἡδέα ὤλεσε φῶτα,

52

On the ex-emperor Michael Kalaphates, when he was arrested and blinded for having banished the empress Zoe from imperial rule; hexameters

So the thrice-hapless city of Byzas was to behold
the dreadful battle between the ship caulker and the
    townsmen,
and the sun was to behold another disaster,
brought about by the exile of the *fair* empress
Zoe, the noble born, whom, when she was still young,   5
the purple received, and the breast of an empress nursed;
Romanos thereafter obtained her as his *wedded wife*,
a highbred man, they called him Argyropolos;
and it was he who loosened her *maiden girdle*.
Her exile bore the city many woes,   10
orphanhood for children, widowhood for women,
blood and wounds, *strife and murder,*
painful deaths, much *sorrow and moaning,*
all because of the infantile mind of her adopted child.
By a bad fate this man reigned over the great city.   15
Intent on evil, he quickly *forgot the covenants,*
and in his rashness he devised a wicked plan.
But in the middle of the city he lost his dear sight

οὕνεχ᾽ ὑπερβασίῃ δηλήσατο ὅρκια πιστά·
20 ὕβρισε δ᾽ ἐς τὸ στέμμα, κατὰ σπονδάς τε πάτησε,
ῥίψας ἐκ βασιλείων δυσβασιλεὺς βασίλισσαν.
Ἀλλὰ τὸν ἀφροσύνῃ ὅρκων τ᾽ ἀθέτησις ἄθεσμος
δεινῶς ἐξαλάωσαν, σκῆπτρα δ᾽ ἀπ᾽ αὐτοῦ ἕλοντο.
Νῦν δὲ βαρυστενάχων γοερὸν βοάει κακοδαίμων
25 οὐλομένην καλέων "βασιλείην, ἣν βασίλευσα."
Κεῖται δ᾽ ἐν δαπέδῳ μέγα ἄθλιος, ὃς πρὶν ἄνασσεν,
ἄκρης δυστυχίης καὶ ὀψιγόνοις ὑπόδειγμα,
φωτὸς ἐελδόμενος, τόπερ ὤλεσεν ἄφρονι βουλῇ.

53

Εἰς τὸ λουτρόν

Οἷον τὸ λουτρὸν χρῆμα θυμῆρες σφόδρα·
παρηγορεῖ γὰρ σῶμα καὶ σμήχει ῥύπους,
ἐλαφρύνει δὲ πάντα τῆς σαρκὸς μέρη
καὶ καινοποιεῖν πᾶν δοκεῖ ταύτης μέλος·
5 πτεροῖ δὲ τὸν νοῦν καὶ διώκει πᾶν βάρος
καὶ τῶν φρενῶν ἅπασαν ἀχλὺν ἐκφέρει·
εἰ δὲ σκοπήσεις, καὶ τὸ χαίρειν εἰσφέρει·
χαίρει γὰρ ὄντως τοῖς λελουμένοις φύσις.

by violating *the truthful oaths* with his offense.
He brought his crown to shame, he trampled upon truces,   20
this baneful emperor, by expelling the empress from the
    palace.
But foolishness and the unlawful violation of oaths
have terribly blinded him and taken away his scepter .
Now this wicked creature sighs heavily, and cries out grief-
    stricken,
calling ruined "this empire that I ruled."   25
He lies now on the ground, the wretched one, who once
    held power,
an example of utter misery for future generations,
craving the light he lost with his foolish aspirations.

53

On the bath

Truly the bath is a delightful thing,
comforting the body and washing off the dirt,
soothing all parts of the flesh,
and seeming to remake all limbs anew.
It gives wings to the mind, expels every burden,   5
and scatters all the fog that clouds the brain.
If you think about it—it also brings joy,
for nature truly rejoices in those washed clean.

54

Εἰς τὸν βασιλέα Κωνσταντῖνον τὸν Μονομάχον

Ἔχεις τὸ λευκόν· εἰς τί μαργάρων χάρις;
Τὸ ξανθὸν αὐχεῖς· χρυσὸς ὄντως εἰς μάτην.
Πλουτεῖς τὸ φαιδρόν· οἱ λίθοι βάρος μόνον.
Κόσμον φέρεις σόν· ἐρρέτω κόσμος νόθος.

55

Εἰς τὸν αὐτὸν βασιλέα, ὡς ἀπὸ προσώπου τοῦ πρωτοσπαθαρίου Ἰωάννου τοῦ Ὑψίνου

Πακτωλὸς ὤφθης ἄλλος, ὦ στεφηφόρε·
ἀλλ' ἦν ἐκεῖνος, ὡς λόγος, χρυσορρόας,
σὺ δ' ὁ κραταιὸς οὐ μόνον χρυσορρόας,
ἀλλὰ πλέον μάλιστα καὶ τιμορρόας·
5 χέουσιν ἐκ σοῦ καὶ γὰρ ἀφθονωτάτως
τιμῶν τε πηγαὶ καὶ ποταμοὶ χρυσίου.

54

On the emperor Constantine
Monomachos

You possess white skin—so why the beauty of pearls?
You boast blond hair—so gold is indeed of no use.
You abound in splendor—gems are merely weight.
You have your own adornments—away with the false ones!

55

To the same emperor,
as if spoken by the *protospatharios*
John Hypsinous

You have appeared as a new Pactolus, O crown bearer.
However, as the story goes, it streamed with gold,
while you, great ruler, stream not just with gold,
but even more with honors too.
From you pour forth abundantly   5
fountains of honors as well as rivers of gold.

Ἐγὼ παρώφθην· οἶδα δ' ὡς οὐκ εἰς τέλος·
οὔκ εἰμι τοίνυν οὐδαμῶς ἀπ' ἐλπίδων,
ἐκεῖνο πᾶσιν ἐκβοῶν καθ' ἡμέραν·
10 "ὁ πάντας ὑψῶν δεσπότης Κωνσταντῖνος
πάντως ἀνυψώσειε καὶ τὸν Ὑψίνουν."
Οὕτως ὄναιο στέμματος καὶ τοῦ θρόνου·
τὰς ἐλπίδας μου μὴ κενὰς θήσεις, ἄναξ.

56

Αἴνιγμα εἰς τὰς ἐν τῷ ὡρολογίῳ ὥρας

Ἡμεῖς ἀδελφαὶ γνήσιαι ψυχῶν δίχα·
ἄλλη μὲν ἄλλης τῷ χρόνῳ πρεσβυτέρα,
ἴσαι δὲ πᾶσαι τοὺς διαύλους τῶν χρόνων·
αἳ καὶ καλοῦμεν οὐκ ἀνοίγουσαι στόμα,
5 βαδίζομεν δὲ μὴ πόδας κεκτημέναι.
Ἐνταῦθά σοι λαλοῦμεν, ὡς ὁρᾶν ἔχεις,
καὶ πανταχοῦ πάρεσμεν, εἰ σκοπεῖν θέλεις.

I have been disregarded, but I know that this is not forever.
Therefore, I am not wholly without hope,
and I cry out to everyone every day:
"May the lord Constantine, who raises up all men,   10
by all means raise up Hypsinous as well."
Hence, may you enjoy your crown and your throne,
but do not disappoint my hopes, my lord.

56

Riddle on the hours of the clock

We are genuine sisters without souls.
Each, in time, is older than the other,
but all of us make equal rounds of time.
We cry out, although we don't open our mouths,
and we stride forth, although we have no feet.   5
We speak to you here, as you can see,
and we're everywhere, if you are willing to look.

57

<Εἰς τὴν μητέρα Ζωὴν τελευτήσασαν· ἡρω>ελεγεῖα

Ἧς φρένες ἦλθον ἄπαντα μακρᾶς ἀνὰ πείρατα γαίης
            ... πινυτῆς,
τῆσδε δέμας μαλακὸν κεῖται ὀλίγῃ ἐνὶ χώρῃ
            ... λάμπει ὅλην
5 ἄμβροτος, ἀθάνατος καὶ ἀγήραος αἰὲν ἐοῦσα
            ... ε καλυπτομένη.
Ὤ μοι, μῆτερ ἐμή, ὅτι σὸς παῖς, ὃν φιλέεσκες,
            ...ατο Χριστοφόρος
αὐτοκασιγνήτοισιν ἑοῖς ἅμα δειλαίοισιν
10   ... γεύσατο καὶ ἀνίης·
ὦ πόσα μοι ἐπέτελλες, ὅσα ψυχὴν ὀνίνησιν
            ... πνεύματος ἡμετέρου·
οὐ γὰρ ἔης μήτηρ σαρκὸς μόνον, ἀλλὰ καὶ αὐτοῦ
            ...υ οὔποτε ὀλλυμένου.
15 Ποίου δὴ προτέρου ἀγαθῶν σῶν μνήσομ' ἔγωγε
            ... λέει ἠδὲ ὑπερφυέα·
οἴδασι ταῦτα ἄπαντες, ὅσοι ὑπὸ ἥλιόν εἰσι,
            <καί σε μα>καρίζουσ', οὕνεκα τοίη ἔφυς.
Ὤιχετο ἐκ φθαρτοῖο φίλη μήτηρ βιότοιο,
20   <ἣν Σ>ολομῶν, σοφίης ἔρνος ἐϋκλεέος,

57

On his mother Zoe who has died; elegiac couplets

Hers is the mind that went over all the limits of the large
 earth
  . . . prudent,
hers too is the tender body that now rests in a small place,
 <while her soul> . . . shines entirely,
being forever immortal, undying, and imperishable,   5
  . . . covered.
Ah, my mother, know that your child, whom you loved,
  . . . Christopher,
together with his own wretched brothers
 has tasted . . . and sorrow.   10
How much advice did you give me, benefitting my soul,
  . . . my spirit;
for you were not only the mother of my body, but also of
  . . . that never dies.
Which of your virtues shall I then first mention?   15
  . . . and extraordinary.
All who live under the sun know this,
 and bless you because you were such a woman.
My beloved mother has left this perishable life,
 she whom Solomon, scion of renowned wisdom,   20

ἐν προτέροισι χρόνοισιν ὑπέγραφε καὶ πρὸ τόκοιο·
<πᾶ>ν γὰρ αὐτὴ ἔης, κεῖνος ὅσα προέφη·
ἀνδρείη, πινυτή, ἀπόροις οἴγουσα ταμεῖα,
βρῶμα νέμουσα δόμῳ, ἔργα δὲ ἀμφιπόλοις,
25 οὐκ ὀκνηρά γε σῖτον ἔδειν ἐθέλουσα κατ᾽ οἶκον,
ἀλλὰ πόνοιο ἔδρᾳ αἰὲν ἐφεζομένη,
βωμὸς ἐοῦσ᾽ ἐλέου καὶ ἐπ᾽ ἀκτεάνους συνιεῖσα.
<Τί>πτε, πάτερ, στενάχεις; Τίπτε βαρυστενάχεις;
Ἐξ ἀρετῶν πασάων ἔμψυχον ἄγαλμά ποτ᾽ εἶχες
30 <οἴ>κῳ ἐν ἡμετέρῳ, μητέρα ἡμετέρην·
εἰ δέ σ᾽ ἀφαιρεῖται κείνην Θεός, ὅς γε δέδωκε,
<τέτ>λαθι καρτερόφρον, καὶ Θεὸν εὐφρανέεις·
Ζωὴ γὰρ μακάρων μοίρη ἐναρίθμιός ἐστι,
<καὶ>ρῷ ἐν εὐφροσύνης γῆθεν ἀποιχομένη·
35 ἔνθεν ἄρ᾽ ἄλγεα δεινὰ πολύστονα πάντα ἀπέδρα.
<Ἀλλ᾽> ἔτι ἐξερέω λώϊον, εἴ γε κλύοις·
ὡς Κυρίῳ Σωτῆρι δοάσσατο κέρδιον εἶναι,
<οὕτω> καὶ γένετο· παῦσ᾽ ὀλοφυρόμενος.

described in earlier times, even before her birth;
    for you were everything he had foretold:
courageous, prudent, opening up your purse for the poor;
    doling out food for the house, and tasks for the servants,
not wanting to eat the bread of idleness at home,   25
    but always sitting on the seat of labor,
being an altar of mercy and an understanding ear for the
      poor.
    Why, father, do you weep? Why do you sigh so heavily?
You once had a living statue of all virtues
    in our house: our mother.   30
If God has taken her away from you, God who gave her,
    endure this with a patient heart and you will gladden the
      Lord.
For Zoe can now be counted among the lot of the blessed,
    having left the earth in a time of gladness:
she has escaped all the sorrowful and terrible pains here.   35
    But I will say something that is even better, if you want to
      listen:
as our Lord the Savior *has thought was better,*
    so has happened; now do not lament anymore.

58

Εἰς τὸν πατέρα λυπούμενον καὶ θρηνοῦντα

<Τί, πάτερ, αὐ>τὸς ἄσχετον πενθῶν κάθῃ,
λούων σεαυτὸν δακρύων καταιγίσι;
<Μήτηρ γὰρ ἡμῶν>, κἂν παρῆλθεν ἐκ βίου,
λαλεῖ δὲ μὴ παροῦσα, μηδ' ὁρωμένη,
5 <Ἠχοῦς λαλιὰν> ὥσπερ ἐκμιμουμένη,
καὶ τοῖς λόγοις δίδωσι τὰς ἀποκρίσεις
                    ... εὐλογωτάτας
κἀντεῦθεν, ὡς ζῇ, πᾶσι πιστοῦται ξένως
...
10 σὺ δὲ προσέξεις καὶ παραψυχὴν λάβῃς
...
λόγοις διδούσης τοῖς ἐμοῖς ἀποκρίσεις
...
<ὁ>ποῖον ἂν φήσειεν ἠχὼ μακρόθεν.

58

To his father who is distressed and grieving

Why, father, do you sit grieving without restraint,
bathing yourself with torrents of tears?
Although our mother has passed on from this life,
she speaks, though she is neither present nor seen,
as if imitating the voice of Echo,   5
and with words she gives answers,
                . . . very reasonable,
and thus she proves to all, inexplicably, that she is alive
. . .
if you pay attention, you will be consoled   10
. . .
as she gives answers to my words
. . .
whatever it is that the echo might say from afar.

59

… <ἴα>μβοι· καὶ οἱ μὲν πρὸς τὴν μητέρα
ἀ… <ἐτ>ερόφωνον, ὡσανεὶ
τῆς μητρὸς τὰ… <θαυ>μασίως κατὰ τὴν
ἠχὼ… τὸν πατέρα διὰ μ… <ἀθυ>μίας
καὶ οἷον παραμυθού<μενον>…
<παρὰ> τοῦ υἱοῦ λεγόμενα

Μ<ῆτερ>,…   …<μέγα>;
      …ἀντέφησε γάρ· "μέγα."
Ἡ…   …<μάλα·>
ἄκουε ταύτης ὡς ἀπεκρίθη· "μάλα."
5 Αἰ<αὶ>…   …<δάκνει·>
ἔφησεν αὖθις, ὥσπερ ἤκουσας· "δάκνει."
Ὡς ἀ…   …<ἔγνων·>
ἔγνω, τί φάσκω, καὶ λέγει πάντως· "ἔγνων."
Ἔμει…   …<τάλας·>
10 ὁποῖος εἰμί, γνοῦσα κραυγάζει· "τάλας."
Σὺ δ<ὴ φιλεῖς με καὶ καλεῖς με σὸν τέκνον;>
Τὸν φίλτατον φιλεῖ με καὶ καλεῖ· "τέκνον."
παντ…   …<πλέον>·
ὡς σφόδρα μου στέργοντος ἐκβοᾷ· "πλέον."
15 Πατὴρ ἐμ<ὸς>…   …<θέλει>·
ὅπερ θέλεις, ἔγνωκε καὶ κράζει· "θέλει."

59

... iambs; some of them to his mother
... with another voice, as if from his
mother ... marvelously, through the
echo ... his father ... distress,
and as if consoled ...
spoken by the son

Mother, ... greatly?
      ..., for she said in turn: "Greatly."
                              ... much.
Listen to her; she has answered: "Much."
Ah, ... bites.   5
She has spoken again, as you have heard: "Bites."
                              ... I have understood.
She has comprehended what I asked, and says: "I have
      understood."
                              ... wretched.
She knows in what state I am, and cries out: "Wretched."   10
You love me and you call me your own child?
She loves me, her most beloved son, and calls me: "Child."
                              ... more.
Since I love her so much, she exclaims: "More."
My father ...   ... wants.   15
She has understood what you want and cries out: "Wants."

Ἀπόκρι<ναι>... ...<δέον>·
καὶ νῦν ἰδοὺ βοᾷ τε καὶ λέγει· "δέον."
Καὶ τρεῖς λόγ<ους>, ...<μάθη>·
20 ἄκουε· καὶ γὰρ ἀνταπεκρίθη· "μάθη."
Εἴπερ τόπος χλ<όης σε νῦν ἐκεῖ φέρει>·
προσέσχες αὐτός; Ἀντέφησε γάρ· "φέρει."
Εἰ φῶς τὸ σὸν πρόσ<ωπον οὐρανοῦ βλέπει>·
χαίρω κατ᾽ ἄκρον· καὶ γὰρ ἐκβοᾷ· "βλέπει."
25 Εἰ τὴν ἄληκτον πνεῦμα σὸ<ν χαρὰν ἔχει>·
δεῖ καὶ σὲ χαίρειν· φησὶ γὰρ μήτηρ· "ἔχει."
Μῆτερ, λαλήσω καὶ π<άλιν σύ μοι λάλει>·
ἐπιτρέπει λαλεῖν με καὶ λέγει· "λάλει."
Θέλω μαθεῖν, αἴσθησις εἰ ψυχ<αῖς ἔνι>·
30 ἔφησεν, "ὡς αἴσθησις ἐν ψυχαῖς ἔνι."
Νοοῦσι δ᾽, εἰ θύοι τις· ἢ γοῦν καὶ <λίαν>;
Ἤκουσας; Ἀντέφησεν ἡ μήτηρ· "λίαν."
Ταύτας δὲ θρηνῶν ὠφελεῖ τις ἢ θύ<ων>;
Εἴρηκεν, ὡς ἤκουσας, ὦ πάτερ· "θύων."
35 Χαίρουσι δ᾽ αὗται ταῖς χοαῖς; ἢ καὶ <πάνυ>;
Πάτερ, προσέσχες; Ἀνταπεκρίθη· "πάνυ."
Δέξαι χοὰς οὖν τοὺς λόγους, εἴ σοι φίλ<ον>·
ἄγαν φιλοῦσα τοὺς λόγους ἔφη· "φίλον."
Λόγοι γὰρ ὄντως βελτίους χοῶν ὅλ<ως>;
40 Συμμαρτυρεῖ μοι καὶ λέγει πάντως· "ὅλως."
Φώνησον ἀνδρὸς εἰς παραψυχήν· "ἄ<νερ>"·
ἰδοὺ σὲ φωνεῖ καὶ καλεῖ τρανῶς· "ἄνερ."
Καί μοι πάλιν σίγησον, εἰ σιγᾶν <πρέπει>·
εἰδυῖα καιρὸν καὶ σιγῆς, ἔφη· "πρέπει."

Answer, ... it is needed.
You see, she now exclaims and says: "It is needed."
And three words, ... learn.
Hear! She answered in turn: "Learn."   20
Is there a green pasture for you that now provides support?
Did you pay attention? She replied: "Provides support."
Does your face see the light of heaven?
I am so glad! For she exclaims: "The light of heaven."
Does your soul possess eternal joy?   25
You have to rejoice too, for our mother says: "Eternal joy."
Mother, I will speak, and you in turn speak.
She permits me to speak, for she says: "Speak."
I want to know whether souls have senses.
She said: "Souls have senses."   30
When someone offers, do they realize? Perhaps even a great
    deal?
Did you hear? Our mother replied: "A great deal."
Do we benefit them with grief or with offerings?
She said, as you have heard, father: "With offerings."
Do they rejoice in libations? Or even greatly?   35
Did you pay attention, father? She replied in turn: "Greatly."
So, accept these words as libations, if you agree.
Since my words please her so much, she says: "Agree."
Are words then better than libations anyway?
She agrees with me, saying: "Anyway."   40
Call then your husband to console him: "Husband."
Hear! She calls you, shouting clearly: "Husband."
And now again keep silent, if silence is befitting.
She knows also the time for silence, saying: "Befitting."

60

Εἰς τὸν πατέρα ἕτεροι παραμυ<θητικοί>

Μαθὼν παρ' αὐτῆς τῆς ἐμῆς μητρός, πάτερ,
ὅποι πάρεστι καὶ τόπους οἵους λ<άχοι,>
καὶ τῶν ἐκείνης νῦν ἀκούσας ῥημάτων
ἢ κρεῖττον εἰπεῖν μᾶλλον ἀντ<ηχημάτων>,
5 μοίρας τε ταύτην γνοὺς τελεῖν σεσωσμένων,
πενθεῖν ἀφεὶς δόξαζε <τὸν Θεὸν πάνυ.>

61

Εἰς τὸν πατριάρχην Μιχαὴλ τῇ ἐπαύριον τῆς χειροτονία<ς αὐτοῦ>

Εὐαγγελισμὸς χθὲς χαρᾶς τῇ Παρθένῳ
ἐκ Γαβριὴλ ὑ<πῆρξε τοῦ πρωταγγέλου·>
ὑπῆρξεν αὖθις καὶ Θεοῦ χθὲς τῷ δόμῳ
<εὐαγγελισμὸς> . . .
5 ὃν αὐτὸς ἡμῖν ἐν μέσῳ στὰς τοῦ θρόνου
. . .
τοῖς Χριστιανοῖς πᾶσιν εἰρήνην νέμων
. . .

114

60

More consolatory verses for his father

You've heard from my mother herself, father,
where she is and what abode she has received.
So, now that you have listened to her words,
or rather listened to her echoes, we should say,
and learned that her lot is counted among the saved,   5
stop grieving, and praise the great God.

61

To the patriarch Michael on the day after his installation

Yesterday there was the annunciation of joy for the Virgin
by Gabriel the archangel.
Yesterday, in the house of God, there was another
annunciation . . .
which you yourself, rising from the throne, in the middle   5
. . . for us,
dispensing peace to all Christians
. . .

62

Εἰς τὸν σιδηροπράτην Λέοντα ἐ. . .
στάντα τῷ βασιλεῖ καὶ ῥα. . . . . .
οὐκ ὀλίγοι προσηγγελ. . .

. . .
Λέοντος οἱ λ. . .

          . . .άσας

χανὼν σὺν αὐτῷ . . .

5   . . .ους

κἀντεῦθεν ἔγνω μ. . .

          . . .ονου

καὶ πορφύρας τὲ μείχο. . .

          . . .ον

10 ἐκεῖθεν εἰς σίδηρα πέμποντα . . .

          . . . <π>άλιν

καὶ χρυσοπάστου μὴ γλίχεσθαι πορφύρας.

62

On the ironmonger Leo . . .
standing before the emperor and . . .
while many were announced . . .

. . .
. . . of Leo
. . .
gaping together with him . . .
. . .   5
. . . and then he understands, . . .
. . .
and . . . of purple . . .
. . .
sending him from there in irons . . .   10
                                        . . . again
and to not lust after the gold-embroidered purple.

63

<Εἰς τοὺς> . . . <πρεσβυτ>έρους καὶ διακόνους, εἰς πλῆθος ἄπειρον ὄντας

. . . <Κυρίου> δόμον,
οἶκον προσευχῆς ὄντα τοῖς πρώην χρόνοις,
. . . ωμένων,
ἔδειξεν οἶκον ἐν βραχεῖ νῦν ἐμπόρων
5   . . . <ε>ἰσόδου·
ὅρα πυλωρούς, ἀμπελουργούς, βο<υκόλους>,
. . . <ἀξ>ινοξόους,
πράτας ὀπωρῶν, ἀρτοποιούς, γηπόνους,
. . . ούς, σκυτορράφους
10 καὶ τῶν παλαιῶν σανδάλων τοὺς ἐμπόρους
. . . τ<ὰς> σπυρίδας
ἤμειψαν αὐτὰς εἰς τύπους στιχαρίων·
. . . ὄντ<ες> ἄλλοι κοσκίνων
φοροῦσι καὶ βαίνουσι κιγκλίδων ἔσω
15   . . . ῦ βήματος καὶ τιμίου,
ὁπαῖς δὲ πολλαῖς τῶν στολῶν ἐστιγμένων
. . . μυριόμματοι νόες,
οὕσπερ Χερουβὶμ οἶδεν ἡ Γραφὴ λέγειν,
. . . ωνης τμῆμα σαπροῦ δικτύου.
20 Ἄλλος δὲ χρῆσιν ἀγνοῶν στιχαρίου
<ὡς στιχαρί>ῳ στέλλεται τῇ διφθέρᾳ,

118

63

On the . . . priests and
deacons, who are of infinite numbers

. . . the house of the Lord,
being *a house of prayer* in earlier times,
. . .
in a short time now turned into a merchant house
      . . . of the entrance.   5
Look at the doorkeepers, the vineyard workers, the
   cowherds,
        . . . , the ax manufacturers,
the fruit sellers, the bakers, the farmers,
      . . . , the cobblers,
and the merchants of old sandals,   10
     . . . the baskets,
they changed them into a kind of *sticharion*.
Others, being . . . of sieves,
wear and walk inside the grills,
     . . . also of the holy altar,   15
their robes riddled with many holes,
      . . . minds with thousands of eyes,
which Scripture calls "Cherubim,"
     . . . a shred from a worn-out net.
Another, not knowing how to use a *sticharion*, 20
is wearing a leather hide as if it were a *sticharion*,

καὶ πλέγμα μᾶλλον ἀνθ' ὁραρίου φέρει.
<Ἄλλος> τὸ "δεῦτε προσκυνήσωμεν" λέγειν
οὔπω γινώσκων, ναυτικός τις ὢν τάχα,
25 <τὸ "δεῦ>τε δὴ πλεύσωμεν" ἄθλιος λέγει,
οὕτως ἐθισθεὶς ἐκβοᾶν καθ' ἡμέραν·
<ᾧ>δαὶ δὲ πᾶσι πρόσφοροι ταῖς σφῶν τέχναις·
ὁ μὲν γὰρ ἄρτον ἱερὸν διαρπάσας
<ἐκ> τῶν τραπέζῃ τῇ Θεοῦ προκειμένων
30 βοᾷ, "τίς ἂν πρίαιτο τὸν σιλιγνίαν;",
<μνησθεὶς> ὁποίαν ἐστὶν ἀσκήσας τέχνην·
ὁ δ' αὖ κρατῆρα χερσὶ μυστικὸν φέρων
<γέμοντα> πάντως αἵματος ζωηρρύτου,
εἴπερ δεήσει τὸ "προσέλθετε" φράσαι,
35 "<φίλο>ι πολῖται, δεῦτε," φησίν, "εἰς πότον·
ἡδὺς γὰρ οὗτος οἶνος, ἡδὺς ἐκτόπως,"
<καπηλ>ικόν τι ῥῆμα τῷ λαῷ λέγων.
Κἂν "τὰς θύρας δέ, τὰς θύρας" εἰπεῖν δέοι,
<βοᾷ τ>ις ἄλλος, "τὸ σκέπαρνον, τὸ ξύλον,"
40 τέκτων τις ὡς ἔοικεν ὢν ὁ γεννάδας.
<Ἄλλος δὲ τοῦ> "πρόσσχωμεν" ἐκλελησμένος
φάσκει, "μαγειρεύσωμεν εἰ δοκεῖ κρέας."
<Οὕτω πλατυνθεὶς> νῦν χορὸς παρ' ἐλπίδα
πρεσβυτέρων τὲ καὶ διακόνων ἅμα
45   . . . κἂν κάμῃ πάνυ.
Ὦ βῆμα θεῖον, ἐκτάθητι πρὸς πλάτος
. . .
καὶ τοῦ τόπου λείψαντος αὐτοῖς εἰς στάσιν
. . .

and wears a woven fabric instead of an *orarion*.
Another, not knowing how to pronounce the phrase
"come, let us worship," being perhaps a sailor,
says, the wretched fool, "come, let us set sail,"   25
being accustomed to shout this every day.
Everyone has at hand the expressions of their trade.
One man grabs the holy bread
from the items displayed on the altar of God,
and exclaims, "Who wants to buy this white bread?,"   30
reminded of the profession that he once practiced.
Another, holding out with his hands the mystic chalice,
filled with the blood of life,
when he should pronounce the phrase "Draw near,"
says, "Dear citizens, come and have a drink,   35
for this wine is delicious, superbly delicious,"
addressing the people in the words of tavernkeepers.
And another, when he should say, "The doors, the doors,"
shouts, "The adze, the wood!"—
probably, the good fellow was a carpenter.   40
Yet another, forgetting the phrase "Let us pay attention,"
says, "Let us cook some meat, if you agree."
The choir of priests and of deacons has now
grown in size, against all odds, to such a degree,
                . . . even if it would make a great effort.   45
O divine altar, stretch yourself out to a greater breadth,
. . .
and leaving enough room for them to stand
. . .

64

Εἰς τὸν πρωτοπαπᾶν Ἰωάννην καὶ τὸν . . . περὶ τοῦ βιβλίου καὶ τοῦ χρυσίου τῶν ἀπο. . .

Τῷ πρωτοπαπᾷ πέμπομεν τὸ βιβλίον
. . .
    . . . τελοῦσι γνησιωτάτων φίλων
. . .
5   . . . ταῦτα τοῖς μακελλίταις
    . . . αλ καὶ φιλούμενος πλέον.

65

Ἐπίγραμμα εἰς τὸν τάφον τοῦ Μανιάκου δι' ἡρωϊκοῦ

Μανιάκης λαλέω ἀπὸ τύμβου ἀνδράσι πᾶσιν·
"οὐ λίπον ἠνορέην ἐπὶ γαίης, ἀλλ' ὑπὸ γαῖαν
οἰχόμενος κατέχωσα, ἐμοὶ δ' ἅμα συγκατέθαψα.
Κεῖται δ' οὐχὶ πέλας μελέων μου ὡς δέμας ἄλλο,
5 βραχιόνων δὲ μάλιστα ἐμῶν περὶ νεῦρα μένουσα,
οὐκ ἐθέλει ἀναβῆναι ἀπὸ χθόνος ἄτερ ἐμεῖο."

64

To the head priest John and the . . .
about the book and the gold
of the . . .

We send this book to the head priest
. . .
    . . . are the . . . of genuine friends,
. . .
    . . . those things to the butchers   5
    . . . even more loved.

65

Inscription in hexameters on the grave
of Maniakes

I, Maniakes, speak from the grave to all men:
"I did not leave my valor on the earth, but buried it
underground as I departed, and I interred it with me.
It lies not far from my limbs, like another body,
staying somewhere near the sinews of my arms,   5
not wishing to ascend from the netherworld without me."

66

Εἰς τὴν Εὐδοκίαν περὶ τοῦ πεμφθέντος αὐτῇ χρυσοῦ <μήλου>..., ὡς ἀπὸ προσώπου φίλου τινός

Α...
κἂν "ἡ καλὴ τὸ μῆλον" ὧδέ τις γράφοι
...
οὔσης καλῆς νῦν ἐν γυναιξὶ σοῦ μόνης.

67

...

Εἰς τὴν γυναικῶν καλλονὴν Εὐδοκίαν.

66

To Eudokia, about the golden apple that was sent to her . . . , as if spoken by a friend

. . .

even if someone would write here, "this apple for the
    beautiful woman,"
< this would be useless: for there cannot be any contest>
when now among women you alone are beautiful.

67

. . .

For Eudokia, the beauty among women.

68

Εἰ<ς τὸν σύγκελλον> . . . Ἀργυροπώλου
περὶ τῆς εἰκόνος τοῦ ἀγίου Κύρου, τῆς ἐν
τῇ . . . ἀντικρὺ τῆς εἰκόνος τοῦ ἀγίου
Παντελεήμονος, πεμφ<θείσης ὑπὸ τοῦ
ἀγίου Ἑρ>μολάου πρὸς τὸν αὐτὸν
σύγκελλον μετὰ τῶν παρόντ<ων
στίχων> . . . <αὕτη ἡ> εἰκὼν τοῦ ἀγίου
Κύρου, ἀπὸ τῆς ἐν τῷ Στρατηγίῳ
οἰκί<ας> . . . αἱρεθεῖσα παρὰ τοῦ
Λυκολέοντος, μετὰ βραχὺ μετηνέχθη εἰς
. . . οἶκον τοῦ Ἀργυροπώλου

POET

Ἡ τοῦ μεγίστου μά<ρτυρος μνήμη Κύρου>
πρόσεισιν, ἐγγύς ἐστιν, αὔριον φθάνει,
καὶ χρή σε πέμπειν το<ῦ Κύρου τὴν εἰκόνα>
εἰς ἥνπερ εἶχεν ἔκπαλαι κατοικίαν,
5 εἰς ὃν κατῴκει θεῖον ἀρ<χαῖον δόμον>.
Δοκεῖ γὰρ αἰχμάλωτος ἐλθεῖν αὐτόθι,
λιπὼν φίλην γῆν καὶ παλ<αιὰν πατρίδα>,
ἢ μᾶλλον ἐξόριστος ἐκ Στρατηγίου,
σύγκελλε, τῷ σῷ προσβα<λὼν Κυνηγίῳ>.

68

To the *synkellos* . . . of Argyropolos
about the icon of Saint Kyros in
the . . . opposite the icon of Saint
Panteleemon, that was sent . . . by Saint
Hermolaos to the same
synkellos with the present
verses. . . . This icon of Saint
Kyros was removed from the house in
Strategion . . . by Lykoleon . . . , and was
shortly thereafter transferred to . . . the
house of Argyropolos

POET

The feast of the great martyr Kyros
approaches, it draws near, it arrives tomorrow,
and you should send the icon of Kyros
to its previous home,
to the divine old house where it dwelled before.   5
For he appears to have come here as a captive,
having left his beloved land and his former country,
or rather, he is now an exile from Strategion,
after being sent to your Kynegion, O *synkellos*.

10 Θηρευτικῆς, βέλτιστε, τί δράσων ἄρα,
ἀνὴρ μοναστής, ἐγκρατοῦς β<ίου φίλος>,
πτῶκας διώξων ἢ συῶν τοὺς ἀγρίους
ἢ καὶ νεβροὺς μάλιστα δειλῶν δορ<κάδων>;
Τοιοῦτον οὐδέν· οὐδὲ γὰρ χρείαν ἔχει.
15 Ἔστω στρατηγὸς τοιγαροῦν ὁ ...
ἔστω στρατηγός, ἀλλὰ μὴ κυνηγέτης·
ὅρα γὰρ αὐτὸν σύμβολον στ<ρατηγίας>
τὸ σταυρικὸν φέροντα τῆς δόξης ὅπλον·
εἰ πλειόνων δὲ τῶν παρασήμων <δέῃ>,
20 τὸν μανδύαν μὲν ἀντὶ σημαίας δέχου,
ξυρῶν δὲ θήκην καὶ ξυροὺς φλεβ<οτόμους>
ὡς κουλεόν μοι καὶ τομὸν ξίφος νόει.
Ἆρ' οὐ στρατηγός ἐστιν; Ἦ σὺ <πῶς λέγεις>;
Ὄντως στρατηγὸς καὶ στρατηγὸς Κυρίου,
25 Θεοῦ στρατηγός ἐστιν ὑψ<ίστου> ...
ὄντως ὁ Κῦρος καὶ στρατηγὸς Κυρίου,
ὄντως ὁ Κῦρος καὶ ...
ὄντως ὁ Κῦρος γνησιωτέρως ἔχει
εἶναι στ<ρατηγὸς Δεσπότου τοῦ Κυρίου>,
30 καὶ βούλεται δὲ σφόδρα τοῦτο καὶ θέλει
...
πέμψον τὸν αἰχμάλωτον ἐκ μετ<οικίας>
...
πέμψον τὸν ἐξόριστον ἐκ Κυν<ηγίου>
35 ...
αὐτὸς γὰρ οὗτος ὁ τρισόλβιος <Κῦρος>
...

What kind of hunting was Kyros then supposed to do, dear   10
    friend,
being a monastic man, a friend of the chaste life?
Was he to pursue hares or wild boars,
or the fawns of timid deer?
Nothing of the kind; for he does not need to.
Therefore, let him rather be a general,   15
let him be a general, but not a hunter.
Look at the cruciform weapon of glory that he carries:
it is a symbol of military leadership.
If you would need more insignia,
regard his woolen cloak as a banner,   20
and consider the box of razors and the vein-opening blades
as the sheath and the edge of a sword.
Well then, isn't he a general? Or how would you describe
    him?
Indeed he is a general and a general of the Lord.
He is a general of God on high . . .   25
Indeed Kyros is a general of the Lord,
indeed Kyros is . . .
Indeed Kyros is able to be more genuinely
a general of our Master the Lord,
and he wants and desires this very much   30
. . .
send the captive from his new home
. . .
send the exile from Kynegion
. . .   35
for the thrice-blessed Kyros himself
. . .

καὶ πρέσβιν ἐξέπε<μψε> . . .

. . .

40 καὶ τὴν πολιὰν εἰς δυ<σωπίαν ἔχων>

. . .

ἔχεις γινώσκειν . . .

. . .

ἐκλιτανεύων . . .

45 . . .

. . .

ἄμφω σεβασθεὶς τὴν . . .

. . .

ἀλλ᾽ εἰ δοκεῖ, πρόσσχωμεν . . .

50 . . .

PANTELEEMON

Πέμπει με πρὸς σὲ π<ρέσβιν> . . .

. . .

ἐργῶδες οὐδέν, ἀλλ᾽ ὅπως διὰ χ<ρόνου>

. . .ευ

55 καὶ τοῖς παλαιοῖς ἐγκατοικήσῃ δόμ<οις>

. . .α

τοσοῦτος ἤδη τῆς ξενιτείας χρόνος

. . .πέδω

φιλεῖ κατοικεῖν ὅνπερ ᾤκει πρὶν δόμον

60 . . .ως

τριβὴν ἐκείνῳ τὴν ἐπὶ ξένης λύων

. . . σθένω

130

and sent out as an envoy . . .

. . .

and using his white hair to entreat   40

. . .

you can recognize . . .

. . .

supplicating . . .

. . .   45

. . .

respecting both . . .

. . .

but if it pleases you, let us pay attention to . . .

. . .   50

PANTELEEMON

<Kyros> sends me to you as an envoy

. . .

not anything difficult, but so that eventually

. . .

and he may dwell in his old house   55

. . .

so long his exile has lasted now

. . .

he desires to live in the house where he used to live

. . .   60

ending for him this sojourn in an alien land,
I am able . . .

συμπρέσβιδάς μοι τάσδε προσδέχου δύο
     . . . <βίβλον> φέρω,
65 εὐαγγέλους ἔχουσαν ἔνδοθεν λόγους
     . . .ν λόγον·
πρέσβεις ἰδοὺ τρεῖς, ἄξιοι πείθειν ἕνα
     . . . <αἰ>χμαλωσίας
τῷ δουλικῷ δὲ καὶ συνήθει χωρίῳ
70   . . . δεσπότης.

HERMOLAOS

Αὐτὸς δέ μοι, βέλτιστε Παντελεήμων,
     . . . κρύπτεσθαι θέλῃς;
Τί καὶ καλύπτῃ τῆς στοᾶς τῇ γωνίᾳ;
     . . .ασαι σὺ τῷ Κύρῳ
75 λιπών με τὸν σὸν καὶ συνοικῶ τῷ ξένῳ;
<Οὐκ ἦν ἐγὼ σὸς> μυσταγωγὸς καὶ φίλος;
Οὐ τοῦ γάλακτος ἔσπασάς μου τῶν λόγων;
<Ἐμοῦ γὰρ οὐκ ἤκ>ουσας ὡς διδασκάλου
κἀντεῦθεν ἔγνως καὶ τὸν ἡδὺν Δεσπότην;
80 <Οὐ πιστὸς> υἱὸς τοῖς ἐμοῖς ὤφθης λόγοις;
Οὐ πρὸς πάλην σε καὶ βίαν τῶν σκαμμάτων
<λόγοις στομ>ώσας καὶ καταφράξας ἅμα
Χριστῷ προσῆξα μάρτυρα στεφανίτην;
<Τί οὖν> ἀφείς με νῦν συνοικεῖς τῷ Κύρῳ,
85 πάντων ἐκείνων ὥσπερ ἐκλελησμένος;
<Πρόσσχες> τὸ βλέμμα τῷ διδασκάλῳ τάχος
καὶ γνούς με τῆς σῆς αἴτιον σωτηρίας,

Accept these two accompanying envoys,
         ... I bring you a book
that contains the evangelic words   65
         ... word.
So, here are three envoys, who are worthy to persuade one,
         ... being hostage
for the place that serves you and is familiar to you,
         ... your master.   70

HERMOLAOS

You yourself, my dear Panteleemon,
         ... want to escape me?
Why do you hide yourself in the corner of the gallery?
         ... you for Kyros
while leaving me, your friend, and choosing a stranger as   75
   companion?
Was I not your initiator and friend?
Have you not suckled the milk of my words?
Have you not listened to me as a teacher,
and in this way become acquainted with our dear Master?
Have you not appeared as a trusted son thanks to my words?   80
Have I not trained you and fortified you with words
for the violence and contests of the arena,
this way bringing you to Christ as a crowned martyr?
Why do you leave me to live now together with Kyros,
apparently forgetful of all those things?   85
Look quickly in the direction of your teacher,
recognize me as the cause of your deliverance,

<πρόσπειθ>ε τὸν σύγκελλον οἷς δύνῃ λόγοις,
Κῦρον μὲν εὐθὺς ἐξάγειν τῶν ἐνθάδε
90 <καὶ τῷ πα>λαιῷ τοῦτον ἐκπέμπειν δόμῳ,
ἀντεισάγειν δὲ τῇδε τῇ κατοικίᾳ
<τὸν Ἑρμό>λαον ἐκ προθύμου καρδίας,
ὡς ἂν συνῶμεν, ὡς ἐν οὐρανοῖς ἄνω,
<οὕτω γ>ε κἂν γῇ καί, συναθλούντων ἅμα,
95 τηρῶμεν ὡς δεῖ τοὺς φιλαλλήλους νόμους.

PANTELEEMON

<Ἤκουσας, ὦ σύγ>κελλε, τοῦ διδασκάλου,
πῶς μοι προσῆψε μέμψιν εὐλογωτάτην
<καὶ Παντελε>ήμονι τῷ σῷ φιλτάτῳ,
σοῦ τὸ πλέον πταίσαντος, ὡς ἐγὼ κρίνω,
100   … <Κῦρο>ν ἀνθ' Ἑρμολάου
ἡμῶν διασπῶν τὴν φίλην συναυλίαν
          …της τέκνα·
καὶ Κοσμᾷ μὲν σύναπτε Σαμψὼν τὸν μέγαν
…
105 δός μοι τὸν Ἑρμόλαον ἐνταῦθα βλέπειν
…
ἐμοὶ γὰρ Ἑρμόλαος ἀρκέσει μόνος
…
<ὑφ'> οὗ προσήχθην ὀρθοδόξων πληθύϊ
110 …
<καὶ τὴν> μεγίστην εὗρον ἐκ Θεοῦ χάριν
…

and persuade the *synkellos* with all the words that lie in your
    power,
to remove Kyros from here immediately,
and send him to his old house.   90
Persuade him to bring instead, with a willing heart,
Hermolaos to this house here,
so that also here on earth we may be together,
just as in the heavens above, and, contending together,
we may respect, as is fitting, the laws of mutual affection.   95

PANTELEEMON

Synkellos, you have heard my teacher,
how he reproached me with reason,
me, Panteleemon, so dear to you,
while you are more to blame, as far as I can judge,
            . . . Kyros instead of Hermolaos,   100
breaking up our dear cohabitation
. . . children of . . . .
Join the great Sampson to Kosmas,
. . .
grant that I may see Hermolaos here   105
. . .
Hermolaos alone will suffice for me
. . .
by whom I was brought to the mass of right-believing
    people,
. . .   110
and found the greatest grace from God
. . .

... .ν μοι γὰρ γραφαῖς κἂν εἰκόσιν

...

115   ... σύ, Κῦρε, καὶ μὴ διστάσῃς

...

KYROS

... <ο>ῖα βούλομαι λέγειν

...

... τὸ πᾶν εὐνουστάτων

120 ...

... <λαμβ>άνοντες ἀξίαν

...ναν ζῇ καὶ μένει

...

... ἐκείνων ὕστερον τεθνηκότων

125 ...

<ὁ θηρ>ιώδης κλῆσιν ἀλλὰ καὶ τρόπους

...

ἐπὶ ξένην ἄγει με κερδᾶναι θέλων

...

130 μηδὲ βραχὺν χρόνον με πλουτήσας ὅδε

...

αὖθις δ' ἀπήχθην ἐν λόφῳ Κυνηγίου
το...
χρόνων δὲ κύκλα πολλὰ πάντως ἐρρύη,
135 ἀφ' <οὗ>...
ἣν νῦν κατοικήσαιμι, Χριστέ μου Λόγε,
το...

. . . for in writings and in images

. . .

. . . you, Kyros, do not hesitate   115

. . .

KYROS

. . . what I want to say

. . .

. . . of the most kind

. . .   120

. . . receiving a rank . . .
. . . lives and remains

. . .

. . . of those who died later

. . .   125

that man, bestial in name but also in manners,

. . .

carries me away to an alien land, wanting to make profit,

. . .

but this man did not enrich me, not even for a short time,   130

. . .

then I was carried away to the Kynegion hill

. . .

many cycles of time have now elapsed,
since I . . .   135

the house where I may now live, my Christ the Word,

. . .

ὁ κλεινὸς Ἑρμόλαος οὗτος ἐσκύλη
λό...
140 τοῦ βήματος τοίνυν με θᾶττον ἐξάρας
στῆσον...
μυστηπόλῳ γὰρ ὄντι τούτῳ καὶ θύτῃ
τὸ βῆμ<α>...

SYNKELLOS

Πλὴν ἀλλ᾽ ἐρῶ σοι καὶ βραχεῖς ἄλλους λόγους·
145 εἴπερ με...
ἕξεις με πρῶτον ἀντὶ δεσπότου φίλον·
ἔπειτ<α>...
καὶ σύμμαχον μέγιστον εἰς πάντα χρόνον·
ζηλωτὰ λο...
150 καὶ δή σε πέμπειν οὐκ ἀποκνήσω τάχος.
Ἄπελθε τοίνυν ἐς <τὸν ἀρχαῖον δόμον>,
ἐμοῦ δὲ καὶ μέμνησο καὶ μεμνημένος
πᾶσι τρόποις φύλαττ<ε τὸν σὸν οἰκέτην>.

the famous Hermolaos was robbed
. . .
lift me now up quickly from the altar, 140
and erect me . . .
to this man who is an initiate and a celebrant,
the altar . . .

SYNKELLOS

I will say to you a few more words now:
since . . . 145
you will have me first of all as a friend instead of a master.
Moreover, . . .
and a formidable ally for all times to come.
Zealous admirer . . .
and look, I will not hesitate to send you away quickly. 150
So, leave now for your ancient home,
but remember me and, while remembering,
protect your servant in all possible ways.

69

Ἐπίγραμμα εἰς τοὺς στίχους περὶ τῆς εἰκόνος τοῦ ἁγίου Κύρου

Στίχων ἀριθμὸς ἰσάριθμ<ος ἐνθάδε>
τῆς τοῖς μαθηταῖς τοῦ φιλανθρώπου Λόγου
ἐν δεξιοῖς βαλοῦσι ληφθ<είσης ἄγρας>.

70

Εἰς τὴν σεβαστὴν Μαρίαν, ὅτε ἐτελεύτησεν· ἡρωϊκά

Οἰχομένης Μαρίης, φύγεν εὔχαρις ἐκ<προλιποῦσα>,
οὐκ ἐθέλουσ' ὀπίσω κείνης ὑπὸ ἥλιον εἶναι,
ἢ καὶ μαρτυρέουσα ἐν ἡλίῳ οὐκ ἔ…
μεῖναι τῇ Μαρίῃ, ἧς εἵνεκα οἴχεται ἐκ γῆς.

69

Epigram on the verses about the icon of Saint Kyros

The number of the verses here is equal to the number
of the catch made by the loving Word's disciples,
who threw their nets into favorable waters.

70

On the *sebaste* Maria, when she died; hexameters

Maria passed away, and grace left before her,
not wanting to stay under the sun after her.
Or perhaps it affirmed thus that under the sun . . .
to remain with Maria, leaving earth because of her.

71

Αἴνιγμα εἰς τὴν τένταν

Ἄπετρος εἰμὶ καὶ κινούμενος δόμος,
ἐν γῇ βεβηκώς, γῇ δὲ μὴ συνημμένος·
οὐ πηλός, οὐκ ἄσβεστος ἐξήγειρέ με,
πρίων δὲ καὶ σκέπαρνον οὐ τέτμηκέ με,
5   εἰ μὴ κορυφὴν καὶ τὰ βάθρα μου λέγεις.
Φῶς ἔνδον ἕλκω, καίπερ ὢν πεφραγμένος,
λοξοὺς συνιστῶντάς με κίονας φέρω.
Τῶν κιόνων μοι πάντοθεν κλονουμένων,
τὸ σχῆμα σῴζων ἀβλαβὴς ἑστὼς μένω.
10 Τὸ καινόν· εἴ με καὶ καταστρέψεις βίᾳ,
οὐκ ἂν καταρράξῃς με, σῷός εἰμί σοι·
ἀνίσταμαι γὰρ καὶ μένω πάλιν δόμος.

71

Riddle on the tent

I am a stoneless house that can be moved around,
I am fixed in the earth, yet not joined with the earth.
Neither clay nor lime have raised me up,
and neither saw nor adze has cut me up,
unless you count my top and bottom. 5
I draw light inside, though I am shut off,
and I have slanting pillars that support me.
When my pillars are swayed from every side,
I keep my form and remain standing undamaged.
The weird thing is: even if you pull me down with force, 10
you would not destroy me; I would stay intact,
for I rise up and remain yet again a house.

72

Εἰς τὸν κηνσουάλιον Κώνσταντα καὶ νοτάριον τοῦ. . .

Λείπεις ὁ Κώνστας, καὶ δοκεῖ τοῖς ἐνθάδε
. . .
ἀργοῦσι πάντα, καὶ γραφαὶ καὶ πᾶς <λόγος>
. . .
5 καὶ χεῖρες ἠρεμοῦσι καὶ μουσῶν <πόνοι>
. . .
καὶ τί γράφειν χρὴ καὶ τὰ λοιπὰ . . .
. . .

73

Εἰς τὸ ταβλίον

Σῴζοιο, Παλάμηδες, εἰ μή τις φθόνος,
ἐκ παιδιᾶς ἄριστα τῆς ἐκ τῶν κύβων
προθεὶς ἐναργὲς εἰκόνισμα καὶ τύπον
τοῦ παντρόφου τὲ καὶ παλιμβόλου βίου,
5 ἢ μᾶλλον εἰπεῖν ζωγραφήσας τὸν βίον
ἄντικρυς ὄντα παιδιᾶς οὐδὲν πλέον.

144

72

On Konstas, census taker and notary of . . .

You are missed, Konstas, and the people here think that
. . .
everything is idle: writings, speech,
. . .
the hands are at rest and the works of the Muses   5
. . .
and why should I write also the rest of . . .
. . .

73

On the tables game

May you live long, Palamedes (if there is no objection),
because by means of the dice game
you have set such a vivid image and perfect example
of life, so volatile and full of turns.
Or, rather, you have painted a picture of life   5
as being just a game and nothing more.

74

Εἰς τὸν Ἡρώδην περὶ τῆς τιμίας κάρας τοῦ Προδρόμου

Ὑπόσχεσιν θεὶς ἥμισυ κράτους ὅλου
ὀρχήσεως, μάταιε, καὶ μόνης χάριν,
πλέον παρ' αὐτὴν τὴν ὑπόσχεσιν δίδως·
οὐ γὰρ δίδως ὡς εἶπας ἥμισυ κράτους,
5   ἀντάξιον δὲ γῆς βασιλειῶν ὅλων,
εἰπεῖν δὲ μᾶλλον, καὶ βασιλείας πόλου,
δῶρον σεβαστόν, τὴν κάραν τοῦ Προδρόμου.
Πληρῶν τὸν ὅρκον τοιγαροῦν ψεύδῃ πλέον·
μᾶλλον γὰρ αὐτὸν καὶ πατεῖς ἄλλῳ τρόπῳ,
10   μεῖζον παρασχὼν ὧν ὑπέσχου, καὶ πλέον.

74

To Herod, about the honorable head of John the Forerunner

Although you promised half of your entire kingdom,
vain fool, all for the sake of just one dance,
you gave even more than you promised;
for you gave not half the kingdom, as you said,
but something that is worth all earthly kingdoms   5
and, yes, even the heavenly kingdom too —
an honorable gift, the Forerunner's head.
By keeping your oath, therefore, you have actually lied;
or rather found another way to break it,
by giving more and better than you promised.   10

75

Εἰς τὴν ἀδελφὴν Ἀναστασώ,
τελευτήσασαν καὶ
ἔτι προκειμένην· ἀνακρεόντεια

Ῥοδοεικέλην γυναῖκα
θάνατος μέλας κατέσχεν·
ἐπὶ τῆς κλίνης δὲ κεῖται
ἀποτμηθὲν ἔρνος οἷα,
5 ἀρετῆς δ' ἄσυλον ὅρμον
περικειμένη καθεύδει,
ἀνακειμένη δὲ λάμπει,
νενεκρωμένη περ οὖσα.
Νεφέλαι ὀμβροτόκοι, δάκρυα χεῖτε,
10 ὅτι καλλίστη ἄφνω ἔσβετο κούρη.
Ἄγε πᾶν φίλοικτον ὄμμα,
δάκρυσον μάλα πρὸ τῆσδε.
Ἄγε πᾶν στόμα, προθύμως
καλά μοι λάλει τὰ ταύτης.
15 Ἀπὸ καρδίας στενάζω
σὸς ἀδελφός, ὦ γλυκεῖα·
ἀπὸ καρδίας στενάζω,
<ἀπὸ καρδία>ς φιλῶν σε.
Κυπάριττος καθάπερ ἐνθάδε κεῖσαι,
20 κασιγνήτη, μέγ' ἄχος ἄμμι λιποῦσα.

75

On his sister Anastaso,
who has died and is still laid out
for burial; in anacreontics

A rose-like woman
has been captured by dark death.
She lies on the bier,
like a severed shoot.
Wearing the inviolable wreath   5
of virtue, she sleeps,
and reclining, she gleams,
though she has died.
O, rain-pouring clouds, shed tears,
for a most lovely maiden suddenly perished.   10
Come, every compassionate eye,
shed tears for her.
Come, every mouth, eagerly
tell me her blessings.
I, your brother, sigh   15
from my heart, O sweet one.
I sigh from my heart,
because I love you from my heart.
You lie here like a cypress,
sister, leaving us great sorrow.   20

Κινύρας λόγων δονεῖτε,
φιλοϊστόρων τὰ πλήθη,
ὁλολαμπρόχρουν δὲ κούρην
στέφετε κρότοις ἐπαίνων·
25 δοκέει κλύειν γὰρ ἥδε,
λαλέειν τις εἰ θελήσει,
ἴχνος οὐδὲν ἐν προσώπῳ
θανάτου φέρουσα πάντως.
Γενεῆς ἡμετέρης ὤλετο κόσμος
30 τριακοστῇ Μαΐου, φεῦ μοι, ἰώ μοι.
Μακάρων ὅπου χορεῖαι,
ἀγέλαι ὅπου κροτούντων,
κατάταξον ἣν προείλου,
Θεέ μου, Ἄναξ ἁπάντων,
35 μετὰ πνευμάτων ἀμέμπτων,
μετὰ ἀγγέλων ἀΰλων,
μετὰ τῶν σέ, παντεπόπτα,
πεφιληκότων δικαίων.
Στενάχω, αἰρομένου σκίμποδος ἤδη·
40 ἐπὶ γὰρ τύμβον ἄγῃ, εὔχροε κούρη.

Pluck the harps of words,
O learned masses,
and crown with the sounds of praise
this all bright-skinned maiden.
For she appears to listen,   25
in case someone should want to speak;
no trace at all of death
does she bear on her face.
The ornament of our family passed away
on the thirtieth of May, alas, woe is me.   30
There where the choirs of the blessed,
and throngs of musicians are,
there, my God, Lord of all,
assign her, your chosen one,
amongst the unblemished spirits,   35
among the immaterial angels,
among the righteous, who love
you, O you who oversee all.
I sigh, now that the bier is already being lifted;
for you are being brought to your grave, fair-skinned maiden. 40

76

Ἐπὶ τῇ ἐκφορᾷ τῆς αὐτῆς

Ἰδοὺ λιποῦσα τὸν σὸν οἶκον ἐκφέρῃ,
οἶκον κατοικήσουσα πικρὸν ἐκτόπως,
κἂν ὁ γλυκασμοῦ καὶ χαρᾶς πλήρης τόπος
τὸ σόν, Θεῷ πέποιθα, πνεῦμα λαμβάνῃ.

77

Εἰς τὴν αὐτὴν ἐπιτάφια

. . .

<τὴν ο>ὐχὶ πένθους ἀλλ᾽ ἐπαίνων ἀξίαν

. . .

<τὰ πάν>τα λευκήν, σῶμα, πνεῦμα καὶ τρόπους

5 . . .

. . . <μετέσ>χες τῶν χοῶν ἀκηράτων

. . .

. . . εὔχομαι Θεῷ Λόγῳ

. . .

10 . . . μέσων τῶν κοιλάδων

76

At her funeral procession

Behold, you are carried out, leaving your house,
to live in that utterly bitter house,
even if that place full of sweetness and joy—
as I trust in God—will take your spirit.

77

Funeral verses on the same woman

. . .
<the woman > who is not worthy of grief, but of praises
. . .
spotless in everything: body, spirit, and manners
. . .

      . . . you partook of the pure libations   5
      . . .
      . . . I pray to God the Word
      . . .
      . . . in the midst of the valleys   10

...

    ... πολὺν μείνας χρόνον

    ... τῶν γυναικῶν ἀθρόον

...

15   ... σελήνη καὶ κατηφείας νέφος

...

    ... ἐβουλόμην σε δάκρυσι κλάειν

...

    ὡς Ἡλιάδες Ἡλίου τὸν υἱέα

20 ...

ἀστακτὶ χεῖν ἤλεκτρον ἐκ τῶν ὀμμάτων

...

τοιοῦδε νεκροῦ καὶ τὸ πένθος εἰκότως.

...

25 οὕτω σε πενθεῖν οὐδὲ χρὴ πενθεῖν ὅλως

...

σὸν πνεῦμα τάττειν ἐν τόποις, ἐν οἷς ἄρα

...

ἄπελθε τοίνυν λῆξιν εἰς αἰωνίαν,

30 εἰ<ς>...

τὴν φιλτάτην ὅπου περ ἡμῶν μητέρα

ὄψ<ει>...

ἣν ὡς ἀφ' ἡμῶν καὶ πρόσειπε γνησίως

καὶ συμ<πλάκηθι>...

35 εἰ συμπλοκαὶ γίνοιντο κἂν μεταστᾶσιν,

εὔχ<ου δὲ>...

τοῖς σοῖς ἀδελφοῖς πᾶσιν ἐξαιτουμένη,

. . .
. . . staying for a long time
. . . of the women suddenly
. . .
. . . a moon and a cloud of gloom   15
. . .
. . . I wanted to bewail you with tears
. . .
. . . as the Heliades did with the son of Helios
. . .   20
shed amber in floods from the eyes
. . .
an appropriate mourning for this deceased.
. . .
to mourn you like this, I do not need to mourn at all   25
. . .
to assign your soul to the places where
. . .
so, leave now for eternal repose,
for . . .   30
where you will see our beloved mother
. . .
speak to her sincerely, on our behalf,
and embrace her . . . ,
if embraces can happen among the dead,   35
and pray . . . ,
interceding on behalf of all your siblings,

καὶ ταῦτ<α δὴ λέγουσα πρὸς τὴν μητέρα>·
"ἥκω λιποῦσα, μῆτερ, ἄνδρα καὶ τέκνα,
40   λιποῦσα τ<ὸν τεκόντα καὶ τοὺς γνησίους>,
λιποῦσα γνωστοὺς καὶ συνήθεις καὶ φίλους,
τούτους ἀφεῖσα καὶ τὸν α. . .
ἐνταῦθα χωρῶ πρὸς τὸ τῇδε χωρίον
καὶ σοὶ συνοικεῖν εὔχομ<αι πάντα χρόνον>
45   ἐν πραέων γῇ καὶ τόπῳ χλοηφόρῳ,
ὅπως ἐπευφραίνοιτο μ<ήτηρ τῷ τέκνῳ>,
ὥς φησι Δαυὶδ ὁ προφήτης Κυρίου."
Σὺ μὲν λαλήσεις ταῦτα πρὸς <τὴν μητέρα>,
ἐγὼ δὲ πρὸς σὲ ποῖον εὑρήσω λόγον;
50   Ἐκεῖνα πάντως φθέγξομαι· τί γ<ὰρ λέγω>;
Ὦ λεῖον ὄμμα καὶ γλυκύφθογγον στόμα,
πῶς μοι δέδεσθε κειρίαις ἐν<ταφίοις>,
τὸ μὲν καλυφθὲν καὶ παρ' ἐλπίδας μύσαν,
τὸ δ' αὖ πεδηθὲν καὶ σιγῇ <κεκλεισμένον>;
55   Ὄντως Θεοῦ θέλημα τοῦτο Δεσπότου.
Ἀλλὰ σκοπῶμεν ὧδε καὶ <προσεκτέον>·
ψυχαῖς ὀρύττει βόθρον Ἕλλην ἀφρόνως,
σφάττει πρόβατον καὶ μελί<κρατον χέει>,
λευκοῖς τε πάττει τὸν βόθρον τοῖς ἀλφίτοις
60   κἀντεῦθεν ἱστᾷ τάσδε τοῦ <βόθρου πέλας>,
καὶ γῇ παριστᾷ καὶ πάλιν πέμπει κάτω·
ἐγὼ δὲ τὴν σήν, αὐτ<αδέλφη φιλτάτη>,
οὐ γῇ παριστᾶν βούλομαι ψυχὴν φίλην,
πόλῳ δ' ἐφι. . .
65   Δράσω τί τοίνυν; Οὐκ ὀρύξω σοι βόθρον,

and saying the following words to our mother:
"I come here, mother, having left my husband and children,
having left my father and family,   40
having left my acquaintances, companions, and friends.
Having left them and . . .
I now come to this place here,
and wish to dwell forever here with you
in the land of the meek, in the green pastures,   45
so that *a mother may rejoice in her child,*
as David says, the prophet of the Lord."
You will say this to our mother,
as for me, what words will I find to tell you?
This I will say for sure; for what else should I say?   50
O gentle eyes and sweetly speaking mouth,
how are you bound in the funereal shroud,
the eyes covered and closed, against all hope,
the mouth bound fast and enclosed in silence?
Truly this is the will of God our Lord.   55
But let us also consider this attentively:
the foolish Hellene digs a trench for souls,
he slaughters a sheep and pours out honeyed wine;
he sprinkles the ditch with white grains of barley
and then he lets the souls approach the trench,   60
he lets them appear on earth and sends them back down
        below.
I, however, dearest sister, do not want
to make your beloved soul appear on earth,
but in heaven . . .
What shall I do then? I will not dig a trench for you,   65

ἀλλ᾽...
ἄνθρωπος οὖσα καὶ φοροῦσα σαρκίον
...
κἂν ἡμέραν ζήσειεν ἐν βίῳ μίαν,
70 ...
ἐξευμενίζων τὸν Θεὸν σοί, φιλτάτη,
...
ἐξ ὧν ὄνησις τοῖς νεκροῖς το...
...
75 ἀλλ᾽ ἐξ ἀλεύρων ἄρτον οἵ<σω>...
...
τὸ σεπτὸν αἷμα τοῦ θ<υσιαστηρίου>
...
ὧνπερ σπάσα<σα>...
80 ...
κούφως δὲ μᾶ<λλον>...
...
ὥσπερ πελειὰς...
...
85 ...
ὦ πᾶν καλὸν λαχοῦσα...
...
ἦν τοῖς ἐπαίνοις πάντες οἰχ...
...
90 ᾄδουσιν ἀγγέλλοντες ἄλλος <ἄλλό τι>·
<ὁ μὲν τὸ>...
ὁ δ᾽ αὖ τὸ σῶφρον καὶ τὸ μέτριον λέγει
...

158

but . . .
since you are human and bear flesh,
. . .
even if he would live one day in real life,
. . .   70
propitiating God for you, my dear,
. . .
from which advantages may . . . for the dead
. . .
but I will bring you a bread made of wheat flour . . .   75
. . .
the honorable blood of the altar
. . .
from which you have drawn . . .
. . .   80
very light . . .
. . .
like a dove . . .
. . .
. . .   85
O you who have received every blessing . . .
. . .
whom everyone . . . with praises
. . .
each has a different virtue to proclaim in song: 90
one . . .
another mentions your prudence and your moderation
. . .

ἄλλος τὸ πρᾷον εἰς τὸ θαῦμα προσφέρων

95 ...

ἐντεῦθεν ἄλλος νοῦν πάλιν τὸν ἀγχίνουν

...

καὶ πιστὰ σοῦ γε ταῦτα πάντα, φιλτάτη,

...

100 τοίνυν ἀνάγκη πᾶσα τούς σοι γνησίους

... τέλος,

μή πως φανῶμεν, εἰ θελήσομεν γράφειν

... πρὸς χάριν·

οὐκοῦν ἐγὼ ξένων σε δοὺς εὐφημίαις.

105 ... δεσπότῃ,

οὐ χρῶτα δρύπτων, οὐ σπαράττων τὴν κόμην,

<οὐ στέρνα κόπτων, οὐ διασχίζων> φάρος,

οὐκ αἰσχύνων πρόσωπα καὶ κάραν κόνει,

... τῷ Πλάστῃ λέγων·

110 ὦ Δέσποτα ζώντων τε καὶ τεθνηκότων,

...ρε μὴ κενουμένη,

Ἀναστασὼ σὴν νῦν μὲν εἰς χλόης τόπον

..., ἔνθα χαιρόντων στίφη·

αὖθις δὲ ταύτην εἰς ἀνάστασιν, Λόγε,

115 ...ους ἐξαναστᾶσαν δίδου

ἐπεντρυφᾶν σαῖς δωρεαῖς ταῖς ἀφθόνοις,

<καὶ φῶς π>ροσώπου σοῦ βλέπειν αἰωνίως,

ὃ πάντες οἱ βλέψοντες ἕξουσι κλέος.

another brings forward your marvelous gentleness
. . .   95
then another in turn your sharp wit
. . .
all of these praises are truthful, my dear,
. . .
well, your family members certainly must   100
. . .
lest we should appear, if we would want to write
just for the sake of . . . .
Therefore, I will hand you over to the praises of strangers.
                               . . . the lord,   105
not scratching my skin, nor rending hair,
not beating my breast, nor tearing my cloak apart,
not blemishing my head and face with dust,
but saying . . . to the Creator:
O Lord of the living and of the dead,   110
                               . . . never being emptied,
. . . your Anastaso now *to the green pastures,*
               . . . , where the throngs of the blissful are;
and then in turn . . . to resurrection, Christ the Word,
               . . . grant that she who lifted herself up high,   115
may enjoy your gifts in abundance,
and see the light of your face in eternity,
which will bring glory to everyone who sees it.

78

<Εἰς τὸν> γραμματικὸν Πέτρον,
αἰτήσαντα <τὰ> εἰς τὴν
ἀδελφὴν ἐπιτάφια ἰαμβεῖα,
κατασχόντα <δὲ χρόνον> πολὺν καὶ
μήπως φθάσαντα ἀποδοῦντα

Ἦ λωτὸν εὗρες ἐμφυτευθέντα ξένως
<ἐμοῖς> ἰάμβοις, Πέτρε, τοῖς ἐντυμβίοις
τοῖς εἰς ἀδελφὴν τὴν ἐμὴν γεγραμμένοις;
... <αὐ>τόχρημα τοὺς στίχους κρίνεις
5 καὶ ῥᾶστα τούτων οὐκ ἀποσπᾶσθαι θέλεις;
... ἀπ' αὐτῶν ὡς ἀναγνοὺς πολλάκις.

79

Ἕτεροι εἰς τὸν αὐτόν, πέμψαντα τοὺς
στίχους καὶ ...

Ἐκεῖνο τοῦ σοῦ Χριστοφόρου πυνθάνῃ,
εἰ ταῦτα πενθῶν, ποῖα γοῦν χαίρων γράφω;

78

On the grammarian Peter, who had asked for Christopher's funeral lament in iambs for his sister, and who kept it a long time and has not yet managed to give it back

Have you perhaps found a lotus flower miraculously
grown upon my funeral iambs, Peter,
which I wrote for my sister?
Do you consider my verses as downright . . . ,
so that you do not want to give them up so easily?   5
Leave them alone, you have read them often enough!

79

More verses for the same person, who had sent back the verses and . . .

This is what you want to know from your friend Christopher:
if I wrote this in mourning, what would I write then when
    happy?

... γνώσεως καὶ τῶν λόγων
τί κομψὸν εἶχε τὰ γραφέντα καὶ μέγα;
5   ... <οὐδ>ενὸς γέμον,
ποίαν δὲ καινὴν καὶ ξενίζουσαν φράσιν
                   ... <πο>ικίλην
πενθοῦντος αὐτοῦ τοῦ γράφοντος, ὡς ἔφης,
...;
10   ὡς ἡ λέγουσα μαρτυρεῖ παροιμία,
...
ὅμως ἂν εὗρες ἄξιόν τι καὶ λόγου,
...
δόξαν χορηγῷ τῶν καλῶν Θεῷ δίδου.

80

Εἰς τὸν ἅγιον Λάζαρον τὸν τοῦ Χριστοῦ φίλον διὰ τὴν σιωπὴν τῶν ἐκεῖθεν

Τῶν ἐν νεκροῖς ἤγγειλας οὐδὲν οὐδ᾽ ὅλως,
ἐκεῖθεν ἐλθών, Λάζαρε, Χριστοῦ φίλε,
οὐ πρᾶξιν αὐτῶν, οὐ δίαιταν, οὐκ ἔθη,
οὐδ᾽ οἷος αὐτοῖς χῶρος οὐδ᾽ οἷος νόμος·
5   καί τις χάρις σοι τῆς ἐγέρσεως χάριν,

　　　　　　　　　... of knowledge and learning,
what elegance, or what greatness did the poem have?
... not full of anything ...　　　　　　　　　　　　　5
Which innovating and unconventional style
　　　　　　　　　　　　　... variegated,
while the author was grieving, as you say,
... ?
As the known proverb attests,　　　　　　　　　　10
...
Yet if you found something that is worth speaking of,
...
attribute glory to God, giver of blessings.

80

On Saint Lazarus, friend of Christ, because he remained reticent about the other world

About the abode of the dead you disclosed nothing,
when you returned from there, Lazarus, friend of Christ:
nothing of their acts, their ways, their customs,
nor what kind of place they have, what kind of laws.
It was gracious of you, in thanks for your awakening,　　　5

εἰπόντι μηδὲν τῶν ἐκεῖθεν μηδ᾽ ὅλως.
Ὄντως ἀληθὴς τυγχάνων Χριστοῦ φίλος,
ἔγνως σιωπᾶν πᾶν ἀπόρρητον φίλου.

81

... Θεοδώραν μνηστεύ ... καὶ τὸ ἦθος

    ... μοι νύμφης πέρι· ἔστι δὲ τ<αῦτα>·
...

    ... ἡλικίην, λαμπρὸν κατὰ φοίνικος ἔρνος
...

5 <εἰ δὲ ἴ>δοις στείχουσαν, ἐρεῖς ἄρα· "αἴθε θεοί μ...
    ..."
ὄμματα παμφανόωντα ὑπ᾽ ὀφρύσι λαμπομένῃσι
...

στήθεα μαρμαίροντα· τὸ γὰρ φάσαν αἴ τάδε εἶδον.

10 ...
χεῖράς τ᾽ ἠδὲ πόδας λαμπροῖο ἀγάλματος οἷον.
...

ταῦτ᾽ ἔχει ἐκ φύσεως μάλα ἀγλαὰ δῶρα ἐκείνη.
...

to say nothing of what is there.
You truly are the genuine friend of Christ,
knowing to keep a friend's every secret in silence.

81

. . . Theodora who is betrothed . . . and character

  . . . about a bride. These are her blessings:
. . .

  . . . a stature like the splendid *shoot of a palm tree,*
. . .

if you saw her walking, you would say: "may the gods . . . 5
. . ."

all-shining eyes under resplendent brows,
. . .

shining breasts, as reported by the women who saw them;
. . .   10

hands and feet as of a splendid statue.
. . .

these are *the glorious boons* that she has from nature.
. . .

82

Εἰς τοὺς νεκροθάπτας, ὅτε τὸ ἐν τῷ ἁγίῳ
Λουκᾷ πολυάνδριον ἐνεπρήσθη,
διαρπάζοντας τὰ τῶν νεκρῶν ἄμφια

Ἀνδρῶνα νεκρῶν πῦρ καταφλέγει κύκλῳ
τὸν ἐγγὺς οἴκου Λουκᾶ τοῦ θεηγόρου,
καὶ συρρυέντα νεκροκηδευτῶν στίφη
δίκην κοράκων πτῶμά που σκεψαμένων
5   μᾶλλον τὰ νεκρῶν ἢ νεκροὺς σῴζειν θέλει.
Μέλει γὰρ αὐτοῖς οὐδ᾽ ὁπωσοῦν λειψάνων,
σουδαρίων δὲ καὶ στολῶν καὶ σανδάλων,
ἐξ ὧνπερ ἐλπίζουσι κερδαίνειν μέγα,
κἂν δυστυχὲς τὸ κέρδος αὐτοῖς ἐκτόπως.
10   Τὰς οὖν στολὰς αἴροντες ἐκ τῶν σωμάτων
γυμνοῦσι νεκρούς, οὓς περιστέλλειν ἔδει,
καὶ τοῦ πυρὸς τὸ κέρδος ἠγαπηκότες
τὸ πῦρ ἑαυτοῖς προξενοῦσι τῆς δίκης.
Ὄλεθρος αὐτοὺς τοιγαροῦν δεινὸς μένει,
15   ἀνθ᾽ ὧνπερ εἰς τὸ κέρδος ἐκδεδωκότες
αὐτὴν παρεῖδον τὴν φύσιν πιμπρωμένην,
ἐκ δυστυχῶν νεκρῶν τε καὶ κεκαυμένων
εὐδαίμονα σπεύδοντες ἐξευρεῖν βίον.

82

On the gravediggers, who robbed the garments of the dead when the cemetery at Saint Luke's was ablaze

A ring of fire devours the burial ground of the dead,
near the church of Luke, God's messenger,
and meanwhile, just as crows eye a corpse,
throngs of gravediggers amass to save
not the dead but the belongings of the dead.   5
They do not care at all about the remains of the dead,
but rather about the head cloths, garments, and sandals,
from which they hope to gain a great profit—
a profit, though, that is extremely baneful for them.
In removing the clothing from the bodies,   10
they strip the dead whom they ought to enshroud;
and in desiring profit from the fire,
they call upon themselves the fire of justice.
A terrible ruin awaits them,
for, as they gave themselves over to gain,   15
they did not heed the nature of fire,
but from burned and miserable corpses sought
eagerly to find a prosperous life.

83

Ἐπίγραμμα δι᾽ ἡρωε<λεγείων περὶ τῶν> ἁγίων τοῦ ὅλου χρόνου

Ἐνθάδ᾽ ἀπειρεσίοιο νοὸς πτ...
    ἐκ βραχέων ἐπέων θήκατο Χριστοφόρος,
ὄφρ᾽ εὖ γινώσκοιντο ὅλου ἁγίων χ<ρόνου ἄθλων>
    τέρματα μακαρίης εἵνεκα μνημοσύνης.

84

Εἰς τὸν Βασίλειον τὸν λεγόμενον Χοιρινόν, πολλάκις αἰτήσαντα ἐκ τῶν συγγραμμάτων αὐτοῦ

Τί πολλὰ γρύζεις τοὺς ἐμοὺς ζητῶν λόγους
καὶ "σαῖς γραφαῖς θρέψον με" συχνῶς μοι λέγεις;
Ἄπελθε πόρρω· χοῖρος οὐ τρώγει μέλι·
ἔχεις βαλάνους δεῖπνον, εἰ βούλει, φίλον·
5   ἂν οὖν μάλιστα καὶ κερατίων δέῃ,
ἡ σύζυγος πλήσει σε καὶ κερατίων.

83

Epigram in elegiac couplets about the saints of the whole year

Here Christopher has set forth in concise verses
    the . . . of a boundless mind,
so that the martyrdoms of the saints of the whole year
    would be made well known, for the sake of their blessed
    memory.

84

For Basil, surnamed "Porky," who had often asked for some of Christopher's writings

Why all this grunting, asking for my words,
and why do you keep saying, "Feed me with your writings"?
Get out of here! A pig does not eat honey.
You have acorns for dinner, your favorite food, if you wish.
And if you want some horns of carob,   5
your wife will fill you with horns as well.

85

Εἰς ἰατρὸν κεν<όδοξον>

Ἰατρέ, μὴ δίωκε τὸν τύφον μάτην·
εἰ γὰρ σκοπήσας ἀκριβῶς ἀνακρίνῃς,
ὅθεν πορίζῃ τὰς ἀφορμὰς τοῦ βίου,
αὐτὸς σεαυτὸν καὶ μυσαχθήσῃ τάχα,
5 τροφῆς χορηγοὺς οὖρα καὶ κόπρους ἔχων.
Χρῆν οὖν ὀφρὺν ῥίψαντα τὴν ἐπηρμένην
κόπρων σκάφας βλέπειν σε καὶ τὰς ἀμίδας,
ὅθεν τραφήσῃ καὶ πόρους ἕξεις βίου,
δυσωδιῶν δὲ καὶ καταφρονητέον
10 . . .
ὡς καί σε φάσκειν τοῦτον Ἰὼβ τὸν <τάλαν>
. . .

86

Εἰς τὸν ἅγιον Διονύσιον ἕν<εκα> . . .

Ἐγώ, Διονύσιε, τολμῶ καὶ λέγειν,
ὡς οὐκ ἐπλάσθης ἐν γυναικὸς κοιλίᾳ,

85

On a conceited doctor

Doctor, do not pursue affectations in vain.
Should you perform a close examination
of how you find the means to make a living,
you likely would be sickened at yourself,
since you procure your food from dung and urine.   5
You would do well to lose your haughty sneer
and consider the chamber pots and bedpans
that nourish you and provide your livelihood.
And you'd better despise the bad odors
. . .   10
so that you say the words that miserable Job once said:
. . .

86

On Saint Dionysios because of . . .

I am so bold, Dionysios, as to say
that you were not born from a woman's womb,

ἀλλ᾽ ἀγγέλοις μάλιστα συντεταγμένος
ἄνωθεν ἦλθες ἐκ πόλου, φύσις ξένη,
5 βροτοῖς ἀπαγγέλλουσα πάντα πρὸς μέρος
τὰ τῶν ἀΰλων ταγμάτων ὅπως ἔχοι.
Οὕτω γινώσκεις τὰς ἀΰλους οὐσίας·
οὕτω θεωρεῖς ἐνθέους θεωρίας·
οὕτω θεωρεῖς τὰς φύσεις τῶν ἀγγέλων·
10 οὕτω, τὸ μεῖζον, ἄγγελος σὺ τὴν φύσιν.

87

Εἴς τινα φίλον ἐξ ἀγροῦ σταφυλὰς πέμψαντα

Σὺ μέν με καρποῖς δεξιοῖ τῆς ἀμπέλου,
ἐγὼ δὲ καρπῷ τῆς συκῆς χαίρω μάλα·
καὶ γὰρ προτιμῶ τὴν συκῆν τῆς ἀμπέλου,
μεμνημένος μὲν καὶ καλῶν συκῆς πάλαι,
5 μεμνημένος δὲ καὶ κακῶν τῆς ἀμπέλου·
ἡ μὲν γὰρ ἐνδύει με γυμνὸν καὶ σκέπει,
ἡ δ᾽ ἐνδεδυμένον με γυμνοῖ τὸν τάλαν·
ἡ μὲν καλύπτει τὴν ἐμὴν πρὶν αἰσχύνην,
ἡ δὲ θριαμβεύει με καὶ καταισχύνει·
10 καὶ μαρτυροῦσι τοῦ γένους ἀρχηγέται,

but that you had a place among the angels
and came down from heaven, an alien nature,
to proclaim to mortals in every detail   5
the immaterial ranks, the nature of each.
This is how you know the immaterial beings;
this is how you contemplate divine contemplations;
this is how you reveal the natures of the angels;
this is how, above all, you too are an angel.   10

87

For a friend who had sent grapes
from the countryside

You treat me with fruits of the vine,
but I still rejoice more in the fig tree's fruit.
For I prefer the fig tree to the vine,
mindful of the fig tree's good deeds of old,
and mindful also of the vineyard's vices.   5
The former clothes and shields me when I am naked;
the latter bares me when I am clothed, poor me!
The first conceals my earlier disgrace;
the other triumphs over me and puts me to shame.
To witness are two forebears of our race: 10

Ἀδὰμ τὸ πρῶτον καὶ τὸ δεύτερον Νῶε.
Σύκοις με γοῦν εὔφραινε, βοτρύων δ᾽ ἅλις·
τῆς ἀμπέλου γὰρ τὴν συκῆν κρείττω κρίνω,
καλόν τι ποιῶν καὶ καλῶς ἄρα κρίνων·
15 τὴν μὲν γὰρ ἐχθρὰν οἶδα, τὴν δ᾽ εὐεργέτιν·
σύκοις με τέρπε· ῥὰξ δὲ πολλὰ χαιρέτω.

88

Εἰς τὸν αὐτὸν σῦκα πέμψαντα

Ἔπεμψας ἡμῖν ἐξ ἀγροῦ τοῦ σοῦ σῦκα,
ἡμεῖς δὲ καρποῖς χαίρομεν τῆς ἀμπέλου,
ὡς τῆς συκῆς κρίνοντες αὐτὴν βελτίω·
ἡ μὲν γὰρ αὐτῶν καὶ κατηράθη πάλαι,
5 ἡ δ᾽ ηὐλογήθη μυστικωτέρῳ τρόπῳ·
καὶ τὴν μὲν οἴσεις θῦμα τῷ Θεοῦ δόμῳ,
ἡ δ᾽ οὐ μετάσχῃ τοῦδε τοῦ θείου κλέους·
καὶ μαρτυρεῖ μοι Δεσπότης Θεὸς Λόγος,
τὴν μὲν συκῆν πρὶν εἰς ἀρὰν κατακρίνας,
10 ὡς μηδὲ καρπὸν ἐξενεγκεῖν εἰσέτι,
τὴν ἄμπελον δὲ τιμιωτάτην κρίνας,
ὡς κλῆσιν αὐτῆς εἰς ἑαυτὸν ἑλκύσαι,
καὶ πρὸς μαθητὰς τοὺς ἄγαν φιλουμένους

the first is Adam, and the second, Noah.
So cheer me, then, with figs—enough of grapes!
I deem the fig superior to the vine.
I do the right thing, so my judgment is also right:
I know one as a foe and one as a helper.   15
Delight me, then, with figs. Away with grapes!

88

For the same friend, who had sent figs

You have sent us figs from your field,
but I am happy with the vineyard's fruit,
as I consider it to be superior to the fig;
for the former was accursed in days of old,
while the vine was blessed in a more mystical way.   5
The one you will offer in the house of God;
the other has no part in such godly honor.
So testifies our Lord, the Word of God,
who has condemned the fig tree to be cursed
to bring no more fruit forth forevermore;   10
the vine, though, he has judged most honorable,
applying to himself its very name;
to those disciples he so greatly loved

οἰκεῖον αἷμα τῆσδε τὸν καρπὸν φάναι.
15 Ἐκ βοτρύων τοίνυν με δεξιοῦ, φίλε,
σύκων ἀποστὰς ὡς ἀρᾶς πεπλησμένων.

89

Εἰς τὸ τίμιον λείψανον τοῦ ἁγίου Παντελεήμονος τὸ ἐκβλύζον τὸ ἁγίασμα

Ἔβλυζε πέτρα ῥεῖθρον Ἰσραηλίταις
ἑνὸς πάθους ἴαμα, τῆς δίψης μόνης·
τὸ σὸν δὲ τοῦτο, μάρτυς, ὀστοῦν ἐνθάδε
πασῶν νόσων ἴαμα ῥεῖθρον ἐκχέει.

he said its fruit was his very own blood.
Therefore, dear friend, offer me grapes, 15
and avoid the figs as the curse-filled fruits they are!

89

On the honorable relic of Saint Panteleemon that dripped with sacred liquid

When a spring flowed out of a rock for the Israelites,
that was a cure for one affliction only: thirst.
But this bone here from you, martyr,
pours out a stream that heals all diseases.

90

<Πρὸς τοὺς ἐ>ν τῷ ἀγρῷ ἀπόντας
φίλους, ἱπποδρομίας ἀγομένης
ἀπολειφθέντας καὶ ἀξιώσαντας
<μανθάνειν τὰ> περὶ αὐτῆς

Ὅπως μὲν εἶχεν ἱππικὸν τὸ χθές, φίλοι,
<ποίους δὲ τοὺς ἀ>γῶνας εὗρε τοῦ δρόμου,
ἀποῦσι καὶ θέλουσι μανθάνειν γράφω,
<ποιῶν> ὑμῖν ἕκαστα δῆλα πρὸς μέρος,
5   ὡς ἄν γε καὶ δόξητε, φίλτατοι φίλων,
<ὡς ἐκ κατόπ>τρου τῶν παρόντων μου λόγων
τῷ χθὲς θεάτρῳ συμπαρεῖναι τοῦ δρόμου
          . . . <ὥσ>περ ἐμφανεστάτως
τοὺς τέσσαρας βλέποντες ἁρματηλάτας
10   . . . ειν ποιουμένους.
Ὕσπληγγα πρώτην, ἥν φασι πρώτην θύραν,
<ἥν μὲν κατασχὼν Λευκὸς ἁρμ>ατηλάτης,
ὁ Ῥούσιος δὲ τὴν τρίτην ἥν προκρίνας,
          . . . <δευτέρ>αν·
15   ἐγειτόνει δὲ Πράσινος τῷ Ῥουσίῳ
. . .
ὕσπληξ δὲ πέμπτη κλῆρος ἦν τῷ Βενέτῳ.
. . .

90

To his friends who were out of town in the countryside, and, having missed the horse race that had been held, asked to be told about it

How yesterday's horse race unfolded, my friends,
and what contests its course witnessed,
I now write to you, who were absent and want to hear about
    it.
I will make everything clear for you in detail,
so that you, my dearest friends, will have the impression,   5
as from the mirror of my present words,
of being present at yesterday's spectacle in the Hippodrome
                        . . . as if very clearly
seeing the four chariot drivers,
made to   10
The first starting box, which is called "the first door,"
was occupied by the White charioteer,
while the Red was assigned to the third,
                       . . . the second.
The Green was next to the Red   15
. . .
The fifth starting box was allotted to the Blue.
. . .

<ὄ>χλου καταψάλαντος, ὡς τούτοις ἔθος,

20 . . .

<ὁ Λευκ>ὸς ἤδη τοῦ δραμεῖν ἦν ἐγγίσας

. . .

. . . τὴν καταρχὴν τοῦ δρόμου

. . .

25 . . . τοὺς πυκνὰ καὶ βλέπων ἅμα

. . .

. . . ἀλλ᾽ οὐκ ἀσκόπως

. . .

. . . <μα>κρὰν παρεκπέσῃ

30 . . .

. . . <ἐ>γκαρσίους

. . .

. . . δὲ τοῖχον θέλων

. . . ραστα συντριβὲν πέσῃ

35 . . .

. . . ῥυτῆρας χερσὶν ἑλκύσας ὅλαις

. . .

<τοῖ>χόν τε φεύγων καὶ στενουμένην τρίβον

. . .

40 ἡ πλὰξ δὲ λευκοῦ ξέσμα τυγχάνει λίθου

. . .

ἤνοιξε χώραν εἰσόδου τῷ Βενέτῳ

. . .

τείνας κατ᾽ αὐτοῦ καὶ βραχὺ προβὰς πρόσω

45 . . .

ἀποπλανήσας τοῦ κατ᾽ εὐθεῖαν δρόμου

The crowd was chanting, as it is accustomed to do,

. . .   20

the White was already near to running,

. . .

               . . . the beginning of the race

. . .

. . . at the same time often looking at the . . .   25

. . .

             . . . but not without purpose

. . .

             . . . to fall far off the mark

. . .   30

             . . . oblique

. . .

. . . wanting to . . . the wall

             . . . was squeezed and fell down

. . .   35

      . . . drawing his reins with all the strength of his hands

. . .

avoiding the wall and narrow track

. . .

the slab which is carved out of white stone,   40

. . .

opened up space for the Blue to pass through

. . .

pulling against him and going slightly ahead of him

. . .   45

swerving away from the straight track

...

τὸν Λευκὸν εἶδε σύνδρομον τῷ Ῥουσίῳ
ἀ...

50 φωναῖς τε συχναῖς καὶ συριγμοῖς χρωμένους·
κ...

ἀφεὶς δὲ τούτους εἰς πρόσω σπεύδων ἔθει·
οἱ...

ἐπεὶ δὲ καὶ παρῆλθον ἐκ τῶν ὀργάνων

55 πρ...

τὸν Ῥούσιον παρῆλθε πολλῷ τῷ μέσῳ
ὁ Β<ένετος>...

καμπτῆρος, ὡς ἔφημεν, ἐκβεβλημένος
ἀπρὶξ ε...

60 καὶ δεξιᾶς σχὼν χερσὶν ἡνίας ὅλαις
στρέφει τε δι...

καὶ τῇ πλατείᾳ προσβαλὼν ἐλᾷ τρίβῳ,
τοῦ Ῥουσίου δὲ ῥ...

καμπτὴρ δὲ τὸν Πράσινον εἶχεν αὐτίκα

65 πρῶτον διϊππάζο<ντα>...,

Λευκὸς δὲ καμπτοῦ τάξιν ἔσχε δευτέραν,
ὁ Ῥούσιος δὲ τρίτος εἵπετο <τρέχων>,
ὁ Βένετος τέταρτος ἀγχοῦ Ῥουσίου.

Τὸν πρῶτον οὖν δίαυλον ο<ὕτω τοῦ δρόμου>

70 οἱ τεσσάρων ἤλαυνον ἱππεῖς ἁρμάτων,
πρῶτα Πράσινος, εἶτα Λευκ<ὸς αὐτίκα>
καὶ δὴ μετ᾽ αὐτοὺς Ῥούσιος, καὶ Ῥουσίου
ὁ Βένετος σύνεγγυς ἡνιο<στρόφος>.

Ἐπεὶ δὲ διπλοῦς ἦν δίαυλος τῷ δρόμῳ,

. . .
he saw the White running together with the Red
. . .
uttering frequent shouts and whistles 50
. . .
he left them and ran forward with speed
. . .
when they had also passed the organs
. . . 55
the Blue overtook with great distance the Red
. . .
as we said, he rushed forward . . . turning post,
tightly . . .
and holding the right rein with all the strength of his hands, 60
he turns and . . .
he enters and rides through this broad passage,
while the Red . . .
The Green immediately reached the turning post,
driving through first . . . 65
the White occupied second place at the turning post,
the Red followed as the third,
and the Blue was fourth, close to the Red.
This way, the first lap of the course
was finished by the four charioteers, 70
first Green, then immediately White,
after them Red, and close to the Red
was the Blue driver.
But when two laps of the course had been finished,

75 εἰς ἓν συνῆλθε Βένετος <τῷ Πρασίνῳ>,
ἄμφω δὲ κοινὴν τὴν ἅμιλλαν εἰχέτην,
πληγαῖς ὁμοῦ νύττοντες ἵππ<ους καὶ ψόφοις>
καὶ τὸν πρόσω σπεύδοντες ἁρπάζειν τόπον.
Ὡς δ' ἥκον, ἔνθα παμμε<γίστη> . . .
80 ἔστηκε χαλκοῦ πυραμὶς διηρμένη,
ἧς πλαίσιον τὸ σχῆμα <τυγχάνει κάτω>,
εἰς ὀξὺ λῆγον εὐφυῶς ἐκ πλαισίου,
βραχὺ προελθὼν <ὁ Πράσινος εἰς πρόσω>,
καὶ τοὺς χαλινοὺς καμπύλως τείνας ἔσω
85 ἵστησι τὸν Β<ένετον> . . .
ἵππους δὲ νύξας ἐκτρέχει σφοδρᾷ ῥύμῃ
ὁ Βένετος . . .
ἐκεῖθεν ἐκβὰς αὖθις ἤρχετο τρέχειν
φω. . .
90 τοὺς γὰρ χαλινοὺς ἐνδακόντες σὺν βίᾳ,
. . .
τοῦτον μὲν ἐκφέρουσιν ἄχρι σφενδ<όνης>
. . .
πλὴν ὁ Πράσινος, ὡς ἔφην ἄνω, . . .
95 . . .
ἐπεὶ δὲ καὶ δίαυλος ἤγετο <τρίτος>,
. . .
βαρύς τε πνεύσας ἐ. . .
. . .
100 ἵππους ἐκείνου τοὺς . . .
. . .
τοὺς ἀστραγάλους . . .

the Blue was tied with the Green,   75
and they both held a contest between them,
spurring their horses with blows and shouts,
and hurrying to take the lead.
When they came to the place where a huge . . .
and high pyramid of bronze stood,   80
having a square shape at its base,
marvelously tapering off from that square to a point,
the Green advanced a bit forward,
and pulling his reins to the inside in a curved line,
he holds the Blue down . . .   85
The Blue spurs his horses and accelerates with a vehement
      rush.
. . .
from there he takes off and starts to run again
. . .
violently biting the reins   90
. . .
they bring him up to the curved ramp,
. . .
But the Green, as I said above, . . .
. . .   95
When the third lap was run, . . .
. . .
he breathed heavily . . .
. . .
his horses   100
. . .
the dice . . .

. . .

καὶ Πράσινον πα<ρῆλθε>. . .

105 . . .

ἐντεῦθεν . . .

. . .

ὡς δ' εἰς . . .

. . .

110 . . .

ἀμφοῖν δὲ τούτων ὁ Πρά<σινος>. . .

. . .

σκοπὸς δὲ Λευκῷ καὶ Βενέτ<ῳ>. . .

. . .

115 ἐκεῖθεν ἔνθεν ἅρμα τούτου συν<τρίβειν>

. . .

ἔμπροσθεν αὐτῶν ἐξελαύνων ὡρά<θη>

. . .

ὃν καὶ διελθὼν καὶ φθάσας νύσσης μέχρι

120 . . .

τοιοῦτον ἔσχε τὸ χθὲς ἱππικὸν τέλος

. . .

ἀπαγγελεῖ τε πρὸς μέρος τοῖς αὐτόθι

. . .

125 ἃ πᾶσίν ἐστι δῆλα τοῖς ἐν τῇ πόλει.

. . .

and he overtook the Green . . .

. . .   105

at that point . . .

. . .

when . . . toward . . .

. . .

. . .   110

the Green . . . both of them

. . .

it was the intention of White and Blue . . .

. . .

to squeeze his chariot from both sides   115

. . .

was to be seen driving in front of them

. . .

passing him and arriving at the finish

. . .   120

such was the end of yesterday's horse race

. . .

reporting in detail to the people there

. . .

what is known to everyone in the city.   125

91

… καὶ Ἰωάννην τὸν ἀδελφὸν αὐτοῦ

…
ποίαν λαβὴν εὕρητε τοῦ πρός με γράφ<ειν>
          … μοι
ἔγωγε τοίνυν τὴν ἀφορμὴν εἰσφέρω
5   … <γρά>φειν·
μωρὸς γὰρ ὄντως, ὡς λόγος, δείξει πόρον.

92

… τε αἰθρίας οὔσης τὰ ἄστρα ὑπερλάμπουσιν

<Ἂν προσβλέπῃς γε τὸν κατά>στερον πόλον,
λειμῶνας εἴπῃς ἢ χλοάζουσαν πόαν
          …εῖαν λίθων
μικρὰ πρὸς αὐτὸν καὶ τὰ τούτων βελτίω
5   … τον πόλον μετ' αἰθρίας,
ἐστιγμένον μὲν οἷον ἐκ τῶν ἀστέρων,

91

. . . and John, his brother

. . .
which occasion did you find to write me?
. . .
I therefore propose an occasion:
$\qquad$ . . . to write;   5
for truly the fool will show the way, as the saying goes.

92

. . . when the stars shine forth in
a clear sky

When you look at the star-studded sky,
you'd say that you see pastures or green grass
$\qquad$ . . . of stones.
<The things on earth>, even the best among them,
<seem> small compared to the sky in clear weather,   5
which looks as if it were stitched with stars,

<εἰπεῖν δὲ μᾶ>λλον ἠμφιεσμένον κύκλῳ
καὶ χρυσοειδῆ κόσμον ἐνδεδυμένον
<καὶ πᾶν καταλ>άμποντα φωτὶ πλουσίῳ·
10 ἄρρητον ὥσπερ ἡδονὴν δέχῃ τότε
<καὶ φαιδρ>ότητος ἐμπιπλήσκῃ τῆς ἄκρας,
χρυσοῦν ἀληθῶς οὐρανὸν δοκῶν βλέπειν·
<βλέπεις γε πο>λλοὺς ἡλίων μικρῶν κύκλους,
τοὺς χρυσομόρφους καὶ φαεινοὺς ἀστέρας,
15 <ἐφ' οἷς ἀνί>σχει καὶ σεληναῖος λύχνος,
ὀφθαλμὸς ἄλλος τῆς δᾳδουχίας μέγας,
<τὴν νύκτα> δεικνὺς ἀκριβῶς ὡς ἡμέραν,
ψυχάς τε τέρπων τῶν ὁδοιπόρων ἅμα
<καὶ πᾶσαν αὐ>τοῖς προξενῶν θυμηδίαν.
20 Ἆρ' οὐχὶ κάλλη ταῦτα τῶν γῆς καλλίω;
<Ἆρ' οὐ δοκεῖ σοι> καὶ πανήγυριν ξένην
ἄγειν ἐπ' αὐτοῖς τὰς φύσεις τῶν ἀγγέλων,
             ... σιωπώσας μένειν,
τὸν Δημιουργὸν ἡσυχῇ θαμβουμένας;

or, rather, garbed all over,
and clad with a gold-like ornament,
illuminating everything with a rich light.
The joy you feel then cannot be expressed,   10
you are filled with supreme brilliance,
convinced the sky you see is truly golden.
You see the many disks of little suns,
the gold-like and brilliant stars,
where the lamp of the moon rises,   15
that second great eye of torch-bearing light
turning the night into day.
It cheers the souls of travelers,
and brings them every joy.
Aren't these beauties better than those on earth?   20
Don't you think that the throngs of angels
celebrate an exceptional feast up there,
            . . . remaining speechless,
silently standing in awe of the Creator?

93

⟨Εἰς τοὺς μελῳδοὺς Ἰω⟩άννην, Κοσμᾶν καὶ Θεοφάνη, ὁμοῦ γεγραμμένους

... ⟨οὐ⟩χὶ χρόας,
οὕσπερ θεωρεῖς τρεῖς μελῳδοὺς ἐνθάδε
...ως
ἀλλ᾽ ἐννεοὶ μένοντες, ὡς ὁρᾶν ἔχεις,
5 ...
ἐπεὶ λαλοῦσι, σάρκες ὄντες, οὐ τύποι.

94

... ⟨πεμφθέ⟩ντων μεσισκλίων

...
... ἐν οὕτω δωρεαῖς κεκρυμμένην
...

...τητος ἡ στοργή, Λέον,
5 ...
⟨καὶ δωρεὰν σὴν ψ⟩αλμικῶς πιανάτω.

93

On the hymnographers John, Kosmas, and Theophanes, painted together

                              . . . not the colors,
the three hymnographers, whom you behold here
. . .
but they remain mute, as you can see,
. . .   5
since they speak, being flesh, not images.

94

. . . the foodstuff that was sent

. . .
. . . hidden in gifts this way
. . .
. . . your affection, Leo,
. . .   5
let him, as the psalm puts it, *regard* your gift *as fat*.

95

Εἰς τὴν ἐκκλησίαν τοῦ ἁγίου Γεωργίου, τὴν ἐν τοῖς Μαγγάνοις

Ἐν ταῖς ἄνω μὲν μαρτύρων κατοικίαις,
ἃς εἰς ἀμοιβὴν τῶν πόνων Θεὸς νέμει,
ποία τὸ κρεῖττον ἔσχεν, οὐκ ἔχω λέγειν·
ἐν τοῖς δόμοις δὲ τοῖς κάτω τούτοις τέως
5   Γεώργιος τὰ πρῶτα κληροῦται γέρα·
κἂν τῶν ἀθλητῶν ἡ θεοστεφὴς φάλαγξ
ὥρας ναῶν ἤριζον ἀλλήλοις χάριν,
πάντων ἂν ἐκράτησεν οὗτος μαρτύρων·
ὑπερφυῆ γὰρ πάντα τοῦδε τοῦ δόμου,
10   καὶ πλῆρες ὧδε χαρίτων τὸ χωρίον
καὶ θεῖον ὄντως, εἰ τἀληθὲς χρὴ λέγειν.
Ἰδὼν Ἰακὼβ εἶπεν ἄν, καθὼς πάλαι·
"ὡς φρικτὸς οὗτος καὶ φόβου γέμων τόπος·
οὐκ ἔστι τοῦτο," φησίν, "ἢ Θεοῦ δόμος."

95

On the church of Saint George in Mangana

Of all the martyrs' dwellings upon high,
which God allots, rewarding each one's pain,
I cannot say which one is best;
but of the abodes down here below, at least,
George has been allotted the first prize.   5
If the God-crowned phalanx of saints
held a contest for most beautiful church,
George would triumph over all the martyrs.
For in this abode everything surpasses nature;
and this place is full of beauty,   10
and truly divine, if truth be told.
Had Jacob seen this, he would say, as of old:
"How awesome is *this place,* inspiring fear!
This can be nothing but the house *of God.*"

96

. . .

Χειρῶν πατοῦσιν ὧδε τοὺς πόνους πόδες.

97

. . .

Ἔθελξας ἡμᾶς ῥημάτων κάλλει πλέον
. . .
κεστῷ γὰρ οἷον τὰ γραφέντα σκευάσας
. . .
5 οὕτω διεξέπεμψας ἡμῖν τοῖς φίλοις
. . .

96

. . .

Feet tread here on the labor of hands.

97

. . .

With the beauty of words, you delighted me more
. . .
adorning your writings as with a magic girdle,
. . .
so you sent out to me, your friend,   5
. . .

98

Εἰς τὸν ἐν μέσῳ τῆς ὀροφῆς τοῦ Ὠάτου Σωτῆρα κάτω βλέποντα

Δοκεῖς προκύπτων καὶ βλέπων γῆν ὑψόθεν
ἕτοιμος εἶναι καὶ κατελθεῖν, εἰ δέοι,
ψυχὴν προθύμως τὴν φιλάνθρωπον πάλιν
ὑπὲρ προβάτων ὡς πάλαι θύσων λύτρον.
5 Τοιοῦτος εἶ σὺ καὶ γεγραμμένος, Λόγε,
τὰ σπλάγχνα γάρ σου χρηστὰ κἀν ταῖς εἰκόσιν.

99

Εἰς τὸ ἱμάτιον τὴν θάλασσαν ἣν ἐφόρει ὁ Στενίτης χ. . .

Ἰδοῦσα φρικτὸν οὐδὲν ὡς Ἰορδάνης,
πῶς ἐστράφης, θάλασσα, νῦν εἰς τοὐπίσω;
Οἶμαι, ῥύπον φεύγουσα τὸν σὸν ἐστράφης,
εἰ καὶ στραφεῖσα τοῦτον οὐκ ἀπεξύσω.

98

On the Savior in the middle of the ceiling of the Oaton hall, who is looking down

As you bend down and look at earth from on high,
you seem prepared to come down, if need be,
eager to sacrifice your loving soul
again, a ransom for your sheep as before.
You keep this quality also when painted, O Word;   5
since in images too, your heart is kind.

99

On the cloak called *thalassa* that was worn by Stenites . . .

Since you saw nothing as awesome as the Jordan,
why, *thalassa, have you* now *turned around?*
I think you've turned around to flee your filth,
but, even by turning, you could not scrape it off.

100

Εἰς τὸν μοναχὸν Νικήταν τὸν φιλόσοφον

Εἰς ἡμέραν μὲν <βρῶμά μοι λόγοι, πάτερ,>
ἐς ἑσπέραν δὲ πέμμα· λοιπὸν οὖν γράφε·
καὶ βρῶμα γὰρ καὶ πέ<μμα σοὺς ἔξω λόγους,>
τρυφῶν ἐν αὐτοῖς νύκτα καὶ μεθ' ἡμέραν.
5   Τοίνυν σιγῆσαι μὴ θέλ<ῃς περαιτέρω·>
εἰ γὰρ σιγήσεις καὶ τὸ σὸν κλείσεις στόμα,
λιμὸς λόγων σῶν τὸν σὸν ἐκτή<ξει φίλον,>
τεθνήξομαι δέ· καὶ τί κερδάνῃς ἄρα;

101

Εἰς τὴν εἰκόνα τοῦ ἁγίου Ἠλιού

Ὡς Ἠλίας ζῇ, πῶς ἀπιστήσεις βλέπων;
Ἰδοὺ γὰρ αὐτὸς ἐνθάδε ζῶν, ὡς βλέπεις.
Ὑποδράμῃ σε καὶ λογισμός τις τάχα,
μὴ καὶ κατελθὼν εἰς Θαβὼρ Ὄρος πάλαι
5   ἔμεινεν εἰς γῆν, οὐκ ἀνελθὼν καὶ πάλιν·
αὐτὸς γάρ ἐστιν οὗτος ὁ ζῶν Ἠλίας.

100

On the monk Niketas the philosopher

Your words, dear father, are my daily food
and my dessert in the evening. Therefore, write;
for I will have your words as both food and sweets,
feasting on them by night and day.
So please, do not keep silent any longer,   5
because, if you are silent, if you close your mouth,
the hunger for your words will starve your friend,
and I will die. What will that profit you?

101

On the image of the holy Elijah

Elijah lives — how could you doubt it when you see this?
For, behold! — here he is alive, as you can see.
Perhaps the notion will occur to you that
after he came down from Mount Tabor, Elijah
stayed on earth, and never went back up.   5
For here he is, the living Elijah.

102

Εἰς τὴν ἀπόκρεων

Μέλλεις ἀπαίρειν ὄψ<ον ἡμῶν καὶ κρέας>,
καὶ δεξιοῦται πᾶς σε πολλῷ τῷ πόθῳ,
καὶ θερμὸν εἰς σὲ νῦν <ἔχει πᾶς τὸν πόθον>,
κατατρυφῶν σου καὶ πλέον τοῦ μετρίου.

103

Εἰς τοὺς ἐν τῇ <οἰκίᾳ αὐτοῦ μῦς>

Οἱ παντοτρῶκται τοῦδε μῦες τοῦ δόμου
οἱ <πάν>τα ...
γάμοις ἑαυτοὺς καὶ τόκοις δεδωκότες
...
5   παροικίαν σφῶν τὴν ἐμὴν κατοικίαν
...
ἅπερ δὲ καὶ πράττουσιν ὡς δεινὰ σφ<όδρα>
...
δρόμους ἄγουσι καὶ περιδ<ρόμους> ...
10   ...

102

On the week before Lent

You'll soon take from us delicacies and meat,
and everyone greets you with much eagerness;
everybody now has a burning desire for you,
indulging in you beyond all moderation.

103

On the mice in his house

The voracious mice of this home
who . . . everything . . .
giving themselves over to marriages and births
. . .
they <turn> my house into their colony,   5
. . .
the things they do, how outrageous they are!
. . .
they make ways and sideways . . .
. . .   10

τέμνουσι τοῖς ὀδοῦσ<ι>...

...

πηδῶσι καὶ βοῶσι...

...

15   ἐνταῦθα βλέψας...

...

ἐκ γωνιῶν πηδ<ῶσι>...

...

μῦας...

20   ...

ἄλλους

...

ὠθ<οῦσι>...

...

25   ...

ἀνατραπέντες πρός τι...

...

τὸν λύχνον οὕτω συγκαταρ...

...

30   καὶ πρὸς φυγὴν βλέπουσι πάντες ἀ<θρόον>

...

καὶ δή ποτε στὰς τῆς φλιᾶς ἐν τῷ μέσ<ῳ>

...

ἔριν τινὰ στήσαντες ὀστέου πέρι

35   ...

ὡς πίονάς τε καὶ παχίστους εἰς ἄκρον

...

τούτους ἰδὼν ἔδοξα δέλφακας βλέπειν

with their teeth, they cut . . .
. . .
they jump and they shout . . .
. . .
seeing here . . .   15
. . .
they jump from the corners
. . .
mice . . .
. . .   20
others . . .
. . .
push . . .
. . .
. . .   25
turning around toward
. . .
they . . . the lamp in such a way
. . .
and suddenly all of them look for an escape route   30
. . .
and once, <a mouse> standing right in the middle of the
        threshold
. . .
they began a fight over a bone
. . .   35
how extremely fat and heavy they are!
. . .
when I saw them, I thought I was looking at pigs.

...μένους.

40 Τοιούσδε πολλοὺς οἶκος οὗτός μου τρέφει

...ύους,

μᾶλλόν γε μὴν αὔξοντας ἐκ τῶν ὠδίνων

...ᾠη

καὶ μῦς ἀναστὰς ἐξαρίθμει τοῦ δόμου

45 ...<δέλφα>κας φύσει,

οἳ πᾶν φαγόντες βρώσιμον τῆς οἰκίας

...ρον

τὰ χαρτία τρώγουσι καὶ τὰ βιβλία

...λόγων

50 σοβεῖν δὲ τούτους οὔμενουν ὅλως σθένω

...οὐ δέκα,

πλῆθος δὲ μᾶλλον οὐκ ἀπηριθμημένων.

...τὰς ἀγρίας

λιμαγχονήσας πρῶτον, ὥσπερ οὖν ἔδει,

55 ...<π>άγην μυοκτόνον

ἔστησα τούτοις καὶ μυάγραν πολλάκις,

<πολλαὶ δ' ἐφηδρεύ>σαντο καὶ γαλαῖ σφίσιν·

ὑπῆρξε δ' αὐτοῖς καὶ σκέπη τις ἡ πάγη

...ξαν ἔσχον εἰς κατοικίαν,

60 μυοτρόφον φανεῖσαν, οὐ μυοκτόνον.

<Καὶ τὰς γαλᾶς> ὁρῶντες οὗτοι καὶ πάγας,

τὰς μὲν γαλᾶς ὁρῶσιν οἷα συννόμους,

<τὰς δ' αὖ πά>γας βλέπουσιν ὥσπερ ἑστίας·

τοσοῦτον ἔξω τυγχάνουσι τοῦ φόβου,

65 <τὴν φυσικὴν μὲν> δειλίαν λελοιπότες,

δέος δὲ πᾶν ῥίψαντες ὡς πορρωτάτω.

. . .
My house nourishes so many such mice   40
. . .
instead, they rather grow bigger after giving birth
. . .
stand up and count the mice of this house,
                              . . . pigs by nature.   45
They devour everything that is edible in the house,
. . .
they gnaw at the papers and the books
                              . . . of words.
I have not the least success in chasing them away   50
                              . . . not ten of them,
but rather a mass that is impossible to count.
                              . . . feral <cats>,
which I first starved, as one is advised to do,
                         . . . I set up a mice-killing snare   55
for them, and often a mousetrap too,
and many cats were lying in wait for them.
However, the snares served as a kind of shelter for them,
                         . . . they used them as a home,
which appeared to be mice-feeding, not mice-killing.   60
And as far as the cats and the traps are concerned,
they saw the cats as companions
and the traps as a kind of buffet.
So far were they from having fear;
they shed their innate cowardice, and   65
threw away all their dread as far as they could.

<Μάτην δ' ἔκαμνον μ>ηχανώμενος δόλους
καὶ τοὺς πονηροὺς μῦας οὐκ ἠδυνάμην
<ἔξω διώκειν> τῆς ἐμῆς κατοικίας,
70 τὰ παγκάκιστα ζῷα καὶ βδελυκτέα.
         . . . ιν αὐτὸς ἐκ βίου
βίον τιθεὶς ἅπασιν ἔξω πραγμάτων.

104

. . . <εἰς τὸν τά>φον τοῦ πρωτοσπαθαρίου
Κώνσταντος καὶ δευτέρου τῶν ἐν
τοῖς . . . · ἡρωϊκά

Ἀνδρὸς δὴ τόδε σῆμα, ὃς οὐ λίπε βέλτερον ἐν γῇ
         . . . ἄλλος,
ἀλλ' ἦν ἐκ σοφίης μέγα ὄλβιος, ἐξ ἀρετῆς δέ
. . .
5 τῷ δ' ἅμα καὶ σοφίην αὐτὴν κατὰ γαῖα καλύπτει,
. . .

In vain I wearied myself by contriving wiles,
as I could not chase away
those vicious mice from my house,
those arch-evil and repulsive creatures!   70
              . . . myself from a . . . life,
I show to everyone a life free from cares.

104

On the grave of Konstans, *protospatharios* and having the second rank among the . . . ; hexameters

This grave belongs to a man who did not leave on earth a
     better
                           . . . someone else,
but he was blessed in wisdom, and in virtue he was
. . .
together with him the earth now covers also wisdom itself,   5
. . .

105

Εἰς τὸ ἐν τῷ ἀμπελῶνι
τῆς Πηγῆς σικυήλατον . . .

<Ὀπω>ρίσασθαι βούλομαι νῦν ἡδέως

. . .

<σὺ δ', ἀμ>πελουργέ, καὶ προθύμως προτρέπεις

. . .

5   . . . μ' ἂν κἂν βιάζεσθαι θέλῃς,

. . .

       . . . <σο>υ τὴν τέχνην βραχεῖ λόγῳ

. . .

         . . . <μ>ισθὸν ἐξ ἐγκωμίων

10 . . .

            . . .ωσας ἱδρῶτας πάλαι

. . .

            . . . τῆς γῆς τὸ πρέπον

. . .

15   . . .ὴν τῶν κοπρίων

. . .

                . . . κλημάτων

. . .

                  . . .υ

20   . . .γγη καὶ χάρακας κυκλόθεν

. . .

105

On the cucumber bed in the vineyard
of the monastery of the Spring . . .

I now dearly want to reap the harvest
. . .
and you, vineyard keeper, you encourage me fervently
. . .
      . . . even if you would want to force me,   5
. . .
      . . . with a short discourse I . . . your art,
. . .
      . . . a compensation consisting of praises,
. . .   10
          . . . sweat of old,
. . .
      . . . the appropriate things of the earth,
. . .
         . . . from dung   15
. . .
         . . . of the vine branches
. . .
. . .
         . . . vine props all around,   20
. . .

. . .τας βλάπτοντα μακράν που τρέπων

. . .

. . . διέρχῃ νύκτας, ἀμπέλων φύλαξ,

25 . . .

τ. . . . πολλὰ συχνοὺς τοὺς λίθους ἐκ σφενδόνης

. . .

ἱστῶν δὲ καὶ φόβητρα κλέπταις ποικίλα

. . .

30 ἐκ πλέγματος μάλιστα τοῦ λινοστρόφου

. . .

πτοῖαν λαβόντα τοῖς ψόφοις καὶ δειλίαν

. . .

βαβαὶ δὲ τούτου σικυηλάτου χάριν

35 . . .

ὅσας δὲ χειρῶν καὶ νεφρῶν ἀλγηδόνας

πῇ μὲν . . .

πῇ δ' ἔνδον αὐτῆς σπέρμα βάλλων σικύων.

Ἔοικε σὸς . . .

40 τὴν τῆς ἀρούρας τῆσδε φημὶ τῆς πέλας

φαίνῃ γὰρ . . .

Εἶεν· πλέον δὲ τοῦτο θαυμάζειν ἔγνων,

πῶς τὸν π. . .

καὶ τῆς χαλάζης τὰς βολὰς ἐν τῷ μέρει

45 ὄφεις . . .

ὁποῖα πολλὰ ταῖς ἀρούραις ἐμμένει.

Πῶς καρτερ<εῖς> . . .

καὶ πῶς τὰ τούτων δήγματα στερρῶς φέρεις

ὡς ἀνδριὰς πρὸς . . .

. . . chasing off faraway the . . . that causes damage,
. . .
you spend . . . nights, guardian of vines,
. . .   25
<you throw> many stones from your sling
. . .
setting up various scarecrows to scare the thieves away
. . .
made from a flax-woven plait   30
. . .
being scared off and terrified by the noises
. . .
alas for the sake of this cucumber bed
. . .   35
how many pains in your arms and back <you endure>,
partly . . . <the cucumber bed>,
partly throwing cucumber seeds inside it.
Your . . . seems like . . .
I mean the one close to the adjacent field here;   40
for you seem . . .
Very well; but I came to admire this even more:
how you . . .
and the showers of hail in that place,
snakes . . .   45
many of that kind beset the fields.
How you put up with . . .
and how you firmly endure their bites,
like a statue confronted with . . .

50 οὐκ ἂν λαθοίμην, οὐ μὰ τὰς σὰς ἀμπέλους·
    μεμνήσομαί σου καὶ <γὰρ ἄχρι θανάτου>·
    πρὸ τοῦ θανεῖν δέ, ζῶντί μοι νῦν εἰσέτι,
    ἐκ τοῦδε τοῦ σοῦ σικυηλάτ<ου δίδου>·
    ἤδη γὰρ οἶδα τῶν ἐπαίνων σοι κόρον,
55 οὓς ἀντὶ μισθοῦ τῶν ὀπ<ωρῶν εἰσφέρω>·
    εἰ δ' οὐ δίδως μέν, προτρέπεις δὲ λαμβάνειν,
    στὰς ἔνδον αὐτὸς δρέψομαι τ<οὺς σικύους>
    καὶ τῶν ὀπωρῶν, εἴ τι κάλλιστον, λάβω·
    κἂν γεῦσιν ὦσιν οἷα δὴ καὶ τ<ὴν θέαν>,
60 ἄλλους ἐπαίνους πλέξομαί σοι δευτέρους
    καὶ τὸν τρύγητον εὔξομαί σε καὶ <πάλιν>
    ἰδεῖν καθὼς πέρυσιν εὐλογημένον,
    ὅπως ἀπείρων ἐκθλιβέντων <βοτρύων>
    γλεύκους ὑπερβλύσωσι ληνοὶ καὶ πίθοι.

106

Εἰς τοὺς ἁγίους Τεσσαράκοντα, μιᾶς κανδήλας ἠρ<τημένης> ἔμπροσθεν αὐτῶν

Εἷς <φω>τὸς ὧδ<ε πᾶσ>ιν ἐξήφ<θη λύχνος>,
οὓς πρὸς πάλην ἀνῆψεν εἷς πυρὸς πόθος
. . .
κἀνταῦθα φῶς ἔχουσι κοινὸν ἓν <πάλιν>.

I could not forget, no, I swear by your vines;   50
for I will remember you until my death.
But before I die, while I still live,
give me some produce from your cucumber bed.
I know that you are already fed up with the praises
which I offer as a payment for your vegetables.   55
But if you do not give them, allowing me instead to take
     them,
I will come in and pick the cucumbers myself,
taking the most beautiful fruits.
If they taste the way they look,
then I will weave for you some more praises, a second time,   60
and I will wish again that you may see
a blessed vintage, like last year,
to make the vats and jars overflow with the wine
of innumerable pressed grapes.

106

On the Holy Forty Martyrs, with one lamp hanging in front of them

One lamp of light has been kindled here for all the men
whom one desire for fire enflamed to the ordeal,
. . .
also here they share again a single light.

107

Εἰς. . .

Ἐγὼ μὲν ὤμην ἄγγελόν σε τυγ<χάνειν>

. . .

πρὸς τοῦτο δ' ἂν νῦν καὶ διϊσχ<υριζόμην>

. . .

5 ἐκ τῆς τελευτῆς, Ἰωάννη, καὶ <τάφου>

. . .

τὸ σῶμα θνητὸν καὶ μό<νον> . . .

. . .

108

Εἰς τὸν κατὰ τὸ Πάσχα γ<ινόμενον> ἀσπασμόν

Τὸ Πάσχα δεσμός ἐστιν εἰρήνης μέγας,
ἧς σύμβολον φίλημα τῷ λαῷ τόδε.

107

On . . .

I was already convinced that you were an angel
. . .
in addition, I could also claim now
. . .
from your death, John, and from your grave   5
. . .
only your body is mortal . . .
. . .

108

On the embrace and kiss that people give each other at Easter

Easter is an important bond of peace,
symbolized by this kiss that people exchange.

109

. . . ⟨μεμ⟩φομένων τοῖς φοβ⟨ουμένοις τὴν θάλασσαν⟩

. . .

μέμφοιτο τοῖς ⟨θάλασσαν ἐκφοβουμένοις⟩

. . .

θεοκ⟨λυ⟩τ⟨οῦσι⟩ . . .

5   . . .

ὅτε . . .

. . .

ἆρ᾽

. . .

10 . . .

ὃς τὴν τελευτὴν ἐγγὺς ἐστῶ⟨σαν βλέπει⟩

. . .

μηδ᾽ ὄντα τὸν σῴζοντα τοῦ κλυδ⟨ωνίου⟩

. . .

15 εἰ τὸν Θεὸν καλοῖεν εἰς σωτηρίαν

. . .

μηδὲν πτοεῖσθαι, κἂν κλύδων αὔξῃ πλ⟨έον⟩

. . .

"ὡς οὐδὲν ἔσται," φησί, "δεινὸν οὐδ᾽ ὅλως"

20 . . .

κἂν οἴακες θραυσθῶσιν εἴτε καὶ τρόπις

109

. . . those berating people who fear the sea

. . .
may berate people who fear the sea
. . .
who call on God . . .
. . .   5
when . . .
. . .
so . . .
. . .
. . .   10
who sees death standing nearby
. . .
and without someone to save him from the waves,
. . .
if they would call on God for rescue   15
. . .
not to be afraid, even if the wave surges higher,
. . .
he says, "there won't be any danger at all"
. . .   20
even if the oars or the keel are shattered

. . .
ἄφρων ὑπάρχεις, ὅστις εἶ, νὴ τὰς φρένας
. . .

25 ἂν δ᾽ ἐμπέσωσιν εἰς μέσον τῶν κυμάτων
. . .τε
ἐρεῖς πρὸς αὐτούς· "μὴ πτοῆσθε" καὶ πάλιν
. . .χρόνου
ἐναντίων μὲν εἰσπνεόντων ἀνέμων
30 <καὶ τῶν κυμάτων πάντοθεν> κυρτουμένων
καὶ τοῖς πλέουσιν οἷα προσκεχηνότων
. . .<τ>ῶν πνευμάτων
ἢ συντριβῆναι ταῖς ὑφάλοις εἰ τύχοι
. . .αι πτύχας.
35 Εἰ δυσχερὲς δὴ τοῦτο καὶ τῶν δυσκόλων,
<καλῶς σὺ ποιεῖς τοῦ δέους ἀ>ποτρέπων·
εἰ δ᾽ οὐδὲν οὕτως εὐχερὲς τῶν ἐν βίῳ,
. . .βλασφημίας,
Θεὸν βοηθὸν μὴ καλεῖν ἐπιτρέπων
40 . . .τελευτῆς ἐλπίσι
μηδὲ πτοεῖσθαι τῆς θαλάσσης τὴν ζάλην.
<Οὐ βούλομαι μὲν σοὶ> λαλεῖν, ἀλλ᾽ εἰσέτι
στόμα πλατυνῶ· καὶ γὰρ αὐτὴ καρδία
<ὥσπερ τις ἀσκὸς> ἔστι μοι γλεύκους ζέων,
45 καθὼς Ἐλιοῦς πρὸς τὸν Αὐσίτην λέγει.
<Παρακα>λοῦντι πρόσσχες ὦτά μοι κλίνας·
οὐ σπένδεται θάλασσα τόλμῃ καὶ θράσει,
<οὐ σπέν>δεται θάλασσα μὴ φοβουμένοις·
τί γὰρ πρὸς αὐτήν, κἂν φοβῇ κἂν μή, τάλα;

222

. . .
you have a foolish mind, whoever you are!
. . .
if they find themselves in the middle of the waves   25
. . .
then you will again say to them, "have no fear!"
                 . . . time,
when contrary winds are blowing in their direction
and when waves are billowing from all sides,   30
as if gaping at the seafarers.
                . . . the winds,
or if they should be shattered against sunken reefs,
                 . . . plates.
If this is strenuous and difficult,   35
you do well deflecting them from fear;
but if there is nothing so easy in life,
                . . . blasphemies,
not allowing to call upon God for help,
                . . . expectations of death,   40
nor to fear the tumult of the sea.
I do not want to talk to you, but still
I will open my mouth; for my heart
is *like a **wineskin bursting with sweet wine**,*
as Elihu says to Job of Ausis.   45
So I ask you to lend me your ear and pay attention;
the sea does not make peace because of courage and bravery,
the sea does not make peace because people do not fear it;
what does it care, poor man, whether you fear it or not?

50 <Οὐκ ἔστι>ν αὐτῆς συμβαλεῖν τὸ ποικίλον,
   οὐκ ἔστι γνῶναι τὰς τροπὰς τὰς μυρίας·
   <τὸ μὲν> γὰρ αὐτὴν παγγάληνον σὺ βλέπων
   ἴδης παρευθὺ κυμάτων πεπλησμένην·
   <τὸ δ'> αὖ θεωρῶν ἠγριωμένην ἄγαν
55 ὄψει γαλήνην, καὶ μετὰ βραχὺν χρόνον
   <ἄλλως> ἔχουσαν ὥσπερ ἠλλοιωμένην,
   ἐξ ἠρεμούσης ἀγρίαν δεδειγμένην.
   <Πεπ>οιθέναι γοῦν οὐδαμῶς δίδωσί σοι,
   ὁπηνίκα πλεῖς, οὐδὲ σὺν θάρρει πλέειν
60   ...τας
   καὶ πρὸς τὸ πνεῦμα τὸ πνέον μορφουμένη
   ...
   <σ>χολῇ βυθῷ τις ἐμπεσὼν ζωὴν ἴδη
   ...
65 <ἰδοὺ> γὰρ αὐτὸν ἐξελεῖται, κἂν κάμη
   ...
   <ἐξασθε>νεῖ γὰρ ὧδε φαρμάκου δόσις
   ...
   <ἐξασ>θενοῦσιν ὧδε καὶ καυτηρίαι
70 ...
   ...<ἀ>πρακτεῖ καὶ σὺν αὐτῇ πᾶς λόγος
   ...
               ...καὶ Γαληνὸς ἐνθάδε
   ...
75   ...οὐκ ἀνοίγων τὸ στόμα
   ...
               ...<τα>χεῖς ἵππους δρόμῳ

We cannot grasp its multiple mutations,   50
nor understand its myriad twists and turns;
for one moment you may see it all calm,
but soon you will notice that it is full of waves;
another time, while looking at a turbulent sea,
you will see calm water, and within a short moment   55
it is again different, as if transformed,
and it appears violent instead of calm.
Therefore, it gives you no reason at all to trust it,
whenever you go sailing, nor to sail with confidence,
. . . <the sea>, . . .   60
is shaped according to the blowing wind
. . .
one who sinks slowly into the deep may see life
. . .
for look, it draws him out, even if he is struggling,   65
. . .
for doses of medicine are powerless here
. . .
also cauterizations are of no avail
. . .   70
. . . in addition, there is no word that is effective
. . .
                              . . . even Galen in this case
. . .
                              . . . not opening the mouth   75
. . .
                              . . . swift horses in their course

...

... κινέειν ἀποτρέπων

80 ...

... βίον πάλιν λέγων

...

...ούμενος τρίβειν

...

85 ...ν γράφειν

...

... ἔχει

...

...ην

90 ... τοῦ βυθοῦ τίς εἶπες

...

... θεῖσα δελφίνων δυὰς τότε

...

<τιθ>εῖσα νώτοις ὡς τὸν αὐλητὴν λόγος

95 ...

εἰς χέρσον ἄξει ζῶντα καὶ κρείττω βλάβ<ης>

...

σῶον φυλάξαν ἐξερεύξεται πάλιν

...

100 μὴ καί τις ἰχθὺς ἄλλος αὐτὸν ἂν λάβοι

...

ἀναρραγεὶς δείξειε τοῖς ἠγρευκόσιν

...

ὡς πρίν τις ἰχθὺς τὸν στατῆρα τῷ Πέτρῳ

105 ...

. . .

       . . . prevent from moving

. . .   80

       . . . saying again that life . . .

. . .

              . . . wear out

. . .

              . . . writes   85

. . .

              . . . has

. . .

. . .

of the depth . . .   90

. . .

a pair of dolphins then put . . .

. . .

carried the flute player on their backs, as the story goes,

. . .   95

and will bring him alive to the land, without harm,

. . .

preserving him safe and sound, he will belch him out again

. . .

lest another fish would take him   100

. . .

and would tear open and show to the fishermen

. . .

as a fish <gave> a coin to Peter previously

. . .   105

τοίνυν ἀπόσχου μέμψεως οὐκ εὐλόγου

. . .

κατηγορῶν παύθητι καὶ σιγὴν ἄγε

. . .

110 ἀλλ᾽ εὔχεται δὴ ταῦτα, "ῥυσθείην," λέγων,

. . .

"καὶ μὴ καταιγὶς ὕδατός με συλλάβοι

. . .

μήτ᾽ αὖ θαλάσσης ἐκροφήσοι με στόμα

115 εἰ . . ."

ὡς καὶ δέεσθαι τοῦ Θεοῦ καὶ Δεσπότου

μη . . .

καὶ ταῦτα μακρὰν ὑδάτων ἑστὼς τέως,

αὐτὸς δὲ . . .

120 ἄνπερ φοβοῖντο, λιπαροῖεν δὲ σφόδρα

τὸν Δημιου<ργὸν> . . .

πολλῆς ἀνοίας τοῦτο, πολλῆς μωρίας.

Οἱ γοῦν Ἰω<νᾶν> . . .

ναῦται μὲν ὄντες καὶ συνήθεις τῆς ζάλης,

125 Θεὸν δὲ πάντ<ως ἀγ>νοοῦν<τες ἐν βίῳ>,

ἄρρητον ἔσχον τηνικαῦτα τὸν φόβον,

ὡς πάντα δοῦναι τῷ βυθῷ <σκεύη τάχει>

καὶ τοὺς θεοὺς σφῶν λιπαρεῖν πολλῷ φόβῳ,

ἴσως τὸν ἀττέλαβον ἢ τὴν ἀ<κρίδα>

130 ἢ μυῖαν ἢ βάτραχον εἴτε καὶ σκνῖπα

ἢ τὴν σελήνην κ<αί τινας τῶν ἀστέρων>·

αὐτὸς δ᾽ ὁ πρωρεὺς προσδραμὼν πτοίας πλέως

καὶ τὸν προφή<την ἐξεγείρας ἐξ ὕπνου>,

therefore, refrain from those unfounded censures
...
stop accusing and keep silent
...
but he makes the following prayer: "*may I be saved,*   110
...
do not let the floodwaters engulf *me,*
...
and do not let the pit of the sea gulp me down,
if..."   115
so to pray to God our Lord
...
and that while you are standing far from the water,
but you yourself...
if they are scared, they will pray more fervently   120
to our Creator...
that is something very foolish and stupid!
The men...Jonah,
although they were sailors and used to the savage sea,
but wholly ignorant of God in their life,   125
were at that moment extremely terrified,
so that they quickly threw all the cargo into the deep,
and prayed, greatly frightened, to their own gods,
perhaps the locust, or the grasshopper,
or the fly, or the frog, or maybe also the insect,   130
or the moon and some stars;
the captain himself, overwhelmed by fear, rushed in,
and awakened the prophet from his sleep,

"Τί," φησί, "ῥέγχεις; Ἐξανάστα μοι τάχει·
135 ἄφες τὸν <ὕπνον καὶ Θεὸν σὸν λιπάρει>,
εἴ πως βυθοῦ σώσειεν ἡμᾶς καὶ ζάλης."

. . .

οἷς πᾶς βίος θάλασσα καὶ πλοῦς καὶ <ζάλη>

. . .

140 Θεῷ γενέσθαι πρέσβυν, ὅνπερ <ἠγνόουν>

. . .

ἀλλ' οὔτε ναῦται τυγχάνοντες . . .

. . .

Θεὸν δὲ πρεσβεύοντες ὕψιστον . . .

145 . . .

πτήξουσι καὶ κλαύσουσι καὶ θ. . .

. . .

κἂν οὐ κελεύεις αὐτός, οὐδὲ . . .

. . .

150 ποῦ θήσομεν δὲ καὶ τὸ τῶν . . .

. . .

κοινῇ τε συντέμνοντ. . .

. . .

ὡς ἔνδον εἰς ῥεῖ . . .

155 . . .

προσῆλθον ἀ. . .

. . .

ᾔτουν βοῶ<ντες> . . .

. . .

160 κἂν ἦν μετ' ἀ. . .

. . .

saying, "Why are you snoring? Get up quickly!
Stop sleeping and pray to your God,   135
to save us somehow from the deep and the tumult!"
. . .
men whose whole life revolved around the sea, sailing, and
    the watery din,
. . .
to become an envoy for the God they disregarded,   140
. . .
but even not being sailors . . .
. . .
they proclaim the highest God . . .
. . .   145
they will cower in fear and weep and . . .
. . .
even if you do not command this, or . . .
. . .
where shall we then put also this . . .   150
. . .
cutting out together . . .
. . .
when inside into the streams . . .
. . .   155
they approached . . .
. . .
they cried out and asked for . . .
. . .
even if he was . . .   160
. . .

ὅταν δ<ὲ> . . .

. . .

τί δ<ὲ> . . .

165 . . .

οὐ . . .

. . .

. . .

μελαγχολᾷς γάρ, δαιμόν<ιε> . . .

170 . . .

φόβον θαλάσσης εἰς λογισμὸ<ν οὐδένα>

. . .

<ο>ὐ πῦρ δέδοικεν, οὐχὶ κρημνόν, οὐχ <ὕδωρ>

. . .

175 τοιαῦτα σοῦ λέγοντος ἐκ πολλοῦ θ<ράσους>

. . .

ὁ δεῖνα θρηνεῖ κυμάτων ὁρῶν ῥύμην

. . .

ὁ δεῖνα πενθεῖ προσδοκῶν βίου πέρας

180 . . .

μαίνῃ φρενῶν σῶν ὥσπερ ἐκλελησμένος

. . .

οὐκ οἶσθ' ὅτε πλεῖς τὸν θαλάττιον πόρον

        . . . <σε θανάτου>

185 οὐδὲν διεῖργον ἢ σανὶς λεπτὴ μόνον

. . .

οὔτ' αὖ γε θρηνεῖν ὡς τὰ μικρὰ παιδία

. . .

εἰ ταῦτα, λῆρε, δογματίζεις καὶ κρίνεις

but when . . .
. . .
why then
. . .   165
. . .
. . .
. . .

you are going out of your mind, my good fellow, . . .
. . .   170
not having any consideration for the fear of the sea
. . .
he does not fear fire, nor a cliff, nor water,
. . .
while you are saying this with much brashness,   175
. . .
one person weeps, as he sees the rush of the waves,
. . .
another grieves, expecting the end of his life
. . .   180
you are raging, as if you have lost your mind
. . .
don't you know you are sailing on a sea voyage
. . .
only a thin wooden board separates you from death   185
. . .
nor again to grieve like little children
. . .
if you, humbug, offer certitudes and make judgments,

190 . . .

καὶ τέμνε τὴν θάλασσαν εἰς διαιρέσεις

. . .

Τί κωλύει σε καὶ πνέουσιν ἀνέμοις

. . . <μά>λα

195 φλοῖσβόν τε παύειν καὶ γαλήνην δεικνύειν

. . . λόγος

βορρᾶν σὺ καὶ θάλασσαν ἔκτισας, λέγων

. . .νου νέος

μηδὲν δεδοικώς, μὴ κλύδωνα, μὴ σάλον,

200 . . . <ἀγρι>ωτάτην.

Εἴπω τι πρὸς σὲ συντομώτερον θέλεις;

. . . <ὥσπερ> τις λάρος,

τί μὴ πρὸς ἡμᾶς καὶ τὸ τοῦ Θεοῦ λέγεις;

"<Ζάλην συν>έσχον τῆς θαλάσσης ἐν πύλαις,

205 τέθεικα δ' αὐτῇ κλεῖθρα καὶ πύλας ὅρους,"

<ὡς αὐτὸς αὐ>τὸν πρὸς τὸν Ἰὼβ φησί που.

Ἀλλὰ πρὸς αὐτῆς κουφότητος ἣν ἔχεις

. . . τοῦτο νῦν λέγε·

οἴει γὰρ εἶναι καὶ Θεός· καὶ τί ξένον

210 . . . <φρεν>ῶν ἡ κουφότης

Θεὸν σεαυτὸν καὶ νομίζειν καὶ λέγειν;

. . .ήσω τὸ στόμα

ἀφεὶς ἀναψύξαι σε πρὸς βραχὺν χρόνον

. . .γειν ἔχων,

215 εὐχὴν δὲ πρῶτον ἐκ μέσης τῆς καρδίας

. . .ε

πέμψοι σε Χριστὸς εἰς βυθοὺς θαλαττίους

. . .
then also split up the sea into divisions,
. . .
What prevents you from <giving orders to> the blowing
    winds,
                    . . . much,
to stop the roaring surf and change it into calm seas,   195
. . .
you have created the north wind and the sea, by saying
                    . . . a young man
not fearing anything, not the waves, not the whirling waters,
                    . . . most turbulent.   200
Do you want me to tell you something more concise?
                    . . . as a kind of gull,
why don't you say to me the words of God?
"I enclosed the tumult of the *sea with gates,*
and I set bounds to it, *bars and gates,*"   205
as he says somewhere to Job himself.
Well now, with that lightheartedness you have,
                    . . . keep saying this now;
since you think that you are also God; what is strange
<if> the levity of your mind <makes you>   210
believe, and proclaim, that you yourself are God?
                    . . . my mouth,
letting you take a breath for a short moment,
. . .
my deepest heartfelt wish   215
. . .
that Christ may send you to the depths of the sea

. . .

    . . . ἐκεῖθεν ἀβλαβὴς ἀναδράμῃς

220 . . .

<καταφρ>ονητὰς κυμάτων ἀπεργάσῃ

. . .

    . . .αὖ γινώσκων ὡς ἀπόχρη καὶ τάδε

. . .

225 . . . <θ>αλάσσης εἰκότως δεδοικότων

. . .

110

Εἰς τὸν πρεσβύτερον Κοσμᾶν περὶ τοῦ ἀποσταλέντος οἴνου

. . .

    . . . νέκταρ ὡς θεοὶ πεπωκότας.

. . .

      . . . and that you come up from there unharmed,

. . .   220

and that you turn the despisers of the waves into

. . .

      . . . recognizing that this suffices

. . .

the people who rightly fear the . . . of the sea   225

. . .

110

For the priest Kosmas, on the wine he had sent

. . .

      . . . having drunk nectar like gods.

III

Αἴνιγμα εἰς τὸ ὄργανον δι' ἡρωϊκῶν

Ἠδ' ἐμὴ ἐν χθονὶ γαστὴρ κεῖται ἠδὲ σαλεύει·
αὐτὰρ ἐγὼν ἀέρος περὶ σῶμα βέβηκα ἀραιόν·
ἄψυχον δὲ ἐόν, λαλέον τρίψυχον ὁρῶμαι·
λῆξαν τοῦ λαλέειν, ψυχὰς ἅμα ὤλεσα τὰς τρεῖς.

II2

Εἰς τὸν ζωγράφον Μύρωνα,
ζωγραφοῦντα τὴν εἰκόνα Μιχαήλ

Εἰ τοῦ Μιχαὴλ τὴν θέαν γράφεις μόνον,
ὤχραν τάραττε καὶ χρόας ἄλλας τρίβε·
εἰ δ' ἀρετὴν σύμπασαν αὐτοῦ σὺν θέᾳ,
ἔμπνουν ἀναστήλωσον αὐτόν, εἰ δύνῃ·
5   σὺν ἀρετῇ γὰρ τοῦτον ἄλλως οὐ γράφεις,
τὸν ἀρετῆς ἔμψυχον ὄντα πυξίον.

III

Riddle on the organ; in hexameters

My stomach lies in the earth and vibrates;
yet, I am mounted around a thin body of air.
While I have no soul, I am seen as having three souls when
    I speak;
but when I stop speaking, I lose my three souls at once.

112

On the painter Myron,
painting the icon of Michael

If you are painting only the appearance of Michael,
then stir the ocher and grind the other colors.
But if you want to paint, together with his appearance, his
    whole virtue,
then erect him alive, if you can;
for you cannot paint him otherwise with his virtue,   5
because he is the living panel of virtue.

113

Εἰς τὴν γέννησιν τοῦ τιμίου Προδρόμου

Θαυμαστὸν οὐδέν, εἰ Θεὸς νικᾷ φύσιν
καὶ στεῖραν ὧδε δεικνύει τεκνοτρόφον·
τοῦ γὰρ παρόντος μικρὸν ὕστερον βρέφους
πάντως ἀκούσεις ἐκβοῶντος τοῖς ὄχλοις,
5   ὡς ἰσχύει καὶ τέκνα, φησίν, ἐκ λίθων
ὁ Δημιουργὸς ἐξεγείρειν Δεσπότης.

114

Πρὸς τὸν μοναχὸν Ἀνδρέαν, ὀστᾶ ἰδιωτῶν ὡς ἁγίων λείψανα ἐξωνούμενον ... τε μέλη ἄπειρα ὡς ἑνὸς καὶ τοῦ αὐτοῦ ἁγίου ... δέχεται

Πολλοὶ λέγουσιν (εἰ δ' ἀληθεῖς οἱ λόγοι,
οὐκ οἶδα), πλὴν λέγουσι καὶ πείθουσί με,
ὡς σφόδρα χαίρεις, ὦ μοναστὰ καὶ πάτερ,

113

On the birth of the venerable
John the Forerunner

It is no wonder if God defeats nature
and here shows a barren woman bearing a child;
for this is the very infant whom you shall hear
soon crying out to the multitudes
that our Creator and our Lord has power   5
to raise up children from stones.

114

To the monk Andrew, who buys up the
bones of ordinary people as the relics of
saints . . . and accepts them . . . and
innumerable body parts as those of one
and the same saint

A lot of people claim (if they speak truly
I do not know), but still they claim and persuade me
that you glow with joy, O monk and father,

εἴ τις σε σεπτοῖς δεξιοῦται λειψάνοις
5 ἀνδρῶν ἀθλητῶν ἢ σεβαστῶν μαρτύρων·
θήκας δὲ πολλὰς λειψάνων θείων ἔχεις,
ἃς ἐξανοίγων τοῖς φίλοις σου δεικνύεις·
Προκοπίου μὲν μάρτυρος χεῖρας δέκα,
Θεοδώρου δὲ πεντεκαίδεκα γνάθους
10 καὶ Νέστορος μὲν ἄχρι τῶν ὀκτὼ πόδας,
Γεωργίου δὲ τέσσαρας κάρας ἅμα,
καὶ πέντε μασθοὺς Βαρβάρας ἀθληφόρου·
καὶ νῦν μὲν ὀστᾶ δώδεκα βραχιόνων
τοῦ καλλινίκου μάρτυρος Δημητρίου,
15 νῦν δ' αὖ καλάμους εἴκοσι σκελῶν ὅλων
τοῦ Παντελεήμονος· ὦ τῆς πληθύος.
Λέγεις δὲ πίστει ταῦτα πάντα λαμβάνειν,
οὐκ ἀμφιβάλλων, οὐκ ἀπιστῶν οὐδ' ὅλως,
αἰδῶ τε πολλὴν τοῖς κιβωτίοις νέμειν
20 καὶ προσκυνεῖν ὡς ὄντα Χριστοῦ μαρτύρων.
Βαβαὶ ζεούσης πίστεως σῆς, Ἀνδρέα,
ἥτις σε πείθει τοὺς μὲν ἀθλητὰς Ὕδρας,
τὰς μάρτυρας δὲ θῆρας οἴεσθαι κύνας,
τοὺς μὲν κεφαλὰς μυρίας κεκτημένους,
25 τὰς δ' αὖ γε μασθῶν πλῆθος ὥσπερ αἱ κύνες.
Ἐκ πίστεως σῆς καὶ πρὸς ἰχθὺν ἐστράφη
Νέστωρ ὁ μάρτυς, ὀκτάπους δεδειγμένος,
καὶ Προκόπιον πίστις ἡ σὴ δεικνύει
Βριάρεων κομῶντα χειρῶν πληθύϊ.
30 Λέγεις ὁ σεμνὸς καὶ Θέκλας τῆς πρωτάθλου
ὀδόντας ἑξήκοντα (φεῦ πλάνης) ἔχειν

if someone hands you venerable relics
of contenders for the faith or pious martyrs;   5
and that you have many caskets of holy relics,
which you open and show to your friends:
ten hands of Prokopios the martyr,
fifteen jawbones of Theodore,
up to eight feet from Nestor,   10
on top of this, four heads of George,
five breasts from that victorious contender Barbara;
and here, a dozen arm bones
from Demetrios the triumphant martyr,
and here are twenty shinbones, all intact,   15
of Panteleemon; what a multitude!
You say that you accept all these in faith,
without the slightest doubt or disbelief,
and that you treat these boxes with much respect,
venerating them as from Christ's martyrs.   20
I say! So fervent, Andrew, is your faith,
persuading you God's champions were Hydras,
and making female martyrs seem like wild dogs,
the former possessing thousands of heads,
the latter with a multitude of breasts, like bitches.   25
Because of your faith the martyr Nestor
has turned into a fish, proving to be an octopus.
Your faith has shown Prokopios
waving a multitude of arms, a Briareus.
You claim to have as well, my pious man, sixty teeth   30
(what a deception!) from the first female martyr Thekla,

καὶ τοῦ μεγίστου Προδρόμου λευκὰς τρίχας.
Αὐχεῖς δὲ καὶ πρὸς πάντας, ὡς νῦν ἐπρίω
ἐκ τῶν γενείων τῶν σφαγέντων νηπίων
35 ἐν Βηθλεὲμ πρὶν τῆς Ἰουδαίας πόλει·
φάσκεις δὲ τιμᾶν ταῦτα, πιστοῖς ὡς νόμος.
Ὢ πίστις ὀρθή, πίστις ἠνθρακωμένη,
ἣ τοὺς πατρῴους οὐκ ἀπαρνεῖται νόμους,
τῶν Μακκαβαίων τὸ ζέον μιμουμένη·
40 ὦ πίστις οὐκ ἔχουσα μῶμον οὐδένα,
τάξεις ἀνατρέπουσα καὶ φύσεις μόνον,
νῦν μὲν γυναῖκα δεικνύουσα πρεσβῦτιν
ὅλην ὀδόντων σχοῦσαν ἑξηκοντάδα,
νῦν δ᾽ αὖ γε λευκαίνουσα τὴν κόμην νέῳ
45 καὶ νηπίοις διδοῦσα πωγώνων πλάτη.
Εἰ ταῦτα πιστῶς ὡς ἀληθῆ προσδέχῃ
καὶ χρημάτων κένωσιν ἡδέως δέχῃ,
οὐκ ἄν γέ σοι λείψειε πλῆθος λειψάνων·
ἔσται γάρ, ἔσται λειψάνων ἔτι πρᾶσις,
50 ἕως ἂν ἠχήσειε σάλπιγξ ἐσχάτη,
κινοῦσα ταῦτα καὶ συναθροίζουσά πως
ἄφθαρτον εἰς σύμπηξιν ἄλλης οὐσίας,
σφίγγουσα τὰ πρὶν ἐκ φθορᾶς λελυμένα,
ἑνοῦσα θᾶττον τὰ πρὶν ἐσκορπισμένα,
55 πνοὴν διδοῦσα πᾶσιν ἐκπεπνευκόσιν
καὶ πάντας εἰς τὸ βῆμα συγκαλουμένη,
τὸ φρικτὸν ὄντως βῆμα καὶ φόβου γέμον,
ἐν ᾧπερ αὐτὸς πράξεως οὐκ ἐνθέου
ὀρθῶς ὑπόσχῃς ἀξίαν τιμωρίαν,

and white hairs from the greatest of all, the Forerunner.
You also boast to everybody that you bought hairs
from beards belonging to the infants slaughtered
in Bethlehem, Judaea's ancient city.   35
You claim to prize these as the law bids believers.
O upright faith! O faith, through trial by fire,
not disobeying our paternal laws,
but copying the Maccabees' devotion!
O faith, not bearing any mark of blame,   40
but merely overthrowing order and nature,
you first reveal an elderly woman
in possession of no less than sixty teeth, and
now you make a young man's hair turn white,
and bestow broad beards on babbling babes.   45
If in good faith you accept these as real,
and empty out your wallet cheerfully,
you will never lack a multitude of relics;
for relics will continue to be sold
until the final trumpet blasts   50
and moves them, somehow gathering them together,
into an incorruptible coalescence of new substance,
pressing back to shape what rot had loosened,
hastily uniting what had been previously scattered,
giving breath to all who had breathed their last,   55
and summoning everyone to the tribunal,
the truly awe-inspiring, dread-laden tribunal,
exactly where you yourself, for your ungodly actions,
will rightly undergo the punishment that befits you,

60 ἀνθ' ὧν παρηνόμησας οὕτως ἀφρόνως,
ὀστᾶ βεβήλων οἷα σεπτῶν μαρτύρων
ὠνούμενός τε καὶ κατακλείων πόθῳ.
Τί καὶ τοσοῦτον ἐκκενοῖς οὖν χρυσίον;
Ἔξεστι καὶ γὰρ δωρεάν σε λαμβάνειν,
65 πρὸς τοὺς τάφους τρέχοντα τοὺς ἐν τῇ πόλει·
εἴπερ δὲ μισθὸν οὐ κομίζεσθαι λέγεις,
ἂν προῖκα ταῦτα λαμβάνῃς ἐκ μνημάτων,
ἴθι πρὸς ἐξώνησιν, ἡδέως ἴθι·
ῥᾷον κενώσεις ἅπαν αὐτὸς χρυσίον
70 ἢ τοὺς τάφους ἅπαντας οἱ νεκροπράται.
Ἔγωγε τοίνυν τοῦτο θαυμάζειν ἔγνων,
πῶς οὐκ ἀπιστεῖς τοῖς πράταις τῶν ὀστέων,
τοὐναντίον δὲ καὶ προσηνῶς προσδέχῃ
ἅπαντας αὐτοὺς καὶ μεθ' ἡδονῆς ὅσης·
75 ἤκουσα δ' αὐτὸς πρός τινος τῶν σῶν φίλων,
ὡς γνοὺς πλάνος τὶς πίστεως σῆς τὸ ζέον,
ὀστοῦν προβάτου μηριαῖον λαμβάνει
. . .
ἅπαν τε κύκλῳ βάμματι χρίσας κρόκου,
80 καὶ θυμιάσας καὶ περιστείλας ἅμα
πρόσεισιν εὐθὺς καὶ δίδωσί σοι λέγων·
"ὀστοῦν ὑπάρχει τοῦτο μάρτυρος Πρόβου·"
(τὸ δ' ἦν προβάτου μᾶλλον, ἀλλ' οὐχὶ Πρόβου)
"δεῖ τοιγαροῦν σοι χρυσίνων ἓξ καὶ δέκα."
85 Λαβεῖν τι χρῆμα θεῖον ᾠήθης, πάτερ,
ἐκ πίστεως καὶ τοῦτο ποιήσας τάχα·
πολλὴ γάρ ἐστι πίστις ἡ σὴ καὶ λίαν

since you so foolishly sidestepped the law,   60
in your eagerness to buy base men's bones
and hoard them like bones of honored martyrs.
What is the point of spending so much gold?
For these relics are free for you to take if you
just run out to our city's cemeteries;   65
but if you claim that you will receive no reward
if you obtain them from the graves for free,
then go and pay for them; please go and do it!
It's easier for you to clean out your wallet
than for the looters to clean out every grave.   70
For my part, I am puzzled by this still:
why do you not doubt the bone sellers,
but, rather, you take the lot of them at face
value—and do it gleefully to boot?
As for me, a friend of yours has told me   75
some con man heard about your fervent faith,
and so he took the thigh bone of a sheep
. . .
he painted it all over with saffron dye,
scented it with incense, wrapped it up,   80
and then went up to you and said straight out,
"This here is the bone of the martyr Probos,"
(it really was a sheep's bone and not Probos's),
"so that will cost you sixteen pieces of gold."
You thought you'd taken something holy,   85
father, doing this out of faith, perhaps.
That faith of yours is great indeed,

καὶ μὴν δυνηθῇ καὶ μεθιστᾶν τὴν κτίσιν·
ὅπου γε μικρὰ πίστις ἀκραιφνεστάτη
90 ὡς κόκκος εἷς νάπυος, ὁ Χριστὸς λέγει,
ὄρη μεθιστᾶν εὐκολώτατα σθένει.
Πλὴν ἀλλ' ἐπεί σε πιστὸν ἔγνων εἰς ἄκρον,
οὐκ ἀμφιβάλλειν οὐδὲ διστάζειν ὅλως
πρὸς τὰς δόσεις θέλοντα τὰς τῶν λειψάνων,
95 παρέξομαί σοι προῖκα χρῆμά τι ξένον·
Ἐνὼχ τὸν ἀντίχειρα τοῦ τρισολβίου,
ὃς τοῦ παρόντος ζῶν μετηνέχθη βίου,
καὶ γλουτὸν αὐτὸν Ἠλιοῦ τοῦ Θεσβίτου,
ὃς ζῶν ἀνῆλθεν εἰς πόλον διφρηλάτης·
100 βούλει παράσχω λειψάνοις τούτοις ἅμα
καὶ δάκτυλόν σοι Μιχαὴλ ἀρχαγγέλου;
Ἔσται, παράσχω τοῦτον ἐκ Χωνῶν ἔχων,
μόνον σύ μοι πίστευε ταῦτα λαμβάνων,
ὥς εἰσι τούτων, ὧν ἐγὼ διδοὺς λέγω.
105 Δώσω σὺν αὐτοῖς καὶ βραχὺ πτερῶν μέρος
τοῦ Γαβριήλ σοι τοῦ μεγίστου τῶν νόων·
ἐν Ναζαρὲτ γὰρ πρὶν κατελθὼν τῇ πόλει
πτερορρυήσας ἐξανέπτη πρὸς πόλον·
ἤχθησαν οὖν ἐκεῖθεν ὧδε τὰ πτίλα,
110 ἐγὼ δὲ ταῦτα πάντ' ἐπέσχον ἐσχάτως
καὶ σοὶ παράσχω, πιστὲ λειψάνων φίλε.
Ἀλλ' οὐδ' ἐκείνων φείσομαι τῶν κρειττόνων,
οὕτω σε πιστεύοντα πρὸς ταῦτα βλέπων,
τὸν ἡδὺν ὄντως ἐν μονασταῖς Ἀνδρέαν,
115 δώσω δέ σοι κἀκεῖνα σὺν προθυμίᾳ,

even able to overhaul creation;
wherever there exists just a bit of pure faith
as tiny as a single mustard seed—Christ says— 90
it has the power to move mountains with greatest ease.
Now since I know you're extremely faithful
and never one to doubt or hesitate
when it comes to gifts of holy relics,
I'll give you something novel for free: 95
the thumb of Enoch the thrice-blessed,
who, while alive, was taken up from this world,
and the buttock of Elijah the Tishbite,
who, while alive, rose to heaven in his chariot.
Would you like me to give you, in addition 100
to these relics, the archangel Michael's finger?
So shall it be, I have it here from Chonai.
Just trust me as you take the things I give:
who I say they're from is who they're from.
And I'll toss in a small piece from the wings 105
of Gabriel—the greatest angelic mind of all.
That day when he came down to the city of Nazareth,
he lost some feathers flying back to heaven.
His plumage has been brought here from that place,
and I got my hands on all these items recently. 110
Now I give them to you—faithful friend of relics!
And I won't spare you even better items,
seeing that you believe so much in them,
O Andrew, truly the sweetest of monks,
these things too I'll give to you with gusto: 115

ἑνὸς Χερουβὶμ ὀμμάτων τριῶν κόρας
καὶ τῆς φλογίνης χεῖρα ῥομφαίας μίαν,
ἣν ἐξανάψας ἐν μέσῳ τῶν λειψάνων
ἄλλου παρ' αὐτὴν οὐ δεηθήσῃ λύχνου·
120 φλὸξ οὖσα καὶ γὰρ ἥδε καὶ φῶς ἐκφέρει,
ὃ πάντα νικᾷ φῶτα λαμπρῶν ἀστέρων·
ἕξεις ἐκείνην τοιγαροῦν σὺ καὶ λύχνον
καὶ λείψανον κάλλιστον, εἴπερ ἄλλό τι·
καὶ πάντα ταῦτα προῖκα καὶ χωρὶς πόνου
125 λοιποῖς συνάψας σοῖς ἀπείροις λειψάνοις,
θήσεις με πρῶτον τοῦ χοροῦ τῶν σῶν φίλων,
εὐεργέτην καλῶν με πάντα τὸν χρόνον·
οὕτω γάρ ἐστιν, ὥσπερ οἶμαι, καὶ πρέπον.
Ὑπογραφεύς σοι ταῦτα τοῦ βασιλέως,
130 ὁ Χριστοφόρος, εἴ με γινώσκειν ἔχεις,
ἀγχοῦ μὲν οἰκῶν τοῦ νεὼ Προτασίου,
ἀμφ' αὐτὸ φημὶ τὸ Στρατήγιον, πάτερ,
ποθῶν δὲ καὶ σὲ γνώριμον σχεῖν καὶ φίλον,
ὡς ἂν γελῴην ἡδέως καθ' ἡμέραν,
135 τῶν θλίψεων εὑρών σε φάρμακον μέγα.

the pupils from three eyes of a Cherubim
and one hand from his flaming sword.
Just light that in the middle of your relics,
and you won't need another lamp beside it,
for, as a flame, it also emits a light   120
that vanquishes all the lights of shining stars;
so with it, you'll possess not just a lantern,
but a marvelous relic, better than all the others.
Since you'll get all this effortlessly for free
to add to your innumerable relics,   125
you'll make me first in your choir of friends,
and call me benefactor all the while;
this seems appropriate, in my opinion.
Christopher the imperial secretary writes this
to you, should you wish to know who I am.   130
I live right by the church of Protasiou,
near the place called Strategion, father.
I long for your acquaintance and friendship,
so that I may have a sweet laugh every day,
having discovered in you a great remedy for sorrows.   135

115

Εἰς τὸν φίλον Νικηφόρον, ἀποστείλαντα πέμματα κατὰ τὸν καιρὸν τοῦ Βρουμαλίου

<Ἐκ ῥη>μάτων με δεξιοῦ, μὴ πεμμάτων·
ἐμοὶ γὰρ ἡδὺ βρουμάλιον οἱ λόγοι,
<ὡς> προσκυνητῇ καὶ λατρευτῇ τοῦ λόγου,
τῶν δὲ σταλέντων πεμμάτων τίς μοι λόγος;
5   <Λοιπόν γε> τοίνυν σύ, γλυκὺς Νικηφόρος,
ἀφεὶς τὸ πέμμα καὶ πλατύνας τὸ στόμα
<τὰ δ᾽ οὔα>τα γλύκαινε καὶ μὴ τὸ στόμα,
ταῖς ἡδοναῖς τέρπων με τῶν σῶν ῥημάτων.

116

... ρα ... τὸ φυτόν

Αὐτὴν ἐκείνην τὴν ἀλήθειαν βλέπων
        ...υσαν μυρσίνη
σύμψηφος εἰμὶ τῆσδε ταύτῃ τῇ κρίσει

115

To his friend Nikephoros, who had sent him cakes around the time of the Broumalia

Greet me with words, not with biscuits!
Words are for me a sweet Broumalion,
as I am a devotee and worshipper of the word.
What do I gain by the cakes that you sent me?
So, listen here, my sweet Nikephoros,   5
forget about the cakes and open wide your mouth,
sweeten my ears, and not my mouth,
delighting me with the pleasures of your words.

116

. . . the plant

Seeing truth itself,
                        . . . with myrtle,
I subscribe to its judgment,

... πάντα προκριν. ...

5 ...

   <πιστῶς λεγ>ούσῃ πάντα καὶ μὴ πρὸς χάριν.

117

Εἰς τὸν μοναχὸν Ἀθανάσιον περὶ τοῦ πεμφθέντος ῥοδοστάγματος

Ὀπὸς ῥόδου τὸ δῶρον, ᾧ χρήσῃ, πάτερ,
οὐκ εἰς σεαυτόν, εἰς δὲ σοὺς μᾶλλον φίλους·
ῥευστὰς γὰρ αὐτὸς οὐ φιλεῖς εὐωδίας,
ὀσμὴν ἀεὶ μένουσαν ἀρετῶν πνέων.

118

. . .

Νικᾷς σὺ σαυτοῦ τὴν φιλεύσπλαγχνον φύσιν
. . .

... preferring everything ...

...

saying everything truthfully and not just to please.

117

About the rose perfume he had sent to the monk Athanasios

This gift of rose oil, father, you may use
not for yourself, but rather for your friends;
for you do not love transitory fragrances,
since you emit the eternal scent of virtue.

118

...

You overcome your own compassionate character
...

119

Εἰς τὸν τάφον τοῦ πρεσβυτέρου Θεοφίλου

. . .

τοῦ μνήματός μου μὴ κινήσῃς τὸν λίθον

. . .

ἄνθρωπος ὢν ἄνθρωπον αἰδέσθητί με

5 . . .

κἀγὼ γὰρ εἰκὼν τοῦ Θεοῦ καὶ Δεσπότου

. . .

ὡς αὔριον σέ· τοῦτο γὰρ τίς ἐκφύγῃ;

120

Εἰς τοὺς μοναχοὺς τῆς μονῆς τοῦ Μανουήλ

Αὐτοὶ λαλεῖτε, πῶς καλεῖν ὑμᾶς δέον·
τὸ μὲν γὰρ ἄλλο σῶμα πάντας ἀββάδας,
τὸ σώματος δὲ τιμιώτερον μέρος

119

On the grave of the priest Theophilos

. . .
do not move the stone of my tomb
. . .
since you are a human, respect me as a human,
. . .   5
for I am as well an image of God and our Lord
. . .
just like you tomorrow; for who will escape that?

120

To the monks of the monastery of Manuel

You say yourselves how you should be addressed;
as for the rest of the body, you're all monks,
but as for the most honored body part,

ἄντικρυς αὐτὸς κοσμικοὺς ὑμᾶς βλέπω·
5 τί γὰρ κεφαλῆς τιμιώτερον μέρος;
Ἢν κοσμικῶς στέλλοντες οὐκ ὀρθῷ στόλῳ
καὶ κοσμικῇ σκέποντες ἐξ ἔθους σκέπῃ
δοκεῖτε τἆλλα πλὴν κεφαλῆς ἀββάδες.

121

Εἰς τὸν ἅγιον Ἰάκωβον τὸν Πέρσην

Καὶ τῶν μελῶν ἕν, μάρτυς, εἰ πέπονθέ σοι,
ἤρκει στεφάνους προξενεῖν σοι μυρίους·
νῦν οὖν τὰ πάντα τῷ Θεῷ θύσας μέλη,
κρείττους ἀριθμοῦ τοὺς στεφάνους προσδόκα·
5 οὐ γὰρ στεφάνων φείσεταί σοι Δεσπότης,
μὴ σχόντι φειδὼ σῶν δι' αὐτὸν αἱμάτων.

I—speaking for myself—just see you as laymen.
For what body part is more honored than the head?   5
But you dress it in worldly fashion with unfitting garb,
and out of habit you cover it with a worldly covering,
and so you seem to be monks except for your heads.

121

On Saint James the Persian

If only one of your limbs had suffered, O martyr,
it would have sufficed to grant you ten thousand crowns;
but now you have sacrificed all your limbs to God,
so you may expect a countless number of crowns.
For the Lord will not begrudge you crowns,   5
since you did not begrudge him your blood.

122

Εἰς τὸν <ἀράχνην>

Ἐκπλήττομαί σου τὴν σοφὴν τεχνουργίαν,
Ἀδωναΐ...
καὶ τὴν κτίσιν σου πᾶσαν εἰς νοῦν λαμβάνων
πῆξίν τε ... <καὶ πάντων πλέον>
5 ἐμαυτὸν αὐτόν, πῶς παρῆγμαι καὶ πόθεν,
καὶ τί πρὶν ἤμην καὶ τί νῦν, <ὁπηνίκα>
τῆς γῆς ὁ χοῦς ὑπῆρξα σὴν κατ᾽ εἰκόνα,
ἁπαξαπλῶς δὲ τῇ νοὸς <θεωρίᾳ>,
βλέπων ἕκαστα καὶ κατασκοπῶν ἅμα,
10 ἄρρητον εἰς ἴλιγγον ἐμπί<πτω λίαν>,
μύω δὲ τὸν νοῦν ὥσπερ οὐκ ἐξισχύων
πρὸς ἥλιον σῆς γνώσεως ἀπ<οβλέπειν>.
Ὅθεν πρὸς ὕμνον εὐθέως ἀνατρέχω,
τῇ σῇ πρὸς ἰσχὺν εὐχαριστῶν <δυνάμει>,
15 ἣν ἐξ ἁπάντων πρὸς μέρος τῶν κτισμάτων
ἔχων ἐπαινεῖν οὐδαμῶς ὥ<ς σοι πρέπει>,
ἐξ εὐτελοῦς γοῦν πλάσματος νῦν αἰνέσω,
οὐκ εὐτελοῦς μὲν οὐδὲ μικροῦ <συνόλως>,
εἴ τις πρὸς αὐτὸ καὶ μόνον βλέπειν θέλοι,
20 πανευτελοῦς δὲ καὶ χαμαιζήλ<ου πάνυ>,
ἂν πρὸς τὰ λοιπὰ πλάσματα βλέψειέ τις.
Πλὴν ἀλλὰ τἄλλα νῦν παραδραμὼν <λέγω>·

122

On the spider

I am amazed by your ingenious handiwork,
Adonai . . . ,
and when I contemplate the whole of your creation,
and its fixing . . . , and most of all
how I myself was made and out of what—   5
what I was once, what I am now—the time
I, earth's mud, came into being in your own image
and now, with intellect's gaze, all at once
see and examine each and every thing—,
I fall into indescribable, utter vertigo;   10
my mind closes in, as though I am not able
to look straight at the sun of your knowledge.
And so I resort immediately to your praise,
and thank you for your power as best I can.
Without the means to praise this power rightly   15
through all parts of creation, one by one,
I will now praise it through one lowly creature—
no, not so lowly, not so small, perhaps,
if you consider it by itself and on its own,
but it is abject and most humble, indeed,   20
if you compare it to the other creatures.
Now, leaving the others aside, I say:

ἴδε πρὸς αὐτὴν τὴν ἀράχνου πᾶς φύσιν
καὶ Δημιουργοῦ γνῶσιν ἐκπλαγ<εὶς νόει>,
25 τοῦ γνώσεως χάρισμα δόντος πανσόφως
ζῴῳ βραχεῖ τε καὶ πανευτελεστά<τῳ>·
ὅρα γὰρ αὐτὸν πῶς ἐς ἀέρα τρέχει
καὶ πῶς ἀνέρπει καὶ καθέρπει πολ<λάκις>
καὶ τοὺς μίτους μὲν εὐφυῶς διαπλέκει,
30 τὰς συνθέσεις δὲ δεξιῶς διαγράφει
καὶ πρὸς τὸ νήθειν ἐκκενοῖ τὴν φροντίδα.
Μακροὺς μὲν οὖν τὸ πρῶτον ἐντείνει στύλους,
ὡς ἂν τὸν ἱστὸν ἀσφαλῶς ἐφεδράσῃ,
αὖθις δὲ γραμμὰς ἐντίθησι καὶ κύκλους,
35 κύκλους ἀραιούς, κέντρον ἓν κεκτημένους·
τοῦ τῶν ἁπάντων ἥττονος καὶ γὰρ κύκλου
κοινὸν τὸ κέντρον πᾶσι τοῖς ἄλλοις κύκλοις.
Καὶ νῦν μὲν ὀρθὰς γωνίας διεκφέρει,
νῦν δ᾽ ἀμβλυγώνους, ὀξυγώνους δ᾽ αὖ πάλιν,
40 ἄνεισι καὶ κάτεισι καὶ συνιζάνει
καὶ σχηματισμοὺς ποικίλους καταγράφει.
Ἴδῃς ἐκεῖνον ἀκριβώσας, εἰ θέλεις,
πῆ μὲν χαλῶντα πρὸς τὸ δόξαν τοὺς μίτους,
πῆ δὲ προσυφαίνοντα δεξιωτάτως
45 καὶ χείλεσι πλέκοντα καὶ ποδῶν βάσει
θαυμαστὸν ἱστὸν κερκίδος πάσης ἄνευ·
ἄγαν δὲ λεπτῶν τῶν μίτων πεφυκότων,
ἔχεις ἐν αὐτοῖς καὶ συνεστῶσαν βλέπειν
θήραν παρ᾽ αὐτῶν τῶν ἀράχνου δακτύλων·
50 εἰς γὰρ τὸ κέντρον τῶν κύκλων κεκρυμμένος,

look, everyone, into the spider's special nature and
observe in astonishment the knowledge of the Creator,
who all-wisely gives the grace of knowledge   25
to such a lowly little creature.
Just look at how it runs and takes to the air, and how
it crawls up and then crawls down again and again,
all while weaving threads ingeniously,
delineating structures dexterously,   30
and concentrating its attention on spinning.
First of all it stretches out long pillars
to make a solid base for its web,
and then it inserts lines and circles,
fine circles that all share one central point,   35
the tiniest of all the circles being
the common center for all of the others.
Now it executes right angles,
and now obtuse, and now, in turn, acute;
it rises and descends, and plunges down low,   40
delineating varied arrays of figures.
Look closer, if you will, and you will make out
how, while it seems to ruin certain threads,
it yet most skillfully intertwines some others
and weaves with its lips and the soles of its feet   45
a wondrous warp without a weaver's shuttle.
And, however delicate the threads,
you can look at them and see they constitute
a hunt made by the spider's very fingers.
For hidden at the center of the circles,   50

δίκην λοχῶντος ἐν τόποις ἀποκρύφοις,
μυίας ἐς αὐτοὺς εἰσιούσας τοὺς μίτους
ὡς ἱέραξ τις πέρδικας συλλαμβάνει
καὶ σφόδρα ταύτας τέρπεται κατεσθίων·
55 πολλὴν δὲ τοῖς βλέπουσιν τὴν θήραν τότε
ὁ μυιαθήρας προξενεῖ θυμηδίαν.
Ἀλλ' ἐξαφεὶς τὸ θαῦμα τῆς θήρας τέως
ἐκεῖνό μοι θαύμαζε κἂν δύνῃ νόει,
ἐκεῖνο φημὶ τὸ ξένον, πῶς ὑγρότης
60 ἐκ κοιλίας ἰοῦσα τοῦ ζῴου μέσης
εἰς νῆμα λεπτὸν πήγνυται παραυτίκα,
καὶ πῶς παγεῖσα μακρὸν ἔστηκε χρόνον,
ἕως τάμῃ τις εἴθ' ἑκὼν ἢ μὴ θέλων.
Ὦ πῶς ἀράχνης καὶ διαβήτου δίχα
65 κύκλους τοσούτους εὐτέχνως διαγράφει,
δεσμεῖ δὲ τούτους καὶ παραλλήλως πλέκει,
καμπὰς συνείρων σφόδρα ποικιλωτάτας;
Ὦ πῶς ἐκεῖνος τοὺς μίτους ἀναπτύει
καὶ πλῆθος ἐκχεῖ νημάτων ἐκ κοιλίας,
70 ποίους τρέφων τοὺς σῆρας ἐν τοῖς ἐντέροις;
Ὦ πῶς τὸ νῆμα λεπτότατον καλλύνει
καὶ πῶς τὸν ἱστὸν εὐπρεπέστατα πλέκει,
πόθεν τὸ νήθειν ἐκδιδαχθεὶς καὶ πότε,
διδάσκαλον δὲ τῆς τέχνης εὑρὼν τίνα,
75 ποίαν σοφὴν γυναῖκα τὰς ἱστουργίας,
ποίαν φίλεργον καὶ πονεῖν εἰθισμένην;
Ὦ πῶς γλυφεῖον οὐδαμῶς κεκτημένος
ὀπὰς τορεύει καὶ σιδηρίου δίχα;

like a warrior lying in ambush,
whenever flies come to those threads,
it seizes them as a falcon seizes partridges,
and, ah, what joy it feels devouring them!
The hunter of the fly lets spectators   55
enjoy their share as well of the thrill of the chase.
To move away now from the marvels of that hunt,
contemplate this, if you can, and marvel
at this strange fact, I mean to say: a liquid
from the middle of the creature's belly   60
hardens into fine thread instantly,
and, once solidified, lasts a long time
until someone cuts it, deliberately or not.
Oh how does the spider, without a carpenter's rule,
skillfully delineate so many circles,   65
connect them, weave them parallel, and
string together so many different twists and turns?
How does it spit these fibers out
and pour a mass of threads out from its belly,
nourishing all those silkworms in its innards?   70
Oh how does it adorn so fine a thread,
and weave its web in such a fitting way?
Where and when did it learn how to spin,
and whom did it find to teach it the art,
which woman, wise in the craft of the loom,   75
which woman loving her work and well-accustomed to toil?
Oh how does it cut out holes, without a knife
or without any other stonemasons' tools?

Ὦ πῶς χαράττειν οἶδε κύκλῳ τῶν κύκλων
80 γραμμὰς ἐπ' αὐτῶν τῶν κύκλων ἐγκειμένας,
ἴσας ἐχούσας πάντοθεν διαστάσεις,
μαθὼν ἐκείνας οὐκ ἀπ' Εὐκλείδου γράφειν,
εἰδὼς δὲ πάντως καὶ πρὸ τοῦ Μαμερτίου
ἢ μᾶλλον εἰπεῖν καὶ πρὸ τῶν Αἰγυπτίων,
85 οὓς εὑρετὰς λέγουσι πρώτους τῆς τέχνης;
Ὦ πῶς συνάπτει ταῖσδε ταῖς γραμμαῖς ἅμα
καὶ ῥομβοειδὲς καὶ σκαληνὸν εὐτέχνως,
οὐκ Ἀρχιμήδην οὔτε μὴν τὸν Ἀρχύταν
ἑωρακώς που, τοὺς σοφοὺς γεωμέτρας,
90 οὐ ταῖς ἐκείνων ἐντραφεὶς ὁμιλίαις,
οὐ σχηματισμῶν ἐκμαθὼν πολλοὺς λόγους,
οὐ τὰς ἀνίσους οὐδὲ τὰς ἴσας θέσεις
οὔτ' ἄλλο μεῖζον ἢ μικρὸν τῶν τῆς τέχνης;
Τίς οὖν Ἐλιὰβ ἐξ ὑπερλέπτων μίτων
95 ἐπ' ἀέρος τοιούσδε πήξει τοὺς δόμους,
οἵους ἀράχνης δημιουργεῖ καὶ πλέκει,
οὕτως ἄριστα συνδέων μοι τοὺς μίτους,
ὡς μὴ λελύσθαι ταῖς πνοαῖς τῶν ἀνέμων
τὸ σαθρὸν αὐτῶν καὶ διησθενημένον;
100 Βεσελεὴλ δὲ ποῖος οὐκ ἀπὸ ξύλων,
ἀλλ' ἐκ μόνων μάλιστα τῶν μηρυμάτων
τοιοῦτον ἔργον τεκτονήσει καὶ ξέσει;
Τίς καὶ τὰ λοιπὰ τῶν ἀράχνου θαυμάσει
καὶ τίς τὰ πάντα τοῦδε πρὸς μέρος φθάσει;
105 Ἐξασθενεῖ πρὸς ταῦτα καὶ νοῦς καὶ λόγος
καὶ πᾶσα πάντων δεινότης τῶν ῥητόρων

Oh how does it know how to carve all around
in circles the radials lying on top of these circles,   80
so they have equal length at all points,
not having learned to draw these lines from Euclid,
yet knowing all of them before Mamertius,
better still, even before the Egyptians,
who are known as the inventors of this art?   85
Oh how does it skillfully join to these lines
at once a rhombus and a scalene triangle,
without ever having had a look at
Archimedes or Archytas, those wise geometers,
nor brought up on their teachings,   90
nor having memorized their many texts on figures,
nor knowing positions even and uneven,
nor any other portion, great or small, of geometry?
Now which Oholiab, out of extremely fine threads,
will set firm upon the air such houses,   95
as those that the spider weaves and fashions —
fastening, oh my, the threads together finely —
so they do not come loose in gusts of wind,
even when they are weakened and decayed?
And what Bezaleel, working not with wood,   100
but only with these strands, would design
and hew to shape such handiwork as this?
Now who will admire the spider's other feats
and come to list them for us one by one?
Mind and speech are at a loss for that,   105
as is all the force of all the rhetors,

καὶ πᾶσα πάντων τῶν σοφιστῶν κομψότης.
Τοιαῦτα τῶν σῶν καὶ τὰ μικρὰ πλασμάτων,
ἀριστοτέχνα Σαβαὼθ Παντοκράτορ.
110   Τοῖς οὖν μεγίστοις οὐδὲ προσβαλεῖν σθένων
ἐκ τῶν μικρῶν ὑμνεῖν σε τολμῶ τὸν μέγαν.

123

Εἰς τὴν Γέννησιν τοῦ Χριστοῦ

Ποίμνης βροτείας τὸν καλὸν σὲ ποιμένα
ἐν γῇ βροτῶν βλέπουσι πρῶτοι ποιμένες·
αὐτὴν γὰρ αὐτὴν τὴν ταπείνωσιν, Λόγε,
δι' ἣν κατῆλθες καὶ δι' ἣν σῴζεις κτίσιν,
5   πρώτην κατηξίωσας αὐτὸς σῆς θέας
—εἴπερ ταπεινὸν σφόδρα χρῆμα ποιμένες.

and all the refinement of all the sophists.
Such are even the lesser of your creatures,
most wondrous artist, Sabaoth, Almighty.
Unable to even come near the greatest things,   110
I dare to praise you, great one, through small things.

123

On the Nativity of Christ

The first mortals to see you on earth, O good shepherd
of the mortal flock, were shepherds;
for it was humility, that very humility, Word of God,
for which you descended and save creation,
which you deemed worthy of seeing you first   5
—since indeed shepherds are something very humble.

124

... φιλ ... κατὰ τὴν ἀρχιμηνί<αν>

...

   ...λοῦνται δεξιώσεις πρὸς φίλους

...

   <πά>ντ<ων> θελόντων· τοῦτο γὰρ τούτου χάρι<ν>.

5 ...

   <ἰ>δοὺ δίδωμι τούσδε δῶρα τοὺς λόγους

...

   γραφῆς καλάμῳ ῥημάτων τελῶ κρότους

...

10 ἐν τῇ καλανδῶν προσδέχου νουμηνίᾳ

...

   ἀλλ' οὐδ' ἔχει τὶ βέλτιον τούτου βίος.

125

Εἰς τὸν μύρμηκα

Τὸν νοῦν ὁ μύρμηξ, τὸ βραχὺ ζῷον, μέγας·
ὦ σῶμα ποῖον οἷόν ἐστι τὴν φρένα·
ἢ μᾶλλον εἰπεῖν, ὦ Θεοῦ γνῶσις πόση,
ὃς κἂν μικροῖς τοιοῦτον ἰσχύει μέγα.

124

... friends ... on the first day of the month

...

.... greetings for friends

...

if all are willing; for that's its charm.

...   5

here, I give these words as gifts

...

I create rhythms of written words with a pen

...

receive on the first day of the calends   10

...

but life has nothing better than this in store.

125

On the ant

The ant, that tiny creature, is great in mind.
What a body this is, compared to its intellect!
Or, better said, how ample is God's knowledge,
with power so great even in things so small.

126

Εἰς τὴν Ἀνάληψιν

Ἐκ γῆς ἀπαίρεις, εὖ τὰ τῆς γῆς θεὶς λίαν·
Ἅιδου γὰρ ἤδη τὰς πύλας κλείσας κάτω,
πύλας ἀνέρχῃ νῦν ἀνοῖξαι τοῦ πόλου,
δι' ὧν τὸ πλάσμα, Σῶτερ, εἰσάξεις ἅπαν
5   καὶ Πατρὶ δείξεις, οἷα τούτῳ τὰ σκῦλα.

127

Εἰς τοὺς ἐξωνηθέντας βόλους τοῦ δικτύου παρ' αὐτοῦ

Ἀναπλέων χθὲς πρωῒ τὴν Προποντίδα,
ἄνδρας κατεῖδον ἓξ ἀγρευτὰς ἰχθύων
βάλλοντας ἀμφίβληστρον ἐν βυθῷ μέσῳ·
καὶ δὴ παρασχὼν χρύσινον τούτοις ἕνα
5   ὠνησάμην τρεῖς δικτύου χαίρων βόλους,
ἕξειν δοκῶν τι καὶ πλέον τοῦ χρυσίνου.
Βάλλουσι τοίνυν· καὶ τὸ μὲν πρῶτον λίθους,

126

On the Ascension

You leave the earth with earthly affairs well settled;
for having closed the gates of Hades below,
you now ascend to open the gates of heaven,
through which, O Savior, you will bring in all humanity,
and show the Father what spoils of war he has.   5

127

On the casts of the fishing net
that he bought

Yesterday morning as I sailed up the Propontis,
I saw six fishermen casting their nets
right down into the midst of the deep.
So I then gave them one piece of gold
and gladly bought three casts of the net,   5
thinking to gain more than a gold piece's worth.
And so they cast their net, first catching stones,

τὸ δεύτερον δὲ ψάμμον εἷλκον ἐκ βάθους·
ὡς δ' ἐγκαθῆκαν τὴν σαγήνην τὸ τρίτον,
10 ἀνεῖλκον οὐδὲν ἄλλο πλὴν ὕδωρ μόνον.
Εἰ γοῦν τινές μοι τῶν φιλούντων τοὺς μύθους
τεκμήριον λέγουσι ταῦτα τῆς τύχης,
ὡς εὐτυχὴς ἔγωγε· τί πλέον θέλω,
εἴ μοι χορηγεῖ ταῦτα μᾶλλον ἡ τύχη,
15 ἃ κόσμος αὐτὸς ἀφθονώτατα τρέφει,
ὕδωρ, λίθους καὶ ψάμμον; Ὦ χρηστῆς τύχης.

128

Εἰς τ... ἐν ταῖς κ... κατὰ τὴν ἑορτὴν τῶν
ἁγίων Ἀποστόλων

Τὰ δεῖπνα ταῦτα...
πανήγυρις προύθηκε τῶν Ἀποστόλων·
πρὶν γὰρ κατακλιθ<εῖσιν Ἰσραηλίταις>
ξένην παρεῖχον βρῶσιν εὐλογημένην
5 μικρῶν ἀπ' ἄρτων <καὶ δυοῖν ἀπ' ἰχθύων>,
ὑπερπεριττεύουσαν ἐκ τῶν κλασμάτων.
Νῦν δὲ τροφὴν νέμουσ<ι τοῖς Χριστωνύμοις>,
ἀπὸ κρεῶν τρέφοντες, οὐκ ἀπ' ἰχθύων,
ναὶ μὴν διδοῦντες καὶ περι...

the next time dragging sand up from the depths,
and then, the third time that they lowered their seine,
they didn't haul in anything but water.   10
So if now somebody who loves stories
tells me that this is a sign of fortune,
then I am a lucky man indeed! What more can I want
than that fortune grants to me the things
the world itself produces in great abundance: 15
water, stones, and sand? Such good fortune!

128

On the . . . in the . . . on the feast of the Holy Apostles

The Apostles' festival has set before us
these meals . . . ;
for they once gave the seated Israelites
a blessed and unusual sort of food
from two fish and some little loaves of bread,   5
with pieces broken off in overabundance.
Now they give out food to Christians,
providing them with meat and not with fish,
yes, even giving them . . .

10 πληροῦντες ἄρτων, οὐχὶ κλασμάτων πάλιν.
Οὕτως ἐκείνων ὡς πρὶν αἱ πα‹ρουσίαι›
καὶ νῦν τροφὰς νέμουσιν αἱ πανηγύρεις.

129

Εἰς τοὺς ψάλτας καὶ τὸν χειρ‹ονόμον›

Γλωσσῶν τὸ πλῆθος εἰς μίαν συμφωνίαν
ἕλκουσι χεῖρες εὐπερίστροφ‹οι λίαν›
καὶ τῷ μέλει διδοῦσι τὴν εὐρυθμίαν.
Ὦ θαῦμα καινόν· ἐκ μόνον κ‹ινημάτων›
5 ἄχορδος αὕτη μουσικὴ θείων λόγων
εἰς ὕμνον ἡμῖν εὑρέθη Θεοῦ Λόγ‹ου›.

130

Εἰς τοὺς ξενῶνας καὶ τοὺς ἐν αὐτοῖς ἀρρώστους· ἡρωϊκά

Αἵδε κλῖναι λαοῖσι . . . ὑπ. . .
καὶ στυγερῆς πενίης, νούσοιο δυσαλθέος ἄλλης

filling them with loaves, not broken pieces.   10
In this way, as at the apostles' previous appearances,
their feasts now distribute food.

129

On the chanters and their conductor

Nimble hands bring the mass of voices
together into a single harmony
and give a lovely rhythm to the tune.
How wonderful and new! From just the motions,
the unaccompanied music of divine words   5
is revealed to us as a hymn for the Word of God.

130

On the hospitals and the sick people there; hexameters

These beds for the people . . .
and of baneful poverty, another torturous disease,

κείανθ' ἐξεί<ης> . . .
Πολλὴν τὴν κομιδὴν νοσέουσι φέρουσι βροτοῖσι,
5 οὐ πενίην δ' . . .
οὔτε γὰρ Ἱπποκράτης πενίης ἄκος, οὔτε Γαληνός,
οὔτε ἐπ. . .
ὧδ' ἐπιδημήσει, ἀφορίζεται οἷον ἐν οἴκῳ.

131

<Εἰς τὴν γλαῦκα, κραυγάζουσαν> . . . καὶ διυπνίζουσαν αὐτόν

Ὦ . . .
ἥτις με μακρὸν οὐκ ἐᾷς ὑπνοῦν χρόνον
. . .
κράζουσα πολλὰ καὶ διυπνίζουσά με
5 . . .
. . .
. . . καὶ λαλοῦσα πρὸς μ. . .
. . .
ᾧ φροντὶς ἐστὶ γνώσεως . . .
10 . . .
σῴζοιό μοι, γλαύξ, εἰσαεὶ σῴζ<οιό μοι>,
. . .

are lying one by one . . . .
They provide much care for sick people,
but they <cannot take away> poverty,   5
for neither Hippocrates is a remedy against poverty, nor
    Galen,
nor . . .
<whoever> will come to stay here, is set apart as if at home.

131

On the owl, hooting . . . and keeping him awake

O . . . <owl>,
you who do not allow me to sleep for a long time
. . .
hooting so often and waking me up
. . .   5
. . .
    . . . and talking to . . .
. . .
who cares about knowledge . . .
. . .   10
may you be well, my owl, may you be well forever,
. . .

ὀξὺν τιθεῖσα καὶ πρόθυμον εἰς πόν<ους>

. . .

15 ἄρτι φθίνοντος ἑβδόμης Σεπτεμβρί<ου>

. . .

ὡς ἂν διυπνίζειν με τῶν νυκτῶν ἔχοι

. . .

ὃς πολλάκις με καὶ πλανᾷ, νὴ τοὺς λόγους,

20 . . .

γέρων ἀληθὲς οὐδὲν ἰσχύων λέγειν

. . .

οὔσης δὲ πέμπτης, ὀγδόην εἶναι λέγει

. . .

25 ἀλεκτρυὼν ὑπῆρχεν ἀμφ᾽ Ὠιδὰς Τρίτας

. . .

κἀμοὶ μὲν εἶπεν αἰσίαν τὴν ἡμέραν

. . .

τέλος δὲ κροῦμα καὶ τὸν ὕμνον δοὺς τέλει

30 . . .

ἔφη τετάρτην οὗτος εἰς ἄλλον χρόνον

. . .

καὶ ταῦτα φάσκων οὐδ᾽ ἐρυθριᾶν θέλει

. . .κρίην

35 εἰ τηλικοῦτος ψευδολεκτεῖ πρεσβύτης

. . .ων,

οὗ καὶ λαλοῦντος οὐκ ἀκούων πολλάκις

. . .α

κεῖμαι καθεύδων ὕπτιος γνοὺς οὐδ᾽ ὅλως.

40 . . . <πολλὰ χαιρ>έτω·

280

making me alert and ready for efforts
. . .
the seventh hour at the end of September   15
. . .
so that it could wake me up during the night
. . .
who often—I swear—even deludes me,
. . .   20
an old man unable to say anything true
. . .
when it was the fifth hour, he said it was the eighth
. . .
there was a rooster around the Third Odes,   25
. . .
to me he said that it was an auspicious day
. . .
but finally, he put an end to his cries and songs
. . .   30
this one said that it was the fourth hour, at another time
. . .
and saying this, he does not even blush
. . .
if such an old man is telling lies,   35
. . .
when he speaks, I often do not hear him
. . .
I lie down, sleeping on my back without knowing anything.
                    . . . adieu to him!   40

ἐγὼ δὲ σὲ κράζουσαν, ὦ γλαύξ, νῦν ἔχων
       . . . νέος
ὕπνου μακρὰν πᾶν ἐκτινάξομαι βάρος
      . . . ωτάτη
45 οὕτω λάλος τὶς καὶ σιγῆς ἀνωτέρα
      . . . κ. . . καὶ πάλιν·
κράζουσα καὶ γὰρ καὶ διυπνίζουσά με
      . . . <οὐδα>μῶς κράζεις μάτην,
ἀλλ' ὠφελήσεις ὥς γε βούλομαι μέγα
50   . . . <προξ>ενήσεις μοι δύο·
συλλέξομαι γὰρ γνῶσιν ἐξ ἀγρυπνίας
      . . .τῆρας, οὓς ἔφην.

132

Εἰς τὸν βασιλικὸν νοτάριον Κωνσταντῖνον, εἰπόντα βδελύττεσθαι τὸν πηλὸν καὶ διὰ τοῦτο τῆς οἰκίας μὴ προϊέναι

Πηλὸν βδελύττῃ καὶ μένεις ἔνδον δόμου;
Καὶ μὴν ὁ πηλὸς οὐδαμῶς ἄπεστί σου,
κἄνπερ προέρχῃ, κἄνπερ ἐν δόμῳ μένῃς·
ὅλος γὰρ αὐτὸς πηλὸς εἶ, Κωνσταντῖνε.
5 Τὸ συγγενὲς γοῦν μὴ βδελύττεσθαι θέλε,
σαυτοῦ γινώσκων πηλὸν οὖσαν τὴν φύσιν.

Now, my owl, I have your shrieks
                              . . . new
I will shed all the weight of sleep
. . .
<an owl> so garrulous and stronger than silence   45
                              . . . and again;
for when you hoot and awaken me,
              . . . you do not at all hoot in vain,
but you will be of great use to me, exactly as I want it,
                   . . . you will provide me with two advantages: 50
I will gather knowledge from my sleeplessness
                        . . . which I mentioned.

132

On the imperial notary Constantine, who had said that he loathed the mud and for that reason did not leave his house

You loathe the mud; is that why you stay home?
The mud will never keep away from you
whether you go out or stay inside the house,
since, Constantine, you are all mud yourself.
Be not so quick to shun what is kindred to you,   5
knowing that your own nature is mud.

133

<Εἰς τοὺς ἁγίους> Τεσσαράκοντα, ἐν διαλλάττουσι σχήμασι ζωγραφηθέντας· ἡρωϊκά

<Ἄθρει ἀθλο>φόρους Θεοῦ ἐνθάδε τεσσαράκοντα,
σχήματι ἄλλον ἐν ἄλλῳ ἐφεσταότας κατὰ λίμνην·
<εἰ δ' ἄρ>α καὶ ἐν σχήμασιν οἵδε μὴ εἶεν ὁμοῖοι,
ἐν βασάνῳ παγέτοιο ὁμόφρονα θυμὸν ἔχουσιν.

134

Εἰς τὸν κατορύττοντα τὸ χρυσίον πλούσιον

Πρὸς μνᾶς κεχηνὼς ὡς γαλῆ τις πρὸς στέαρ,
τὸν χρυσὸν αὔξεις· πλὴν κατακρύπτεις βόθρῳ,
ὡς οὐχὶ σαυτῷ, γῇ δὲ τοῦτον συλλέγων,
ὁ γῆν ὑπελθεῖν ἄξιος σὺ καὶ πάλαι.

133

On the Holy Forty Martyrs,
painted in various
postures; hexameters

Behold, here stand the forty who bore travails for God,
each in a different posture as they stand in the lake.
And though they are not alike in their postures,
they stand like-minded in their icy torture.

134

On the rich man who buried
his gold

Gaping at money like *a cat* gaping *at fat,*
you accumulate gold; but you bury it in a hole,
gathering it not for yourself, but for the earth—
the earth you've long been worthy to go under.

135

Εἰς τοὺς μοναχοὺς τοῦ Προέδρου
διὰ τὰς ὕσκας

Νόμον λαβόντες ἡδονὰς φεύγειν βίου,
τῶν ἡδονῶν πίπλασθε μᾶλλον εἰς κόρον,
ὕσκας τίθεσθε βρῶσιν ἡδεῖαν μάλα.
Καὶ τίς γὰρ ἄλλη βρῶσις ὕσκας ἡδίων;
5   Ἧς ἐμφορεῖσθε καὶ πατεῖτε τὸν νόμον,
ἔσθοντες, οὐ φεύγοντες ἡδονὰς βίου.

136

... ἀπελεύσεως τοὺς νοταρίους

...
θρίαμβον ἦγον παῖδες ἐν μέσῃ πόλει
...
ἐς Μαρκιανοῦ καὶ Μαρτυρίου δόμον
5   ...
ἐν ἐσχάτῳ δὲ καὶ μεγίστων μαρτύρων
... ἔβλεπον τοὺς ν<οταρίους>...

135

To the monks of the Proedros monastery about the sturgeons

You've adopted the rule to shun all life's pleasures,
yet stuff yourselves with them to saturation,
and serve yourselves a lovely dish of sturgeon.
What food is more delicious than the sturgeon?
You fill yourselves with it and break the rule   5
by eating and not shunning life's pleasures.

136

. . . of the procession, the notaries

. . .
the boys held a triumph in the center of the city
. . .
to the church of Markianos and Martyrios
. . .   5
and, at the end, also great martyrs
. . . they saw the notaries . . .

. . .

. . . ὅμων δὲ σφόδρα τοῖς παναθλ<ίοις>

10 . . .

. . .<ἐ>κείνους γαυριῶντας καὶ μάλα

. . .

ξένοις χαλινοῖς καὶ περιτραχηλίοις

. . .

15 ἀλλοτρίοις χαίροντες οἷα γνησίοις

. . .

ἐν οἷς φρενῶν δείλαιος ἐξέστη χρόνοις

. . .

καὶ πρὸς τοσαύτην μέμψιν οὐκ αἰδουμένους

20 . . .

ὄντως μάτην ἔχαιρον εἰς βραχὺν χρόνον

. . .

ἄλλος χιτῶνα λαμπρόν, ἄλλος ἐμβάτας

. . .

25 ἄλλος γυναικὸς κόσμον, ἄλλος ἄλλό τι
ᾠχ<εῖτο> . . .
πλῆθος τοσοῦτον οὔμενουν αἰδουμένους

. . .

λαβὼν τὸ χρησθὲν πᾶν ἕκαστος τῶν φίλων

30 . . .

κἂν ἐνδύσηται πορφύραν τις ὢν πένης

. . .

κἂν εἰς κεφαλὴν στέμμα θῇ μέλλων πάλιν

. . .

35 μέμψοιτο δ' ἄν τις εὐλόγως τοῖς πατράσι

'   . . .

. . . heavily the deeply wretched

. . .   10

them prancing around

. . .

marvelous reins and neckpieces

. . .

delighting in others' possessions as if they were their own   15

. . .

times in which a wretched man lost his mind

. . .

they, not ashamed at such a great cause of blame

. . .   20

truly in vain they rejoiced for a short time

. . .

one wore a brilliant robe, still another boots,

. . .

another women's ornaments, another wore yet something   25
    else.

. . .

not at all ashamed at such a large crowd

. . .

each of the friends took everything that was used

. . .   30

Even if a pauper would dress himself in purple,

. . .

and, moreover, would place a garland on his head,

. . .

anyone would blame their fathers with good reason,   35

τρέ...
οὗτοι γὰρ ἀφραίνουσι τῶν παίδων πλέον
ὡ<ς>...
καὶ συγκαλύπτειν τήνδε παντοίοις τρόποις
40 σπλ...
καὶ τοὺς ἑαυτῶν παῖδας ὑβρίζειν μάλα
τιμῶν ἀ...
κἂν μὴ νοῶσι παῖδες ὄντες εἰσέτι
καὶ τοῦ κα...
45 ὅταν γὰρ αὐτῶν σήμερόν τινας βλέπων
λαμπρειμ<ονοῦντας>...
εἰς αὔριον βλέψαιμι τούτους ἀθρόον
σαπρούς, ῥυπώ<δεις>...
μετεκπεσόντος ὀστράκου, τὸ τοῦ λόγου.
50 Οὐκ αἰσχύνη τ...
ἀλλ' οἱ τεκόντες ὥσπερ ἐκλελησμένοι
οὐδ' αἰσθάνοντ<αι τῆς μεγάλης αἰσχύνης>,
ἣν προξενοῦσι τοῖς ἑαυτῶν φιλτάτοις,
χρυσοὺς πρὸς ὥ<ραν>...
55 αὐχμῶντας οὓς ἔχουσι πάντα τὸν χρόνον,
οἷον τί ποιεῖν καὶ <φιλοῦσιν οἰκέται>·
ἰδεῖν σε καὶ γὰρ εἰκὸς αὐτοὺς πολλάκις
κοσμοῦντα<ς>...   <οἰκίας>
ἅπαξ, κατ' αὐτὸ Πάσχα, χρωμάτων χρίσει
60 θύρσοις τε δάφ<ν>...
τὸν δ' ἄλλον αὐτὰς οὐδ' ἐρευνῶντας χρόνον,
πλήρεις ἀράχνης τυγχανούσας <καὶ ῥύπου>.
Σκοπῶμεν οὖν κἀκεῖνο καὶ προσεκτέον·

...
for they are more foolish than the boys,
because ...
and hiding this in all possible ways
...   40
and insulting their own children
... of honors,
even if they do not understand, being boys after all,
...
for when, while seeing some of them today   45
wearing bright clothes ...
I will see tomorrow that they are suddenly
worn out, filthy, and ...
when *heads become tails,* as the saying goes.
No shame ...   50
But the parents, as if being forgetful,
do not feel the great shame
that they cause to their beloved ones,
<dressing them> in gold for the occasion,
while they leave them unwashed the rest of the year.   55
Servants love to do something similar;
for it is usual to see them
adorning ... houses,
just once, for Easter, painting them in colors,
and ... with staffs of laurel, but   60
during the rest of the year they do not even examine their
      houses,
leaving them full of cobwebs and dirt.
Let us now look at the following point and consider it:

εἴ τις τάλαντα βαστάσας τ. . .
65 ἐκ τῶν τοσούτων χρημάτων ὧν βαστάσει,
εἰς κέρδος ἕξει μηδὲ πολλο<στὸν μέρος,>
ἔντιμος ἔσται πᾶσιν ἀνθρώποις ὅδε
ἐκ τοῦ μόνον τάλαντα πολλὰ <βαστάσαι;>
Ἵππῳ δ' ἐρυθροῖς κωδίοις ἐστρωμένῳ
70 ὀχούμενος τὶς μὴ <κρατεῖν τούτου σθένων>,
εὐφημίαις ἐντεῦθεν ἕξει καὶ κρότους;
Οὐκ ἄν τις <εἴποι> . . .
εἰ μὴ μέμηνε καὶ διέφθορε φρένας.
Καὶ παῖδα τ. . .
75 κἂν εὐπάρυφον τὴν καταστολὴν φέρῃ,
κἂν . . .
οὐκ ἂν φρονῶν τὶς ἄξιον τιμῆς κρίνῃ
. . .
λαβόντα τοῦτο πρός τινα βραχὺν χρόνον.
80 . . .
αὐτοῖς ἐκείνοις τοῖς ἐπὶ σκηνῆς πλάνοις.
. . .
. . .
. . .τῆς αὐτ. . . τ. . . προ. . .
85 . . .
οἷοίπερ ἦσαν καὶ πρὸ τῆς σ<κηνῆς πάλαι>
. . .
ὁποῖον εἰς χθὲς εἶχεν ἡ πομ<πὴ τρόπον>
. . .
90 ἄγαν πενιχραῖς ἐν στολαῖς ἐσταλμέν<οι>
. . .

292

if someone having carried talents . . .
will not make a minimal gain   65
out of so much money that he may have carried,
will all people then admire that man,
just because he carried many talents?
If someone rides a horse, covered with red sheepskins,
but is not able to hold it in check,   70
will he then receive praises and applause?
No one would be able to say . . .
unless he is insane and out of his senses.
And a boy, . . .
even when he would wear garb with a fine purple border,   75
or even when . . .
a sensible person would not deem him worthy of honor
. . .
if he takes this for a short time.
. . .   80
for those very impostors on the stage.
. . .
. . .
. . .
. . .   85
as they previously were, before the stage
. . .
in a similar way as the procession of yesterday
. . .
wearing very shabby clothes   90
. . .

κρείττους ἐκείνων σφόδρα τῶν λαμπρ<εν>δύ<των>

. . .

ἀλλοτρίοις δὲ μηδαμῶς κεχρημένοι

95 . . .

τὸ δ᾽ ᾆσμα τούτων τοὺς σοφοὺς νοταρίους

. . .

πρὸς τὴν χάριν σπεύδουσιν αὐτῶν ἐκ πόθου

. . .

100 ἐπεγγελῶντες κερτομοῦντες μυρία

. . .

τρισαθλίους κρίνοντες, οὐ τρισολβίους

. . .

οὓς αὔριον βλέψουσιν αὐτοὶ πρωΐας

105 . . .

πτωχοὺς πενιχρούς, ὡς ἔθος, σαπρενδύτας

. . .

ἀφαιρεθέντος ψευδεπίπλαστα πτίλα

. . .

110 τὸ πεζικὸν δὴ ταῦτα καὶ πλείω τάχα

. . . λόγος,

ὥς που προσῆκον, ἐκφράσειε πρὸς μέρος

. . .

τὰ πάντα τούτου πρὸς φίλους ἄνδρας λόγων

115 . . .

εἶτ᾽ αὖθις ἄλλη καὶ μετ᾽ αὐτὴν ἡ τρίτη

. . . <συν>ωρίσι

διῆεσαν χαίροντες ὢ χαρὰν πόσην·

<ἀνθ᾽ ὧν γὰρ ἐχρῆν πικρὰ πάντας> δακρύειν

superior to those who are brilliantly dressed
. . .
they did not make any use of possessions of others
. . .   95
their song . . . the wise notaries
. . .
they are eager to rush to their grace
. . .
jeering at them with a thousand mockeries   100
. . .
considering them thrice-wretched, not thrice-happy
. . .
whom they themselves will see tomorrow morning
. . .   105
poor and needy, as usual, and shabbily clad
. . .
robbed them of their fake plumage
. . .
those on foot perhaps even more   110
                         . . . words,
if in any way appropriate, could describe this in detail
. . .
all this to men who are friends of words,
. . .   115
Then again a second, and after this, a third
                          . . . on pairs of horses
they went forth, reveling in great mirth.
Instead of this, they should all have wept bitterly,

120   καὶ σφόδρα πενθεῖν ὡς ἐπεγγελωμένους
                . . .νοίας ἄρα,
  ἔχαιρον αὐταῖς ταῖς ἑαυτῶν αἰσχύναις.
     . . . <λευκὸν> ὡς γάλα,
  ὃν ἀμπέχεσθαι τοῦ θέρους μόνου δέον
125   . . . <ἐστολι>σμένος τότε,
  χρήσαντος οἶμαι πρὸς γέλωτα τοῦ φίλου
     . . . καιροῦ ξένον·
  ὃ δ' ἦν κροκωτὸν τὸν χιτωνίσκον φέρων.
     . . . <γῆ>ς ἄκρας ἐψαυέτην,
130   γελοῖον αὐτὸν δεικνύοντες τοῖς ὄχλοις.
              . . . ἐξηρτημένος
  ἐνωτίων τί πλῆθος, ὦ τῆς αἰσχύνης.
     . . . <π>λοκάμους συνθέτους.
  Αἴσχιστον ἦν θέαμα τοῖς θεωμένοις
135   . . .ταῖς κεχρημένος
  ὤμων σύνεγγυς εἶχεν ἐμβατῶν ἄκρα
     . . . δῆμος . . .στείας μάλα
  ὕβρ<ι>ζεν ὕβρεις καὶ κατηρᾶτο πλέον
  <παιδός γ' ἐ>κείνου τοῖς γονεῦσιν ἐνδίκως.
140   Ἄλλος χαλινοὺς θελκτικωτάτους ἔχων
  <χαλκῶν φα>λάρων πάντοθεν πεπλησμένους.
  Παῖς σφόδρα μικρός, ὡς τριῶν εἶναι χρόνων,
  <ἵππῳ κατ>ίσχνῳ καὶ δυσειδεῖ τὴν θέαν
  ὠχεῖτο χωλεύοντι καὶ ποδῶν ἕνα
145   . . . οὗτος τοῦ βρέφους
  καὶ ψωριῶν τε καὶ γέμων ἦν τραυμάτων
     . . .πον ἔσθ' ὅτε

and grieved deeply, because they were derided   120
...
they rejoiced in those very things that put them to shame.
                         ... white as milk,
that should be worn during summer only,
                  ... he was wearing at that time,   125
using this, I think, to make his friend laugh
                  ... out of season.
The other was wearing a saffron-colored short tunic,
         ... both of them touched the surface of the earth,
making a fool of him for the crowd.   130
                            ... attached,
what a mass of earrings, oh what a shame!
                  ... interlaced plaits.
It was a most appalling sight for the onlookers
... wearing ...,   135
he had his shoulders close to the tips of his shoes,
                   ... the crowd
cursed and heaped insults on
the parents of that boy, and rightly so.
Another one had the most beautiful reins   140
everywhere full of bronze disks.
A very young child, as if three years old,
rode on a scrawny horse, which was ugly in appearance
and had one lame foot,
                   ... of the child   145
was full of scabs and wounds
                  ... sometimes

ἔκνηθε πλευρὰ καὶ σκέλη καὶ γαστέρα

... <τ>ὸν ἱππέα·

150 ὅ δ' οἷα παῖς ἔκλαιε δειλιῶν σφόδρα.

... <μ>άλα

βοῶν ἄναρθρα καὶ κατεψελλισμένα,

... υ

ἐξ ἀργύρου μύωπας εἶχεν εἰς πόδας

155 ...

ἐν ᾗ καθῆστο σεμνὸς αὐτὸς ἱππότης

...

πολλοὶ δὲ τούτων ἦσαν ἐγκεχρισμένοι

... <οὐ>κ ἀπρεπ<ῶν> ε...

160 ...

...ω ᾤκτειρα καὶ πιστευτέ<ον>

...

... <π>ρόσωπα δυστυχῶς γεγραμμ<ένα>

...

165 <ἐσ>θῆτα τοίνυν τίς θεωρήσας φίλου

...

ἵππον δέ τις κάλλιστον ἄλλος γνωρίσας

...

πόσην ἔχουσι τὴν ὕβριν τὰ παιδία

170 ...

πόσην δὲ μᾶλλον οἱ γονεῖς τὴν αἰσχύ<νην>

...

καὶ τοὺς ἑαυτῶν στηλιτεύοντες βίους

...

175 χαλκᾶς φέροντας ἐν κεφαλαῖς τιάρ<ας>

it scratched his sides, his legs and his stomach
                    . . . the rider;
as a child he wept in great fear.   150
. . .
crying inarticulately and lisping,
. . .
he had silver spurs on his feet
. . .   155
at which sat this solemn horseman
. . .
many of them were anointed
            . . . not indecent . . .
. . .   160
. . . I had pity and it should be believed
. . .
. . . faces that were painted in a miserable way
. . .
one looked at the clothes of his friend   165
. . .
another one recognized a very beautiful horse,
. . .
how disrespectful are those boys
. . .   170
rather, how much shame do the parents
. . .
and making a fool of their own lives,
. . .
wearing tiaras of bronze on their heads   175

. . .

καί τι κρομύων πλέγμα καί τι σκορδίων

. . .

βραχεῖς δὲ τούτους ἦγον ἵπποι καὶ λίαν

180 . . .

τοίους δὲ σεμνοὺς κοσμίους καὶ τιμίους

. . .

οἷς συγκαθυβρίζοντο πάντες εἰκότως

. . .

185 ἔχοντες ἦσαν εἰς ἀφορμὴν αἰσχύνης

. . .

οἱ πάντα καλοὶ καὶ σεμνοὶ συνιππόται

. . .

ἐν τῷ τραχήλῳ μαργάρους φέρων ξένους

190 . . .

ταῖς χερσὶ δ' αὐτοὺς τῇδε καὶ τῇδε τρίβων

. . .

ἔρριψεν εἰς γῆν καὶ παρῆλθεν αὐτίκα

. . .

195 ὁ παιδαγωγὸς ὀψὲ τοὺς ἀλλοτρίους

. . .

πληρῶν βοῆς τὰ πάντα καὶ κραυγῆς ὅσης

. . .

ἀρχαγγέλων πλήρωμα προστιθεὶς ἅμα

200 . . .

πρὸς χρῆσιν ἐκδοθέντας ἡμερησίαν.
Κα. . .

ἔφιππος ὢν ὕπνωττεν, ὃς καὶ τοῖς ὄχλοις

. . .

and a braid of onions and garlic

. . .

some tiny horses bore them

. . .   180

these solemn, orderly and honorable men

. . .

appropriately, everyone shared in these insults

. . .

they had as the cause for their shame   185

. . .

the riders in their company, excellent and respectable in
     every aspect,

. . .

wearing marvelous pearls at his neck,

. . .   190

with his hands, he rubbed them this way and that

. . .

he threw them to the ground and passed immediately

. . .

the elementary instructor . . . the others too late   195

. . .

filling everything with his shouts and yells

. . .

adding at the same time a mass of archangels

. . .   200

handing them over to daily use.

. . .

he slept on his horse, giving the crowd <an occasion>

ἡδὺν πα<ρεῖχε τὸν γέλωτα καὶ κρότον·>
205 πολλοὶ δὲ τούτων ἤσθιον τῶν ἱππέων,
οἱ μὲν πλα<κοῦντας>...
οἳ δ' ἰσχάδας καὶ μῆλα καὶ σιλιγνίας.
Ὡς οὖν παρ<ῆλθον>...
εὐθὺς μετ' αὐτοὺς τὸν διδάσκαλον βλέπω
210 ὄπισθεν ἱππ<εύοντα>...
γέροντα κυρτόν, ἔκλυτον, πωγωνίαν,
ὃς καὶ κατ...
καὶ προσκυνῶν ἦν πυκνὰ πᾶσι τοῖς ὄχλοις.
Γελῶ<σ>ιν...
215 τοῦτον χθὲς ὁ θρίαμβος εἶχε τὸν τρόπον.
Ἐγ<ὼ δὲ>...
ἔνδον παρελθὼν τῆς σχολῆς τῶν παιδίων
...
ἐσχισμένους χιτῶνας ἠμφιεσμένους
220 ...
τοὺς χθὲς μύρου πνέοντας εὐωδεστάτου
...
τὸν παῖδα δ' αὐτόν, ὃς τρίβων τοὺς μαργάρους
...
225 πληγαῖς πρεπούσαις παιδίοις ἐστιγμένον
...
ὄνειρον εἶναι τὴν χθὲς εἶπον ἡμέραν.
...
ἀφεὶς ἐκείνους ᾠχόμην παραυτίκα
230 ...
καθ' ὃν τελεῖσθαι ταῦτα μέλλει καὶ πάλιν.

for sweet laughter and applause.
Many of these horsemen were eating,   205
some of them flatcakes . . .
others figs and apples and white bread.
When they thus passed by, . . .
I see immediately after them the schoolmaster,
riding behind . . .   210
a dissolute old hunchback with a beard,
who also . . .
and who frequently kneeled before the whole crowd.
They laugh . . .
Thus was the triumphal procession of yesterday.   215
I, instead, . . .
entering the school of the boys
. . .
<them> wearing ripped tunics
. . .   220
those who yesterday were emitting a fragrant smell
. . .
that very boy, who was rubbing the pearls
. . .
bruised by beatings suitable for boys.   225
. . . ,
I said to myself that yesterday was a dream.
. . .
I left them and went away at once
. . .   230
when these events would happen again.

137

Εἰς τὸν σπόγγον

Χαῦνόν τι σῶμα θαῦμα πῶς ὕδωρ φέρει,
καὶ πῶς ἀπείροις ταῖς ὀπαῖς τετρημένον
ἔνδον φυλάττει τῶν ὀπῶν ὑγρὰν φύσιν.
Ὦ ποῖα ποιεῖς, δημιουργικὴ φύσις,
5 σὺν πᾶσιν ἄλλοις, οἷς τελεῖς ξενοτρόπως,
καὶ ῥευστὰ χαύνοις συγκρατοῦσα πανσόφως;

138

Εἰς τὸν Κυριακὸν καὶ Θεόδωρον τοὺς θυμελικοὺς ἀποκαρέντας

Οἱ πολλὰ πρὶν τέρψαντες ἡμᾶς ἐν βίῳ
φυγῇ βίου τέρπουσι νῦν Θεὸν Λόγον.

137

On the sponge

What a marvel, how this porous object holds water,
and how, although pierced by countless holes,
it keeps the liquid element inside these holes.
O what things can you work, creative nature,
besides everything else you accomplish in such wondrous   5
    ways,
if you also, so ingeniously, make porous objects hold fluids?

138

On the actors Kyriakos and Theodore, who were tonsured

Before, in this earthly life, they delighted us a great deal;
now, by abandoning this earthly life, they delight God the
    Word.

139

\<Εἰς τὰ ὑπὸ τοῦ Ἡρώδου ἀναιρεθέντα Ἅγια\> Νήπια

Πρῶτοι χέαντες αἷμα, Χριστέ, σ\<οῦ χάριν\>
. . .
ὁμήλικες σοὶ κέρδος ἔσχον ὡς μέγα.
. . .
5 ὅθεν φανέντες μάρτυρες πρῶτοι, Λόγε,
. . .

140

Εἰς τὴν γαμετὴν τοῦ στρατηγοῦ Λέοντος

. . .
\<κ\>οιμωμένου λέοντος ἐν σαῖς ἀγκάλαις
. . .
λέων γὰρ οὗτος ἦν βρυχήσηται μόνον,
5 . . .

139

On the Holy Innocents massacred by Herod

The first to shed their blood for your sake, Christ,

. . .

those of the same age as you received a great profit.

. . .

therefore, appearing as the first martyrs, Word,　　　　5

. . .

140

On the wife of the general Leo

. . .

a lion sleeping in your embrace

. . .

for he is a lion even when he only roars

. . .　　　　5

141

Εἰς τὴν βίβλον
τοῦ ἁγίου Ἰωάννου τοῦ Χρυσοστόμου,
τὴν λεγομένην Μαργαρῖται

Ναί, μαργαρῖται χειλέων σῶν οἱ λόγοι,
οὐκ αὐχένας κοσμοῦντες, οὐ στέρνων πλάτη,
μορφὰς δὲ μᾶλλον, Ἰωάννη, τὰς ἔσω·
ψυχῶν γάρ εἰσι κόσμος, οὐχὶ σωμάτων.

142

Εἰς τὸν πρωτοσπαθάριον Νικήταν
περὶ τῆς ὀφθαλμίας.

. . .
ἀφαιρεθεὶς δὲ τὰς ἀναγνώσεις ἄκων
      . . . <ἄν>ερ,
ὃν φωτί μοι φώτιζε τῶν σῶν ῥημάτων
5 . . .
ὀφθαλμίαν μοι τὴν μίαν λύσεις τέως

141

On the book
of Saint John Chrysostom,
the so-called *Pearls*

Yes, the words from your lips are truly pearls,
not adorning necks, or the expanse of a bosom,
but rather the interior forms, John;
for they are the adornment of souls, not bodies.

142

To the *protospatharios* Niketas,
about his eye disease

. . .
against my will deprived of reading,
. . . man,
whom please enlighten for me with the light of your words,
. . .   5
you will now dispel this one eye disease for me

. . .
εἰς ᾠὰ θερμὰ καὶ μάραθρά μοι πάρες
. . .
10   εἰ μὴ λαλοῦσι ψεῦδος Ἀσκληπιάδαι
. . .
οὐχὶ φθονοῦντες, ἀλλὰ μηδὲν εἰδότες.

143

<Εἰς τὸν ἀνδριάντα τοῦ Ἡρ>ακλέως,
τὸν ἱστάμενον ἐν
τῷ παλατίῳ τῶν Ἀρετῶν

. . . ἐκ λίθου·
φωνῇ δὲ πρὸς πίστωσιν ἐνδέει μόνη
. . . χεὶρ ἡ τεχνίτου
τοῦ παντελῶς ἔμψυχον Ἡρακλῆν ξέσαι.

. . .

permit me to have hot eggs and fennel

. . .

if the disciples of Asklepios do not tell lies,   10

. . .

not by jealousy, but by complete ignorance.

143

On the statue of Hercules
that stands in
the palace of Aretai

. . . of stone;
it lacks only a voice to give proof of this.
. . . the hand of a craftsman
for carving out a Hercules who is fully living.

144

<Εἰς τὸν ἅγιον Βονηφ>άτιον διὰ τὸν μετὰ τὴν ἀποτομὴν γέλωτα

… αὐτὴν τὴν φύσιν
γελᾷς, Βονηφάτιε, καὶ τετμημένος
… <ὑ>πὲρ Θεοῦ Λόγου
οἱ μαρτυροῦντες ζῶσι, καὶ τεθνηκότες.

145

<Εἰς … γρ>αός

Ταῖς ἱερείαις τῆς Πανάγνου Παρθένου
…
καὶ τὴν <π>ενιχρὰν τήνδε γραῦν ἐγγραπτέον
… ιον.
5 Ἄν οὖν μέλη σοι σεμνότης, ὡς λέγεις,
… <σεμνό>της.

144

On Saint Bonifatios because of his laughter after his beheading

. . . at nature itself
you laugh, Bonifatios, even when beheaded,
. . . for the Word of God
the martyrs live, even when they are dead.

145

On . . . an old woman

Among the holy devotees of the Holy Virgin
. . .
this poor old woman should also be inscribed
. . . .
Therefore, if you care about dignity, as you claim,   5
. . . dignity.

THE POEMS OF
JOHN MAUROPOUS

I

Πρόγραμμα εἰς τὴν ὅλην βίβλον

Πάλαι διδαχθεὶς ὡς ἄριστον πᾶν μέτρον,
τά τ᾽ ἄλλα πάντα μετριάζω, καὶ λόγους·
οἱ γὰρ περιττοὶ τῶν περιττῶν εἰκότως
χρῄζειν δοκοῦσι πραγμάτων τε καὶ λόγων·
5 ἐμοὶ δὲ—μικρῷ—πραγμάτων μικρὸς λόγος.
Καὶ τῶν λόγων οὖν μικρὸν ἀρκείτω μέρος,
εἰς δεῖγμα καὶ γνώρισμα τῶν ὅλων λόγων,
οὓς εἰς κενὸν κέκμηκα πολλάκις γράφων
(ἐῶ γὰρ εἰπεῖν οἷς ἐχρησάμην λέγων)·
10 τίς γὰρ περισσεία τε καὶ τί τὸ πλέον
ἐν παντὶ μόχθῳ τῷ βροτοῖς μοχθουμένῳ,
κἂν πολλὰ φυσήσωσιν ἐν τῷ νῦν βίῳ,
λέγοντες ἢ γράφοντες εἰς ἀπληστίαν,
ὄμβρους ἀμέτρους ἐκχέοντες ῥημάτων,
15 βροντῶντες, ἀστράπτοντες ἐξ εὐγλωττίας;
Πλεῖστον μὲν ὕψος οὐρανοῦ καὶ γῆς βάθος,
πλείστη δὲ τούτων εὐρυχωρία μέσον·
πνείτωσαν εἰς ἄπειρον· ἄφθονος τόπος·
οὐδεὶς στενώσει τήνδε τὴν ἀπειρίαν·

I

Preface to the entire book

I learned long ago that *all measure is supreme,*
and so I measure all things, words as well;
for excessive people seem to be in need,
as one might expect, of excessive things and words;
but as a small man I have small regard for things.   5
And thus let also a small share of words suffice
as a token and a sample of all my discourses,
which oftentimes I vainly toiled to write
(I refrain from mentioning those which I used in speeches);
for *what profit is there,* what additional advantage,   10
in all the labors mortal men exert,
even if they might get all puffed up in the here and now,
insatiable in what they write or speak,
gushing forth boundless torrents of verbiage,
while they thunder and flash in eloquence?   15
Heaven is plenty high, earth plenty deep,
and in between is plenty of vast space;
let them blow endlessly—there's room galore.
Nobody will confine this boundlessness;

20 πολλὰς φορὰς ἤνεγκεν ἤδη πνευμάτων,
    πλείους δ' ἐνεγκεῖν ἐστιν ἠὐτρεπισμένη,
    ἕως ἀποπνεύσουσιν ἐσχάτην μίαν,
    ἕως λυθῶσιν εἰς ἀδηλίας χάος,
    μηδὲν κατορθώσαντα πλὴν κενοὺς πόνους.
25 Ἀλλ' οἱ μὲν ὡς θέλουσιν· οὐδεὶς γὰρ φθόνος·
    ἐγὼ δὲ τούτους ἐξελών μου τοὺς λόγους
    πολλῶν ἀντ' ἄλλων—ἐμμέτρων, οὐκ ἐμμέτρων—
    μόνους φέρων δίδωμι τοῖς λόγων φίλοις,
    ὡς γεῦμα μικρὸν δαψιλοῦς ἀνθοσμίου·
30 οἷς ἡδονὴ γένοιτο ταῦτα μετρία,
    κόρος δ' ἀπέστω καὶ μέθη καὶ ναυτία.
    Ἔχοντες οὖν μοι τοὺς βραχεῖς, φίλοι, λόγους,
    αὐτοὶ δι' ἔργων μᾶλλον ἢ μακρῶν λόγων
    εὔχεσθε πᾶσιν εὐαρεστεῖν τὸν φίλον,
35 πλέον δὲ πάντων τῷ λογιστῇ καὶ Λόγῳ,
    ᾧ κἂν Λόγος λέγοιτο, πραγμάτων λόγος·
    ὃς ἔργα σῴζων ἐκ πυρὸς τὰ σὺν λόγῳ,
    εἰς καῦσιν ἐκδίδωσιν ἀπράκτους λόγους
    ὡς χόρτον, ὡς ἔρημον ἱκμάδος ξύλον.
40 Ἔγωγε τοίνυν ἔργα τῷ Λόγῳ φίλα
    φέροιμι, καὶ λάβοιμι τὴν σωτηρίαν·
    λόγων δὲ πολλῶν καὶ γραφῶν ἄλλοις μέλοι.

it has borne many gusts of wind already   20
and is prepared to bear still many more,
until they have all gusted out their last,
until they peter out in the abyss of obscurity
with nothing to show for all their empty toils.
Let them do as they please; I bear them no grudge.   25
I, however, have chosen these words of mine
out of many others — some poetry, some prose —
and offer just these gifts to friends of words
as a small taste of an array of wines.
May they be enjoyed in moderation,   30
without overindulgence, drunkenness, or nausea.
So, friends, now that you have my scanty words,
pray that through deeds and not through long speeches
your friend may be well pleasing to all men,
especially to the Word who judges all   35
and cares for deeds, though he is called the Word;
he saves from fire the works made with reason,
but gives up idle words to be burned
like grass or wood devoid of moisture.
May I, instead, bring offerings of works   40
dear to the Word, and may I find salvation;
let others worry about many words and writings.

Εἰς πίνακας μεγάλους τῶν ἑορτῶν· ὡς ἐν τύπῳ
ἐκφράσεως

2

Εἰς τὴν ἁγίαν τοῦ Χριστοῦ Γέννησιν

Τί τοῦτο; Φῶς ἤστραψεν ὡς ἐξ αἰθέρος,
ἀὴρ δὲ μεστὸς μουσικῆς συμφωνίας·
πρόσσχωμεν ὡς μάθωμεν. Ὦ μυστηρίου·
παρεμβολή τις ἀγγέλων κράζει μέγα,
5 "Θεῷ," λέγουσα, "δόξα τῷ σαρκουμένῳ."
"Καὶ πῶς Θεὸς σάρξ; Ποῦ τὸ θαῦμα, καὶ πόθεν;
Τὸ θαῦμα ποῦ;" Βάδιζε σὺν τοῖς ποιμέσιν·
ἐκεῖ γὰρ αὐτοῖς, ὡς ὁρᾷς, ἠπειγμένοις
καταφρόνησις γίνεται τῶν θρεμμάτων·
10 τούτοις συνελθὼν ἐμφοροῦ μοι τοῦ πόθου.
Ἄντρον θεωρεῖς, ἄντρον ἠμελημένον·
ἐν ᾧ φάτνη τις καὶ βρέφος καὶ παρθένος.
Οὐκοῦν Θεὸς σὸς τοῦτο τὸ βραχὺ βρέφος.
"Θεὸς πένης; Ἄοικος; Ἐν φαύλῳ ράκει;
15 Εἰς φῶς προελθὼν ἄρτι; Φεῦ, τί μοι λέγεις;"
Ψεῦδος μὲν οὐδέν, ἀλλ᾽ ἀληθῆ μανθάνεις·
καὶ μάρτυς ἀστὴρ ὃν κατ᾽ οὐρανὸν βλέπεις,
ἐκεῖθεν ἧκον τὸ βρέφος σοι δεικνύων,

On large paintings of the Feasts: in the manner of an
ekphrasis

2

On the holy Nativity of Christ

What's this? A light has shone as from the ether.
The air is filled with harmonious music;
let us take heed and learn—such mystery!
A company of angels shouts out loud:
"*Glory to God* who has become incarnate."   5
"How is God flesh? Where is this marvel, and whence?
Where is this marvel?" Walk with the shepherds;
as you see, they are rushing to that place,
forgetful of the tending of their flocks.
Go with them, let desire invigorate you!   10
You see a cave, an overlooked cave;
in it a manger, an infant, and a virgin—
and yes, that little baby is your God.
"God is poor? Homeless? In humble rags?
He's just seen the light of day? Ah! What is this you tell me?" 15
This is no lie. You are learning the truth.
A witness is the star you see in the sky,
showing you from where the infant came,

οὗτοί τε, συντρέχοντες ὡς πρὸς δεσπότην,
20 ὧν καὶ τὸ τερπνὸν ᾆσμα τῆς εὐφημίας.
Οἷς συμμελῳδεῖν, οὐκ ἀπιστεῖν σε πρέπον·
εἰς γὰρ χάριν σὴν ταῦτα πάντα συντρέχει—
Θεὸς βροτωθείς, ὡς θεώσῃ σὴν φύσιν·
πένης ὑπὲρ σοῦ, πλούσιον σὲ δεικνύων·
25 ἐπικροτοῦντες ἄγγελοι ταῖς ἐλπίσι·
μήτηρ ἄνανδρος· παρθένος βρεφοτρόφος·
μάγων τὰ λαμπρὰ δῶρα· ποιμένων δρόμος·
χαρᾶς τὰ πάντα μεστὰ καὶ θυμηδίας.
Τούτοις μὲν οὖν σύγχαιρε καὶ συμπροσκύνει.
30 Ἔα δὲ τόνδε τὸν κατηφῆ πρεσβύτην·
δάκνει γὰρ αὐτὸν ἄλλο τι κρυπτὸν πάθος.
Ἕξει δὲ τούτου μικρὸν ὑπνώσας λύσιν,
καὶ συγκροτήσει πᾶσιν ἡμῖν ἡδέως.

3

Εἰς τὴν Βάπτισιν

Ἀνὴρ κομήτης, αὐχμὸν ἄγριον τρέφων,
τρίχας καμήλου καὶ δορᾶς ζώνην φέρων,
ἄσαρκος, ἡμίγυμνος, ἀγγέλου τύπος,
ἥκει προφήτης καινὸς ἐξ ἐρημίας·

and these men running together as to their lord,
with their sweet song of praise. 20
You should join in their song, without any lack of faith.
It's for your good that all these things convene:
God made mortal to make your nature divine,
poor for your sake to make you rich,
the angels cheering in their expectation, 25
the husbandless mother, the virgin nursing a child,
the magi's splendid gifts, the shepherds coming at a run;
everything is full of joy and cheer.
So rejoice with them and join their worship,
and leave this downcast elderly man alone; 30
a different, secret feeling nags at him,
but after a short sleep he'll be released
and happily join us all as we rejoice.

3

On the Baptism

A long-haired man, dressed in savage squalor,
wearing *camel hair and a belt* made out of hide,
fleshless, half-naked—the image of an angel—,
arrives as a new prophet from the desert;

5 πρῶτον δ' ἑαυτοῦ Χριστὸν εἶναι μηνύων,
δείκνυσιν αὐτὸν πᾶσι τοῖς ἠθροισμένοις,
νέμει δὲ καὶ βάπτισμα τοῖς μυουμένοις.
Τούτῳ προελθὼν Χριστός, ὡς ἐγνωσμένος,
αἰτεῖ λαβεῖν βάπτισμα, τοῖς ἄλλοις ἴσα.
10 Ὁ δ' εὖ γινώσκων ὅστις οὗτος καὶ πόθεν,
πεῖραν τὸ πρᾶγμα, πεῖραν ἡγεῖται μόνον,
ὅθεν κραταιῶς ἀντιτείνει τῷ λόγῳ.
Πλὴν ἀλλ' ὑπείκει Δεσπότου προθυμίᾳ,
τρέμει δ' ὅμως τὴν χεῖρα, καὶ ψαύει μόλις,
15 ἄνω θεωρῶν, ὡς ἴλιγγον ἐκφύγοι·
μᾶλλον δὲ κἀκεῖ φρικτὸν ἄλλο τι βλέπει.
Περιστερὰ κάτεισιν εἰς γῆν ὑψόθεν,
ἣν οὐρανοὶ πέμπουσιν ἐκ τῶν σχισμάτων·
φωνὴ δ' ἐκεῖθεν πατρικὴ βροντᾷ μέγα,
20 Υἱὸν καλοῦσα Χριστὸν ἠγαπημένον.
Καὶ μαρτυρεῖ τὸ Πνεῦμα, τούτῳ προστρέχον
δι' ὃν κατῆλθεν, ᾧ σεμνῶς ἐφιζάνει.
Πτηνῷ δ' ἔοικεν ὀξυκινήτῳ φύσει·
περιστερᾶς γὰρ εἶδος, ὡς ἁπλουστέρας.
25 Συνεὶς δὲ ταῦτα καὶ ποταμὸς ἠρέμα
ἱστᾷ τὸ ῥεῖθρον τοῦ δρόμου καὶ προσμένει,
οὕτω γε τιμῶν τὴν τοῦ Θεοῦ παρουσίαν,
καὶ τὴν καλὴν κάθαρσιν ἀντιλαμβάνων,
ὡς πρῶτος αὐτὸς τὴν χάριν δεδεγμένος,
30 ἀρχὴ γένηται τῷδε τῷ μυστηρίῳ.
Τοῦτο βροτῶν φῶς, τοῦτο δευτέρα πλάσις·
χάρισμα καὶ σφράγισμα καὶ σωτηρία·

he says that Christ was before him,   5
and points him out to all the gathered throngs,
and administers baptism to the initiates.
Christ approaches him, as he is discerned,
and asks to be baptized like all the rest.
Well knowing who this man is and from where,   10
he takes this for a test and nothing more
and thus makes firm resistance to the request.
He nonetheless yields to the Lord's desire,
but his hand quivers and he barely touches him.
He looks above to stave off dizziness—   15
or no, because he sees there another awesome sight.
A dove comes down to earth from on high,
sent from heaven's furrowed clefts,
from which the Father's voice resounds like thunder,
proclaiming that Christ is his beloved Son.   20
The Spirit bears witness, hastening to the man
on whose account it descended, and perching solemnly on
     him.
It resembles a swiftly moving winged creature,
as gentle as a dove, whose form it takes.
The river is aware of this; it calmly stills   25
the flowing of its course and waits,
and thus shows honor for God's presence,
foreshadowing the noble purification,
so that as the first to receive this grace,
it may initiate this sacrament.   30
This is the light of mortals, the second creation.
It is a gift, a seal, a salvation.

τοῦτο κροτοῦσιν ἄγγελοι, τοῖς γηΐνοις
ἥδιστα συγχαίροντες ὡς θεουμένοις.
35 Ἀπευχαριστῶ πολλὰ τῷ λελουμένῳ·
τοῦτο γὰρ οὐδὲν εἰς ἀμοιβήν μοι πλέον.

4

Εἰς τὴν Μεταμόρφωσιν

Φρίξον, θεατά, τὴν ὁρωμένην θέαν,
καὶ στῆθι μακράν, εὐλαβῶς κάτω βλέπων,
μήπως καταστράψῃ σε Χριστὸς ἐγγύθεν,
καὶ ζημιωθῇς σαρκικῶν φῶς ὀμμάτων
5 ὡς Παῦλος ἄλλος, ἀστραπῇ βεβλημένος.
Ὁρᾷς μαθητὰς ἐνθάδε προκειμένους;
Οὐ γὰρ φέρειν ἔχουσι τὴν λαμπηδόνα.
Βλέπει δὲ Μωσῆς τὴν χάριν σὺν Ἠλίᾳ·
γνόφος γὰρ αὐτοῖς προξενεῖ παρρησίαν.
10 Σὺ δ' εἰ λαλούσης ἐκ γνόφου φωνῆς μόνον
θείας ἀκούσεις, εὐτυχεῖς, καὶ προσκύνει.

The angels cheer for this and happily share
the joy of earthly men, who are made divine.
I give my many thanks to the man who was cleansed;   35
there is no better reward for me than this.

4

On the Transfiguration

Shiver, viewer, at the sight you see;
keep a distance—with your eyes downcast in reverence,
or Christ will strike you with lightning from close by,
and you'll be deprived of the light of your bodily eyes,
struck by lightning, like another Paul.   5
Do you see here the disciples lying down?
The brilliance is too much for them to bear.
Yet Moses sees the grace, as does Elijah;
the darkness grants that they may freely speak.
But you, if you but hear the divine voice that   10
speaks from darkness, then you're blessed and should
    worship.

5

Εἰς τὸν Λάζαρον

Ὁ τῆς γραφῆς νοῦς; Ἀλλ' ἄκουε καὶ βλέπε.
Ἦν τις δίκαιος Λάζαρος, Χριστῷ φίλος·
τοῦτον θανόντα γῆ καλύπτει καὶ τάφος.
Αἱ σύγγονοι θρηνοῦσι τὸν τεθαμμένον·
5 τοῦ γὰρ φιλοῦντος ἀγνοοῦσι τὸ κράτος.
Πάρεστιν αὐτός· αἱ δὲ συντονωτέρως
κλαίουσι, κωκύουσι, προσπίπτουσί τε,
καθυστερεῖν λέγουσι τὴν παρουσίαν.
"Ὄψεσθε," φησί, "τὴν ἐμὴν ἐξουσίαν,"
10 ὁ Δημιουργός· "ποῦ δ' ὁ τοῦ φίλου τάφος;"
"Ἰδοὺ σέσηπε· τὸν τεταρταῖον βλέπεις,"
ἀπεκρίθησαν. Καὶ σκόπει τὸν Δεσπότην·
ὑποκριτὴς ἄριστος ὁ ζωηφόρος.
Σχολῇ βαδίζων δυσφορεῖ καὶ δακρύει·
15 ἐξ οὐρανοῦ τε δῆθεν αἰτεῖ τὴν χάριν.
Σὸν ἔργον, ὦ Κράτιστε. Τί βλέπεις ἄνω;
Ἐγγὺς δ' ὁ μάρτυς· εἰ κελεύσεις γὰρ μόνον,
τρέψεις τὸ πένθος εἰς ἑορτὴν αὐτίκα.
Οὐκοῦν κελεύει. "Δεῦρο" δ' "ἔξω," κραυγάσας,
20 ζωὴν ἑτοίμως ἐμπνέει τῷ κειμένῳ·
τοιαῦτα Χριστὸς οἶδε ποιεῖν τοῖς φίλοις.
Ἐξάλλεται γ' οὖν ζῶν ὁ νεκρὸς ἐκ τάφου.

5

On Lazarus

The meaning of the painting? Listen and look.
A just man, Lazarus, was a friend to Christ;
earth and a grave covered him when he died.
His female relatives mourn the man they buried,
unaware of the power of his friend.   5
He appears, and all the more intensely
do the women weep and shriek and fall before him,
saying that he has arrived too late.
"You will see my power," the Creator tells them,
"but where is my friend's grave?"   10
"Look how he rots; you see four days have passed,"
they answer him. Now pay attention to our Lord—
how fine an actor is the bringer of life.
He grieves and weeps and slowly walks about;
he pretends to beg for favor from heaven.   15
Your work, Almighty. Why do you turn your eyes on high?
The witness is near; if you but give the command,
you will turn mourning into celebration.
So he gives the command. He shouts, "Come out,"
and readily breathes life into the dead man.   20
Such things can Christ do for his friends.
The dead man then leaps out alive from the tomb.

Καὶ δὴ βαδίζει, κειρίαις ἐσφιγμένος.
Πλὴν ἀλλ᾽ ἀνεῖται, καὶ λυθεὶς ἀποτρέχει,
25 τὸ δεῖπνον (οἶμαι) σκευάσων ὁ γεννάδας
εἰς δεξίωσιν προσφιλοῦς εὐεργέτου,
δι᾽ ὃν πάλιν ζῇ, καὶ τροφῆς δεῖται πάλιν.

6

Εἰς τὰ Βαΐα

Ἄνοιγε τὰς σάς, ὦ Θεοῦ πόλις, πύλας,
ἃς ἠγάπησε Κύριος Παντοκράτωρ·
ἰδοὺ γὰρ αὐτὸς ἔρχεταί σοι Δεσπότης,
πρᾷος, δίκαιος, μέτριος, ταπεινόφρων,
5 ἔχων ὄχημα πῶλον εὐτελοῦς ὄνου,
καὶ τοὺς μαθητὰς ἐκ ποδῶν ὁδοιπόρους.
Παῖδες προπεμπέτωσαν αὐτὸν ἐν κρότοις·
δεῖ γὰρ τὸν ἀγνὸν ἐξ ἀγνῶν τιμὴν ἔχειν.
Κλάδους προσσειέτω δὲ νικητηρίους
10 ὃς τοῦ παρόντος χθὲς κατεῖδε τὸ κράτος.
Ὁ δ᾽ ἄλλος ὄχλος τοὺς χιτῶνας στρωννύων,
ὕμνους προσᾳδέτωσαν ἱκετηρίους·
Σωτὴρ γὰρ ἥκει πᾶσιν ὁ ζωηφόρος,
ὅσοι λαβεῖν θέλουσιν αὐτοῦ τὴν χάριν.

Indeed, he walks, still wrapped in his shroud.
Then he casts it off and runs off, set free.
The good man goes, I think, to fix a meal   25
to welcome his beloved benefactor,
who made him live again—and hungry once more.

6

On Palm Sunday

Open wide your gates, O city of God,
your gates beloved of the Lord Almighty.
Behold! He is coming now, your Master,
mild and just, moderate and humble,
a simple donkey foal is his vehicle,   5
and his disciples make their way by foot.
Let children clap their hands and escort him,
for the pure one should be honored by the pure.
Whoever saw his power yesterday
should wave the branches of the victory feast.   10
The rest of the crowd should spread out their garments,
and sing to him with hymns of supplication.
For the life-bearing Savior comes to all,
as many as desire to receive his grace.

15 Σὺ δ', ὦ ποθεινή, πρὸς τί τὰς σαυτῆς πύλας,
Σιών, ἀνοίξεις, ἔνδον ἐμπεπλησμένη
λῃστῶν ἀπηνῶν, δυσσεβῶν, μιαιφόνων,
οὓς οὐδ' ὁ νεκροὺς ἐξανιστῶν ῥᾳδίως
Ἅιδην τε νικῶν οὗτος ἐντρέψει τάχα;
20 Τοῖς γὰρ φόνον πνέουσιν αἰδὼς οὐκ ἔνι·
καὶ μᾶλλον, εἰ φθόνος τις αὐτοὺς ἐκφλέγει.
Ὅμως δ' ἄνοιγε, καὶ δέχου τὸν Δεσπότην·
καὶ γὰρ πάρεστι, τοῦ παθεῖν (οἶμαι) χάριν,
ἐπείπερ οἶδε καὶ παθὼν φεύγειν πάθος.
25 Οὐ δή τις ἡμῖν ἐστιν ἐντεῦθεν φόβος·
ὡσάννα τοίνυν· σῶσον, εὐλογημένε,
οὕτω προσηνὴς εἰσελαύνων καὶ φέρων
βροτοῖς ἅπασιν ἐκ παθῶν ἀφθαρσίαν.

7

Εἰς τὴν Σταύρωσιν

Νὺξ ταῦτα· καὶ γὰρ ἥλιον κρύπτει σκότος,
ἀχλὺς δὲ πληροῖ πάντα καὶ βαθὺς ζόφος.
Πῶς οὖν θεωρῶ, Δημιουργὲ Χριστέ μου,
σταυρούμενόν σε; Φεῦ· τί τοῦτο; Καὶ πόθεν
5 Σωτῆρα κόσμου προσδοκῶν σε μακρόθεν,

But why, O Sion, city of heart's desire,   15
will you open your gates when you are filled within
with savage brigands, impious men, and killers,
who cannot easily be brought to repentance
even by the one who awakens the dead and conquers Hades?
People who breathe murder have no shame,   20
especially if some envy inflames them.
But now open the gates, and receive your Lord.
He is here, I believe, for Passion's sake,
since he escapes the passions even in his Passion.
So, therefore, we do not have any fear.   25
Hosanna! Bring salvation, blessed one,
entering in such a kindly way and bringing
all mortals incorruption from passions.

7

On the Crucifixion

It is night here; darkness hides the sun.
Mist and deep gloom fill everything.
How can it be then, Creator Christ, that I now see
you crucified? Alas, what is this? Why is it that,
while I long expected you to be the world's Savior,   5

νῦν ὡς κακοῦργον εἰς ἀρᾶς ξύλον βλέπω;
Ἀπῆλθεν εἶδος· κάλλος οὐκ ἔχεις ἔτι·
μήτηρ δὲ θρηνεῖ καὶ σὸς ἠγαπημένος,
μόνοι παρόντες τῶν πρὸ μικροῦ σοι φίλων.
10 Φροῦδοι μαθηταί· καὶ πτερωτοὶ δ' οἰκέται,
μάτην περιτρέχουσι μεστοὶ δακρύων·
οὐ γὰρ βοηθεῖν εὐποροῦσι τῷ πάθει.
Μέγας δ' ἄπεστι σὸς Πατὴρ Παντοκράτωρ,
μόνον λιπών σε ταῦτα πάσχειν, ὡς λέγεις,
15 καίτοι προεῖπες οὐχὶ λειφθῆναι μόνος,
συνόντος αὐτοῦ καὶ τὰ νῦν πάσχοντί σοι·
ἀλλ' οὐκ ἄπεστι· πνεῦμα σὸν γὰρ λαμβάνει,
συνευδοκῶν τε καὶ συνών σοι, καὶ φέρων
Υἱοῦ τελευτὴν ἠγαπημένου βλέπειν.
20 Δεῖ γάρ με, δεῖ, σοὶ συνθανεῖν, εὐεργέτα,
ὡς συμμετασχῶ τῆς ἐγέρσεως πάλιν.
Οὕτως ἔδοξε· τοῦτο τῆς εὐσπλαγχνίας
ὑμῶν πρὸς ἡμᾶς ἡ μεγίστη χρηστότης.
Εὐγνωμονοῦμεν· πλὴν τάχυνον ἐκ τάφου.
25 Σπεύσεις δὲ πάντως· ἥλιος γὰρ ἐνθάδε,
ὁ πρὶν ζοφωθεὶς καὶ κρυβείς, εἰς σὴν χάριν
ἔλαμψε φαιδρὸν αὖθις ἀνθ' ἑωσφόρου,
σὲ τὸν μέγιστον ἥλιον προμηνύων
ἐκ γῆς ἀνασχεῖν φῶς τε πέμψειν αὐτίκα.
30 Ἴδοιμεν οὖν λάμποντα καὶ σέ, Χριστέ μου,
ὥσπερ τὸ σὸν ποίημα, τὴν νῦν ἡμέραν,
δι' ἧς ὁρῶμεν τούσδε τοὺς θείους τύπους,
καὶ σοὶ συναστράψωμεν ἐκ γῆς καὶ τάφων.

I now see you as a criminal on accursed wood?
Your comeliness has gone, your beauty vanished.
Your mother and your beloved disciple lament you;
they alone are present of all your former friends.
Disciples—gone; followers—taken wing;   10
while these two walk round in vain, filled with tears,
unable to help your suffering.
Your great Almighty Father, absent too,
leaves you alone to suffer these things, as you say,
though you had foretold you would not be left alone,   15
and that he'd join you in your present ordeal.
But no! He has not left; he takes your spirit,
sympathizing with you, being with you, enduring
the sight of his dying beloved Son.
I too must, yes must, die with you, O benefactor,   20
in turn, to take part in your resurrection.
Thus it is decreed. This is the greatest
kindness that your mercy grants to us.
We thank you for this; now hurry from the grave.
You will surely hasten, for the sun is here;   25
previously hidden and obscured, it now brilliantly shines
        again
for your sake, instead of the morning star,
proclaiming you to be the greatest sun,
which soon will rise from earth and send its light.
So may we see you too shining, my Christ,   30
just like the present day, your creation,
through which we look upon these divine forms,
and may we shine with you from earth and the tombs.

8

Εἰς τὴν Ἀνάστασιν

Σκόπει, σκόπει τὸ θαῦμα τοῦ τεθαμμένου,
ἕως θεατόν ἐστι, πρὶν παραδράμῃ,
μήπως ἀπιστῇς ὕστερον λαλουμένῳ,
θέλων προσάπτειν τοῖς ὑπὲρ φύσιν φύσιν.
5 Τοίνυν, μαθητὰ τῶν ἀπορρήτων, ὅρα
καὶ ζῶντα Χριστὸν αὖθις· εὖγε τοῦ τάχους·
ὡς ὀξὺς εἰς ἔγερσιν ὁ ζωηφόρος,
τάφον κατοικεῖν νεκρὸς οὐκ εἰθισμένος.
Τριήμερον γοῦν, οὐ τριέσπερον, βλέπεις,
10 κἂν ζωοποιῇ τετραημέρους φίλους.
Νῦν δ᾽ ἐξαναστὰς τοὺς γενάρχας ἑλκύει
χερσὶ κραταιαῖς ἐκ παλαιῶν μνημάτων.
Πρῶτον δ᾽ ἀνορθοῖ τὸ προπεπτωκὸς πάλαι·
ἔπειτα τὸν βρίθοντα τόνδε πρεσβύτην,
15 μεθ᾽ ὧν ἅπασαν ἐξεγείρει τὴν φύσιν,
δι᾽ ἣν κατελθὼν μέχρι σαρκὸς καὶ τάφου,
Ἅιδην πατεῖ τύραννον ἀνθρωποφθόρον·
πλὴν ὡς ἀπαρχὴν τοῦ γένους τοῦ σοῦ δέχου
Ἀδάμ, Δαβίδ τε, καὶ σοφὸν Σολομῶνα·
20 οὓς ἡ γραφή σοι ζῶντας ὧδε δεικνύει,
ὡς τοῦ διδόντος τὴν ἔγερσιν πατέρας·
αὐτὸς μὲν οὖν τοὺς ἄνδρας ἐκ νεκρῶν ἔχεις,

8

On the Resurrection

See! See the marvel of the buried man,
while it can still be seen, before it passes away,
so you will not doubt one who speaks of it later,
in your desire to apply nature's laws to the supernatural.
So, disciple of the mysteries, 5
see Christ among the living again! Hurrah, for such speed!
So avid is the bearer of life to wake,
unused to dwelling as a corpse in a tomb.
After three days, not three evenings, you see him,
though he revives his friends after four days. 10
Now his strong hands drag out of the ancient tombs
our first forefathers and stand them upright.
First he raises what fell long ago,
then raises this weighty, venerable man,
and thus he resurrects all humankind. 15
For their sake he came down to the flesh and the grave,
and now tramples Hades, the man-destroying tyrant.
Accept now as the first of your kindred
Adam, David, and Solomon the wise.
The image shows them to you alive, 20
as forefathers of the one who gives new life.
Now you have these men risen from the dead,

Εὔαν γυναῖκες, τὴν ἁπάντων μητέρα.
Οὗτοι δὲ τυφλούσθωσαν ἐκ φόβου τέως
25 φρουροὶ μάταιοι, δυστυχεῖς ὑπηρέται·
βάλλει γὰρ αὐτοὺς ἀστραπαῖς ὁ Δεσπότης,
ὡς μὴ θεαθῇ δυσσεβῶν ὄψει πάλιν.
Σὺ δ᾽ ἀξιωθεὶς ὧν ὁρᾷς θεαμάτων
ἐπικρότησον· σὴν ἀνάπλασιν βλέπεις·
30 καὶ χαῖρε, χαῖρε· Πάσχα τοῦτο Κυρίου.

9

Εἰς τὴν Ψηλάφησιν

Χριστός, μαθηταί, Χριστός ἐστι καὶ πάλιν·
θαρσεῖτε. Μὴ κλονεῖσθε τῇ ξένῃ θέᾳ,
μηδὲ πτοεῖσθε τὰς ἀδήλους εἰσόδους·
οὐδεὶς γὰρ ὑμᾶς ὄψεται κεκρυμμένους.
5 Ἀλλ᾽ αὐτὸς ἀκράτητον εἰληφὼς φύσιν
οὕτω διέδρα καὶ τάφον κεκλεισμένον.
Ἀλλ᾽ ὢ τί τοῦτο; Νῦν γὰρ ὥσπερ ᾐσθόμην,
οὐχ οὗτος ὁ πρὶν εὔστομος δημηγόρος;
Οἷον κάτω νένευκεν ἐκπεπληγμένος.
10 Ἡ χεὶρ δὲ ναρκᾷ, καὶ παρειμένα τρέμει,
πλευρὰν φλέγουσαν ψηλαφᾶν ὡρμημένη.

and women have their Eve, the mother of all.
And these—let them be blinded now with fear;
these useless guardians and wretched servants.   25
The Lord strikes them with lightning bolts,
so impious eyes will not see him again.
But you, deemed worthy of the sights you see,
clap your hands! You see your renewal.
Rejoice, rejoice, this is the Lord's Easter.   30

9

On the Appearance to the Disciples

Christ, disciples! Christ is here again!
Take heart! Do not be upset by this strange sight;
fear not his inexplicable entrance;
while you are hidden, nobody will see you.
Wielding his invincible nature,   5
he escaped also the sealed tomb.
But what is this? I noticed only now,
is this not he who was such an eloquent speaker?
How he looks downward now, astonished!
His hand goes numb and trembles haltingly,   10
urged on to touch the body's flaming side.

Χριστὸν προδήλως, ὦ φιλοπρᾶγμον, βλέπεις,
ὡς ἡ παροῦσα μαρτυρεῖ σοι δειλία.
Νῦν οὖν πέπεισο, καὶ λιπὼν τοὺς πρὶν λόγους
15 θαύμαζε καὶ κήρυττε τὸν ζωηφόρον.

10

Εἰς τὴν Ἀνάληψιν

Οὐκ ἦν ὁ Χριστὸς σαρκικῶν ἐκ σπερμάτων,
κἂν σὰρξ προῆλθε μητρικῶν ἐξ αἱμάτων,
ἀλλ' ἐκ Θεοῦ φύς. Καὶ κατελθὼν ὑψόθεν,
εἰς οὐρανοὺς ἄνεισι πρὸς Θεὸν πάλιν.
5 Καὶ σῶμα θεῖον ἐκ ταφῆς ἀφθαρτίσας
φέρει σὺν αὐτῷ, καὶ καλύπτεται νέφει.
Οὗτοι δ' ἄνω βλέπουσιν ἐκπεπληγμένοι,
καὶ χεῖρας ἐκτείνοντες ὡς πρὸς αἰθέρα,
ζητοῦσιν ὥσπερ τὴν σύναρσιν ἐκ πόθου
10 φίλοι μαθηταὶ καὶ τεκοῦσα Παρθένος.
Ὅθεν καταστέλλουσιν αὐτοὺς ἠρέμα
λόγοι προσηνεῖς ἀγγέλων εὐαγγέλων,
οὕτω λέγοντες, Χριστὸν ἥξειν καὶ πάλιν,
ὥσπερ κατεῖδον ἄρτι γῆθεν ἡρμένον·
15 πέρας γὰρ εἶναι τοῦτο τοῦ μυστηρίου.
Ταῦτα προδήλως ὁ γραφεὺς τῶν εἰκόνων
τύποις διδάσκει, τὴν ἀλήθειαν σέβων.

340

Clearly, O inquisitive man, you see Christ,
as your present lack of courage attests.
So now have confidence; cast off your earlier words
and marvel, and proclaim the bringer of life.   15

10

On the Ascension

Christ did not emerge from bodily seed,
though he came forth as flesh from mother's blood.
He is God's offspring, come down from on high,
and now he ascends again to God in heaven.
He takes out of the tomb with him the holy   5
body he made deathless, and is enveloped in cloud.
And these people, his dear disciples and the Virgin
who gave birth to him, look up astonished,
stretching out their hands, as to the ether,
to eagerly ask, it seems, to ascend with him.   10
And so, sweet words from angels of good tidings
serenely reassure them,
telling them that Christ will come again,
as they just saw him, raised from the earth;
this will be the mystery's completion.   15
The painter of these images clearly teaches
us this with forms, honoring the truth.

II

Εἰς τὴν Πεντηκοστήν

Τὴν ἐσχάτην τε καὶ μεγίστην ἡμέραν,
γράφει πρὸς ἀκρίβειαν ἡ σοφὴ τέχνη,
καθ' ἣν τὰ φρικτὰ θαυματουργεῖται τάδε.
Διώροφόν τι τοὺς ἀποστόλους φέρει,
5 ἄφνω δ' ἄνωθεν ἦχος ἐμπίπτει μέγας,
καὶ φῶς τε καὶ πῦρ συγκάτεισιν ὑψόθεν,
γλώσσας ἀπαρτίζοντα τὰς ὁρωμένας,
ἃς οὐκ ἔγνω τις γηγενῶν πλὴν ἐνθάδε.
Τούτων δ' ἕκαστος προσλαβὼν αὐτῶν μίαν
10 φωνὰς δίδωσι τοῖς παροῦσι ποικίλας,
ἄλλως πρὸς ἄλλον ἐκλαλῶν τὴν νῦν χάριν.
Ἡ συνδρομὴ δὲ πρὸς τὸ θαῦμα τῶν ὄχλων
διδασκάλους δείκνυσι τοὺς καθημένους
ἅπασιν αὐτοῖς προσλαλοῦντας γνησίως,
15 εἰ καὶ συνῆλθον ἐκ γενῶν ἀλλοθρόων·
πλήθη γὰρ ἐθνῶν εἰσὶ συμμεμιγμένων.
Σὺ δ' εἰ ξενίζῃ πρὸς τὸ τῆς θέας ξένον,
ἄκουε καὶ πίστευε τοῖς λαλουμένοις·
καὶ δοὺς σεαυτὸν τοῖσδε τοῖς πυριπνόοις,
20 Θεὸν τὸ Πνεῦμα τοῦ Θεοῦ δόξαζέ μοι,
τὸ ταῦτα πάντα θαυματουργοῦν ἐνθέως —
φῶς, πῦρ, πνοήν τε καὶ σοφοὺς ἀγραμμάτους.

II

On Pentecost

Ingenious art here paints in precise detail
the final and most important day
on which these awesome marvels are performed.
The apostles stand on a two-storied structure,
and suddenly from on high a great sound descends;   5
with it, light and fire come down from heaven,
taking on the shapes of visible tongues,
which no man has ever seen except here.
Each apostle takes one of these tongues,
and speaks in various languages to those there,   10
telling of the present grace to everyone differently.
The multitudes assembled for this marvel
demonstrate that the seated are teachers
who speak in their own tongue to them all,
even though they came from foreign places,   15
the masses forming a mix of many nations.
If you are astonished at this wondrous sight,
listen and believe the things that are said;
surrender to these fire-breathing men,
and give glory to God's Spirit as a God,   20
who worked all these wonders divinely:
light, fire, breath, and learned unlettered men.

12

Εἰς τὸν Ἠλίαν τρεφόμενον ὑπὸ κόρακας

Ζηλωτά, παιδεύθητι μακροθυμίαν,
καὶ μὴ τὸ πῦρ ἄνωθεν, ἀλλ᾽ ὕδωρ βρέχε·
καὶ σὲ τρέφει κόραξ γάρ, οὐ καταφλέγει.
Ὅθεν διδαχθεὶς ὡς κακὸν λιμὸς μέγα,
5 ἄρδευε τὴν γῆν, καὶ τὰ γῆς ζῷα τρέφε·
χρήζεις τροφῆς γὰρ καὶ σὺ τοῖς ἄλλοις ἴσα.

13

Εἰς τὴν κατὰ τὸν ἅγιον Παῦλον καὶ τὸν Χρυσόστομον ἱστορίαν

Σίγα, θεατά, καὶ βραχὺν μεῖνον χρόνον,
μήπως ταράξῃς τὴν καλὴν συνουσίαν,
καὶ ζημιώσῃς κόσμον ἐνθέους λόγους·
ἐξ οὐρανοῦ γὰρ ἄρτι τούτους τοῦ τρίτου
5 ἥκει κομίζων Παῦλος αἰθεροδρόμος·

344

12

On Elijah being fed by the ravens

Zealous one, learn how to have patience,
and let water, not fire, rain from on high;
the raven too is feeding you, not burning you.
So, having learned what great evil hunger is,
irrigate the earth, and feed earth's creatures;   5
for you too need the same food as all the rest.

13

On the picture of Saint Paul and
Saint Chrysostom

Be silent, viewer, wait a little while,
so you do not disturb this beautiful encounter
and deprive the world of inspired words.
Paul, speeding through the air, comes from the *third
heaven,* bringing these words down with him;   5

κινεῖ δὲ χεῖρα πρὸς γραφῆς ὑπουργίαν
οἰκουμένης τὸ θαῦμα, τὸ χρυσοῦν στόμα.
Ζήλου τὸ λοιπὸν ὃν πρὸ τῶν θυρῶν βλέπεις,
τούτῳ τε συνθαύμαζε καὶ συγκαρτέρει.

14

Εἰς τὸν ἅγιον Χρυσόστομον

Ἢ γλῶσσαν εὑρὼν πῦρ πνέουσαν, ζωγράφε,
μόνην ἀφῆκας, εὐλαβηθεὶς τὴν φλόγα;
Ἢ πάντα τολμῶν προσγράφεις καὶ τὸ φλέγον;
Καὶ φθέγγεται μὲν καὶ λαλεῖ παραινέσεις,
5   ἀλλ' ἐστὶν ἰσχνόφωνος ἐξ ἀσιτίας.
Ἐμὸν τὸ λεῖπον· οὐ γὰρ οὓς παρεσχόμην.
Νῦν οὖν ὑποσχὼν γνώσομαι τί μοι λέγει.
Βαβαῖ· καταφρονεῖν με πείθει τοῦ βίου.

the golden mouth, the world's marvel, then
moves his hand to the work of writing them down.
So strive to be like the man you see at the door;
and marvel with him, and with him be patient.

14

On Saint Chrysostom

Perhaps you encountered a fire-breathing tongue, O painter,
so that, dreading the flame, you left only this unpainted?
Or, in your utter boldness, do you add also the fire?
Yes, he calls aloud and utters admonitions,
but his voice is weak from fasting.   5
It is my fault—I did not lend my ear.
But now listening attentively, I will grasp what he tells me.
Alas! He persuades me to reject this life.

15

Εἰς τὸν ἅγιον Γρηγόριον τὸν Θεολόγον

Τί σοι τὸ σύννουν βλέμμα βούλεται, πάτερ;
Λέξειν τι καινὸν ἐκβιάζῃ μοι τάχα;
Ἀλλ' οὐκ ἂν εὕροις· πᾶν γὰρ ἀνθρώποις ξένον
ἐγνώρισαν φθάσαντες οἱ σοί μοι λόγοι.

16

Εἰς τὸν Μέγαν Βασίλειον

Ἐπιπρέπει τις σεμνοποιὸς ὠχρότης
ἐξ ἐγκρατείας τῷ σοφῷ διδασκάλῳ.
Ἀλλ' εἰ λαλήσει (ζῆν δοκεῖ γὰρ καὶ τύπος),
τρυφὴ τὸ χρῆμα, φαιδρότης καὶ τερπνότης.
5 Οὐκοῦν τὰ χείλη πρὸς λόγους κίνει, πάτερ,
τοὺς καὶ λίθους θέλγοντας· ἀλλὰ μὴ λέγε
ἅπερ διδάσκων εἰς συναίσθησιν ἄγεις·
δάκνειν γὰρ οἶδε ταῦτα, κἂν στάζῃ μέλι,
τοὺς ἕλκεσι βρύοντας· ἐξ ὧν στυγνότης,
10 πρὸς ἣν ἐπαρκεῖς καὶ γραφεὶς οὕτω μόνον.

15

On Saint Gregory the Theologian

What signifies your thoughtful look, O father?
Perhaps you strain to tell me something new?
You will find nothing, for your words have
already taught me all that is new for mankind.

16

On Basil the Great

A dignifying pallor befits
the wise teacher because of his abstinence.
But should he speak—for even his image seems to be alive—
then all is joy, brilliance, and delight.
So, father, move your lips to utter words,   5
which charm even the stones; but do not say those
teachings by which you lead us toward self-awareness,
because such words, though dripping honey, can sting
men teeming with sores; and hence the gloominess
which you, just by being painted this way, can instill.   10

17

Εἰς τοὺς τρεῖς ἅμα

Τριὰς μὲν εὗρεν ἰσαρίθμους συμμάχους,
ὑπερμάχους δ' ἔστησε πίστις ἐνθάδε,
ἀνάξιον κρίνασα καὶ πόρρω λόγου
ὧν τοῖς λόγοις σύνεστι, μὴ καὶ τοῖς τύποις.
5 Ὅθεν γραφέντες ζῆν δοκοῦσι καὶ λέγειν
ἅπερ φέρουσιν αἱ θεόγραφοι βίβλοι.
Ταύτην ἀμοιβὴν τοῖς διδασκάλοις νέμει
εὔνους μαθητὴς οἰκέτης Ἰωάννης.

18

Εἰς τὸν ἅγιον Νικόλαον

Αὐτόν, πάτερ, σὲ προσκυνῶ τε καὶ βλέπω,
αὐτὸν κρατῶ σε· σὸν δὲ θαῦμα καὶ τόδε.
Ἀνὴρ ἐναργῶς πρεσβύτης. Ἐκ χρωμάτων
σαφὲς τὸ σῶμα· πνεῦμα δ' ἄν σοι καὶ λόγον
5 ἐμὸν παρέσχον, εἰ λαβεῖν κατηξίους.
Οὕτως ἔχειν πόθος με πείθει καὶ λέγειν.

17

On the three together

The Trinity has found like-numbered allies,
and faith has stationed her defenders here,
for she has deemed it foolish and unworthy
to be with them in words but not in images.
So, painted, they appear to live and to speak   5
the words that their divinely inspired books contain.
Their well-intentioned servant and student John
offers this to his teachers as his due payment.

18

On Saint Nicholas

It's you yourself to whom I bow and whom I see, father;
it's you I hold. This too is your miracle.
Plainly, you are elderly. Through colors
your body is discerned. I'd give you my breath,
my speech as well, if you should deign to take it.   5
Desire makes me behave and speak this way.

19

Εἰς τὸν ἅγιον Κωνσταντῖνον
τὸν ἐν τῷ Καμηλῷ

Κόσμῳ νεκρωθεὶς καὶ Θεῷ ζήσας, πάτερ,
ἀπεκρύβης ζῶν, καὶ θανὼν ἀνευρέθης.
Κράζεις δὲ σιγῶν, καὶ βοᾷς ἐκ τοῦ τάφου,
σάλπιγγα τὰς σὰς θαυματουργίας ἔχων.
5 Ἐντεῦθεν ὁ πρὶν πᾶσιν ἠγνοημένος
νῦν καὶ βασιλεῖς προσκυνητὰς ἑλκύεις,
ὧν ἔργον ἡ στέφουσα τὴν σορὸν χάρις,
πᾶν τερπνὸν ὕλης καὶ τέχνης πᾶν ποικίλον
φέρουσα, καὶ τέρπουσα τοὺς θεωμένους.
10 Δι' ἧς ἄριστα τὴν νοητήν σου δίδως
δόξαν θεωρεῖν, ἐν Θεῷ κεκρυμμένην,
ἕως παρ' αὐτοῦ τὸ πρὸς ἀξίαν λάβοις.

19

On Saint Constantine
in Kamilas

Dead to the world, alive to God, father,
you hid while living, and you were discovered after your
    death.
You shout while silent and cry out from the grave;
your trumpet is the miracles you work.
And thus you, who were once unknown to all,   5
now attract emperors to venerate you.
The beauty crowning your coffin is their work,
bearing all delight of materials, all varied charms of art,
delighting those who see it.
Through this beauty you grant that your spiritual   10
glory may be seen in perfection, though hidden in God,
until you shall receive your due from him.

20

Εἰς τὴν Θεοτόκον δακρύουσαν

"Ὦ τοῦ πάθους, Δέσποινα, καὶ σὺ δακρύεις;
Καὶ τίς βοηθὸς τῶν παρ' ἡμῖν δακρύων,
εἰ καὶ σὺ πάσχεις ἄξια θρηνῳδίας;
Τίς ἐλπὶς ἄλλη; Τίς παράκλησις; Φράσον."
5   "Καὶ μὴν ἐχρῆν σε μᾶλλον εὐθύμως ἔχειν,
ἄνθρωπε, χρηστοῦ τοῦ τέλους προκειμένου·
ἄλλοις γὰρ ἄλλο φάρμακον σωτηρίας,
ἐμὸν δὲ πένθος κοσμικοῦ πένθους λύσις."

21

Εἰς τοὺς ἁγίους Ἀναργύρους

Ἰδού, τί τερπνὸν ἢ γέμον θυμηδίας
ὡς αὐταδέλφων φιλτάτων συνοικία;
Ἢν ἡ παροῦσα μαρτυρεῖ τούτοις στάσις,
καθ' ἣν ὁμοῦ σύνεισιν οἱ γεγραμμένοι.
5   Ἀνάργυρος μὲν ὁ τρόπος τοῖς συγγόνοις·
τέχνη δ' ἰατροί· θαυματουργοί τε πλέον.

20

On the weeping Mother of God

"What suffering is this, O Lady, that you too weep?
Who, then, will be our helper in our tears,
if you too suffer things worthy of lament?
What hope is left? What consolation? Tell us."
"Yet you ought rather to rejoice, O man,   5
since the longed-for end draws near.
Others have other remedies that bring salvation,
but my grief is deliverance from worldly sorrow."

21

On the Holy Anargyroi

Behold, what is as pleasant or as joyful,
as loving brothers living together?
This composition bears witness to this concord,
joining their painted images together.
The brothers' manner is to accept no money;   5
as far as their art, they are doctors, but wonderworkers to
    boot.

Ἥν οὖν θέλεις, ἄμισθον ἐξαιτοῦ χάριν·
θεία γὰρ ἐγγύς, εὐτυχὴς δὲ καὶ τέχνη.

22

Εἰς τὸν ἅγιον Παῦλον ὑπαγορεύοντα, καὶ Λουκᾶν καὶ Τιμόθεον παρεστῶτας καὶ γράφοντας

Ὁ ζῶντα Χριστὸν ἐν μέσῃ ψυχῇ φέρων
ἐκεῖθεν ἕλκει τοὺς ἀπορρήτους λόγους,
οὓς καὶ διδαχθεὶς σκέπτεται πῶς ἐκφράσοι·
τοῖς ἀξίοις γὰρ πᾶσιν ἐξειπεῖν θέλει.
5 Ἀλλ' οἱ παρόντες εὐφυεῖς ὀξυγράφοι
ὡς μυστικοὺς γράφουσι τοὺς λόγους τέως·
φθόγγος γὰρ οὔπω γῆν προῆλθεν εἰς ὅλην,
κἂν πᾶσαν ἐπλήρωσεν ὕστερον κτίσιν.

So, whatever favor you desire, ask for free,
for the divine favor is near, and their art is successful.

22

On Saint Paul dictating,
and Luke and Timothy standing by him
and writing

He who bears the living Christ deep in his soul
draws ineffable thoughts from there.
He learns them, and ponders how to express them,
wishing to tell them to all worthy people.
But the skillful secretaries who are present   5
for now write down the words as if in confidence;
for his voice had not yet spread to all the earth,
even though later it filled the entire world.

23

Εἰς τὴν κηδείαν τοῦ Χρυσοστόμου καὶ τὴν κατὰ τὸν Ἀδέλφιον ἱστορίαν

Τὸν ἄγγελον μὲν ἐν βροτοῖς ὁ πρεσβύτης
ζητῶν ἔκαμνε, καὶ ποθῶν ἐδυσφόρει,
ἐπείπερ εἶδεν ὡς βροτὸν τεθνηκότα,
οὕτω τε νεκρὸν πρὸς ταφὴν ἀπηγμένον.
5 Ἐν οὐρανοῖς δὲ τὸν ποθούμενον βλέπει,
τοῦ προσκυνητοῦ σφόδρα πλησίον θρόνου·
οὗτος πρέπων γὰρ ἦν Ἰωάννῃ τόπος,
σὺν τοῖς Χερουβὶμ ὡς ἐχρῆν τεταγμένῳ.

24

Εἰς τὸν ἀρχάγγελον Μιχαήλ

Φῶς, πνεῦμα καὶ πῦρ οἴδαμεν τοὺς ἀγγέλους,
παντὸς πάχους τε καὶ πάθους ὑπερτέρους.
Ἀλλ᾿ ὁ στρατηγὸς τῶν ἀΰλων ταγμάτων
ἔστηκε γραπτὸς ὑλικῶν ἐκ χρωμάτων.

23

On the funeral of Chrysostom and the picture of Adelphios

The old man struggled to find the angel
among mortal men. Longing for him,
he was distressed to see him dead, as a mortal man,
carried off to the tomb, a corpse.
But he sees the man he longed for in heaven,   5
right beside the throne that all must worship;
for that is the place befitting John,
joining, as is right, the ranks of the Cherubim.

24

On the archangel Michael

Light, spirit, fire—we know what angels are,
beyond all substance and all suffering.
But the commander of the immaterial cohorts
stands here painted in material colors.

5 Ὦ πίστις, οἷα θαυματουργεῖν ἰσχύεις·
ὡς ῥᾷστα μορφοῖς τὴν ἀμόρφωτον φύσιν·
πλὴν ἡ γραφὴ δείκνυσι τὸν γεγραμμένον
οὐχ ὡς πέφυκεν, ὡς δ' ἔδοξε πολλάκις.

25

Εἰς τὸν ἀσπασμὸν Πέτρου καὶ Παύλου

Ἐξιστόρει μοι, Παῦλε, τὸν μέγαν Πέτρον·
λέγεις γὰρ ἐλθεῖν εἰς Σιὼν τούτου χάριν.
Δίδου δὲ καὶ φίλημα, σύμβολον πόθου,
περιπλακεὶς ἥδιστα τῷ ποθουμένῳ.
5 Ἀντάσπασαι δὲ καὶ σύ, Πέτρε, γνησίως
τὸν σὸν διώκτην, τοῦ πάλαι λυθεὶς φόβου,
ἐπείπερ οὕτως εἶδες ἠλλοιωμένον·
Χριστοῦ μαθητής ἐστι, καὶ ζήλου πνέει,
ἀλλ' οὐκ ἀπειλῆς, ὡς πρὸ τούτου, καὶ φόνου.
10 Ὅθεν συνεργὸν προσλαβὼν τὸν γεννάδαν,
σκέπτεσθε κοινὴν σκέψιν, ὡς σεσωσμένην
Χριστῷ παραστήσαιτε τὴν οἰκουμένην.

O faith, what wonders you have the power to work!　　　5
How easily you shape shapeless nature!
And yet, the image shows the painted subject
not as he was by nature, but as he often appeared.

25

On the embrace of Peter and Paul

Tell me, Paul, about the great Peter,
for you say you came to Sion for his sake.
Give him a kiss as well, a symbol of love,
and give your beloved friend a sweet embrace.
And Peter, embrace your persecutor warmly in turn,　　　5
for you were set free from your former dread
the moment you saw that man transformed.
He is Christ's disciple, breathing zeal
instead of *threats and murder,* as before.
Therefore take this noble man as a comrade,　　　10
and devise a common plan for how
to save the world and present it to Christ.

26

Εἰς τὸν Σωτῆρα

Τοὺς οὐρανοὺς ἔχοντα, Δέσποτα, θρόνον,
καὶ γῆν πατοῦντα, καὶ τὸ πᾶν πληροῦντά σε
ἐνταῦθα πίστις εὐσεβὴς περιγράφει·
ἣν σοι γεωργεῖ καρδία Γεωργίου,
5 ὃς αὐτάδελφον εὐτυχῶς αὐχεῖν ἔχει
πιστὸν Μιχαήλ, τὸν νέον γῆς δεσπότην.

27

Πρόγραμμα εἰς τὸν τῆς Κοιμήσεως λόγον

Σοὶ τοῦτο πλεκτὸν ἐξ ἀκηράτου στέφος
λειμῶνος, ὦ Δέσποινα, κοσμήσας φέρω,
ἀλλότριον πρόσφθεγμα, σοὶ μάλα πρέπον·
ἅπαντα γὰρ σὰ δοῦλα, καὶ τὰ τῶν ξένων.
5 Λόγων ὁ λειμών, τῆς Ἐδὲμ φυτὰ τρέφων,
βρύων τε πολλοῖς ἄνθεσιν καὶ ποικίλοις,

26

On the Savior

Having the heavens as your throne, O Lord,
treading the earth and filling the universe—
this is how a pious faith here depicts you,
a faith that is tended here in the heart of George,
who may take pride in the blessing of being a brother   5
to the faithful Michael, the earth's new lord.

27

Preface to the oration on the
Dormition of the Virgin

I have adorned this *woven crown from an*
unfading meadow and bring it to you, my Lady.
It is a stranger's greeting, yet it suits you;
for all things serve you, even if they come from strangers.
The meadow is of words, nurturing Eden's plants,   5
and teeming with varied multitudes of flowers,

ὧν οὐ μαραίνει τὴν καλὴν ὥραν χρόνος,
οὐδ' ἄλλος οὐδεὶς τὴν χάριν φθείρει τρόπος,
ἀλλ' εἰς ἀεὶ θάλλει τε καὶ λάμπει πλέον
10 τῶν ἄρτι φαιδρὸν ἐξανισχόντων ῥόδων.
Ἐκεῖθεν ἐδρέφθησαν ἡμῖν καὶ τάδε,
τοῖς νῦν γεωργεῖν αὐτὸν ἠξιωμένοις·
ἐκεῖθεν οὗτος ὁ στέφανος ἐπλάκη,
οὐκ ἀξίως μέν (καὶ γὰρ οὐδὲ πᾶν τόδε
15 ἐπάξιόν σου), τοῦ πόθου δ' ἐπαξίως,
ὃς πᾶσαν εἰσήνεγκεν ἰσχὺν ἐνθάδε,
οἷς εἶχε, τιμᾶν τὴν ὑπέρτιμον θέλων.
Σὺ δὲ πρὸς αὐτὸν εὐμενὲς βλέψασά μοι,
δέχου παρ' ἡμῶν, ὡς βασιλὶς μέν, στέφος,
20 ὡς τοῦ Λόγου Μήτηρ δέ, τὸ πρὸς τῶν λόγων·
τῆς δουλικῆς τε χειρὸς ἀντειλημμένη
εὔθυνε πρὸς σέ, καὶ δίδου παρρησίαν,
ὡς ἄν σε λαμπρῶς ᾧ φέρει στέψῃ στέφει.
Εἰ δ' οὖν, τὸ δῶρον δεξιᾶς σῆς ἀξίου,
25 αὐτή τε σαυτὴν εὐπρεπῶς τούτῳ στέφε·
ἢ μᾶλλον εὐπρέπειαν αὐτὴ τῷ στέφει
προσψαύσεως σῆς ἀξιουμένῳ δίδου.
Ἡμᾶς δὲ τοὺς λόγοις σε τιμῶντας μόνοις
ἔργοις σὺ πάντως ἀντιτίμησον πλέον,
30 οἴκῳ τε τῷ σῷ γειτονοῦντας ἐνθάδε
καὶ τῆς ἐκεῖ σου στῆσον ἐγγὺς οἰκίας,
ἣν ἀμφέπουσιν οἱ χοροὶ τῶν ἀγγέλων,
ἣν προσκυνοῦσι πᾶσα τάξις τῶν ἄνω.
Ταύτην ἀμοιβὴν τοῦ πόθου καὶ τοῦ λόγου

whose youthful beauty cannot be faded by time
and whose grace no other, no other force can waste;
rather, it blooms eternally, more radiant
than roses that just began their splendid bloom.   10
It is from this meadow that I have plucked these, too,
now that I have been deemed worthy to cultivate it.
From that place this crown has been woven,
though not in worthy fashion (for not even this whole work
is worthy of you), but still worthy of my zeal   15
that has instilled all the power here,
trying its best to honor the Lady who is above honor.
May you look benevolently upon it.
As a queen, accept from me a crown,
but as Mother of the Word, accept this crown of words.   20
Clasp your servant's hand and draw it near
to you; and grant it the freedom
to brightly crown you with the crown it offers.
If not, deem the gift worthy of your right hand,
and crown yourself with it in dignity.   25
Or rather, give the garland dignity
by deeming it worthy of your touch.
While I have given you honor with words alone,
repay it to me all the more with deeds.
I live near your abode on earth,   30
but bring me near as well to your heavenly home,
the one which angelic choirs surround,
the one to which all heavenly ranks bow.
May I receive from you this reward for my

35 λάβοιμεν ἐκ σοῦ, καὶ τὸ τῆς δόξης στέφος,
   κἂν ταῦτα μεῖζον ἢ καθ' ἡμᾶς ἐλπίσαι.

28

Πρόγραμμα εἰς τὸν περὶ
τῶν Ἀγγέλων Λόγον

Κἂν ἄλλο μεῖζον εὐπόρουν τι προσφέρειν,
ὡς οἱ ῥέοντες τὰς βαρυπλούτους δόσεις,
ἐφεισάμην ἂν οὐδαμῶς ὡς τιμίου·
ὡς τίμιον μᾶλλον δέ, σὺν προθυμίᾳ
5 ἤνεγκα δῶρον προσφιλὲς τοῖς τιμίοις.
Ἀλλ' οὐδενὸς μὲν ἔσχον ἄλλου φροντίδα,
οὐδεὶς δ' ἔτρωσε τὴν ἐμὴν ψυχὴν ἔρως
τῶν γῆν ὁρώντων καὶ μενόντων ἐνθάδε,
πλὴν ἢ μόνων λόγων τε καὶ μαθημάτων,
10 ἅ μοι συνῆξαν οἱ μακροὶ μόλις πόνοι,
ὑμᾶς συνεργοὺς προσλαβόντες γνησίους,
ἀρχιστράτηγοι τῶν ἀΰλων ταγμάτων.
Ὅθεν στενὸς μὲν εἰμὶ τἆλλα καὶ πένης·
τῆς δ' οὖν προσούσης κτήσεώς μοι μετρίαν
15 ἕλεσθε μοῖραν, ὦ Θεοῦ προστάται,
καὶ τὴν χάριν δέχεσθε τῆς συνεργίας·

desire and my words, and also the crown of glory,   35
though even hope for these is beyond me.

28

Preface to the Oration
on the Angels

If I could offer also something of greater value,
like those who overflow with opulent gifts,
I would not have spared it as something valuable;
and yet, with fervor I have brought something more
        precious,
this gift, dear to those held in esteem.   5
Nothing else mattered to me,
no other love consumed my soul
for things that see and dwell upon the earth,
except for love for literature and learning,
which long toils could scarcely reap for me,   10
gaining you as genuine supporters,
the commanders of the immaterial hosts.
Thus, I'm otherwise poor and in dire straits;
but from all of my possessions, choose then,
O God's attendants, a modest part,   15
and accept it, in thanks for your support;

λόγος γὰρ ὑμῖν οὗτος ἀντὶ τῶν λόγων
ἐκ γείτονος δώρημα μετριωτάτου.
Ὃς καὶ τὸν ὑμῶν οἶκον ἐκ τοῦ πλησίον
20 κάλλιστον ἐντρύφημα προσβλέπειν ἔχων,
ὑμᾶς δι' αὐτοῦ—τοὺς ὑπὲρ θνητὴν θέαν—
δοκεῖ θεωρεῖν ἀστραπηβόλους ὅλους,
δεικνύντας, εἰς γνώρισμα τῆς παρουσίας,
φωτὸς τὰ κύκλῳ πάντα πεπληρωμένα.
25 Ὃ καὶ πρὸς ἡμᾶς τοὺς ἀναξίους φθάσαν,
εἰς τοῦτον ὡδήγησε τὸν βραχὺν λόγον.
Ἀλλ' ἀντὶ τοῦ ῥέοντος εἰς αὔρας λόγου
τῷ ζῶντι καὶ μένοντι συστήσοιτέ με,
καὶ τὴν καθ' ὑμᾶς δόξαν ἀντὶ τῆς κάτω
30 ποθοῦντι μᾶλλον τὴν ἄνω δείξοιτέ μοι.

29

Εἰς τοὺς λόγους τοῦ Θεολόγου
τοὺς μὴ ἀναγινωσκομένους

Τίς ὁ θρασυνθεὶς πρῶτος εἰπεῖν τοὺς λόγους
ἥκιστα τούτους ἀναγινωσκομένους;
Τίς κοσμολαμπὲς φῶς καλύπτει γωνίᾳ;
Τίς ἀστέρας λάμποντας ἐγκρύπτει νέφει;

for this discourse is a gift from a modest neighbor,
given in exchange for the gift of words.
Being able to see your abode from close at hand,
a delight so fine to look upon, through it   20
I seem to see you, who are beyond mortal sight,
all flashing with lightning,
revealing—so your presence may be known—
all things about you filled with luminescence.
This light has reached me too, unworthy though I am,   25
and guided me to write this brief oration.
But rather than the words that fly to the winds,
introduce me to the living, enduring Word,
and since I desire your glory, not earthly glory,
show me the glory from above.   30

29

On the orations of the Theologian
that are not read aloud

Who was so bold to be the first to say
that these discourses were the ones least read?
Who hides in a corner a light that lights the world?
Who obscures shining stars with a cloud?

5   Τίς μαργάρους στίλβοντας εἰς γῆν χωννύει;
    Φεῦ κλήσεως μὲν βασκάνου ψευδωνύμου,
    εἰ δ' ἔργον εἶχε, ζημίας παγκοσμίου.
    Νῦν δ' οὐ γὰρ ἔστιν ἔργον, ἀλλ' ἄλλως λόγος.
    Τὸ φῶς ὁράσθω φαῖνον ἐν τῇ λυχνίᾳ·
10   πᾶσι προκείσθω, πᾶσι κοινῇ λαμπέτω
    ὅσοι βλέπειν ἔχουσι τῶν ἄλλων πλέον.
    Ὡς εἴθε πάντες εἶχον εἰδέναι τάδε,
    εἴθε προσεῖχον τοῖσδε πάντες τοῖς λόγοις·
    οὕτω γὰρ ἂν πρόχειρος ἡ σωτηρία
15   παρῆν ἅπασιν ἐκ μιᾶς ταύτης βίβλου·
    ἐῶ γὰρ εἰπεῖν ὡς σοφοὺς ποιεῖ, μόνη
    ἀρκοῦσα πρὸς παίδευσιν ἀνθρώποις ὅλην.
    Πλήρης μέν ἐστι δογμάτων ἀποκρύφων,
    πλήρης δὲ θείων καὶ σοφῶν μυστηρίων,
20   πλήρης δὲ χρηστῶν ἠθικῶν διδαγμάτων,
    πλήρης δὲ κομψῶν τεχνικῶν μαθημάτων·
    μουσεῖον αὐτόχρημα, γνῶσιν ἔμπνεον.
    Ταύτης ἄμεμπτον τὴν γραφὴν καταρτίσας,
    πολλοῖς τρυφὴν προὔθηκα μὴ κενουμένην.

Who buries gleaming pearls in the earth?   5
Alas for the slanderous, false designation;
if it had effect, there would be worldwide harm.
But, all the same now, it has no effect. It is just a name.
May the light that shines in the lamp be seen,
set before all, illuminating all those   10
able to see more than the others.
If only everyone could understand this,
if only everyone would heed these discourses,
then deliverance for humankind
could be easily attained through this single book.   15
I refrain from saying that it makes men wise;
alone it suffices for men's entire education.
For it is full of secret teachings,
full of divine and wise mysteries,
full of useful moral instructions,   20
full of elegant lessons in the art of speaking:
the Muses' very home, inspiring knowledge.
I have had this knowledge impeccably written down,
and offer it to the multitudes for inexhaustible pleasure.

30

Πρόγραμμα εἰς τοὺς νόμους

Ὦ κόσμε, κόσμε, τῶν κακῶν τὸ χωρίον,
πλῆρες ταμεῖον δαψιλοῦς μοχθηρίας,
θάλασσα μεστὴ συμφορῶν τρικυμίας·
ὅσης δεηθεὶς καὶ τυχὼν συνεργίας,
5 ὡς ὀψὲ γοῦν γένοιο σαυτοῦ βελτίων,
εἴληφας οὐδὲν εἰς διόρθωσιν πλέον.
Ὦ πολλὰ μοχθήσαντες ἄνθρωποι μάτην
καὶ πολλὰ φροντίσαντες ἀνθρώπων χάριν,
ἵνα πρέποντα ζῶμεν ἀνθρώποις βίον,
10 ὦ δογματισταὶ καὶ σεμνοὶ νομογράφοι,
σύμπνοια κοινὴ πατρικῶν φρονημάτων,
φύσημα δήμων, ἀξίωμα συγκλήτων,
γνῶμαι σοφῶν τε καὶ νόμοι βασιλέων,
φαύλων κολασταί, τῶν καλῶν ἐπαινέται,
15 λύμης διῶκται, προστάται σωτηρίας,
οἷς ἠκρίβωται πᾶς προμηθείας τρόπος —
ὑμᾶς μὲν οὐδὲν ἐλλιπόντας ὧν ἔδει
πρὸς ὀρθότητα τῶν καθ' ἡμᾶς πραγμάτων,
ἔχει κρατήσας καὶ καλύψας ὁ χρόνος·
20 θνητοὺς γὰρ εὗρεν, εὐκατέργαστον φύσιν.
Ἡ δ' ἐστὶν ἀκράτητον, ἡ πονηρία,
καθ' ἧς ἄπρακτοι καὶ κενοὶ πάντες πόνοι

30

Preface to the laws

World, O world, abode of wickedness,
a storehouse filled with villainy in abundance,
sea teeming with the squalls of calamity;
how much help you needed, and received,
so that you might become better, albeit late;   5
yet you accepted nothing more for your correction.
O men who labored hard to no avail,
and devoted much thought for the sake of men,
so that we might lead a life fitting for men,
O issuers of decrees and solemn lawgivers,   10
O common union of fatherly care,
pride of the people, dignity of the senate,
opinions of the wise and laws of the kings,
chastising the wicked, praising the good,
banishing outrage, protecting salvation,   15
by whom each way of foresight is perfected,
you who lack nothing that is needed
to set our affairs aright,
time has defeated you and covered you over,
finding you mortal, a nature easily vanquished.   20
But wickedness, she is invincible,
by her doings all your efforts at all times

ὑμῖν κατεβλήθησαν ἐν παντὶ χρόνῳ·
οὐ γὰρ πέφυκεν ἠρεμεῖν ἡ σχετλία.
25 Ἀεὶ δὲ ποιεῖν μᾶλλον ἢ πάσχειν θέλει·
ἄτρωτός ἐστι πᾶσιν ὅπλων ὀργάνοις·
ἄτρεστός ἐστι τοῖς φόβοις τῶν δογμάτων·
ἄληπτός ἐστι τοῖς βρόχοις τῶν γραμμάτων·
μᾶλλον δὲ τοῖς μὲν γωνίας σκότος τόπος,
30 τῆς δὲ πρὸς ἄκρα γῆς τὸ πάντολμον θράσος.
Οὐκ οἶδε κάμνειν· οὐ δαμάζεται πόνοις.
Οὐκ οἶδε θνήσκειν· οὐ μαραίνεται χρόνῳ.
Μᾶλλον μὲν οὖν ῥώννυσιν αὐτὴν ὁ χρόνος·
τόλμης γὰρ ἤδη καὶ θράσους πεπλησμένη
35 ἕλκει, σπαράσσει καὶ ταράσσει τὸν βίον·
ἄγει τὰ πάντα καὶ φέρει, καὶ συστρέφει.
Ἀμήχανόν τι δεινὸν ἀνθρώποις ἔφυ
καὶ τῶν φοβήτρων τῶνδε καρπὸς ἡ βλάβη·
τὸ θηρίον γὰρ ἀγριαίνεται πλέον
40 ὥσπερ λέων τις ἐξ ἀμυδρῶν νυγμάτων.
Τίς οὖν φυγή, τίς, συμφορᾶς ἀμηχάνου;
Μία τις ὡς ἔοικε τοῦ κακοῦ λύσις—
φεύγειν πρὸς ἄλλον ἡμερώτερον βίον.
Μᾶλλον δὲ κἀκεῖ—φεῦ πονηρῶν ἐλπίδων.
45 Εἰ γὰρ τὰ νῦν μοι σπέρματα ζωὴν λύει,
τῶν σπερμάτων ἐκεῖθεν οἱ καρποὶ τίνες;
Σὺ σῷζε, Χριστέ· σῷζε δὴ σύ, Χριστέ μου,
σὺ καὶ χάρις σή· ποῦ γὰρ ἀλλαχοῦ τόπος;
Τίς ἐλπὶς ἄλλη, τίς πόρος σωτηρίας,
50 εἰ μὴ σύ, Πλάστα, ῥύστα τῶν ἀγνωμόνων;

374

are reduced to vanity and pointlessness,
for evil is not able to remain still.
It always strives to act and not to submit;   25
it is unharmed by any weaponry;
it cannot be scared by the fear of dogmas;
it cannot be caught by the snares of written words.
Rather, a dark corner is the place for the lawgivers,
while evil's bold rashness reaches the ends of the earth.   30
It does not know fatigue; toils do not tame it.
It does not know death; it does not wither with time.
On the contrary, time gives it strength—
already full of nerve and boldness,
it drags, tears apart, and perturbs our life.   35
It ravages and upsets everything.
It's terrible for men, unassailable, and
the only result of these deterrents is more harm,
for they just make the wild beast angrier,
exactly like a lion lightly pricked.   40
What refuge is there, then, from this inescapable calamity?
There seems but one solution for this evil:
to flee to another more peaceful life.
Yet, also there—alas, wicked hopes!
For if the seeds I plant now dissolve my life,   45
what will be the fruits of my seeds in heaven?
Save me, Christ, yes save me, O my Christ,
you and your grace; for where else can we turn?
What other hope, what way of salvation,
is there but you, O Maker, savior of ingrates?   50

31

Εἰς λιτὸν εὐαγγέλιον ἐνίστορον

Ὢ τῶν ἀπίστων καὶ ξένων θεαμάτων.
Πάλιν Λόγος σάρξ, καὶ βροτὸς Θεὸς πάλιν·
Χριστὸς γὰρ αὐτὸς ἦλθεν αὖθις ὑψόθεν,
ἢ δὶς παχυνθείς, ἢ τὸ πρὶν φέρων πάχος·
5   οὐκ ἐξ ἁγνῆς μὲν (ὡς τὸ πρόσθεν) παρθένου,
οὐδ᾽ εἰς Ἰουδαίαν τε καὶ Παλαιστίνην,
ἀλλ᾽ ἐνθάδε, ξένην τε καὶ καινὴν πλάσιν
πλασθείς, ἀπ᾽ ἄλλων χρωμάτων, οὐχ αἱμάτων.
Ὁ τοῦ λόγου δ᾽ ἔλεγχος ἐκ τῶν πραγμάτων·
10   πάρεστι καὶ γὰρ θαυματουργοῦντα βλέπειν
καὶ δρῶντα καὶ πάσχοντα καὶ νῦν ὡς πάλαι.
Πάρεστι καὶ λέγοντος ἃ πρὶν τοῖς φίλοις
τρανῶς ἀκούειν εἰς βροτῶν σωτηρίαν.
Καινὸν τὸ θαῦμα, καὶ νέα γὰρ ἡ χάρις.
15   Ὅθεν νεάζει καὶ θεόφθεγκτος βίβλος,
κἂν ἀρχαΐζῃ τοὺς τύπους τῶν γραμμάτων,
ὡς ἐν χρόνῳ φέρουσα τὸν πρὸ τοῦ χρόνου.
Τίς οὖν τοσοῦτον ἀξιώματος βάρος,
τίς τὸν φέροντα πᾶσαν ἐν χειρὶ κτίσιν,
20   μονὴν ποθοῦντα, καρτερήσει βαστάσαι;
Οὐ γὰρ ξένος τις εἰς ξένους ἥκει πάλιν,
Ζακχαῖον αἰτῶν τὸν μικρὸν μικρὰν στέγην,

31

On an illuminated gospel book in uncials

O what an incredible and novel sight!
The Word made flesh again, God again mortal.
For Christ himself has come again from on high,
either incarnated anew or in his earlier body,
not from a chaste virgin as the first time,   5
not in Judaea and Palestine, but here,
shaped in a remarkable and novel creation,
made of different colors, not of blood.
The proof of my words lies in reality,
for one may see him here working wonders,   10
acting and suffering now as before.
One may also hear him clearly say the same words
he said to his friends, for mankind's salvation.
The marvel is novel, and the grace is new.
So this book, speaking divine words, is new,   15
even if its letter forms are archaizing,
since it brings into time the one who existed before time.
Who then will bear the weight of such an honor,
and who will dare to carry the one who holds
all creation in his hand, yet longs for a home?   20
He comes not as before, a stranger to strangers,
when he asked the short Zacchaeus for a small room,

ὡς οὐδὲ τρώγλης εὐπορῶν ἀλωπέκων,
ἀλλὰ πρόδηλος τῶν ἁπάντων Δεσπότης,

25 ἄψαυστος, ἀπρόσιτος, ἄστεκτος φύσει,
πληρῶν ἅπασαν ὡς ἀχώρητος κτίσιν.
Ἀλλ' ὡς Θεὸς μὲν ταῦτα καὶ τούτων πέρα·
ὡς σὰρξ δὲ καὶ νῦν οὐκ ἀπαξιοῖ στέγην.
Οὐκοῦν ξενίζει δεσπότης τὸν Δεσπότην,

30 ὁ καὶ θαλάσσης τὸ κράτος καὶ γῆς ἔχων
τὸν Δημιουργὸν τοῦ οὐρανοῦ καὶ τῶν κάτω·
οὐδεὶς δ' ἐρίζει τῷ ξενιστῇ τοῦ γέρως·
ἐξίσταται γὰρ πανταχοῦ τῶν τιμίων
τοῖς κρείττοσι πρόθυμος ἡττόνων φύσις.

35 Ἥττων δὲ πᾶς τις τοῦ κρατοῦντος ἐννόμως,
ἄλλως τε, κἂν τύχοι τις οὐ δῶρον τύχης,
ἀλλ' ἐκ Θεοῦ σχὼν τοῦ κράτους τὰς ἡνίας,
ὡς ὁ κραταιὸς δεσπότης Κωνσταντῖνος
ὁ Μονομάχος. Οὗ κρατήσας ὁ φθόνος

40 ἀντεκρατήθη καὶ νενίκηται πλέον,
Θεοῦ κραταιὰν χεῖρα δόντος ὑψόθεν,
καὶ πρὸς μεγίστην δόξαν ἐξ ἀτιμίας
ἄραντος αὐτὸν μέχρι καὶ λαμπροῦ στέφους,
ἀεί τε συμπράττοντος ἃ πράττειν θέμις,

45 καὶ συνδιευθύνοντος αὐτῷ τὸ κράτος,
δέος μὲν ἐχθροῖς, ἡδονὴν δ' ὑπηκόοις,
καὶ θαῦμα παντὸς τοῦ βίου καὶ τοῦ χρόνου.
Ἀλλ' ὦ κραταιὲ δέσποτα στεφηφόρε,
δέχου τὸν ἐξάγοντα φῶς ἀπὸ σκότους,

50 τὸν ἐξ ἀναγκῶν δόντα σοι σωτηρίαν,

378

since he did not even possess a fox hole;
no, he appears clearly as Lord of all,
untouchable, inaccessible, unapproachable by nature,   25
filling all creation, yet uncontained.
But that, and things beyond that, he does as a God;
now, as flesh, he does not refuse shelter.
So a lord hosts the Lord here,
and the master ruling over the sea and the earth   30
hosts the Creator of heaven and things beneath.
No one will contest the host's gift,
since everywhere those who are lower by nature
readily cede the things they prize to the higher.
And by law everyone is inferior to the ruler,   35
above all if he should hold the reins of power,
not as a gift of fortune, but from God,
as does the powerful lord Constantine
Monomachos. Envy, having first defeated him,
is now in turn defeated and routed still more,   40
since God gives a strong hand from above,
raising him from insignificance to great glory,
as far as the illustrious crown,
always giving him aid in virtuous deeds,
and helping him to wield power,   45
which terrifies his enemies, gladdens his subjects,
and provides a marvel for all life and time.
O strong crown-bearing lord,
accept the one who brings out light from darkness,
who has delivered you from dire need,   50

καὶ πρὸς τοσοῦτον ὕψος ἐξάραντά σε·
δέχου τε πιστῶς, καὶ σέβε πρὸς ἀξίαν,
βλέπων, ἀκούων, προσκυνῶν, κρατῶν, φέρων
αὐτὸν Θεόν τε καὶ Θεοῦ φρικτοὺς λόγους,
55   τὸ τῶν βροτῶν φῶς, τὴν τρυφὴν τῶν ἀγγέλων,
τὸν καὶ βασιλεύσαντα καὶ στέψαντά σε
καὶ συμβασιλεύοντα καὶ σκέποντά σε·
ᾧ συγξένιζε καὶ φίλους καὶ μητέρα,
αὐτόν τε τὸν σὸν σύμμαχον καὶ προστάτην,
60   ᾧ τὰ τρόπαια κλῆσιν ἀξίαν ἔθου·
πάντες γὰρ εἰς ἓν συνδραμόντες ἀθρόοι,
σύνεισι Χριστῷ, καὶ δέονται σοῦ χάριν·
πάντες σὲ λαμπρύνουσι· πάντας οὖν δέχου.
Οὗτοι στέφος σοι, μάργαροι, λαμπροὶ λίθοι,
65   κοσμοῦντες ὡς κάλλιστα τὴν ἁλουργίδα.
Οὗτοι κατ' ἐχθρῶν ὅπλα σοι νικηφόρα,
μεθ' ὧν κρατεῖς τε καὶ κρατήσεις εἰς τέλος,
ἐν οἷς φυλάξεις εὐτυχές σου τὸ κράτος,
καλὴν παρ' αὐτῶν καὶ πρὸ τῆς ἐν ἐλπίσι
70   τῆς εὐσεβείας τὴν ἀμοιβὴν λαμβάνων.

and who has lifted you up to such a height.
Accept him faithfully, and honor him worthily,
seeing, hearing, venerating, supporting, carrying
God himself and the awesome words of God,
the light of mortals, the delight of angels,   55
God who rules as a king and who has crowned you,
who shares your rule and protects you.
Welcome, together with him, his friends and mother,
and certainly himself, your ally and protector,
to whom you have given a worthy name as a trophy.   60
For all together rally to one point,
they are together with Christ, and ask you for favor.
All bring glory to you; so accept them all.
These are your crown, your pearls, your shining gems,
adorning most beautifully your purple robe.   65
These are the victorious weapons against your foes,
with them you rule, and you will rule forever,
in them you will maintain your rule in good fortune,
receiving from them a fine reward for your piety
even before the reward for which you hope.   70

32

Εἰς Σταύρωσιν χρυσῆν

Κἀνταῦθα Χριστός ἐστιν ὑπνῶν ἐν ξύλῳ.
Φέρει δὲ χρυσὸς τοῦ πάθους τὴν εἰκόνα,
ἀνθ' οὗ πραθείς, ἔσωσε τοὺς κατ' εἰκόνα.

33

Πρὸς τὸν ἐπιλαβόμενον τοῦ ἰάμβου τοῦ "ἀνθ' οὗ πραθείς" ὡς τῆς προθέσεως οὐ καλῶς προσκειμένης

Εἰ Χριστὸν ἐχθροῖς ὤνιον μιαιφόνοις
ἐχθρὸς μαθητὴς ἀντέδωκε χρυσίου,
τί νῦν ἁμαρτάνουσιν οἱ πεπεισμένοι
πάλαι "πραθῆναι" Χριστὸν "ἀντὶ χρυσίου";
5 Πῶς δ' οἱ λέγοντες καὶ γράφοντες τὴν πρᾶσιν,
ὅπως συνέστη καὶ καθ' ὅντινα τρόπον,
ἔξω φέρονται τοῦ προσήκοντος λόγου,
σκάφην καλοῦντες τὴν ὑμνουμένην σκάφην;

32

On a golden Crucifixion

Here too, Christ is asleep on a wooden cross.
The gold bears the image of his passion;
sold for gold, he saved those *in his image*.

33

Against the man who criticized the verse "sold for gold," because the preposition is not rightly construed

If the hostile disciple traded Christ for gold,
in sale to his murderous enemies,
why would they be mistaken who are convinced
that Christ was "sold for gold" long ago?
Those who speak of a sale, in speech and writ,   5
how it was concluded and in what way,
how would they stray from the appropriate terms,
calling a spade the proverbial spade?

Τί δ᾽ ἄν τις εἴποι τὴν πρᾶσιν πλὴν ἢ μόνον
10 ὅπερ πέφυκεν, ἀντὶ λήψεως δόσιν,
μόνον προσέστω κέρμα τῷ πεπραγμένῳ,
ὡς ἂν πρὸς ἀντάλλαγμα μὴ συνεμπέσοι.
Ἐγὼ μὲν οὕτω τὴν πρᾶσιν μαθὼν λέγω·
ἄλλοι δ᾽—ἴσως βλέποντες ἡμῶν τι πλέον—
15 οὐκ "ἀντὶ χρυσοῦ" φασὶ πεπρᾶσθαι τόδε,
ἁπλῶς δὲ "χρυσοῦ" δεῖν γράφειν τε καὶ λέγειν.
Τῆς ἀκριβείας τῶν διδασκάλων ὅση!
Πῶς οὖν ἐκεῖνον τὸν Θαλῆν τις θαυμάσοι;
Σοφοὶ μὲν οὗτοι, καὶ τὸ δόγμα τῶν πάνυ·
20 ὑπερφυῶς γὰρ ἐστὶ τῶν ἀποκρύφων.
Τί δ᾽ ἡ πρόθεσις ζημιοῖ προσκειμένη;
Ἐρήσομαι γὰρ τὸν δικαστὴν τοῦ λόγου.
Ἢ πῶς παροῦσαν μακρὰν ἐξωθεῖς βίᾳ,
ἣν οὐ παροῦσαν αὖθις ἕλκεις εἰς μέσον;
25 Πῶς γὰρ νοήσεις τὸ "πραθῆναι χρυσίου,"
μὴ προσλαβὼν ἔξωθεν αὐτὴν ἀγράφως;
Δεῖ γάρ με πάντως πρὸς σὲ τῶν σῶν τι φράσαι.
Ἀλλ᾽ ὡς ἔοικε τῆς σαφηνείας χάριν
ἄχρηστος ἡ δύστηνος ὑμῖν εὑρέθη·
30 τὸ γὰρ σαφές τε καὶ πρόδηλον ἐν λόγοις
λογογράφοις ἥδιστον, οὐ σχεδογράφοις,
καὶ ταῦτα κλῆσιν τὸ σχέδην κεκτημένοις.
Γρίφους δὲ σοὶ πλέκοντι τοὺς ἐν τῷ σχέδει
ἐπαχθές ἐστι πᾶν πρόχειρον καὶ σχέδην.
35 Ἀλλ᾽ "εἵνεκεν" τε καὶ "χάριν" καὶ τοιάδε,
ἢ τὴν "ὑπὲρ" δεῖν ἀντὶ τῆς "ἀντὶ" φράσεις

When speaking of a sale, what else could one mean than
the thing it is, something one gives for something received,   10
except that the sale should involve money,
lest it should coincide with barter?
As I've learned, I call such a thing a sale.
Others, however, perhaps seeing more than I do,
contend that he was not sold "*anti chrysou*,"   15
but that one should write and say merely "*chrysou*."
So great is the hair-splitting of schoolmasters!
How would one then admire the famous Thales?
These men are wise, and their assertion is superb,
for it belongs to the exceptionally esoteric.   20
But what harm is done when this preposition is added?
I will ask the judge of words.
Why do you violently banish afar the preposition when it is
        present,
although you again draw it back when it is absent?
For how would you understand the "*prathenai chrysiou*,"   25
without implying an unwritten preposition?
It is time to speak to you in terms familiar to you.
As it appears, you considered that unfortunate preposition
useless for the sake of clarity,
because clarity and transparency in writing   30
are cherished by speech writers, but not by writers of school
        exercises,
although they carry "gently" in their name.
You too, weaving riddles into your exercises,
despise everything that is elementary and gentle.
Would you claim perhaps that "because of" and "thanks to"   35
or "instead of" need to be added to round off

εἰς συμπέρασμα τοῦ λόγου προσλαμβάνειν;
Μάλιστα μέν πως· ἀντὶ γὰρ τούτου τόδε
ἄμεινον εἰπεῖν μᾶλλον εἶναι τὴν πράσιν,
40 ἢ τοὺς τοσούτους ἐκπεριτρέχειν κύκλους.
Ἔπειτα πολλὴ συγγένεια πρὸς τάδε
τῇ προθέσει πρόσεστι μαρτυρουμένη,
ἀνθ' ὧν πέφυκε λαμβάνεσθαι πολλάκις.
Πῶς οὖν στερηθῇ τῶν ἑαυτῆς ἐνθάδε;
45 Νικᾷ δ' ἀμφοῖν. Ὥστε συγχωρητέα.
Εἰ δ' ἄλλος αὐτὴν ἐξελαύνει τις λόγος,
ἢ δεῖξον, ἢ σίγησον, ἢ δόξεις μάτην
ἐπηρεάζειν τοὺς ἀνευθύνους λόγους.
Οὐκ εὐλόγως δὲ τοῦ λόγου τὸν προστάτην
50 λόγοις μάχεσθαι σφόδρα τῶν ἀνευλόγων.

34

Πρὸς τοὺς ἀκαίρως
στιχίζοντας

"Ἄριστον εἶναι πᾶν μέτρον," προεῖπέ τις.
Κἀγὼ δὲ μετρεῖν πρᾶξιν εἰδὼς καὶ λόγον,
μέτροις ὁρίζω καὶ λόγους τοὺς ἐμμέτρους.
Μέτρον δ' ἂν εἴη πᾶν τὸ συμμέτρως ἔχον·
5 μέτρον δ' ἄμετρον οὐδαμῶς μέτρον λέγω.

the expression, instead of "for"?
I already thought so. Instead of that, it is better
to use this word to make clear what a sale really is,
better than to run so many circles. 40
Moreover, there are many attestations
that this preposition is related to these locutions,
instead of which it is often used.
How would it then be stripped of its own properties here?
It wins by both arguments. So it will have to be admitted. 45
If another text omits it, either show it,
or keep quiet. Otherwise you will give the impression
of disparaging irreproachable discourses for nothing.
That the champion of words should fight with words
in an unreasonable way is something totally deprived of 50
    reason.

34

Against those who versify in an inappropriate manner

"*All measure is supreme,*" someone stated of old.
I too know how to measure my deeds and words,
and so I define metered words by measure.
Measure would be all that is moderate;
an unmeasured meter I call no meter. 5

Σκόπει τὸ ῥητόν, καὶ "σύνες τί σοι λέγει"
(ἐκ Πινδάρου σοι τοῦτο τοῦ σοφωτάτου),
καὶ μοὶ μέτρει μέν, ἀλλ᾽, ἄριστε, σὺν μέτρῳ·
καὶ τὸν λόγον γὰρ σὺν λόγῳ χειριστέον.
10 Κακῶς δὲ μὴ σὺ τῷ καλῷ κέχρησό μοι·
ἀμετρία γὰρ πανταχοῦ κακὸν μέγα,
μάλιστα δ᾽ ἡ φθείρουσα τὴν μέτρου φύσιν.

35

Ἐπιτύμβιοι εἰς τὸν φίλον
Μιχαὴλ τὸν διάκονον

Ἡ τῆς Μεγίστης ἡδύτης Ἐκκλησίας,
τὸ τῆς κρατούσης νῦν ἀηδίας ἅλας,
ὁ πᾶς γλυκασμὸς τῆς καθ᾽ ἡμᾶς πικρίας
ἀπῆλθε, τὸν δύστηνον ἐκλιπὼν βίον·
5 ἡμῖν δὲ τὸ ζῆν συμφορὰν ἀφεὶς μόνον,
αὐτὸς διαδράς, οἴχεται σεσωσμένος·
οὐ γὰρ δίκαιον ἦν τὸ φῶς ὑπὸ σκότους
ἔτι κρατεῖσθαι, καὶ διαυγάζειν μάτην,
πάντων φιλούντων οὐ τὸ φῶς, τὸ δὲ σκότος.
10 Ὅθεν μετέστη πρὸς τὸ συγγενὲς σέλας·
τῷ Πατρὶ τῶν φώτων γὰρ ἠνώθη πάλιν,

Consider that saying, and "*understand* what it says to you"
(this latter quote is from Pindar, the wisest of poets), and
for my sake write, dear friend, in meter—but with measure;
for words ought to be handled with reason too.
Do not treat the good in an evil manner;   10
for lack of measure is always a great evil,
above all when it spoils the nature of meter.

35

Funeral verses for his friend
Michael the deacon

The sweet savor of the Great Church,
the salt in the unsavoriness that now prevails,
the sweetening of the bitterness among us,
has passed away, departing this wretched life.
He left behind for us only the affliction of living,   5
while he himself escaped, having been saved;
it was not right that light should still be overshadowed
by darkness, and shine in vain,
since all men now love not the light, but darkness.
And so he has now passed on to the kindred light;   10
for he is again made one with *the Father of lights,*

ἐξ οὗ τέλειον δῶρον ἦλθεν εἰς βίον.
Ἀλλ' αὐτόθεν με, τῶν ἐμῶν φῶς ὀμμάτων,
φώτιζε τὸν σόν, Μιχαήλ, Ἰωάννην.

36

Ἐπιτύμβιοι εἰς τὸν Πρωτεύοντα

Ἓν ἦν τὸ κοσμοῦν τὸν ταλαίπωρον βίον,
ὁ νεκρὸς οὗτος, πρὶν νεκρὸς πεφηνέναι·
ἕως ἔτι ζῶν, φῶς ὑπῆρχε τοῦ κόσμου,
ἕως ὑπὲρ γῆς εἶχε τὴν λαμπηδόνα,
5 ὑφ' ἧς ὅλην ηὔγαζε τὴν οἰκουμένην,
ὁποῖα φαιδρὸς λύχνος αὐχμηρὸν τόπον·
Θεοῦ γὰρ οὗτος δῶρον ἦν φερωνύμως,
ἤθει, λόγῳ, τρόπῳ τε καὶ λαμπρῷ βίῳ
τὴν εὐγένειαν τὴν ἄνωθεν δεικνύων.
10 Οὗτος λόγοις ἄριστος ἐκ μαθημάτων,
οἷς ἐτράφη τε καὶ συνῆν καθ' ἡμέραν.
Οὗτος κράτιστος ἐν νόμοις ἐκ τοῦ τρόπου,
λέγων δίκαια καὶ κατευθύνων κρίσεις,
καὶ ταῖς πάγαις ἄληπτος ὢν τῶν λημμάτων,
15 ὑφ' ὧν πέφυκε πᾶς μαλάσσεσθαι τόνος.
Οὗτος γένει τε καὶ τύχῃ φρονεῖν ἔχων

from whom he came into this life as a perfect gift.
But, from where you are, O light of my eyes,
bring light, Michael, to me, your own dear John.

36

Funeral verses for Proteuon

Just one thing adorned this wretched life:
this dead man, before he appeared dead;
while still alive, he was the light of this world,
as long as he spread upon the earth his luster,
by which he illuminated the entire world,   5
like a radiant lantern in a dark place.
For he was a gift of God, as his name says,
in character, speech, manner, and brilliant life,
revealing a nobility that came from the heavens.
Through study, he was most excellent with words,   10
nurtured by learning and living by it daily.
Through character, he reigned supreme in law,
justly giving decrees and judging cases.
He was incorruptible by all of bribery's snares,
to which all effort usually succumbs.   15
He could have boasted of family and fortune,

εἰς γῆν ἑώρα καὶ ταπεινὸν ἐφρόνει
ὡς ἄν τις οἰκτρὸς εὐτελέστατος πένης·
καὶ γὰρ πένης ἦν· ἀλλὰ πολλοὺς πλουσίους
20 ἀντλῶν ἐδείκνυ χερσὶ δαψιλεστάταις.
Οὗτος ξένην ὥδευσεν ἀνθρώποις τρίβον,
καὶ μίξιν εὗρε τῶν ἀμίκτων πραγμάτων,
ἄσκησιν εἰς ἓν καὶ πολιτείαν ἄγων,
καὶ τὴν μὲν ὡς ἄσαρκος ἐκπονῶν λάθρα,
25 τῇ δὲ προδήλως, εἴ τις ἄλλος, ἐμπρέπων·
νύκτωρ διαθλῶν ἐν προσευχαῖς ἀγρύπνοις,
καὶ πρὸς τὰ κοινὰ συντελῶν τὴν ἡμέραν·
μένων ἄχραντος ἐν μέσῳ τῶν πραγμάτων,
ὡς μάργαρός τις ἐν μέσῳ ῥυπασμάτων·
30 πρᾷος, γαληνός, ἐγκρατής, σώφρων πλέον,
ἡδύς, προσηνής, ἵλεως, πᾶσιν φίλος·
θείου φόβου τε καὶ πόθου πεπλησμένος,
οὐδὲν κάτωθεν οὐδὲ τῆς ὕλης φέρων,
ἀεὶ δ᾽ ἑαυτὸν τοῖς Θεοῦ δούλοις νέμων
35 δοῦλον, ξενιστήν, καὶ ποριστήν, καὶ φίλον.
Οὗτος—τί μὴ τάχιστα συντεμὼν λέγω;—
ἔμψυχος εἰκὼν ἀρετῆς ἦν καὶ τύπος,
καὶ τοῖς καλοῖς ἅπασιν πρωτεύων μόνος
τὴν κλῆσιν ἐκράτυνεν ἐκ τῶν πραγμάτων.
40 Καὶ ταῦτα μὲν χθές. Νῦν δὲ τί; Σκιᾶς ὄναρ.
Τὰ πάντα φροῦδα, πάντα φάσμα φασμάτων,
φανέν τι μικρὸν καὶ παρελθὸν αὐτίκα.
Ἢ μᾶλλον εἰπεῖν, ταῦτα μὲν ζῇ καὶ πάλιν·
οὐ γὰρ πέφυκεν ἀρετὴ θνήσκειν ὅλως.

but he humbly looked down to earth,
like a wretched, worthless pauper.
And poor he was; but he made many rich
with the generosity of his bountiful hands.   20
He pursued a path alien to many,
and found a mix of things that do not mix,
combining ascetic life with politics,
secretly performing the former like a fleshless being,
and shining forth in the latter above all others.   25
At night he labored in vigilant prayers,
but the day he spent serving the common good,
remaining pure amid worldly affairs,
like a pearl in the midst of filth.
He was gentle, calm, restrained, and, even more so, chaste;   30
sweet, pleasant, kind, and friendly to all.
He was filled with fear of and desire for God,
concerned with nothing earthly nor anything material,
always devoting himself to the servants of God,
himself a servant, a host, a donor, a friend.   35
This man—why not be short and to the point?—
was a living image and model of virtue,
and alone prevailing in all good things,
he confirmed his name in reality.
That was yesterday. Now *what? A shadow's dream.*   40
It is all gone—all a phantom of phantoms,
appearing for a while, then vanishing.
Or rather, these things live yet again:
for it's not in virtue's nature to die completely.

45 Ἔχει δὲ τὸν χοῦν ἡ φθορὰ πάλιν μόνον
ἀφ᾽ ἧς ὑπέστη καὶ πρὸς ἣν ὑποστρέφει.
Οὐκ οὖν τι δεινὸν ἔσχεν ὁ κρυβεὶς τάφῳ,
ἀλλ᾽ ὁ στερηθεὶς τοῦ καλοῦ τούτου βίος,
τοιοῦτον οὐδὲν ἄλλο τι βλέπειν ἔχων,
50 καίτοιγε πολλῶν ἄρτι χρῇζων εἰκότως,
ἐπικρατούντων πανταχοῦ τῶν χειρόνων.
Ὅθεν τὸ πρᾶγμα πένθος ἡγεῖται μέγα,
καὶ τὸν θανόντα κόπτεται καὶ δακρύει,
εἰδὼς μεγίστην ἣν ὑπέστη ζημίαν.

37

Ἐπιτύμβιοι εἰς τὸν χαρτοφύλακα

Πένθους ὁ καιρός· συμφορᾶς τὸ χωρίον·
καὶ δυστυχοῦσιν ἀρετή τε καὶ λόγοι·
τὸ σφῶν γὰρ αὐτοῖς οἴχεται μέγα κράτος,
ἤδη πεσόντος (ὡς ὁρᾷς) Ἰωάννου,
5 Ἰωάννου πεσόντος (οἴμοι) τοῦ πάνυ.
Ὦ καρδία, σείσθητι καὶ θραύσθητί μοι,
πλήττοντος οὕτω καιρίαν σε τοῦ λόγου.
Ἀνὴρ σοφὸς τέθνηκεν· ὦ τῆς ζημίας.
Ἀνὴρ δίκαιος, εὐλαβής· φεῦ τοῦ πάθους.

394

Decay now clutches in its hands only the dust,   45
from which he came and to which he returns.
The loss is not suffered by him who lies in the grave,
but by life, deprived of so good a man;
never will it see his like again,
though it needs now many such men,   50
since evil men everywhere prevail.
So life looks on this loss as a great sorrow;
it mourns and bewails the deceased,
knowing what a great blow it has suffered.

37

Funeral verses for the master of archives

It is a time of mourning, a place of calamity.
Virtue and culture are in distress,
since their great bulwark has departed.
As you see, John has now died,
John, that famous man, alas, has died.   5
O my heart, shake and break into pieces,
since these words deal you such a fatal blow.
A wise man has died; O what a loss!
A just and prudent man; O what a disaster!

10 Ὁ χαρτοφύλαξ· ὦ στυγνῶν ἀκουσμάτων.

Ὁ χαρτοφύλαξ, οὗ τὸ πρὶν μέγα κλέος,
τὸ καὶ πρὸς αὐτὸν οὐρανὸν τρίτον φθάνον
καὶ τὴν ἄπειρον γῆν ὅλην περιτρέχον,
εἰ καὶ βραχεῖ νῦν συγκαλύπτεται τάφῳ.

15 Τάφος γὰρ αὐτὸν ἔσχεν ὡς θνητὸν ἕνα,
κἂν οὐκ ἐῴκει τὴν φύσιν θνητὴν ἔχειν·
βροντῶν μὲν ὥσπερ ἐκ νεφῶν ἐν τοῖς λόγοις,
ἔργων δὲ λαμπρότησιν ἀστράπτων πάλιν,
καὶ πρὸς Θεοῦ μίμησιν ἠκριβωμένος,

20 τοσοῦτον ἡμᾶς τοὺς χαμαὶ λιπὼν κάτω,
ὅσον συνῆπτε πλησιάζων τοῖς ἄνω
λαμπροῦ βίου τε καὶ λόγου κοινωνίᾳ.

Τὰ νῦν δὲ ταῦτα μικρὸς ἤλεγξε χρόνος,
διαρρυέντων ἀθρόον πάντων ἅμα,

25 καὶ τὸν χθὲς αὐγάζοντα φαιδρὸν ἀστέρα,
δύντα πρόωρον, οὗτος ἔκρυψεν τόπος.

Ἀστὴρ μέν, ἀλλ᾽ ἤστραπτεν ἡλίου πλέον.
Πρόσγεια λάμπων, ἀλλὰ νικῶν τοὺς ἄνω,
καὶ τὸ κράτιστον, νοῦν τε καὶ λόγον, φέρων,

30 οἷς ἦγεν, οἷς ἔθελγε καὶ λίθων φύσιν.
Τοιοῦτον ἦν τὸ θαῦμα τῆς χθὲς ἡμέρας,
τοσοῦτον εὐτύχημα τοῦ παντὸς βίου
καὶ τοῦ καθ᾽ ἡμᾶς εἶδεν ἥλιος χρόνου.
Νῦν δ᾽ ὡς ἔβλεψε τὴν ἐναντίαν τύχην,

35 καὶ τὴν κάτω σβεσθεῖσαν ἔγνω λαμπάδα,
οὐδ᾽ αὐτὸς ἡμῖν καρτερεῖ λάμπειν ἔτι,
ἀλλὰ σκυθρωπός ἐστι καὶ πάθους γέμει·

The master of archives—this is so painful to hear.   10
The master of archives, whose earlier fame was so great
that it reached *the third heaven*
and went around the whole vast world,
even if he is now covered by a small grave.
Yes, a grave now holds him, as a mortal,   15
although he did not seem to have a mortal nature;
thundering in his discourses as if from the clouds,
and in turn flashing with the brilliance of his deeds,
he perfected himself in imitation of God,
and left us behind down here on earth as much as   20
he joined us to the ones above by approaching them,
in combining a brilliant life and learning.
But now a brief flash of time has refuted this.
Everything suddenly fell apart,
and this spot now conceals the shining star   25
that shone yesterday, setting all too soon.
A star, yes, but one that gave more light than the sun,
illuminating the mundane, yet eclipsing the celestial,
and offering what is best: mind and words.
With these, he gave guidance, and charmed even stones.   30
Such was the marvel of yesterday,
such was the good fortune of our whole life
and our time, as witnessed by the sun.
Now the sun has seen the contrary fortune, and
understands that the light below has been quenched.   35
So it cannot any longer bear to shine for us;
instead, it remains somber and full of sadness.

δεῖ γὰρ στυγνάζειν πᾶσαν ἄρτι τὴν κτίσιν,
ὡς τὴν ἑαυτῆς δόξαν ἐστερημένην.
40 Ὁμώνυμός σοι ταῦτα, δοῦλε Κυρίου,
ψυχῆς ἐμῆς μέλημα, φῶς τῶν ὀμμάτων,
μαθημάτων κοινωνὲ καὶ διδασκάλων,
ᾧ καὶ συνέζης καὶ συνέπνεις ἐν βίῳ,
πρὸς ὃν τὸ φίλτρον εἶχες ἐξῃρημένον,
45 ὁμώνυμός σοι τήνδε τὴν μονῳδίαν,
θρηνῶν ἑαυτὸν οἷς τὸ σὸν θρηνεῖ πάθος.
Πέπτωκε κέδρος; Ἡ πίτυς στεναζέτω.
Εἰ γὰρ σὺ θᾶττον ἡρπάγης ἐκ τοῦ βίου,
σώφρων, ἄμεμπτος, ἐγκρατής, ἁγνός, νέος,
50 τί χρή με τὸν δύστηνον ἐλπίζειν ἔτι;

38

Εἰς τὸν βεστάρχην Ἀνδρόνικον
ἐπιτύμβιοι

Ἐκεῖνος οὗτος, ὁ χθὲς ἐν βίῳ μέγας,
πλούτῳ, λόγοις, δόξῃ τε λάμπων καὶ νόμοις,
ὃν εἶχε κόσμος κόσμον ἐν μέσῃ πόλει,
ὃς φαιδρὸν ἀντέλαμπεν ἐκ γῆς ἡλίῳ,
5 Ἀνδρόνικος—φεῦ· πῶς προσείπω, καὶ τίνα,

All of creation must now be gloomy,
because it is bereaved of its glory.
These are words from your namesake, O servant of the Lord,   40
care of my soul, light of my eyes,
you who shared schools and teachers with me,
while still alive, you shared life and breath with me,
having for me exceptional affection.
Yes, from your namesake is this lament,   45
mourning himself with the same words as he mourns your
     suffering.
The cedar has fallen? The pine must grieve.
For if you who were chaste, blameless, restrained, pure,
     young,
were snatched from this life so soon,
what hope is left then for wretched me?   50

38

Funeral verses for the *vestarches* Andronikos

This is that man, so great in this life yesterday,
shining in wealth, words, glory, and laws,
a jewel for the world in the midst of the city,
emitting from earth a light that matched the sun,
Andronikos—alas; how shall I speak and address him,   5

οὗ μηδὲ κλῆσιν ἀξίαν ἄν τις φράσοι;
Πλὴν ἀλλὰ κεῖται, καὶ τέλος ζωῆς ἔχει,
βίου τε τοῦ ῥέοντος, ἀλλὰ καὶ φθόνου.
Αὕτη δὲ μορφὴ τοῦ παρελθόντος μόνη,
10 τὸν τοῦ καλοῦ σῴζουσα σώματος τύπον.

39

Ἕτεροι εἰς τὸν αὐτόν

Εἰ καὶ σοφοὶ θνήσκουσι, τίς λόγων λόγος;
Εἰ καὶ δυνάστας πτῶσις οὕτως ἀθρόα
φέρει συναρπάζουσα, τίς δόξης ἔρως;
Τί πλοῦτος ἡδύ, τίς δυναστείας χάρις,
5 εἰ πάντα θνήσκει προσβολῇ μιᾶς νόσου;
Τούτων ἁπάντων εἰς τὸ πρωτεῖον φέρων,
πρὶν ἐλπίσοι τις, πρὶν μάθοι τὸ πᾶν πάθος,
ἄφνω νεκρός, φεῦ, κρύπτεται βραχεῖ λίθῳ
Ἀνδρόνικος. Τάλαινα, δυστυχεῖς, πόλις.
10 Ὁ νοῦς ὁ λαμπρός, ἡ νοημάτων βρύσις,
τὸ τῶν λόγων ἄγαλμα, τῶν νόμων κράτος,
ἡ τοῦ κράτους εὔκλεια καὶ τῶν ἐν τέλει,
ὁ γοῦν τοσοῦτος ἁρπαγεὶς ἐκ τοῦ βίου,
τί τερπνὸν ἡμῖν οἴχεται λιπὼν ἔτι;
15 Τί δ' ἄλλο χρηστόν; Ἥλιε, στύγναζέ μοι,
τοιοῦτον οὐδὲν ἄλλο προσβλέπειν ἔχων.

for whom no one could find any fitting title?
But now he lies down, and has reached the end of his life—
of this fleeting life, but also of envy.
And this image is only an image of what has departed,
preserving the appearance of his beautiful body.　　　　10

39

More verses for the same man

If the wise die too, what good is learning?
If a downfall so sudden bears away
even rulers, why should we yearn for glory?
What sweetness is in wealth, what pleasure in power,
if all things can die by the blow of a single illness?　　　　5
One man took the prize in all these blessings.
Before one could expect it, or grasp entirely what had
　　　　happened,
Andronikos was suddenly dead, covered by a small stone,
alas. Wretched city, you are doomed.
This splendid mind, this well of ideas,　　　　10
this statue of learning, this pinnacle of laws,
the glory of the state and of the rulers,
such a great man is now snatched from his life.
What joy has he left us, now that he has gone?
What other benefit? Sun, cloud yourself,　　　　15
since you will never again see such a man.

40

Εἰς τὸν ἑαυτοῦ τάφον

Θαύμαζε μηδέν, ἀλλὰ φρίσσε τὴν θέαν·
βλέπεις γάρ, ὢν ἄνθρωπος, ἀνθρώπου πάθος.
Τὸ πτῶμα κοινόν, ἀλλ᾽ ἄνισος ὁ χρόνος,
καὶ τὸν σὸν ἄλλοις ὕστερον δείξει τάφον.
5   Ἕως δὲ μέλλει, γνῶθι τὴν σαυτοῦ φύσιν,
καὶ σωφρονίζου συμφοραῖς ἀλλοτρίαις.

41

Ἄλλοι

Ζωῆς ἀπελθὸν φάσμα καὶ χθὲς ἡμέρα,
ψευδεῖς ὄνειροι καὶ πλάνοι, σῴζοισθέ μοι,
παίξαντες ἡμᾶς ἐν σκιαῖς βραχὺν χρόνον,
εἶτα προδόντες καὶ λιπόντες ἀθρόον·
5   οὐδὲν γὰρ ἦτε πλὴν ἐνυπνίων χάρις,
κλέπτουσα καὶ σφάλλουσα τοὺς πλανωμένους.

40

On his own grave

Do not be surprised, but shiver at this sight,
since you, a human, are seeing a human's suffering.
The downfall is the same for all; it is time that is unequal,
which will later show also your grave to others.
Before this happens, know your own nature,   5
and be chastised by the misfortunes of others.

41

More verses

Phantom of life, now gone, and days past,
deceitful and false dreams, farewell.
You have fooled me for a short time, in the shadows,
and then betrayed and abandoned me all of a sudden;
for you are nothing more than the beauty of dreams,   5
deceiving and deluding those led astray.

42

Εἰς πολυάνδριον

Ἄστοργε μῆτερ, ὦ πικρᾶς ἀσπλαγχνίας,
ὑφ' ἧς τὰ σαυτῆς τέκνα συγκατεσθίεις,
οὐδεὶς δ' ἔνεστιν οἶκτος. Ἀλλ' ἐπ' ἐσχάτων
σάλπιγξ ἀπαιτήσει σε πάντας ἀγγέλου.

43

Ἐπίγραμμα εἰς τὸν Πλάτωνα καὶ τὸν Πλούταρχον

Εἴπερ τινὰς βούλοιο τῶν ἀλλοτρίων
τῆς σῆς ἀπειλῆς ἐξελέσθαι, Χριστέ μου,
Πλάτωνα καὶ Πλούταρχον ἐξέλοιό μοι·
ἄμφω γὰρ εἰσι καὶ λόγον καὶ τὸν τρόπον
5 τοῖς σοῖς νόμοις ἔγγιστα προσπεφυκότες.
Εἰ δ' ἠγνόησαν ὡς Θεὸς σὺ τῶν ὅλων,
ἐνταῦθα τῆς σῆς χρηστότητος δεῖ μόνον,
δι' ἣν ἅπαντας δωρεὰν σῴζειν θέλεις.

42

On a common graveyard

Loveless mother, what a bitter lack of mercy,
that made you devour your own children
and show no pity. But at the end of time,
the angel's trumpet will ask you for all of them back.

43

Epigram on Plato and Plutarch

If, perhaps, you should want to release
some of the heathen from your threat, dear Christ,
then choose Plato and Plutarch, for my sake;
for both of them, in their words and also actions,
have clung most tightly to your laws.   5
And if they did not know you as God of all,
in this case, they only need your benevolence,
that makes you wish to save all men, expecting nothing in
    return.

44

Εἰς τὴν καθημερινὴν λειτουργίαν τῆς Ἁγίας Σοφίας

Οὐκ ἦν δίκαιον τὴν σκιὰν μὲν τοῦ νόμου
φέρειν ἄπαυστον τῷ Θεῷ λειτουργίαν,
σχολῆς δὲ καιρὸν τὴν ἀλήθειαν βλέπειν·
ὃ καὶ κατορθοῖ δεσπότης Μονομάχος.

45

Ἄλλοι

Δαβὶδ μελῳδῶν εὐσεβῆ νόμον γράφει,
ἐν παντὶ καιρῷ τῷ Θεῷ δόξαν νέμειν.
Πληροῖ δὲ τοῦτον εὐσεβὴς Μονομάχος,
ἀεὶ τὸ θεῖον εὐσεβεῖσθαι θεσπίσας.

44

On the daily liturgy of the Hagia Sophia

It was not right that the shadow of the law
showed a continuous liturgy for God,
while the truth should experience a time of respite.
This, too, lord Monomachos has set right.

45

More verses

David wrote a pious law in song:
it is right to give God glory at all times.
The pious Monomachos fulfills this law,
ordaining that the divine be always honored.

46

Εἰς χρυσόβουλλον τῆς Λαύρας

Χρυσοῖς γραφῆναι γραμμάτων ἔδει τύποις
τὸν ἐν λόγοις κάλλιστον ὡς χρυσοῦν ὅλον.
Εἴ τις δὲ τέχνη πρὸς τὸ καὶ μέλι γράφειν,
ἐκεῖσε βάπτων γραψάτω τις τὸν λόγον,
5 ὡς ἂν πρέπουσαν ὄψιν ἐντεῦθεν λάβοι
τὸ στίλβον αὐτοῦ καὶ γλυκάζον ἠρέμα.
Ἀλλ᾽ οὐ θεατός ἐστι τοῖς ἀναξίοις,
ἀλλ᾽ οὐδ᾽ ἀκουστὸς τοῖς ἀγροικικωτέροις·
ὅθεν φυλάξει τὴν χάριν κεκρυμμένην
10 χρυσοῦς φύλαξ κάτωθεν ἐμβεβλημένος,
μόνοις δὲ ταύτην ἐκφανεῖ τοῖς ἀξίοις,
σήμαντρα χειρὸς εὐγενοῦς δεδεγμένην.

46

On the golden bull of the Lavra

It is in golden letters that one should write
this loveliest of texts, as it is pure gold.
And if there is a technique for writing with honey,
let someone dip his pen in it and write this text,
so that its radiance and gentle sweetness   5
may have the most appropriate appearance.
But it cannot be seen by the unworthy,
nor can it be heard by the boorish.
Thus the golden guardian placed at the bottom
will preserve its hidden grace,   10
showing it only to the worthy,
having received the signature of a noble hand.

47

Εἰς τὴν ἑαυτοῦ οἰκίαν,
ὅτε διαπράσας ταύτην ἀπέλιπεν

Μὴ δυσχέραινε σὺ πρὸς ἡμᾶς, οἰκία,
ἔρημος οὕτω καὶ κενὴ λελειμμένη·
σὺ γὰρ σεαυτῇ πρόξενος τοῦ νῦν πάθους,
ἄπιστος οὖσα τοῖς ἑαυτῆς δεσπόταις,
5   καὶ μηδένα στέργουσα τῶν κεκτημένων,
μήδ' εἰς τέλος σῴζουσα τὴν ὑπουργίαν·
οὐ γὰρ πέφυκας τοῖς ἔχουσι προσμένειν,
ἀεὶ δ' ἀμείβειν ἄλλον ἐξ ἄλλου θέλεις,
ἀποστατοῦντος οἰκέτου κακοῦ δίκην.
10 Πρὶν οὖν προδῷς σὺ καὶ λίπῃς τὸν δεσπότην,
οὗτος σὲ φεύγει σωφρονῶν ὡς δραπέτιν.
Πρὸ τοῦ παθεῖν ἄκων δὲ τὴν σὴν ζημίαν
ἑκὼν σε ῥίπτει, καὶ λιπὼν ἀποτρέχει.
Πλὴν οὐ πάθους ἄμοιρος οὐδ' οἴκτου δίχα·
15 οἰκτίζεται γὰρ καὶ λίαν σε, φιλτάτη,
ὡς κτῆμα τερπνόν, ὡς πατρῴαν ἑστίαν,
ὡς ἐκ γένους δῶρόν τε καὶ κλῆρον μόνην.
Καὶ μοὶ στρέφει τὰ σπλάγχνα καὶ τὴν καρδίαν
ὁ πρὸς σὲ θερμὸς ἐκ συνηθείας ἔρως·
20 σὺ γὰρ τιθηνὸς καὶ τροφός μοι, φιλτάτη,
σὺ παιδαγωγὸς καὶ διδάσκαλος μόνη·

47

On his own home,
when he sold and left it

Now do not get upset with me, my home,
by being left empty and abandoned this way.
You were the cause of your present suffering,
unfaithful as you were to your own masters.
You had no love for any of your owners;   5
you failed to do your duty till the end.
It's not in your nature to abide with your owners;
instead you like to trade one for another,
behaving like a vile treacherous servant.
Before you can betray and desert your master   10
like a fugitive, he wisely leaves you.
Before he unwillingly feels the harm you would inflict,
of his own accord he casts you off and runs away.
Still, he is not without pain or without pity;
for he mourns for you, dearest, and he mourns a lot,   15
as his dear possession and his paternal hearth,
as the one thing that his family gave or willed to him.
My ardent love for you, the result of long intimacy,
ties up my stomach and heart in knots.
You were the one, dear house, who raised and nurtured me.   20
You were the only tutor and teacher I ever had.

ἐν σοὶ πόνους ἤνεγκα μακροὺς καὶ κόπους,
ἐν σοὶ διῆξα νύκτας ἀγρύπνους ὅλας,
ἐν σοὶ διημέρευσα κάμνων ἐν λόγοις,
25 τοὺς μὲν διορθῶν, τοὺς δὲ συντάττων πάλιν,
κρίνων μαθηταῖς καὶ διδασκάλοις ἔρεις,
ἕτοιμος ὢν ἅπασιν εἰς ἀποκρίσεις,
καὶ προστετηκὼς ταῖς γραφαῖς καὶ ταῖς βίβλοις.
Ἐν σοὶ συνῆξα γνῶσιν ἐκ μαθημάτων,
30 ἐν σοὶ δὲ ταύτην τοῖς θέλουσι σκορπίσας,
πολλοὺς σοφοὺς ἔδειξα προῖκα τῶν νέων.
Τούτοις ὅλον με, πατρική, θέλγεις, στέγη.
Τούτοις με κάμπτεις καὶ κατακλᾷς, φιλτάτη.
Λόγος δὲ νικᾷ πάντα καὶ Θεοῦ πόθος·
35 τρίτον δ' ἀρίθμει τῆς τελευτῆς τὸν φόβον.
Οἷς ὡς μύωψιν ἀθρόον πεπληγμένος,
ἄπειμι φεύγων ἔνθεν οὗ Θεὸς φέρει,
ἄλλων πάροικος ἀντὶ τοῦ χθὲς δεσπότου,
προσήλυτός τις οἰκτρὸς ἀντ' ἐγχωρίου,
40 ἀνέστιός τε καὶ ξένης χρήζων στέγης
ὁ τῆς ἑαυτοῦ μὴ φθονήσας τοῖς ξένοις.
Ἐπεὶ δ' ἀπαίρειν καιρὸς εἰς ἀλλοτρίαν,
σὺ χαῖρε πολλά, χαῖρέ μοι σύ, γνησία,
ξένη δὲ μᾶλλον, ἔκ γε τῆς νῦν ἡμέρας.
45 Ὅμως δὲ χαῖρε, χαῖρε, μῆτερ δευτέρα,
ἡ καὶ τιθηνήσασα καὶ θρέψασά με
καὶ πρὸς τέλειον μέτρον ἐξ ἔτι βρέφους
ἀπαρτίσασα καὶ καταρτίσασά με.
Νῦν δ' ἄλλους ἕξεις οὓς παιδεύσεις καὶ θρέψεις.

Inside your walls I endured lengthy labors and pain,
inside your walls I spent whole sleepless nights,
inside your walls I labored all day long on words—
revising some works, and composing others.   25
I arbitrated disputes for both students and teachers,
ready to respond to everyone,
engrossed in my writing and books.
Within your walls I gathered knowledge from their
        teachings,
within your walls I shared it with whoever asked,   30
making many young men wise for free.
All this is why you cast a spell over me, family house,
and this, dear house, is why you bend and crush me.
Yet learning and love for God will conquer all,
and thirdly we may list the fear of death.   35
So, as if suddenly bitten by gadflies,
I depart from here to where God leads,
the former owner now a paying guest,
the former native now a pitiful wanderer,
without a hearth, and borrowing a stranger's roof,   40
I who never turned a stranger away from my own.
Well, time to move on to another place.
So farewell, then, you, my true home,
which has to be another's from this day on.
So farewell, now, farewell, my second mother,   45
since it was you who nursed me and raised me,
preparing and equipping me
from infancy toward the perfect standard.
Now you'll have others to educate and raise.

50 Ἄλλοις παρέξεις πρὸς λόγους εὐκαιρίαν,
εἴπερ λόγους στέργουσιν, ἡμῖν δ' οὐκέτι.
Σῴζου δέ, σῴζου καὶ σύ, πιστὴ γωνία,
ἐν ᾗ λαθὼν ἔζησα τὸν πρὸ τοῦ βίον.
Ὑμεῖς τε, χρηστοὶ γείτονες, σῴζοισθέ μοι,
55 καὶ τῷ μακρυσμῷ μὴ σκυθρωπάζοιτέ μου·
πάντων γὰρ ἡ χεὶρ τοῦ Θεοῦ δεδραγμένη
ῥᾷον τίθησι καὶ τὰ μακρὰν πλησίον,
ἕως συνάξει πάντας εἰς κρίσιν μίαν.

48

Ὅτε τὴν οἰκίαν ἀπέλαβεν

Ἔχω πάλιν σε καὶ βλέπω τὴν φιλτάτην.
Πλὴν οὐκέτι κλῆρόν σε πατρικὸν λέγω,
Χριστοῦ δὲ μᾶλλον δῶρον ἠγαπημένον
χάριν τε λαμπρὰν εὐσεβοῦς βασιλέως,
5 οἵ με γλυκεῖαν προστεθεικότες βίαν,
παλίντροπον στρέφουσιν αὖθις ἐνθάδε,
ὁ μέν, καθ' ὕπνους δεξιὰν θείαν νέμων,
καὶ πρὸς τὰ τῇδε πολλάκις δοκῶν ἄγειν·
ὁ δέ, προδήλως τὴν ἀνάγκην προσφέρων
10 καὶ τῆς πατρῴας τὴν ἀνάκλησιν στέγης

414

You'll give them now a chance to read and write,   50
if letters interest them — no more for me.
Farewell, farewell, you dear faithful retreat
where I spent my earlier life in seclusion.
I bid farewell, good neighbors, to you too;
do not let my departure cause offense.   55
It is the hand of God that holds all things,
and so with ease will bring the distant near,
till all are gathered for a final judgment.

48

When he recovered his house

I have you back and can look at you, my dearest.
It is only that I no longer call you a family estate,
but a cherished gift from Christ
and a pious emperor's splendid boon.
These two have exerted sweet coercion,   5
turning my course back to this place again;
Christ, showing this divine omen in my sleep,
often appearing to lead me toward this place;
the emperor, crying out my need
and staunchly calling for the return   10

σφοδρῶς ἀπαιτῶν ὡς ἀσύγγνωστον χρέος,
ἕως ἔπεισαν ἐγκατοικῆσαι πάλιν.
Καὶ δὴ κατοικῶν ἐξ ὑπαρχῆς δευτέρας
οὐκ οἶδα μεχρὶ ποῦ τε καὶ πόσον χρόνον
15 νέος καλοῦμαι τῆς παλαιᾶς δεσπότης.
Καὶ θαῦμα τὴν ἄπιστον εὐκινησίαν,
(ναί, τὴν ἄπιστον) ἣν ἐκινήθην, ἔχω,
οὕτως Θεοῦ στρέφοντος οἷς οἶδε τρόποις
καὶ ποικίλως ἄγοντος ἡμῶν τὸν βίον,
20 εἰς ὃν πεποιθὼς εἰμι καὶ θαρρεῖν ἔχω
ὡς καὶ τὸ λεῖπον εὐθετήσει τοῦ βίου,
τοῖς δεξιοῖς τούτοις με πρὸς σωτηρίαν
ὡς ἀσθενῆ τε καὶ μικρόψυχον φέρων·
τὸ καρτερεῖν γὰρ οὐκ ἐμὸν τἀναντία.
25 Οὐκοῦν ἀποτρέποις γε ταῦτα, Χριστέ μου,
μόνοις δὲ τοῖσδε τὴν ἐμὴν ζωὴν ἄγοις,
ὡς χρηστός, ὡς εὔσπλαγχνος, ὡς εὐεργέτης,
εἶτα πρὸς ἄλλον χειραγωγήσοις βίον
ἄλυπον, ἀστένακτον, ἔξω φροντίδων.
30 Τίς γὰρ φόβος σοι τῷ κρατοῦντι τῶν ὅλων
ἓν πλάσμα σῶσαι δωρεὰν ἔργων δίχα;

of my paternal roof, as an unwaivable debt,
till both persuaded me to live there again.
Inhabiting it now for a second time,
I do not know till when and for how long
I can be called the new master of my old home.   15
This mobility is wondrous beyond belief,
—beyond belief, yes!—I own the house I left.
So God changes our course, he alone knows how,
and directs our life in varying directions.
I am confident, and I trust, that God   20
will also guide the rest of my life,
and lead me to salvation with these good omens,
feeble and fainthearted though I am;
for I do not bear adversities well.
So may you keep these away, dear Christ, and   25
may you guide my life by these good omens only,
since you are good, merciful and benevolent.
And may you guide me then toward the next life,
the life without pain, without sighs, without cares.
What fear would you have, as the ruler of all,   30
to save one creature, without works, for free?

49

Εἰς τοὺς ἁγίους πατέρας ἱστορημένους, ἐν οἷς ἦν καὶ ὁ Θεοδώρητος

Ἀνιστόρησας τοὺς σοφοὺς διδασκάλους
καὶ τὸν Θεοδώρητον αὐτοῖς συγγράφω
ὡς ἄνδρα θεῖον, ὡς διδάσκαλον μέγαν,
ὡς ἀκράδαντον ὀρθοδοξίας στύλον.
5 Εἰ δ' ἐκλονήθη μικρὸν ἐκ τινὸς τύχης,
ἄνθρωπος ἦν. Ἄνθρωπε, μὴ κατακρίνης·
οὐ γὰρ τοσοῦτον δυσσεβὴς ἦν ὁ κλόνος,
ὅσον μετεῖχε τῆς ἐριστικῆς βίας.
Τί γὰρ Κύριλλον πανταχοῦ νικᾶν ἔδει,
10 καὶ δογματιστὴν ὄντα καὶ λογογράφον;
Ὅμως δὲ τοῦτο καὶ διώρθωται πάλιν.
Τὰ δ' ἄλλα πάντα τῶν μεγίστων ποιμένων
βλέπων τὸν ἄνδρα μηδενὸς λελειμμένον,
ἐνταῦθα τούτοις εἰκότως συνεγγράφω.

49

On a depiction of the holy fathers, among whom was also Theodoret

Making an image of the wise teachers,
I also depict Theodoret among them,
since he was a divine man, a great teacher,
and an unshakable pillar of orthodoxy.
If perhaps he wavered because of some incident,   5
well, he was human. So, being human, don't you condemn
    him.
His wavering was not so impious,
but was rather due to the violence of the dispute.
Why should Cyril always win,
being both a dogmatist and an author?   10
But this has also been set straight.
In my view, this man is in all respects
equal to the greatest shepherds, and therefore,
it is fitting that I represent him in their company.

50

Εἰς τὸ τυπικὸν τῆς Λαύρας

Δέδοικα μήπως θεσπίσας ἄλλοις τάδε,
αὐτὸς δὲ τούτων οὐδὲν ἐξειργασμένος
κατηγόρους εὕροιμι τοὺς ἐμοὺς νόμους.
Ἀλλ' ὁ Κριτής μου καὶ Θεὸς καὶ Δεσπότης,
5 μὴ τοῖς ἐμοῖς με, τοῖς δὲ σοῖς κρῖνον νόμοις·
οὐ τοὺς δικαίους—φεῦ γάρ· οἴχομαι τάλας—
τοὺς συμπαθεῖς δὲ καὶ φιλανθρώπους λέγω,
οἷς προῖκα σῴζειν οἶδας ὡς εὐεργέτης.

51

Εἰς τὸν διαρρήξαντα τὸ οἰκεῖον χειρόγραφον

Τὴν πάρδαλιν μὲν δυσμενῶς ἔχειν λόγος
πρὸς ὄψιν ἀνδρός, κἂν γεγραμμένην λάβοι,
εὐθὺς διασπᾶν καὶ γραφὴν μισουμένην.
Οὗτος δ' ὁ δεινὸς τῆς Ἀραβίας λύκος

50

On the *typikon* of the Lavra

I fear that, by decreeing the present laws for others,
I may find that my own laws prosecute me,
since I have fulfilled nothing of them.
But, my Judge and God and Lord,
judge me according to your laws and not mine.   5
I mean not the just laws—for alas, I would be damned—
but the compassionate and merciful ones,
by which you, benefactor, know how to save as a gift.

51

On the man who ripped apart his own manuscript

The story goes that a leopard gets angry
at the sight of man, even a painted image,
and won't hesitate to maul the hated picture.
But this fearsome *wolf of Arabia*

5   μορφὴν μὲν ἄλλην οὐ διέσπασε ξένην,
    αὐτὸς δ' ἑαυτὸν ἔξανεν γεγραμμένον.
    Ἕν οὖν τὸ λεῖπον· τὰς τομάς, θεῖα δίκη,
    ἃς ὁ γραφεὶς πέπονθεν, ὁ γράψας πάθοι.

52

Εἰς τὸ αὐτὸ χειρόγραφον,
συγκολληθὲν πάλιν

    Πιστευέτω πᾶς τῇ νεκρῶν ἀναστάσει.
    Ὀστᾶ πρὸς ὀστᾶ συντεθήσεται πάλιν,
    καὶ πῆξιν αὖθις σωμάτων ἕξει λύσις,
    ἐπεὶ τὰ λεπτὰ ταῦτα τῶν σπαραγμάτων
5   εἰς ἓν συνήφθη καὶ συνηρμόσθη πάλιν,
    καὶ τὸν σπαράκτην θῆρα πᾶσιν δεικνύει.

did not shred the image of another,   5
no, he mangled a portrait of himself.
There is only one thing left to do: O divine justice,
may the painter suffer the same injuries as the man in the
    picture.

52

On the same manuscript
that was glued back together

Let all believe in the resurrection of the dead.
Bones will again be attached to bones,
and disjointed bodies will again be reunited,
since also these shredded fragments
are again joined together and assembled,   5
showing to all that the man who ripped them is a wild beast.

53

Εἰς τὰς ἐγγράφας λοιδορίας τὰς κατὰ τοῦ βασιλέως καὶ τοῦ πατριάρχου

Ἄνθρωπε, ῥῖψον ὃ κρατεῖς τε καὶ βλέπεις·
δεινὸς γὰρ αὐτοῖς ἐγκάθηται σκορπίος,
ἰοῦ φέρων ὄλεθρον ἀνθρωποκτόνου.
Τὸ κέντρον ἦρε· μή σε πλήξῃ καιρίαν.
5   Καὶ πῶς γὰρ ἂν φείσαιτο τῶν ἐλαττόνων
ὃς οὐδὲ χριστοὺς εὐλαβεῖται Κυρίου;
Βάλλει βασιλεῖς, οὓς σέβονται καὶ λίθοι,
οὓς οἶδε τιμᾶν καὶ χορὸς τῶν ἀγγέλων,
ὧν ἡ περιττὴ καλλονὴ καὶ χρηστότης
10   καὶ θῆρας αὐτοὺς ἡμεροῖ τοὺς ἀγρίους.
Βάλλει, τιτρώσκει πατριάρχας, ἀγγέλους,
ὧν δαίμονες φρίττουσι τὴν ἀϋλίαν,
οἷς οὐδ᾽ ὁ Μῶμος αὐτὸς ἂν μέμψαιτό τι.
Οὕτως ἀναιδής ἐστι καὶ φόνου πνέει.
15   Πλὴν τοῖς ἅπαξ παθοῦσι καὶ πεπληγόσι
θαυμαστός ἐστι ἰατρείας τρόπος·
εἰ γάρ τις αὐτὸν συλλαβὼν τέμοι μέσον,
ἐκεῖθεν ἕξει τοῦ κακοῦ θᾶττον λύσιν·
τὸν γὰρ βαλόντα καὶ βοηθεῖν τῷ πάθει
20   ἰατρικὸς λόγος τε καὶ παροιμία.
Εἰ δὲ κρατήσας φείσεται τοῦ θηρίου,

53

On the written insults against
the emperor and the patriarch

Man, throw away what you hold and see:
a fearsome scorpion is hidden there,
carrying a deadly venom, lethal for humans.
He has raised his stinger: don't let him inflict a fatal wound.
For why would he spare lesser ones,   5
if he does not even respect the Lord's anointed?
He strikes emperors, whom even stones revere,
whom even the choir of angels holds in honor,
whose abundant charm and goodness
even calms down wild beasts.   10
He strikes, he wounds patriarchs, angels,
whose ethereality even demons fear, and
whom even Momus himself could not blame for some fault.
So shameless is he, breathing murder.
But for those who have once suffered and been wounded,   15
medicine has an amazing remedy.
For if one would grab him and cut through the middle,
he would quickly find deliverance from this evil.
It is a medical maxim and proverb
that the one who causes evil also helps to cure it.   20
But he who captures and then spares the wild beast,

ἄνθρωπον αὐτὸν οὐδαμῶς ἐγὼ λέγω,
θεὸν δὲ μᾶλλον καὶ Θεοῦ καλῶ τύπον,
ὃς καὶ φονευταῖς οἶδε συγγνώμην νέμειν.

54

Ὅτε πρῶτον ἐγνωρίσθη
τοῖς βασιλεῦσιν

Πάλαι μὲν ἦν μοι, δέσποτα στεφηφόρε,
ἄκουσμα φρικτὸν βασιλεὺς αὐτοκράτωρ,
γῆς καὶ θαλάσσης κύριος καὶ δεσπότης,
ἐξουσιαστὴς καὶ δυνάστης τοῦ βίου,
5   ὃν ἂν θέλοι κτείνων τε καὶ σῴζων πάλιν,
ὡς τῶν ἁπάντων τὸ κράτος κεκτημένος·
ἀφ' οὗ δὲ τῆς σῆς ἡμερωτάτης θέας
καὶ τῶν μελιχρῶν ἠξιώθην σου λόγων,
καὶ τὴν καλὴν ἔβλεψα τῶν ἠθῶν χάριν,
10   καὶ τοὺς πόθου γέμοντας ἔγνων σου τρόπους,
οὐκ ἔστιν εἰπεῖν ἡλίκος μοι καὶ πόσος
γλυκασμὸς ἐστάλαξεν εἰς τὴν καρδίαν.
Καί που με δεινὸς πρὸς τὸ πρᾶγμα νῦν ἔρως
ἄφνω κατέσχε καὶ βιάζεται λέγειν
15   ὡς τερπνὸν οὐδὲν ἄλλο πλὴν βασιλέως,
ἀλλ' οὗτός ἐστι χρῆμα κάλλιστον μόνος

I would call him not a human,
but rather god and an imprint of God,
because he is able to forgive even murderers.

54

When he made his first acquaintance
with the ruling family

Once, crown-bearing lord,
I was terrified to hear the words emperor, single ruler,
lord and master of earth and sea,
holding power and might over life,
killing and sparing whomever he wished,   5
because he possesses power over all.
But from the moment I was deemed worthy
of your serene countenance and charming words,
and saw your graceful demeanor,
became familiar with your manners filled with love,   10
I cannot say how much, what immense
sweetness dripped into my heart.
And now somehow, a powerful desire for this
suddenly took hold of me and forces me to say
that there is nothing so fine as the emperor;   15
he alone is the most beautiful

πάντων ἀκουσμάτων τε καὶ θεαμάτων.
Οὕτως ἄρα, κράτιστε τῶν βασιλέων,
ἡ σὴ προσηνὴς καὶ φιλάνθρωπος θέα
20 ἔθελξεν, ἠλλοίωσεν, ἐξέστησέ με,
ἄλλα φρονεῖν ἔπεισεν ἀντὶ τῶν πάλαι,
ὅλως δὲ καινὸν ἐκ παλαιοῦ καὶ νέον
ἔδειξε, διπλοῦν ἔργον ἐξειργασμένη·
ὁμοῦ μὲν ἐπλήρωσεν ἡδονῆς ξένης,
25 ὁμοῦ δὲ λαμπρότητος ἐμπέπληκέ με·
ἄμφω γὰρ αὕτη τὰς ἐνεργείας φέρει,
λαμπηδόνος γέμουσα καὶ θυμηδίας.
Καὶ Μωσέως μὲν τὸ πρόσωπον (ὡς λόγος)
ἐδόξασε πρὶν ἡ Θεοῦ θεωρία,
30 ὡς καὶ κάλυμμα τὸν θεόπτην λαμβάνειν,
ἐπειδὰν αὐτὸν προσλαλεῖν ἄλλοις ἔδει·
οὐ γὰρ φορητὴν εἶχε τὴν αὐτοῦ θέαν,
εἰ μὴ καλυφθεὶς ἦλθεν εἰς ὁμιλίαν.
Ἐμοὶ δὲ σύ, κράτιστε τῶν βασιλέων,
35 εἰς ὄψιν ἐλθὼν καὶ θεαθεὶς μετρίως,
οὐ τὸ πρόσωπον οὐδὲ τὴν ὄψιν μόνον,
ὅλον δὲ δόξης ἐμπέπληκας αὐτίκα.
Καίτοι μέγαν σε τῶν καθ' ἡμᾶς δεσπότην
ᾔδειν πρὸ τούτου καὶ Θεοῦ θεῖον τύπον,
40 καλῶς στρέφοντα τοῦ κράτους τὰς ἡνίας
καὶ σὺν Θεῷ σῴζοντα τὴν οἰκουμένην,
θεὸν δέ, πανσέβαστε, καὶ πλάστην νέον
ἢ δημιουργὸν ἄλλον οὐκ ἠπιστάμην.
Νῦν δ' ὀψὲ μὲν νοῦν, ἀλλ' ὅμως ἐκτησάμην,

of all things to be heard or seen.
Thus, most powerful of emperors,
your gentle and kind appearance
has charmed me, changed me, and exalted me.   20
It persuaded me to have different thoughts than before,
renewed me and made me young instead of old,
thus accomplishing a twofold result:
it filled me with a novel pleasure,
and at the same time I was filled with radiance.   25
Your appearance causes these two effects,
so full it is of light and joy.
As the story goes, the sight of God brought glory
to the face of Moses,
so that he who had seen God covered his face   30
whenever he had to talk about him to others;
for they could not endure the sight of Moses,
unless he entered into conversation with veiled face.
But when you, mightiest of emperors,
come into my sight and I catch even a glimpse of you,   35
you fill me entirely with your glory,
not only my face or my eyes.
I knew before that you were the great ruler
of our world and a divine imprint of God,
guiding well the reins of the state,   40
and saving the world together with God, but,
most venerable one, I did not know you were a new god
and creator, or a new demiurge.
But now, albeit late, I have acquired understanding

45 καὶ πρᾶγμα, θαῦμα, θαῦμα θαυμάτων πέρα,
εἰς δεῦρο λανθάνον με, μανθάνω μόλις.
Σὺ γὰρ θεός τις (ὡς ἔοικε) τὴν φύσιν.
Ἢ πῶς νεουργεῖς (εἰπέ) τοῖς κατ' εἰκόνα,
καὶ ῥᾷστα πλάττεις καὶ μεταπλάττεις πάλιν,
50 γνώμας ἀμείβων, καὶ μεθαρμόζων τρόπους,
τρέπων λογισμούς, καὶ μεθιστῶν καρδίας,
ἄγων, φέρων, στρέφων τε πάντα ῥᾳδίως
ἐκ φθέγματός τε καὶ θέας τῆς σῆς μόνης;
Καὶ τοὺς μὲν ἄλλους οὐ τοσοῦτον θαυμάσω,
55 οὓς ταῦτα ποιεῖς ἐν βραχεῖ καὶ συντόμως,
οὐκ ἀπροθύμους ὄντας οὐδ' αὐτοὺς ἴσως·
ἡμᾶς δὲ πῶς ἤμειψας οὕτως ἀθρόον;
Ἢ πῶς τοσοῦτον ἴσχυσε βραχὺς χρόνος;
Ἅπαξ προσωμίλησας ἡμῖν ἐγγύθεν,
60 ἅπαξ προσεῖδες, μικρὸν ἀντώφθης πάλιν·
ἀπῆλθες εὐθὺς συμμεθαρμόσας ὅλους·
καινὴν γὰρ ἐντέθεικας ἡμῖν καρδίαν,
καὶ πνεῦμα καινὸν ἔκτισας τοῖς ἐγκάτοις.
Ἄγροικος ἦν χθές, ἀστικὸς δὲ νῦν μάλα·
65 κάτω νενευκώς, ἀλλὰ νῦν ἄνω βλέπων·
ἄθυμος, ἀλλ' εὔθυμος, ἡδονῆς γέμων·
μικρός, κατηφής, νῦν δὲ λαμπρὸς καὶ μέγας·
καὶ ταῦτα μηδὲν εἰς τροπὴν φέρον πάθος
παθεῖν ἀπ' ἀρχῆς εὖ παρεσκευασμένος.
70 Ὡς ἄν τι δώσω δεῖγμα τοῦ νέου πάθους,
ἄτυφος ὢν πρίν, νῦν δὲ κομπάζων τάδε,
οὕτω με παντάπασιν ἐξ ἄλλου τέως

and I am just becoming aware of something wondrous,   45
wonder of wonders, that was hidden from me until now.
For you must be a god by nature, so it seems to me.
Or how else, tell me, do you renew those in your image,
how do you so easily mold and remold them,
changing their opinions, transforming their habits,   50
altering their thoughts, transforming their hearts,
guiding, bringing, turning everything easily
by your voice and appearance alone?
I will not admire the others as much,
whom you altered so quickly and suddenly,   55
even if they too were perhaps rather willing.
But how did you change me so suddenly?
How can such a short time have had such an impact?
You spoke to me once from nearby,
you looked upon me once, and I looked back briefly.   60
You went away instantly, but left me wholly changed.
You planted a new heart in me,
you shaped a new spirit within me.
I was boorish yesterday, but now I am urbane;
I looked downcast, but now I look upward;   65
I was somber, but now I am cheerful, full of gladness;
I was of no account and disheartened, but now I am glorious
        and great!
And this happened while I was well prepared from the
        beginning
not to allow any passion to change me.
Just to give an example of this new passion: 70
I was averse to bragging before; now I pride myself on this.
In this way has your all-mighty grace in every respect

ἔδειξεν ἄλλον ἡ παναλκής σου χάρις·
μικρὸν γὰρ αὕτη μικρὸν ἐλλάμψασά μοι,
75 εἶτα κρυβεῖσα θᾶττον ἐκ τῶν ὀμμάτων
ὡς ἀστραπῆς τις ὀξύτης καὶ λαμπρότης,
ὅμως κατεκράτησεν ἡμῶν εἰς τέλος,
καὶ τὴν καλὴν ἄμειψιν ἐξήμειψέ με.
Τί δ᾽ ἂν πάθοι τις, εἰ πάλιν τούτου τύχοι,
80 καὶ τῆς ὁμοίας δεύτερον τύχοι θέας,
ὡς ἡ κέλευσις βούλεται τοῦ δεσπότου;
Ἦ δῆλον ὡς ἄνθρωπος οὐ δόξειέ τις,
ἀλλ᾽ ἄγγελός τις, ἢ θεὸς παραυτίκα,
ὅλος θεωθεὶς τῇ Θεοῦ κοινωνίᾳ.
85 Πειράσομαι δὴ καὶ πάλιν καὶ πολλάκις
σοί τε προσελθεῖν καὶ τυχεῖν ὁμιλίας,
εἴ πως λάβοιμι τήνδε τὴν εὐκληρίαν.
Ἀλλ᾽ ἓν δέδοικα (καὶ τὸ σὸν θεῖον κράτος
αἰτῶ βοηθὸν προσλαβεῖν εἰς τὸν φόβον),
90 μή που με δεινὸν ὄμμα Γοργοῦς ἀγρίας
πρὸ τῆς πύλης βλέψειεν ἠγριωμένα,
μὴ Κέρβερός τις ἐξυλακτήσοι μέγα,
μηδὲ Βριμώ τις ἐμβριμωμένη δάκοι·
καὶ πῶς γὰρ οἴσω δήγματος πληγὴν μίαν,
95 ἄνθρωπος ἰσχνόσαρκος ἐκτετηγμένος;
Ἐγὼ δὲ δειλός εἰμι καὶ πρὸς ἄλλο τι.
Λειτουργικῶν γὰρ πνευμάτων ὄψεις τρέμω,
καὶ τῶν πτερωτῶν ἀγγέλων σου τὴν θέαν·
ψυχὰς γὰρ ἁρπάζουσιν ἐκ τῶν σωμάτων.
100 Ἐξ ὧν με ῥῦσαι, ψυχοσῶστα προστάτα,

made me a person different than before.
Just briefly your grace shone upon me,
then it hid itself quickly from my eyes,   75
like a sharp and blazing lightning flash,
yet it holds me in its grip forever,
and has utterly changed me for the good.
What would someone feel, if this fell to his lot again,
and he obtained for the second time such a sight,   80
as the commandment of my lord wishes?
It is clear that he would no longer seem to be a man,
but an angel, or a god indeed,
wholly divinized by contact with God.
Therefore, I will try, often and repeatedly,   85
to approach you, and be awarded a conversation,
if I may ever receive this privilege.
But there is one fear I have (and I ask
your divine power to help me in this fear):
let not the terrible eye of an angry Gorgon   90
look at me savagely, in front of the gate,
or let a Cerberus bark loudly at me,
or a snorting Brimo bite me;
for how could I endure just one blow or bite,
being a thin-skinned and emaciated man?   95
Above all, I am cowardly;
I tremble at the sight of your *ministering spirits,*
and of your winged angels,
for they steal the soul from the body.
Protect me from them, soul-saving protector,   100

καὶ μήτε τούτων ἐκταραξάτω μέ τι,
μηδ' ἄλλο μηδὲν προσβάλοι τῶν φασμάτων
ἢ τῶν φοβήτρων τῶν πρὸ τῶν προαυλίων.
Ἐπὰν δὲ ταῦτα σὺν Θεῷ διαδράσω,
105 καί που γένωμαι πλησίον τοῦ σοῦ θρόνου,
μηδὲν Χερουβεὶμ ῥομφαίαν πυρὸς φέρον
κατὰ στόμα τρώσοι με καὶ φλέξοι πάλιν,
ἀλλ' ὥσπερ αὐτὸς ἥμερον πλουτεῖς φύσιν,
καὶ τὴν ὁδόν μοι πᾶσαν ἥμερον δίδου.
110 Ὡς εἴ γε ταύτην ἀσφαλῶς διαδράμω,
ὅρμος τις ἡδὺς τἆλλα πάντα καὶ φίλος,
τῆς σῆς γαληνότητος ἐμπεπλησμένα.
Τὰ νῦν δὲ Χριστόν, πιστὲ χριστὲ Κυρίου,
ἔχοις σύνοικον καὶ συνεργὸν τοῦ κράτους,
115 τὸν καὶ βασιλεύσαντα καὶ στέψαντά σε
καὶ συμβασιλεύοντα καὶ σκέποντά σε·
οὗτος γὰρ ὥσπερ τοῖς τρισὶν νεανίαις
συνῆν τέταρτος ἐν μέσῳ φλογὸς πάλαι,
οὕτω πάλιν τέταρτος ἔστω κἀνθάδε
120 δροσισμὸς ὑμῖν ἐν βασιλείοις μέσοις·
τὸν ἥλιον σὲ πρῶτα σῴζων, καὶ νέμων
ζωὴν ἄλυπον, εὐτυχῆ, νικηφόρον
καλοῖς τε τοῖς σύμπασιν εὐθηνουμένην·
ἔπειτα ταύτην τὴν σελήνην τοῦ κράτους,
125 τὴν κοσμολαμπῆ καὶ διαπρεπεστάτην,
τὴν οὐδὲν ἄλλο πλὴν ὃ κέκληται μόνον—
ζωὴ γὰρ ὄντως ἡ Ζωὴ τοῦ νῦν βίου—
τρίτην δέ μοι σύνταττε καὶ τὴν δευτέραν,

and let none of them pester me,
and let no other terrifying apparition
from the forecourts attack me.
And when I can pass through them, with God's help,
and approach your throne,   105
let no Cherubim holding a flaming sword
pierce my mouth and set me ablaze,
but, just as you have a tranquil nature,
grant me a way that is wholly tranquil.
And if I can pursue this way safely,   110
there shall be a sweet and friendly haven,
as all the rest is filled with your tranquility.
For now, faithful one anointed by the Lord, may you have
Christ as your comrade and colleague of your reign;
he has made you emperor and crowned you,   115
he rules together with you, and protects you.
Just as he joined those three young men of old
as a fourth man, in the midst of flames,
let him now be again the fourth person here,
a drop of dew for you in the midst of the palace.   120
May he first save you, the sun, and give you
a painless, fortunate, and victorious life,
prospering in all fine things;
and then her, the moon of your reign,
who illuminates the world magnificently,   125
being nothing else than the name that is given her—
for Zoe is truly the life of our present time—
and add a third person, that second woman,

τὸ φαιδρὸν ἄστρον τοῦ πανολβίου στέφους,
130 ἢ τὴν ἐκείνης αὐταδέλφην ἀξίαν,
ὃ παντὸς ἄλλου μεῖζον εἰς εὐδοξίαν.

Ὁ Χριστὸς οὖν τέταρτος ὑμῖν ἐν μέσῳ
ἀεὶ παρέστω καὶ πρὸς ἀλλήλους μίαν
σύμπνοιαν ἐργάζοιτο καὶ συμψυχίαν,
135 διδοὺς ἅπασι μακρὸν ἐνθάδε χρόνον,
δόξαν δ' ἐκεῖθεν τὴν ἑαυτοῦ προσνέμων
καὶ τὸ στέφος, κράτιστε, τῆς ἀφθαρσίας.

55

Εἰς τὰς δεσποίνας

Δισσαῖς ἀνάσσαις αὐταδέλφαις Αὐγούσταις
δώρημα κοινὸν ἐξ ἑνὸς δούλου τόδε.

Εἰς τὴν ἐμὴν δέσποιναν οὐ χωρεῖ τόπος,
ἀλλ' ἡ κατ' αὐτὴν δόξα καὶ τὸ νῦν κλέος
5 ἅπασαν ἐπλήρωσε τὴν οἰκουμένην,
καὶ πανταχοῦ φαίνει τε καὶ λάμπει πλέον
τῆς κοσμολαμποῦς πανσελήνου λαμπάδος,
ὥστε πρόδηλος πᾶσιν ἡ ταύτης χάρις,
κἂν ἔνδον αὐτὴ τῶν ἀνακτόρων μένῃ.
10 Ἀλλ', ὦ μεγίστη κυρία τοῦ νῦν γένους

436

the shining star of our blissful crown,
or else, the sister worthy of the other one, 130
something that above all else confers glory on her.
So, may Christ be the fourth person in your midst,
may he always be present, and may he create
agreement of thought and soul among you,
granting all of you many years on earth, 135
and assigning you his own glory in heaven,
and, O most powerful one, the crown of immortality.

55

For the empresses

For the two sisters, empresses and Augustae,
this is a common gift from one servant.

One place is not sufficient for my lady
since her glory and her present renown
have filled up the entire universe, 5
and shine everywhere, illuminating more
than the moonlight shining on the earth,
so that her grace is clear to all,
even when she herself remains within the palace.
But, greatest lady of this generation 10

(πρὸς γὰρ σὲ τρέψω τὸν βραχὺν τοῦτον λόγον,
κἂν μὴ βλέπειν ἔχω σε, πῶς δέχῃ τάδε),
ὦ τῶν τοσούτων ἐκγόνη βασιλέων
ὅσους ἀριθμεῖν οὐκ ἔνεστι ῥαδίως,
15 τὸ σκῆπτρον ἡμῶν, ἡ πρόνοια, τὸ κράτος,
τῆς εὐγενείας λείψανον, τῆς πορφύρας
κάλλιστον ἄνθος, χρῶμα τῆς ἁλουργίδος,
ὀφθαλμὲ κόσμου, πλοῦτε, δόξα, λαμπρότης,
πᾶν εἴ τι τερπνὸν ἄλλο τῶν τιμωμένων,
20 ὦ τῶν καθ' ἡμᾶς πραγμάτων σωτηρία,
ζωή τε τοῦ σύμπαντος εὐτυχεστάτη,
οὕτω πλατύνου γῆς ἀπ' ἄκρων εἰς ἄκρα,
φαίνουσα πᾶσιν, ἐγγύθεν καὶ μακρόθεν·
οὕτως ὁρωμένη τε καὶ κεκρυμμένη
25 πλήρου τὰ πάντα φωτὸς ἀκραιφνεστάτου·
οὕτως δὲ πυκνὰς πέμπε τὰς λαμπηδόνας,
ἔχουσα συλλάμπουσαν ἐκ τοῦ πλησίον
ἄλλην σεαυτήν, τὴν ἐμὴν μὲν δεσπότιν,
σὴν δ' αὐταδέλφην γνησίαν καὶ φιλτάτην,
30 ᾗ συμμετέσχες καὶ γένους καὶ τοῦ στέφους,
ᾗ συμμερίζῃ τοῦ κράτους τὰς ἡνίας.
Ἐπεύχομαι δὲ πλεῖστον ἐνταῦθα χρόνον
ὑμῖν δοθῆναι καὶ τὸ συγχαίρειν ἅμα.
Καὶ δὴ συνευφράνοισθε, καὶ βλέποιτέ μοι
35 καὶ τὸν φαεινὸν ἥλιον καὶ φωσφόρον,
τὸ κοσμικὸν φῶς, τὴν γαλήνην τοῦ βίου,
ἔαρ τὸ φαιδρόν, τῆς χαρᾶς τὴν ἡμέραν,
τὸν εὐγενῆ μέν, εὐτυχῆ δὲ δεσπότην,

(I now turn this short discourse to you,
though I cannot see how you'll receive it),
scion of so many emperors
that no one could easily enumerate them,
our scepter, our providence, our power,   15
remnant of nobility, loveliest flower
of purple, hue of the imperial robe,
the world's eye, wealth, glory, brilliance,
whatever delightful among things to be honored,
O salvation of our current affairs,   20
life most blessed of the universe,
thus may you stretch from earth's one end to the other,
shining on all from near and far;
in this way, seen as well as hidden,
may you fill all things with the purest light;   25
may you thus often send forth your rays,
having close to you another self,
who shines with you: my mistress,
your genuine and dearest sister,
with whom you share ancestry and crown,   30
with whom you hold the reins of state.
I wish long ages here on earth
be granted you with happiness to share.
May you, indeed, rejoice together and look
upon the brilliant and light-bringing sun,   35
the light of the world, the serenity of our life,
the glorious spring, the day of joy,
a lord who is noble and yet fortunate,

τὸν εὐτυχῆ μέν, εὐσεβῆ δὲ τὸ πλέον,
40 τῆς γῆς τὸ θαῦμα, τὸν μέγαν Μονομάχον,
ὃν ἡ πρόνοια κοσμικῶν κακῶν λύσιν
ἔδειξεν ἡμῖν καὶ καλῶν πάντων βρύσιν.
Οὕτως ἄλυπον ἐκπερῶσαι τὸν βίον,
ἔχοιτε τοῦτον λύχνον ἄλλον ἐν μέσῳ,
45 ἄσβεστον ἐκπέμποντα λαμπαδουχίαν·
πρὸς ὃν βλέπουσαι νύκτα καὶ μεθ' ἡμέραν,
ὁμοῦ τε συντέρποισθε, καὶ σῴζοισθέ μοι.

56

Ἐν τῇ μνήμῃ τῶν ἁγίων
Σεργίου καὶ Βάκχου,
ὅτε καὶ δῶρα ἔπεμψαν

Οἱ γειτονοῦντες μάρτυρες τοῖς δεσπόταις
ὡς γείτονας στέργουσι τοὺς ἐν γειτόνων,
φιλοβασιλεῖς ἐκ μακρῶν ὄντες χρόνων,
καὶ συμφορὰς ἔλυσαν αὐτοῖς πολλάκις,
5 ἀφαρπάσαντες ἐξ ὀλέθρων ἐσχάτων·
ἐφ' οἷς παρ' αὐτῶν εὖρον ἀντιμισθίαν
τὸν πανσέβαστον τοῦτον οἶκον ἐνθάδε·
ὃς εὐπρεπὴς μέν ἐστι δόξα τῷ κράτει,

who is fortunate and yet even more pious,
the marvel of this earth, great Monomachos.   40
Providence has shown him as the solution
of all evil on earth and source of all good.
May you complete a painless life,
and have him as another lamp in your midst,
emitting inextinguishable torchlight;   45
by looking upon him night and day,
may you equally share in his delight, safe and healthy.

56

On the commemoration day of
Saints Sergios and Bacchos,
when they also sent gifts

The martyrs who are neighbors of our rulers
love their neighbors as neighbors,
since they have supported emperors from very early on,
and often have they resolved their misfortunes,
saving them from the deepest downfall.   5
For this, the saints have received compensation from them:
this most venerable home here,
an appropriate glory for the state,

πόλει δὲ κόσμος, τοῖς δ' ἀνακτόροις φύλαξ.

10 Τοῦτον βασιλεῖς δεξιοῦνται πλουσίως·
τοῦτον σέβουσιν οἱ σεβαστοὶ δεσπόται,
ἄλλος παρ' ἄλλου τὸν τύπον δεδεγμένοι,
καὶ τὴν ἀμοιβὴν τῶν ἐπ' αὐτοῖς θαυμάτων
τοῖς μάρτυσι νέμουσιν ἐκ τοῦ πλησίον.

15 Οὗτοι φιλοῦντες ἔκπαλαι τοὺς τοῦ κράτους,
μᾶλλον φιλοῦσι τοὺς καθ' ἡμᾶς δεσπότας
ὡς εὐσεβεστέρους τε καὶ σοφωτέρους·
σοφώτεροι γάρ εἰσιν οἱ πρὸς ἀξίαν
τὰ θεῖα τιμᾶν εἰδότες πάντων πλέον.

20 Οὗτοι κατευθύνουσιν αὐτῶν τὸ κράτος,
αἴγλῃ περιστέφοντες εὐτυχημάτων·
οὗτοι κατ' ἐχθρῶν συμμαχοῦσι τοῖς φίλοις,
καὶ προσφιλεῖς τιθοῦσι τοῖς ὑπηκόοις,
πᾶσι προσηνεῖς, πᾶσιν ἠγαπημένους·

25 οὗτοι δὲ καὶ νῦν, οἷάπερ φίλοι φίλοις,
γνωρίσματα στέλλουσιν εὐνοίας τάδε,
καὶ τοῦτον αὐτοῖς μηνύουσι τὸν τρόπον
ἤδη παροῦσαν τὴν ἑαυτῶν ἡμέραν,
καθ' ἣν θανόντες εὐκλεῶς οἱ γεννάδαι,

30 δόξῃ κατεστέφθησαν ὡς νικηφόροι,
καὶ συγκαλοῦσιν εἰς μίαν θυμηδίαν,
οὓς ἐξ ἔθους ἔχουσι τιμᾶν γνησίως,
ὡς ἂν συνευφραίνοιντο τοῖς στεφηφόροις
κοινῶς ἑορτάζοντες οἱ στεφηφόροι.

35 Πείθεσθε τοίνυν, ὦ φαεινοὶ δεσπόται,
καὶ τῆς χαρᾶς δέχεσθε τὴν κοινωνίαν.

an adornment for the city, a guardian for the palace.
Emperors honor this building lavishly,   10
and the revered rulers pay it respect.
The emperors receive the example from each other,
and give their neighbor saints
the reward for their miracles.
The saints have always been well disposed toward the rulers,   15
but they love especially our present lords
because they are more pious and wise;
for those who know how to worthily honor the divine,
and more than any other, are the wisest.
The saints guide their reign,   20
and crown it with a bliss of good fortune;
they join their friends in the fight against enemies,
and make them popular with their subjects,
friend to everyone, and loved by all.
Also now they send these gifts as tokens of benevolence,   25
as friends do for friends,
and in this way they announce to them
that their own day is already present,
when these virtuous men died gloriously,
and were crowned with glory as victors.   30
The saints summon to a common feast
those whom they genuinely honor, as is their habit,
so that the crowned ones can celebrate
and rejoice in company of the crowned ones.
So comply, O shining lords,   35
and accept to share in the joy.

Ἐνταῦθα μὲν νῦν ὡς φίλοι καὶ πλησίον,
ἐν οὐρανοῖς δὲ μικρὸν ὕστερον πάλιν,
ὅταν λαβόντες ἄλλο βέλτιον στέφος,
40 τούτοις τε συγχαίροιτε καὶ τοῖς ἀγγέλοις.

57

Εἰς τὴν ἐν Εὐχαΐτοις εἰκόνα τοῦ βασιλέως

Καὶ τὸν κραταιὸν δεσπότην Κωνσταντῖνον,
τῆς γῆς τὸ θαῦμα, τὸν μέγαν Μονομάχον,
ἐνταῦθα πρᾶξις εὐσεβὴς ἀναγράφει·
τὰς δωρεὰς γὰρ τῶν πρὸ τοῦ βασιλέων
5 σάλον παθούσας ἐξ ἐπηρείας μέγαν
χρυσῆς ὑπεστήριξε κιόνος βάσει,
τὸν χρυσόβουλλον ἀνταναστήσας λόγον
ὡς ἀντέρεισμα καρτερὸν πρὸς τὴν βίαν,
δι' οὗ τὸ μέλλον ἀσφαλέστερον νέμει
10 τῇ μάρτυρος πόλει τε καὶ παροικίᾳ·
ὅθεν δίκαιον ἀντιλαμβάνει γέρας,
εἰς τοὺς καθ' ἡμᾶς ἐγγραφεὶς εὐεργέτας.

Here and now, you are the saints' friends and neighbors,
and in the near future, in heaven,
when you will have received another crown, a better one,
may you rejoice with them, and with the angels.   40

57

On the image of the emperor
in Euchaïta

A pious deed depicts here
also the powerful lord Constantine,
the marvel of the earth, great Monomachos.
The gifts of the previous emperors,
shaken gravely by devastation,   5
he supported with the base of a golden pillar,
by setting up a golden bull,
as an enduring buttress against destruction,
thus granting a safer future
to the city, abode of the martyr.   10
Therefore, he receives a rightful gift in exchange,
by being depicted among our own benefactors.

58

Εἰς τὴν θήκην τοῦ Τιμίου Ξύλου τοῦ βασιλέως

Σταυροῦ πάλιν φῶς, καὶ πάλιν Κωνσταντῖνος.
Ὁ πρῶτος εἶδε τὸν τύπον δι' ἀστέρων,
ὁ δεύτερος δὲ τοῦτον αὐτὸν καὶ βλέπει,
καὶ χερσὶ πισταῖς προσκυνούμενον φέρει.
5 Ἄμφω παρ' αὐτοῦ τὸ κράτος δεδεγμένοι,
ἄμφω σέβουσιν αὐτὸν ὡς εὐεργέτην.

59

Εἰς τὸν ἅγιον Θεοφύλακτον

Θεὸς φύλαξ σοι· τοῦτο γὰρ κλῆσιν φέρεις.
Ἐμοὶ δὲ καὶ σὺ σὺν Θεῷ φύλαξ, πάτερ,
σώζων ἀσινῶς, ἀσφαλῶς διεξάγων,
καὶ τὴν ζάλης γέμουσαν ἡμερῶν νόσον,
5 ἣν εἰς τέλος πράϋνον εὐχῶν φαρμάκοις,
καὶ πάντα μοι σύμπραττε πρὸς τὸ συμφέρον,

58

On the emperor's reliquary of the wood of the True Cross

Again the light of the cross, again a Constantine.
The first Constantine saw its image through the stars,
the second sees the cross itself,
and carries the adored object in faithful hands.
Both have received their power from it,   5
and both revere it as their benefactor.

59

On Saint Theophylact

God is your guardian; hence the name you bear.
But you, together with God, are also my guardian, father,
saving me from harm, conducting me safely,
and subduing the disease full of confusion,
which you may alleviate forever with the medicine of prayers,   5
and assist me to my advantage in everything I do,

ἔργοις βεβαιῶν τὴν ἐπώνυμον χάριν,
ἐφ' ἣν πεποιθώς, ἱστορῶ σε καὶ γράφω.

60

Αἴνιγμα εἰς πλοῖον,
ὡς ἐξ ἑτέρου

Ζῷόν τι πεζόν· ἀλλὰ νηκτὸν εὑρέθη.
Ἔμψυχον, ἀλλ' ἄψυχον. Ἔμπνουν, ἀλλ' ἄπνουν.
Ἕρπον, βαδίζον, καὶ πτεροῖς κεχρημένον.
Ἄκουε καὶ θαύμαζε, καὶ δίδου λύσιν.

61

Εἰς τὸν τὸ αὐτὸ δι' ἑτέρων ὡς ἕτερόν τι
προβαλόντα

Ἐδεξάμην σε καινὸν οὐ φέροντά τι·
οὐ πρόσφατος γὰρ ὥσπερ αὐχεῖς, ἀλλ' ὅλος

confirming with deeds the gift that you carry as a name,
in which I have faith, and hence I represent you and paint
   you.

60

Riddle on the ship, as if said by someone else

It is an animal on feet, but it turns out to swim.
It has a soul, but is soulless. It has a spirit, but is spiritless.
It creeps, walks, and uses wings.
Hear and marvel, and give the solution.

61

To the person who presented the same riddle in other words and as another riddle

I found out that you brought nothing new:
you're not fresh, as you boast, but absolutely

ἕωλος, ἐξίτηλος ἐν λόγοις πάρει,
νηὸς λυθείσης τῷ χρόνῳ, σαπρὰ ξύλα
5 ὡς ναυαγός τις συλλέγων τε καὶ λέγων.
Ἄνθρωπ', ἄπελθε. Τὴν σκάφην ἀνατρέπεις·
φθείρειν γὰρ αὐτὴν μᾶλλον ἢ σῴζειν ἔφυς,
κάκιστα πηγνύς, ῥᾳδίως δ' ὅμως λύων,
ἤ, μᾶλλον εἰπεῖν, συνδιασπῶν τῷ χρόνῳ·
10 οὕτω σέσηπεν ἡ σοφή σου Πυθία.
Χρησμὸς δὲ καινὸς οὐδαμῶς, κενὸς δ' ὅμως.
Ἥρως δὲ δόξας, λῆρος εὑρέθης μόνον.

62

Εἰς τὸ Δεσποτικὸν αἷμα

Ἐν οὐρανοῖς μὲν προσκυνητὰς ἀγγέλους
ἔδει τὸ λύτρον τῆς ἐμῆς ψυχῆς ἔχειν,
ἀλλ' ἦν ἄμεινον τὸν δι' ὃν παρεσχέθη
τοῦτον τὸ δῶρον προσκυνεῖν ἐν γῇ κάτω.
5 Ὅμως δὲ τοῦτο προσκυνοῦσι καὶ νόες,
ἐνταῦθα σεπτῶς νῦν τεθησαυρισμένον·
πρέπει γὰρ αὐτοὺς αἷμα τιμᾶν Δεσπότου,
εἰς ἓν δι' αὐτοῦ τοῖς βροτοῖς συνημμένους.

450

obsolete and worn out in words.
Like some castaway, you gather and collect
rotten wood from a ship that is wrecked by time.   5
Go away, man! You're overturning my skiff.
You're destroying it rather than saving it—
assembling badly, dismantling with ease—
more like ruining it with the help of time.
This is how your wise Pythia has wasted away.   10
Your oracle isn't original, it's arid.
You looked like a hero, but you're just idle talk.

62

On the blood of the Lord

It is right that angels in the heavens
should worship the ransom for my soul,
but better still that the one for whom it was offered
should worship this gift here on earth below.
Yet the angelic minds also worship it,   5
stored here in reverence as a treasure;
for it is fitting for them to honor the Lord's blood,
since through it they are made one with mortals.

63

Εἰς τὴν Θεοτόκον,
ὡς ἐν ὕπνῳ ἀπεκαλύφθη

Οὐκ ἦν καθεύδειν τὴν φιλάνθρωπον κόρην,
τῶν εὐσεβούντων ἀγρυπνούντων ἐν φόβοις,
οὐδὲ προδοῦναι τοῦ κράτους τὰς ἡνίας
εἰς χεῖρας ἐχθράς, δουλικὰς καὶ βαρβάρους.
5 Ἀλλ᾽ εἰς δύσιν σπεύδουσα καὶ πρὸς τὴν ἔω
τῷ γῆς κρατοῦντι συμμαχεῖ στεφηφόρῳ,
εὔζωνον οὕτω τὸν δρόμον ποιουμένη.
Καὶ μαρτυροῦσιν οὓς ἀφυπνίζει φίλους.

64

Εἰς τὴν αὐτήν

Δραμοῦσα τὸ πρὶν ἐξ ἑῴας εἰς δύσιν,
καὶ σὺν δίκῃ κτείνασα τὸν μιαιφόνον,
πρὸς τὴν ἑαυτῆς αὖθις ἐκτρέχει πόλιν
ἡ παντάνασσα, καὶ τροποῦται βαρβάρους,
5 νίκην ἀεὶ νέμουσα τῷ στεφηφόρῳ,
ὅθεν παριστᾷ καὶ γραφεῖσα τὸν δρόμον.

63

On the Mother of God,
when she revealed herself during sleep

The compassionate maiden could not sleep
while the pious were awake with fear,
nor could she hand over the reins of power
to hostile, servile, and barbaric hands.
Instead, she rushes to the west and to the east,   5
in alliance with the crown-bearing ruler of the earth,
thus making the way unencumbered.
The friends she awakens confirm this.

64

On the same

After running previously from east to west,
and rightfully killing the murderer,
the mistress of all now quickly returns
to her own city, and repels barbarians,
thus always awarding victory to the crown bearer;   5
therefore, also in image, she shows her journey.

65

Εἰς τοὺς δύο ἁγίους Θεοδώρους

Ὡς ἀγχίνους ἦν ὁ γραφεὺς τῶν εἰκόνων.
Διπλοῦς γὰρ αὐτός, πνεῦμα σάρξ τε, τυγχάνων,
διττοὺς ἑαυτῷ τοὺς ὑπερμάχους γράφει,
τῷ μὲν τὸ σῶμα, τῷ δὲ τὴν ψυχὴν νέμων.

66

Εἰς τινὰ τιμηθέντα ἐξαίφνης

Μυστογράφος χθὲς εὐγενὴς νεανίας,
καὶ σήμερον πάρεστιν ἐξάκτωρ νέος.
Τὸ μὲν παρῆλθεν, ἄλλο δ᾽ ἦλθεν ἁθρόον·
καὶ τοῦτο δ᾽ αὖθις μακρὸν οὐ μένει χρόνον.
5   Ἀπῆλθεν ἡ χθές, ἡ δ᾽ ἐνεστῶσα τρέχει·
καὶ τὴν παροῦσαν αὔριον χθές τις φράσει.
Κἀνταῦθα τοίνυν νῦν μὲν ἐξάκτωρ φίλος,
δείξει δὲ τοῦτον ἄλλο τι χρόνος τάχα,
ταῖς κλήσεσιν δ᾽ ἔπειτα συγκατασβέσει.
10 Τοιοῦτόν ἐστι πᾶν τὸ θνητὸν καὶ ῥέον·

65

On the two saints Theodore

How intelligent was the painter of these icons!
Being himself dual, of soul and flesh,
he paints for himself two allies,
commending to one his body, to the other his soul.

66

On someone who was suddenly promoted

This noble youth was yesterday a clerk
and is today a newly made tax collector.
The former is gone; the latter came of a sudden,
and this, in turn, will not last for long.
Yesterday is gone; today speeds by.   5
Tomorrow, people will also call today "yesterday."
Now, to be sure, the tax collector is a favorite,
but time perhaps will show he's something else,
and will later let him fade away with his titles.
Such are all beings mortal and fleeting: 10

σκιὰ κρατούσαις χερσὶν οὐ κρατουμένη.
Τίς οὖν παρατρέχοντα ῥοῦν παραδράμοι;

67

Εἰς τάφον

Κοινὸς τριῶν εἷς φιλτάτων οὗτος τάφος.
Μηδεὶς δὲ καὶ τέταρτον ἄλλον ἐμβάλοι·
ἕξει γὰρ οὗτος, ὅς τις ὤν που καὶ τύχοι,
τόλμης ἀμοιβὴν τὴν Θεοῦ φρικτὴν δίκην.

68

Εἰς σχέδος

Τεσσαράκοντα συμμάχους θείους ἔχω,
τεσσαράκοντα φράσσομαι παραστάταις.
Τίς πρὸς τοσούτους χεῖρας ὁπλίτας ἄροι;
Τίς πρὸς φάλαγγα μαρτύρων στήσοι μάχην;
5 Ὅρα, σχιδευτά, πρὸς τίνας μοι συμπλέκῃ,
πόσῳ στρατῷ δὲ συμβαλεῖν τολμᾷς μάχην.

a shadow that cannot be held by the hands that hold it.
Who, then, will run by the stream that itself runs by?

67

On a grave

This is one common grave for three dear people.
No one should put a fourth in it.
Whoever he happens to be, he will have
God's terrible justice as a reward for his boldness.

68

On a dictation exercise

I have forty divine allies,
I am defended by forty supporters.
Who will take up arms against so many hoplites?
Who will begin battle against a phalanx of martyrs?
Look out, dictation botcher, whom you fight against,   5
and what a great army you dare to engage in battle.

69

Εἰς τὸ λοῦμα τῶν Βλαχερνῶν

Ἔβλυζε καὶ πρὶν νᾶμα τῷ λαῷ πέτρα·
Χριστὸν δὲ ταύτην μυστικοί φασιν λόγοι,
ὃς καὶ ποτίζει νέκταρ εἰς ἀφθαρσίαν.
Μήτηρ δὲ Χριστοῦ δευτέρα πάλιν πέτρα·
5   ζηλοῖ τὸν υἱόν, καὶ ῥέει ζωῆς ὕδωρ.
Πάντες δέχεσθε συντρέχοντες τὴν χάριν.

70

Εἰς τὴν διὰ κινναβάρεως χαραγὴν
τῶν σχεδῶν

Ἡ δεσπότου χεὶρ τοῦ σοφοῦ Μονομάχου
ἀληθινὸν νοῦν ἐντίθησι τοῖς νέοις,
ἄνθει καταχρῴζουσα πορφυροχρόῳ,
βασιλικῆς γνώρισμα λαμπρὸν ἀξίας.

69

On the bathhouse of Blachernai

Of old a rock gushed forth a stream for the people.
Mystic writings explain that it was Christ,
who also gives nectar to drink for immortality.
The mother of Christ, in turn, is a second rock:
she imitates her son and streams the water of life.   5
Hasten all together to receive this gift.

70

On the cinnabar writing
of the dictations

The hand of the wise lord Monomachos
instills a true mind in the youth,
giving it the color of a purple flower,
the splendid sign of imperial dignity.

71

Εἰς τὸ βιβλίον τῆς διακονίας τοῦ τροπαιοφόρου

Πιστὸς βασιλεύς, εὐσεβὴς αὐτοκράτωρ,
σεβαστὸς ὀρθόδοξος ὁ Μονομάχος,
τὸ πρὸς σὲ φίλτρον οἷον ἐν ψυχῇ φέρω,
ἔργοις ἔδειξα, λαμπρὲ τροπαιοφόρε,
5 ἅπαντα ταῦτα σὴν ἀπαρτίσας χάριν·
ὧν ἡ γραφὴ δείκνυσιν αὕτη τοὺς τύπους,
ἐμοὶ πρὸ πάντων μαρτυροῦσα τὸν πόθον,
ἔπειτα ταῖς σαῖς πανσεβάστοις Αὐγούσταις.

72

Εἰς τὸ αὐτό

Ἄλλων βασιλεύς, σὸς δὲ πιστὸς οἰκέτης,
ὁ τὸ κράτος σαῖς ἐκ Θεοῦ λιταῖς ἔχων.
Ἀδελφὸν οὖν δίδωμι τοῖς ὑπηκόοις,
χαίρων ἐμαυτὸν εἰς τὸ σοὶ δόξαν φέρειν,

71

On the book for liturgical services in the church of the victorious martyr

I, faithful king and pious emperor,
the revered and orthodox Monomachos,
have shown the great love I hold for you in my soul
through deeds, radiant trophy bearer,
as I have, for your sake, completed all this.   5
This very painting shows our images,
bearing witness to my devotion before all,
and in addition that of your most revered Augustae.

72

On the same

I am the king of all others, but of you I am a faithful servant,
obtaining my power from God by your entreaties.
So I give what is akin to my subjects,
gladdening myself by bringing you glory,

5 καὶ τὰς Αὐγούστας ὡς συνεργοὺς λαμβάνω
πρὸς τὴν ἴσην πρᾶξίν τε καὶ λειτουργίαν.
Ἀλλ' ἀντίδος, μέγιστε τροπαιοφόρε,
ἅπασιν ἡμῖν τὴν ἄνω σκηπτουχίαν.

73

Ἀμοιβαῖοι εἰς τὸν Ἀσώματον

"Τίς τὴν ἄμορφον ἐξεμόρφωσεν φύσιν;"
"Ἡ δοξάσασα τὸ στέφος Θεοδώρα."
"Καὶ πῶς ἀνιστόρησεν ἄγνωστον θέαν;"
"Πίστις κατορθοῖ πάντα ταῦτα ῥᾳδίως."
5 "Ποῖον δὲ μισθὸν ἡ πανευσεβὴς θέλει;"
"Ποθεῖ πρὸ πάντων ψυχικὴν σωτηρίαν."
"Ἀρχιστράτηγε, σπεῦδε, πλήρου τὸν πόθον."
"Ἡ πίστις αὐτῇ προξενήσει καὶ τόδε."

and I take the Augustae as my helpers,   5
for the same deed and the same service.
But you, greatest trophy bearer, give in exchange
to all of us the rule from above.

73

Dialogue verses on the Incorporeal One

"Who has given form to a formless nature?"
"She who has brought glory to the crown: Theodora."
"And how has she pictured an unknowable sight?"
"Faith can easily accomplish those things."
"And what reward desires this pious woman?"   5
"Above all, she longs for the salvation of her soul."
"Archgeneral, quickly fulfill her wish."
"Faith will procure her this too."

74

Ἄλλοι εἰς τὸν αὐτόν

Ἔχουσα θερμὸν προστάτην ἐνταῦθά σε
ἡ πανσέβαστος Αὐγούστα Θεοδώρα,
ἐκεῖ πλέον σε προστατεῖν αὐτῆς θέλει,
ἀρχιστράτηγε τῶν ἄνω στρατευμάτων,
5 ὅταν βασιλεὺς οὐρανῶν κρίνων κάτω
τοὺς γῆς βασιλεῖς εἰς κρίσιν φρικτὴν ἄγῃ.
Ὅθεν παρ' αὐτῆς νῦν λαβὼν δῶρον τόδε,
θερμῶς τότε πρόστηθι τῆς δωρουμένης.

75

Εἰς δέησιν ὑπὸ τοὺς πόδας τοῦ Χριστοῦ κειμένου τοῦ βασιλέως, ὡς ἐκ τοῦ βασιλέως

Σὺ δεσπότην με τῶν σεαυτοῦ κτισμάτων
καὶ τῶν ἐμῶν ἄρχοντα συνδούλων ἔθου.
Ἐγὼ δὲ δοῦλος εὑρεθεὶς ἁμαρτίας,
τὰς μάστιγάς σου, Δέσποτα Κριτά, τρέμω.

74

Other verses on the same

The most revered Augusta Theodora
has you as her ardent protector in this world,
but desires your protection more in the world beyond,
archgeneral of the celestial armies,
when heaven's king makes judgment here below   5
on earthly kings and leads them to dreadful judgment.
So accept this gift from her now, and
ardently advocate for the donor in the world to come.

75

On an entreaty scene in which the emperor is lying prostrate at Christ's feet, as if spoken by the emperor

You have appointed me as the lord of your creatures
and as the ruler over my fellow slaves.
But since I have been found to be a slave of sin,
I tremble before your scourges, Lord and Judge.

76

Ὡς ἐκ τῆς Θεοτόκου

Μήτηρ σε, τέκνον, ἱκετεύει παρθένος·
σὸν οὗτος ἔργον, κἄν τι προσκέκρουκέ σοι,
σὸν πλάσμα, σὸν ποίημα· σοῦ πλὴν οὐδένα
θεὸν γινώσκει. Δὸς σὺ τὴν σωτηρίαν.

77

Ὡς ἐκ τοῦ Προδρόμου

Ἄνθρωπος ἦν, εὔσπλαγχνε· συγγνώμην ἔχε·
ζῷον μὲν εὐόλισθον εἰς ἁμαρτίαν,
ὅμως δὲ τὴν σὴν πίστιν οὐκ ἠρνημένον.
Ἡ πίστις αὐτόν, μακρόθυμε, σωσάτω.

76

As if spoken by the Mother of God

Your virgin mother implores you, child:
this man is your work, and even if he has offended you,
he is your creation, your artifact. He knows no other god
than you. Grant him salvation.

77

As if spoken by John the Forerunner

He was a human, O compassionate one. Show mercy.
He is a living creature prone to sin,
but still he did not deny faith in you.
Let faith then save him, O patient one.

78

Ὡς ἐκ τοῦ Χριστοῦ

Αἰδώς τε μητρὸς καὶ παράκλησις φίλου
κάμπτουσιν οὐκ ἄκοντα καὶ πείθουσί με.
Ὦ πιστὲ δοῦλε, τὴν χάριν τούτοις νέμων,
εἰς τὴν χαρὰν εἴσελθε τοῦ σοῦ Κυρίου.

79

Ἄλλοι εἰς τὸν Σωτῆρα, ὡς ἐκ τοῦ βασιλέως

Τῶν ἀστάτων μὲν οὐδὲν αἰτήσαντί μοι
ὅμως δέδωκας πάντα, Δημιουργέ μου.
Ζωὴν δὲ τὴν μένουσαν ἐξαιτουμένῳ
μᾶλλον παρακλήθητι, καὶ δὸς τὴν χάριν.

78

As if spoken by Christ

Reverence for my mother and the entreaty of my friend
win me over, not against my will, and persuade me.
Faithful servant, thank them,
and enter into the joy of your Lord.

79

More verses to the Savior,
as if spoken by the emperor

While I have not asked for any transitory things,
you have given me all of them, my Creator.
But now that I beg for eternal life,
be swayed by mercy and grant the favor.

80

Εἰς τὴν ἐν τῷ Σωσθενίῳ
εἰκόνα

Σὴ χεὶρ κραταιὰ τοὺς κραταιοὺς δεσπότας
ἔστεψε, Χριστέ, καὶ παρέσχε τὸ κράτος·
σὴ χρηστότης θάλασσαν οὐ κενουμένην
ἔδειξεν αὐτοὺς πλουσίων χαρισμάτων.

5 Ὧν ἀφθόνως ἅπασα γῆ πληρουμένη,
σοὶ τῷ βραβευτῇ τοῦ κράτους δόξαν φέρει,
σὲ τὸν συνεργὸν ἱκετεύει τοῦ κράτους
ἀεὶ παρεῖναι, συμμαχεῖν, ἐνισχύειν,
ζωὴν χορηγεῖν καὶ χαρὰν τοῖς δεσπόταις.

10 Μάρτυς δὲ τούτων ἡ γραφὴ τῆς εἰκόνος·
οἱ γὰρ μονασταὶ τῆς μονῆς τῆς τιμίας
τοῦ Σωσθενίτου τοῦδε τοῦ πρωταγγέλου,
πολλῶν τυχόντες δωρεῶν καὶ πλουσίων,
ταύτην ἀμοιβὴν τοῖς καλοῖς εὐεργέταις
15 ἀντεισφέρουσιν, ἱστοροῦντες εὐτέχνως
σέ, Χριστέ μου, στέφοντα τούτους ἐνθάδε.

80

On the icon in the monastery of Sosthenion

Your powerful hand has crowned the powerful rulers,
Christ, and has given power to them.
Your goodness has made them a sea
that never can be drained of opulent graces.
The whole earth, filled generously with these graces,   5
offers you glory, as the judge awarding this power,
and implores you, the supporter of this reign,
to be ever present, an ally, a giver of strength,
and to grant life and happiness to the rulers.
The painting of this icon testifies to this,   10
because the monks of this honorable monastery
of the archangel of Sosthenion,
having received many rich gifts,
contribute in exchange this reward
for their good benefactors, artfully depicting   15
you, my Christ, crowning them here.

81

Εἰς τὸν τοῦ βασιλέως τάφον
ἐπιτύμβιοι

Ὄναρ τὰ θνητὰ πάντα καὶ ματαιότης·
εὔκλεια, δόξα, πλοῦτος, αὐτὸ τὸ κράτος·
ὁ γὰρ πρὸ μικροῦ βασιλεὺς κεκλημένος,
ὁ γῆς ἀκούων κύριος καὶ δεσπότης,
5 καὶ ζῶν μὲν ἄλλον εἶχε μείζω Δεσπότην,
καὶ νῦν τεθνηκὼς ὡς Κριτὴν τοῦτον μένει,
λόγους ἀπαιτήσοντα τῶν πεπραγμένων.
Τέως δὲ νεκρός ἐστι καὶ κωφὴ κόνις,
ἄφωνος, ἄπνους, χοῦς μόνον λελυμένος.
10 Ἡ πρὶν δὲ δόξα καὶ τὸ τοῦ θρόνου κράτος,
τὰ σκῆπτρα, τὰ τρόπαια, τὸ στέφους κλέος,
ἄπαντα ταῦτα, φεῦ, παρῆλθεν ἀθρόα
ὡς καπνός, ὡς ὄνειρος, ὡς ἄνθος χλόης.
Ἀλλ', ὦ χορηγὲ τῶν καλῶν, Θεοῦ Λόγε,
15 ὁ δοὺς τὰ ῥευστὰ ταῦτα τῷ τεθαμμένῳ,
σὺ καὶ τὰ κρείττω τῶν ἀπελθόντων δίδου·
θεὸν γὰρ ἄλλον οὐκ ἔγνω πλὴν σοῦ μόνου,
καὶ πρὸς σὲ πάσας ἔστρεφεν τὰς ἐλπίδας.
Κἂν αὐτὸς ὡς ἄνθρωπος ἡμάρτηκέ σοι,
20 ἡ πίστις οὖν, εὔσπλαγχνε, τοῦτον σωσάτω.

81

Funeral verses on the grave of
the emperor

All things mortal are a dream, are vanity:
renown, glory, wealth, and power itself.
The man who was recently called emperor,
the one titled lord and master of the earth,
when living had another, greater Lord,   5
and now, dead, he awaits him as his Judge,
who will call him to account for his deeds.
Until then he is a dead body, senseless earth,
without voice, without breath, just loosened dust.
The glory of past days, the power of the throne,   10
the scepter, the triumphs, the prestige of the crown—
all that, alas, has now suddenly disappeared
like *smoke,* like *a dream,* like *blossoms of the grass.*
O Word of God, who awards all good things,
who gave this entombed man these fleeting glories,   15
give him also rewards better than those that have passed
        away;
for he knew no other god but you alone,
and to you he attached all his hopes.
Even if he, as a human, sinned against your laws,
let faith save him, O compassionate one.   20

82

Ἕτεροι, ὡς ἐκ τοῦ βασιλέως

Ἔδει με, Χριστέ, μηδὲ φῶς ἰδεῖν βίου,
τὴν σὴν παροξύναντα μακροθυμίαν·
ποία γὰρ ὠφέλεια κερδῆσαι κόσμον,
ψυχῆς δὲ πικρὰν δυστυχῆσαι ζημίαν;
5 Ἧς οὐδὲ μικρὰν ἔσχον αὐτὸς φροντίδα,
ἀλλ᾽ ὥσπερ ἄλλον οὐκ ἔχων βασιλέα,
οὕτω κατετρύφησα τῆς ἐξουσίας.
Τῶν σῶν δὲ σεπτῶν, Δέσποτα, προσταγμάτων
τὰ τῶν ἐμῶν προὔθηκα, φεῦ, θελημάτων,
10 ὑφ᾽ ὧν παχυνθεὶς καὶ πλατυνθεὶς ἐν βίῳ,
ἄρτι στενοῦμαι τῷ βραχεῖ τούτῳ λίθῳ,
εἰς ὃν γυμνὸς νῦν ἀντὶ τῶν πάλαι θρόνων
καὶ τῶν ἀπείρων ὧν ἐπεκράτουν τόπων
ὥσπερ πένης τις δυστυχὴς ἀπερρίφην.
15 Τῆς πρὶν δὲ λαμπρότητος ἀντηλλαξάμην
τὸ στυγνόν, οἴμοι, τοῦτο τοῦ τάφου σκότος.
Ὁ χθὲς βασιλεύς, ὁ χθὲς ἐν δόξῃ μέγας,
ὁ χθὲς δοκῶν γῆς καὶ θαλάσσης δεσπότης,
τοιοῦτον ἐτρύγησα τῆς ἁμαρτίας
20 ἐνταῦθα καρπόν, τῶν δ᾽ ἐκεῖ πλείων φόβος.
Ἐξ ὧν με ῥῦσαι, Δημιουργὲ Χριστέ μου,
ῥῦσαι με τῇ σῇ δωρεὰν εὐσπλαγχνίᾳ,

82

More verses, as if spoken by the emperor

I should never have even seen the light of life,
Christ, since I have put your patience to the test.
What benefit is it to gain the world,
but suffer bitter harm to your soul?
For my soul I had not the slightest care,   5
but, as if I had no other lord,
I enjoyed my power to the full.
Instead of your esteemed commands, Lord,
I preferred the commands of my own volition,
by which I swelled and puffed myself up when alive,   10
whereas now I am confined to this small stone tomb,
thrown naked into it like a wretched pauper,
instead of the thrones from past days,
instead of the vast places I ruled.
The previous brilliance I exchanged, alas, for   15
the gloomy darkness of this grave.
Yesterday's emperor, yesterday's glorious man,
yesterday's so-called lord over earth and sea,
such is *the fruit of my sin* that I enjoyed here on earth,
in this place, while my fear for the other place only increased.   20
Save me from that, Christ, my Creator,
save me with your freely granted compassion,

ἥτις με θάλπει, καὶ πρὸς ἣν βλέπω μόνην·
ἄλλη γὰρ ἐλπὶς οὐδαμοῦ σωτηρίας.

83

Ἄλλοι

Τί μοι τὸ κέρδος τοῦ ταλαιπώρου βίου;
Ἔζησα μικρὸν ἐν πολυστρόφοις τύχαις·
εἶδον τὰ τερπνὰ πάντα καὶ τἀναντία·
πρὸς δόξαν ἤρθην, ἐκφυγὼν Ἅιδου πύλας·
5 καὶ βασιλεὺς ἤκουσα, φεῦ, καὶ δεσπότης.
Τὰ νῦν δ' ἐγὼ μὲν ἐν στενῷ κεῖμαι λίθῳ,
ἄψυχος, ἄπνους, εἰς κόνιν λυθεὶς μόνην.
Ἐκεῖνα δ' ἦν ὄνειρος, οὐδέν τι πλέον.
Ἀλλ' ὁ πλάσας με ταῖς ἀχράντοις χερσί σου,
10 ἀνάπλασον πάλιν με τὸν λελυμένον,
καὶ δὸς βοηθὸν χεῖρα, δός μοι κειμένῳ,
καὶ δεῖξον αὖθις φῶς τὸ σόν, Πλαστουργέ μου.

which comforts me and is all I look for,
because there is no other hope for salvation.

83

More verses

What did I gain by this miserable life?
I lived a while amid whirling fortunes;
I saw all the pleasures, and the opposite too;
I was lifted to glory, fleeing the gates of Hades;
and, alas, I was called emperor and lord. 5
But now I lie in a narrow stone grave,
without soul, without breath, dissolved into dust merely.
All those things past were a dream, and nothing more.
But you, who created me with your pure hands,
give substance again, to me, dissolved; 10
give, please, give a helping hand to me, lying here;
and show me again your light, my Creator.

84

Ἄλλοι

Σὺ Βασιλεύς, ὕψιστε, καὶ σὺ Δεσπότης,
ζωῆς ὑπάρχων Κύριος καὶ θανάτου·
ἐγὼ δὲ θνητὴν ἐκ φθορᾶς λαβὼν φύσιν,
μέλλων τε θᾶττον εἰς φθορὰν ὑποστρέφειν,
5 μάτην βασιλεὺς ὠνομαζόμην ἄρα,
χαίρων ὀνείροις καὶ σκιαῖς ἀσυστάτοις.
Ἃ πρὸς μικρὸν τέρψαντα καὶ παίξαντά με,
ἀπῆλθον, ἐξέπτησαν ἐν βραχεῖ χρόνῳ·
ἐμοὶ δ' ἀφῆκαν τὰς ἐπ' αὐτοῖς εὐθύνας,
10 καὶ τοὺς λόγους, φεῦ, τῶν κακῶς πεπραγμένων·
οὓς μὴ βαρύνῃς, Δημιουργέ μου, τότε,
ἀλλ' ὡς Κριτὴς εὔσπλαγχνος ἱλάσθητί μοι.

85

Ἄλλοι

Ὦ τῶν ματαίων καὶ κενῶν φρονημάτων.
Πρόσκαιρος ὢν ἄνθρωπος ἐφρόνουν μέγα,

84

More verses

You are Emperor, O highest one, and you are Lord,
being Master over life and death,
whereas I have taken my mortal nature from decay,
destined to return quickly to decay.
So it was in vain that I was called emperor,   5
and took pleasure in dreams and fleeting shadows,
which for a while charmed and deluded me,
but then disappeared, and quickly flew away.
They left me with liability because of them
and with the accounts, alas, of bad deeds.   10
May you not make these accounts heavier, my Creator,
but may you, as a clement Judge, have mercy on me.

85

More verses

O vain and empty presumptions!
I, a man of few days, I had grandiose thoughts;

καὶ γῆς βραχὺς χοῦς γῆς ἐπεσκόπουν ἄκρα,
ζητῶν τὰ κύκλῳ τῆς ὅλης οἰκουμένης
5 εἰς ἓν συνάψαι τοῖς ὅροις τοῖς τοῦ κράτους.
Ἀλλ᾽ ἐκράτησεν ἡ πρὸ τοῦ κρατουμένη,
καὶ πρὸς στενὸν μέρος τι συγκλείσασά με,
ἐνταῦθα τέφραν ἀντὶ δεσπότου φέρει.
Σὺ δ᾽ ὁ πλάσας με ταῖς ἀχράντοις χερσί σου,
10 ἀνάπλασον πάλιν με πρὸς σωτηρίαν.
Καὶ τοῖς βλέπουσι συμπαθῶς μου τὸν τάφον
φάνηθι καὶ σὺ συμπαθὴς ἐν τῇ Κρίσει.

86

Εἰς τὴν εἰκόνα τῶν τριῶν ἁγίων, ἣν ἐδωρήσατο τῷ μοναχῷ Γρηγορίῳ

Ἐμοὶ τί μεῖζον τῶν ἐμῶν διδασκάλων;
Ὧν οὐδὲ κόσμον πάντα προκρίνειν ἔχω.
Ὅμως δὲ φίλτρον ἀνδρὸς ἡγιασμένου,
αἰδοῖ κρατῆσαν, οἴχεται τούτους ἄγον.
5 Ἀλλ᾽ ἐντρύφα μοι τῷ καλῷ δώρῳ, πάτερ,
ἥδιστα τόνδε τὸν συνώνυμον βλέπων
καὶ τοὺς συναυγάζοντας αὐτῷ φωσφόρους.
Ἐμοὶ δ᾽ ἀπ᾽ αὐτῶν μικρὸν ἐξαιτοῦ σέλας,
ἀεὶ κατευθῦνόν με πρὸς σωτηρίαν·
10 τούτου γὰρ οὐδὲν βούλομαι λαβεῖν πλέον.

480

a small clump of earth, I eyed earth's frontiers,
seeking to bring what's in the whole world's circle
together within the bounds of my power.   5
But the earth, previously conquered, then conquered me,
and has now confined me in this narrow place,
holding ashes here instead of an emperor.
But you who have created me with your pure hands,
give me substance again, and bring me salvation.   10
And may you also appear benign at the Last Judgment
to the people who look benignly upon my grave.

86

On the icon of the three saints that he gave to the monk Gregory

What could matter more to me than my teachers?
I wouldn't prefer the whole world above them.
And yet my friendship and respect for a holy man
prevailed and carries them away.
May you delight in your beautiful gift, father,   5
and enjoy looking at your namesake
and the two luminaries who share in his radiance.
Just ask them for a small flame for me,
which may always guide me toward salvation;
that is the thing I most want to obtain.   10

87

Εἰς τὴν εἰκόνα τοῦ βασιλέως καὶ τοῦ πατριάρχου

Οἱ προκριθέντες τῇ σοφῇ Θεοῦ κρίσει
ἄρχοντες ἡμῶν καὶ γραφαῖς τιμητέοι·
ὁ μὲν γὰρ ἄρχει σωμάτων ἀνθρωπίνων,
ψυχῶν δὲ ποιμὴν οὗτος ἐκλελεγμένος·
5 ἄνωθεν ἄμφω τὸ κρατεῖν εἰληφότες,
ἄμφω καλῶς ἄρχουσι τῶν ὑπηκόων·
ὅθεν γραφέντες, τοῦ κράτους τοὺς αἰτίους
καὶ προστάτας ἔχουσι συγγεγραμμένους.

88

Εἰς τὸν προφήτην Δανιήλ

Θῆρες λέοντες ἦσαν ἐχθροί σοι πάλαι,
ἀνὴρ Λέων δὲ νῦν σὸς οἰκτρὸς ἱκέτης.
Ὡς οὖν παρ' αὐτῶν οὐδὲν αὐτὸς ἐβλάβης,
οὕτω, προφῆτα, τοῦτον ἐκ βλάβης ῥύου.

482

87

On the icon of the emperor and the patriarch

The men who are chosen by God's wise judgment
to be our rulers should be honored with images too.
One of them reigns over human bodies,
the other is chosen as the shepherd of souls.
Both have received their power from above,   5
both preside well over their subjects.
Therefore, when painted, they have the sources of their
        power
painted together with them, as their protectors.

88

On the prophet Daniel

Of old, lions, being beasts, were your enemies.
But now Leo, a man, is your pitiful suppliant.
Just as you were not harmed by the beasts,
prophet, save likewise this man from all harm.

89

Ὑπὲρ ἑαυτοῦ πρὸς Χριστόν

Πολλὴ χάρις σοι τῶν λόγων, Θεοῦ Λόγε,
οἷς εὐδόκησας δωρεάν με πλουτίσαι,
ὑφ᾽ ὧν λογισμοῖς σώφροσιν κεχρημένος,
ἔταξα ῥητὰ ταῖς ἐμαῖς χρείαις μέτρα,
5 ἀρκεῖν ἔμοιγε ταῦτα κρίνας τὰ τρία,
τροφήν, σκέπην στέγην τε, καὶ μηδὲν πλέον,
δι᾽ ἃ κλονεῖται πᾶσα σήμερον κτίσις,
ἐπείπερ ἐξήμειψεν ἡ τρυφῆς βία
τὴν χρῆσιν αὐτῶν εἰς παράχρησιν πάλαι.
10 Χρῆσιν δ᾽ ἔγωγε τὴν ἀναγκαίαν ἔχων,
ὑπερπερισσεύω τε καὶ χαίρω πλέον
τῶν τοῖς ἀπλήστοις ἀντεπαντλούντων πίθοις.
Τί γὰρ τὸ κέρδος τῶν ἀμετρήτων πότων
τοῖς εἰς ἄπαυστον δίψος ἐκκεκαυμένοις;
15 Διαρραγεῖεν πρῶτον ἂν τῇ πλημμύρᾳ
ἢ τοῦ πάθους ἴαμα προσλάβοιντό τι·
ἐπεὶ δὲ τοῦτο συμφορὰ μισουμένη,
τὸ μηδὲ διψᾶν κρεῖττον ἢ τὸ μετρίως,
ἐφ᾽ ᾧ λαβὼν ἄνωθεν αὐτὸς τὴν χάριν,
20 καὶ σύντομον σχὼν τῶν ὀρέξεων πέρας,
πολλὴ χάρις σοι τῶν λόγων, λέγω, Λόγε,
οἷς εὐδόκησας δωρεάν με πλουτίσαι.

89

In defense of himself, addressed to Christ

Many thanks to you, Word of God, for the words
with which you thought fit to endow me as a gift.
Thanks to these words, I used wise thoughts,
putting clear limits to my needs.
These three things I considered to satisfy my needs: 5
food, clothing, a roof, and nothing else.
These now shake the whole world upside down,
since the force of pleasure has made people
abuse, instead of use, them.
Since I make only the necessary use of them,   10
I have more abundance and I am happier
than those who keep drawing from inexhaustible jars.
What benefit can innumerable drinks bring you
if you are burning with an unquenchable thirst?
They would rather burst from excess   15
than get some remedy for their problem.
Since this is a loathsome misfortune,
to have no thirst being better than having moderate thirst,
I have received in this respect a favor from above,
a swift end to my desires,   20
and thus many thanks to you, I say, O Word, for the words
with which you thought fit to endow me as a gift.

Πρὸς οὓς τὸ πλεῖστον ἀσχολῶν τῶν φροντίδων,
εἰς τἄλλα τὸν νοῦν δυσχερῶς ἐπιστρέφω·
25 οἷς ἐντρυφῶν νύκτωρ τε καὶ μεθ’ ἡμέραν,
ἄλλης τρυφῆς ἥκιστα ποιοῦμαι λόγον·
ἀρκεῖ γὰρ αὕτη ψυχαγωγεῖν πλουσίως,
βρύουσα πᾶσαν ἡδονήν τε καὶ χάριν.
Πλὴν ἀλλ’ ἄγοις οὕτω με καὶ φέροις, Λόγε,
30 ἄτρεπτον, ἀκλόνητον, ἡδραιωμένον,
εἴσω μένοντα τῶν τεταγμένων ὅρων,
ὡς ἄνθεσιν μέλισσαν ἐν βίβλοις στρέφων,
ὡς τέτιγγα δρόσῳ με τοῖς λόγοις τρέφων,
μόνοις τε πείθων τοῖς παροῦσιν ἐμμένειν,
35 καὶ μηδὲν αἰτεῖν ἄλλο πλὴν σωτηρίαν,
εἰς ἣν με θᾶττον προσλάβοις, εὐεργέτα,
κἂν μηδὲ τοῖς νῦν σφόδρα δυσκόλως ἔχω.
Κρείττων γὰρ εὐπλοίας τε καὶ κούφων πόνων
ὅρμος ποθεινὸς καὶ τὸ τῶν πόνων τέλος·
40 ὧν μοι τυχεῖν γένοιτο ῥᾷστα, Χριστέ μου.

Devoting most of my care to words,
I can barely turn my mind to other matters.
Enjoying them night and day,   25
other forms of pleasure are my last concern.
The pleasure of words suffices to profoundly enrapture me,
bursting as it is with all delight and grace.
But may you, Christ the Word, guide and support me this
      way:
unmovable, unshakable, firm,   30
staying within the imposed limits,
as I flit among my books, like a bee among flowers,
feeding me with words, like a cicada with dew,
persuading me to remain content with the present
      circumstances only,
and to ask for nothing else than salvation,   35
to which may you bring me quickly, benefactor,
even if I do not have serious problems in my present life.
For better still than a good voyage and light troubles
is the longed-for haven and the end of troubles;
which I hope to obtain with the greatest ease, my dear   40
      Christ.

90

Ἄλλοι περὶ ἑαυτοῦ πρὸς τὸν Χριστόν

Πολλὴ χάρις σοι τῶν λόγων, Θεοῦ Λόγε,
οἷς εὐδόκησας δωρεάν με πλουτίσαι·
πολλὴ χάρις σοι τοῦδε τοῦ τερπνοῦ βίου
καὶ τῆς ἔμοιγε φιλτάτης ἀπραξίας.
5 Ἴσως ἄδοξός ἐστιν, ἀλλ᾽ ἐλευθέρα·
ἴσως κρότων ἄμοιρος, ἀλλὰ καὶ φθόνων.
Κτῆσίς τις οὐ πρόσεστιν; Οὐδὲ φροντίδες,
αἳ μᾶλλον ἐκτήκουσι σάρκας δεσπότου
ἢ τῶν προσόντων ἡ μετουσία τρέφει.
10 Ἄπεστι κέρδος; Ἀλλὰ καὶ μοχθηρία,
ἢ πάντα κέρδους ἐξανιχνεύει πόρον,
ἢ κερμάτων χνοῦν οἶδεν ἐκλείχειν μόνη.
Οὐ προσκυνεῖ τις οὐδὲ θωπεύει τάχα;
Οὐ προσκυνοῦμεν οἷα θῶπες οὐδένα,
15 ἀλλ᾽ εὐγενῶς ἅπαντας ὡς κατ᾽ εἰκόνα.
Προεδρία ποῦ; Καὶ προσεδρεία πότε;
Ἧς πολλαπλῆν σύνοιδα τὴν ἀηδίαν
πρὸς τὴν ἐκείνης ἡδονὴν μετρουμένην.
Πλοῦτος ῥέει; Πῶς; Οὐχὶ καὶ παραρρέει;
20 Μάλιστα. Καὶ τίς ἀστάτου φίλου λόγος;
Ἔα πλανᾶσθαι τοὺς θέλοντας εὐκόλως·

90

More verses about himself, addressed to Christ

Many thanks to you, Word of God, for the words
with which you thought fit to endow me as a gift.
Many thanks to you for this delightful life
and this tranquility, so dear to me.
It may lack glory, but it is free.   5
It may be bereft of applause, but of jealousy as well.
It does not bring wealth? Nor does it bring worries either
that wear out its master's body
more than the enjoyment of possessions can nourish it.
Profit is absent? But also wickedness as well,   10
which tracks down every means for gain,
and only knows how to lick the powder of coins.
Nobody will revere me or flatter me, perhaps?
We do not revere anyone as flatterers,
but each human respectfully, as made in God's image.   15
Where is the presidency? And the precedence?
I am fully aware that its repugnance is manifold,
compared to the delights of tranquility.
Wealth flows away? How? Doesn't it also flow by?
Certainly. And what is there to say about a fickle friend?   20
Let those who want to be easily led astray, do so.

σὺ δ᾽ εὖ βεβηκώς, κτῆμα τοιοῦτον πόθει,
ἀεὶ πεφυκὸς τῷ φιλοῦντι προσμένειν.
Ἀλλ᾽ ὄγκον αἴρει; Καὶ καταστέλλει πάλιν
25 ὡς πνεῦμα φύσης ἀσκὸν ἐστερημένον.
Ἀλλὰ τρυφὴν δίδωσιν; Ἀλλὰ καὶ φθόην.
Ὦ ποῖον εἶπας; Καὶ γὰρ οὐ ψευδῶς ἔφην·
σὺ δ᾽ ἐξέταζε τἄλλα τῶν κακῶν ὅσα,
ἐν οἷς ὁ πλοῦτος δεξιοῦται τοὺς φίλους.
30 Τίς οὖν συνήσει; Τίς διοπτεύσει τάδε;
Πολλὴ χάρις σοι τῶν λόγων, Θεοῦ Λόγε,
οἷς εὐδόκησας δωρεάν με πλουτίσαι,
οὓς ἀξίωμα, πλοῦτον, εὔκλειαν, θρόνον,
καὶ πᾶν ὅ,τι κράτιστον, ἡγοῦμαι μόνους·
35 οἳ τὰς ὀρέξεις τῶν ἐμῶν θελημάτων
ῥεμβασμὸν οὐκ ἐῶσι πάσχειν ῥᾳδίως,
πίνοντες αὐτοὶ πάντα τῆς ψυχῆς πόθον,
ὡς τοὺς ποταμοὺς ἡ θάλασσα τοὺς πέριξ,
εἰ μή τι σαρκὸς ἀσθένεια προσλάβοι,
40 ὡς τέλμα μικρὸν ἐκτραπὲν ῥείθρου μέρος·
ἐξ ὧν ἔγωγε τὰς ἀφορμὰς λαμβάνων,
τούτους ἐμαυτῷ τοὺς νόμους ἔχω γράφειν,
ἐν οἷς κρατοῦμαι, καὶ κρατῶ τῶν ὧν θέμις.

You, firmly anchored to the earth, should desire such a
    possession
that always stays with the person who loves it.
It lifts pride? But pride, then, shrinks again
like the air in a bag, when it lacks wind.   25
It gives pleasure? Yes, but also decay.
What do you say now? Well, I haven't told a lie.
You should examine how many other woes there are,
with which wealth welcomes its friends.
Who will then understand? Who will see through this?   30
Many thanks to you, Word of God, for the words
with which you thought fit to endow me as a gift.
I consider words as my only dignity, wealth, glory, throne,
and all that may be superior.
They do not allow the desires of my will   35
to easily descend into daydreaming.
They absorbed all the longings of my soul,
as a sea absorbs the rivers around it,
unless a physical sickness takes something for itself,
as a small pond does with a part of the river that flows astray. 40
Taking from words my point of departure,
I am now able to write down for myself these laws,
that rule me and through which I rule what's rightly mine.

91

Εἰς ἑαυτόν

"Πλουτοῦσι πολλοί." "Παῦε. Καὶ τίς μοι λόγος;
Πτωχοὺς γὰρ ἕξει πάντας ἐξ ἴσου τάφος,
ἁβρούς, μέσους, ἥττους τε καὶ πενεστάτους.
Τὰ νῦν δὲ παῖξαι μικρὸν αὐτοῖς ἐνδίδου,
5 ἕως κενὰς φέροντες αἴσθωνται χέρας."
"Πολλοὺς θρόνοι φέρουσιν ὑψηλοὺς ἄνω."
"Ἐγὼ δὲ γῆθεν ἔκπαλαι πεπλασμένος,
εἰς γῆν τε νεύω, καὶ κάτω ζητῶ μένειν,
πολλῷ δὲ τὴν ἔπαρσιν ἐκκλίνω φόβῳ,
10 μήπως σκοτωθεὶς ὑψόθεν χαμαὶ πέσω,
τῆς αὐθαδείας ἀξίαν διδοὺς δίκην·
ὅθεν ταπεινὴν ἀσφάλειαν ἐκλέγων,
πεζῇ βαδίζω, πεζὸν ὢν ζῷον φύσει,
πᾶσιν μὲν οὐκ ἄποπτος ὡς ἐκ τῶν ἄνω,
15 πολλοῖς δὲ καὶ κάτωθεν ὢν ἐγνωσμένος,
ὃ μεῖζον οἶδα μᾶλλον εἰς εὐδοξίαν,
ὅταν τις αὐτὸς ἐκ ταπεινοῦ χωρίου
πρὸς ὕψος ἐκτείνοιτο καὶ δοκῇ μέγας
ὥσπερ κολοσσός, μῆκος οἰκεῖον φέρων,
20 καὶ μηδὲν εἰς δίαρμα χρῄζων τοῦ τόπου.
Ὅσοι δὲ κομπάζουσι βαθμοῖς καὶ θρόνοις,
οὗτοι κολοιῶν οὐδέν εἰσι βελτίους

91

To himself

"Many are rich." "Stop it! Why should I bother?
The grave will have us paupers all the same:
the wealthy, the middle, the lesser, and the poorest.
Allow them now to play for a bit,
until they realize they're empty-handed."   5
"The thrones bear many lofty ones up high."
"But since I was made of earth long ago,
I nod to earth and seek to stay below.
I avoid being lifted, fearing greatly
that I'll grow dizzy and fall to the ground from above   10
to suffer just punishment for my presumption.
And so I choose a humble security;
I walk on foot, being a pedestrian creature by nature,
not seen by all, perhaps, from up above,
but recognized by many from below—   15
much better, I know, for good renown—
such as when out of a lowly place somebody
stretches to the sky, seeming tall
as a colossus, yet keeps his normal height,
not needing any more space to raise himself.   20
All those who boast of offices and thrones,
they are not any better than the jackdaws,

μέγα φρονούντων ἐν πτεροῖς ἀλλοτρίοις,
ὧν ἡ πάλιν ψίλωσις αἰσχύνει πλέον·
25 τῶν προσθέτων γὰρ χρωμάτων τῇ συγκρίσει
εἰς μεῖζον ἐξάγουσι τὴν ἀμορφίαν."
"Ἀλλὰ κροτοῦσι πᾶς ὄχλος τοὺς ἐν μέσῳ."
"Εἰπὼν ὄχλον, βέλτιστε, μὴ ζήτει πλέον·
ὄχλος γὰρ οὐδὲν ἄλλο πλὴν ὄντως ὄχλος,
30 βοὰς ἀτάκτους τοῖς κρατοῦσι προσνέμων
ὡς πρόσφορον μείλιγμα τῆς ἐξουσίας,
πλέον δὲ μηδὲν συντελῶν τῶν χρησίμων,
μᾶλλον μὲν οὖν μέγιστα καὶ βλάπτειν ἔχων·
φυσᾷ γὰρ αὐτοὺς τοῖς ἐπαίνοις πολλάκις,
35 πείθων ἀκούειν ὡς ἀληθεῖς τοὺς λόγους·
οἱ δ' εἰσὶν οὐδέν, πλὴν μόνον κενοὶ ψόφοι,
ἐπηρεασταὶ τῶν κενῶν φρονημάτων,
ψεῦσται, πλάνοι, γόητες, ἀνδράσιν γέλως,
βόθρος δ' ἀνάνδροις· οἷς ὁ πιστεύων ἄνους.
40 Κραυγῆς δὲ πολλῆς οὐ πάνυ φροντιστέον·
καὶ ψῆρες ὀξύφωνον, ἀλλὰ κουφόνουν.
Τούτοις ἔγωγε τοῖς λογισμοῖς καὶ λόγοις
ἄγων ἐμαυτὸν ἐκπεραίνω τὸν βίον."

so conceited in the feathers of others,
and all the more ashamed when plucked of their plumage;
for their ugliness is all the more exposed,   25
in contrast to the colors that they added."
"But every crowd applauds those in the center."
"Saying 'crowd', my dear friend, seek no further.
The crowd is nothing more than that: the crowd,
granting its unruly shouts to rulers—   30
ephemeral flattery of power.
As for the rest, it brings no useful gain,
but rather has tremendous power for harm,
often puffing rulers up with words of praise,
convincing them to hear these words as true.   35
But they are nothing more than empty sounds,
treating hollow minds abusively—
liars, frauds, cheats—a joke to real men,
a snare for the unmanly, believed by a fool.
Nor should one pay heed to the frequent shouting;   40
starlings, too, have a loud voice but an empty mind.
But, guided by these thoughts and words,
I'll carry on my own life to the end."

92

Εἰς ἑαυτόν

"Ἕλκουσι βαθμοί." "Πρόσσχες. Ἀθρόα ζάλη."
"Ψῆφοι φέρονται." "Συστροφὴ καταιγίδων."
"Θρόνοι καλοῦσιν. Ὦ κυβερνῆτα, βλέπε."
"Ὁρᾷς ὅσος κύκλωθεν ἠγέρθη κλύδων;"
5 "Σπεῦσον βοήθει." "Κλύζεταί σοι τὸ σκάφος.
Λαβοῦ, τάλαν, τάχιστα τῶν σῶν οἰάκων."
"Λαβοῦ, λογισμέ, πρὶν παραχθῶμεν βίᾳ."
"Ἦ που τι κἀμὲ συμπονεῖν ἐπιτρέπεις;"
"Ὡς οὖν κελεύεις πείθομαι. Καὶ δὴ λέγε."
10 "Σὺ τὴν σεαυτοῦ κοσμίως βάδιζέ μοι·
ἀρκεῖ γάρ, ἂν κάλλιστα καὶ ταύτην δράμοις·
βαθμῶν δ' ἐκείνων καὶ θρόνων πρὸς οὓς πτύρῃ,
πολλοὶ μὲν ἦσαν ἐγκρατεῖς χθὲς καὶ πάλαι,
πολλοὶ δ' ἔσονται, συρρέοντες τῷ χρόνῳ,
15 ᾧ καὶ συνεκλείπουσι πάντες ἐν μέρει,
ἕως καταντήσουσιν εἰς κοινὸν τέλος,
μηδὲν παρ' αὐτῶν κερδάναντες ἄλλό τι
πλὴν τὰς ἐπ' αὐτοῖς εὐθύνας καὶ τοὺς λόγους,
πλέον πικραίνειν ὕστερον πεφυκότας
20 ἢ σήμερον τέρπουσι τοὺς κεκτημένους·
τέρπουσι καὶ γὰρ ὥσπερ ἄνθρακες βρέφη,
τοὺς πρὸς μόνον τὸ στίλβον ἐκθαμβουμένους

92

To himself

"Offices attract!" "Watch out, a sudden squall!"
"Votes are cast!" "A whirling storm."
"Thrones call, O steersman, look!"
"Do you see how great a wave rises all around?"
"Come quickly to help." "Your vessel is tossed around.   5
Take hold of your helm quickly, poor man!"
"You take the helm, reason, before we are carried away by
     force!"
"If you will indeed allow me to help out?"
"As you wish, I will obey. Well then, speak."
"You should walk your own way as befits you.   10
It suffices if you follow that way well.
Those offices and thrones that alarm you,
many were master of them before,
and many will be, passing by with time,
and all will vanish in turn, together with time,   15
until they end up at a common end,
having gained nothing from offices and thrones
except the responsibilities and justifications these bring
     with them,
which will vex them more in the future,
than they today delight their possessors.   20
For indeed they delight them as coals do children,
who are fascinated only by their glow,

καὶ μὴ σκοποῦντας ὡς ἔχει καὶ τὸ φλέγον,
πρὶν ἂν παθών τις νοῦν ἐνέγκοι καὶ μάθοι."
25 "Ἔστω, καλῶς εἴρηκας. Ἀλλὰ γὰρ πόθεν
τὸ σὸν τάλαντον ἐμπορεύσῃ τοῦ λόγου;"
"Ποῖον λόγου τάλαντον; Οὐκ ἔχω λόγον,
οὕτω καμνόντων (ὡς ὁρᾷς) τῶν ὀργάνων,
ὡς μηδὲ λεπτὸν φθέγμα πέμπειν εὐκόλως·
30 τοσοῦτον ἐκράτησε τῶν πρώην ὕθλων
ἡ νῦν με συστέλλουσα παιδαγωγία,
ὑφ' ἧς πέπαυμαι τοῦ θεατρίζειν μάτην
καὶ πολλὰ ληρεῖν ἐν σχολαῖς καὶ συλλόγοις·
εἴσω δὲ νεύων μετριάζω πρὸς λόγους,
35 μηδὲν περιττὸν μηδ' ἄκαιρον ἐκφέρων,
μόνοις δὲ φωνὴν τοῖς ἀναγκαίοις νέμων,
οὕτω τε, σαίνων καὶ λεαίνων τὴν νόσον,
τὸ ζωτικόν μοι πνεῦμα συνθάλπω μόλις,
ἄλλως τε κἂν πάλαι τις ἦν εὐγλωττία,
40 καὶ καρπὸν οὐκ ἄχρηστον ἐξήνεγκέ σοι,
καλῶς γεωργήσασα πολλοὺς τῶν νέων—
πάντας γὰρ οὐ τίθημι, μὴ καὶ κομπάσω·
πλὴν ἀλλὰ πλείστους—ἦρεν ἐκ μαθημάτων,
πλείστοις δὲ καὶ πρὸς ἦθος εἰσήνεγκέ τι,
45 οὗ μᾶλλον ἡ παίδευσις εὐτυχεστέρα
τῆς τῶν περιττῶν ἐν λόγοις κομψευμάτων.
Τούτους ἔγωγε τοὺς σοφισθέντας νέους
κέρδος μέγιστον τῷ ταλάντῳ προσφέρω,
ὧν νῦν θεωρεῖς ἔστιν οὓς διδασκάλους
50 βαθμοῖς τε λαμπροῖς ἐμπρέποντας ἀξίως.

498

and do not realize that they also are burning,
until someone has an accident, and then thinks twice and
    learns."
"So be it, you have spoken well. But then still,   25
how will you cash in on your talent for words?"
"Which talent for words? I do not have words any more,
now that my body is ailing, as you see,
so that I have trouble uttering even a short syllable.
So much have the tales of old been defeated   30
by the discipline that now controls me,
thanks to which I have ceased to show off in vain,
and to talk much nonsense in schools and assemblies.
Instead, I look now to the inside, measuring my words,
not pronouncing anything superfluous or inappropriate,   35
and only giving voice to necessary things.
Thus, caressing and soothing my disease,
I barely keep my life's breath warm.
Yes, before, there was a certain eloquence,
and it yielded fruits for you that were not useless,   40
since it well reared many youths—
I won't say all of them, let's not boast,
still, most of them—it lifted them with education,
and, for most, it made a contribution to their morals,
and education in that area is more fruitful   45
than vain demonstrations in words.
I certainly provide these educated young men
with a great profit, thanks to my talent,
and you can see some of them now being teachers
and honorably excelling in brilliant offices.   50

Ἀργοῦντα δ' ἄρτι μηδαμῶς μέμφου σύ με·
ξηρὸς γάρ εἰμι τῇ πυρώσει τοῦ πάθους,
καὶ πραγματείας ὡς γεωργίας ξένος,
ὅθεν σχολάζων προστέτηκα τοῖς βίβλοις,
55 εἶναι μαθητής, οὐ διδάσκαλος, θέλων·
ῥᾷον γὰρ οἶδα τοῦτο πολλῷ τῷ μέσῳ,
καὶ πᾶσιν ἄλλως ἀσφαλέστερον τρόποις."
"Κρύψεις δέ σου τὸν λύχνον ἐν τῇ γωνίᾳ;"
"Τί τοῦτό φης, ἄνθρωπε; Πῶς καλεῖς λύχνον
60 τὸν οὐκ ἔχοντα τὸ προσῆκον φῶς λύχνῳ;
Ἦν λύχνος, οἶδα, καὶ γὰρ οὐκ ἀρνητέον·
ἀλλ' εἰς τροφὴν ἔλαιον ἀρκοῦν οὐκ ἔχων,
ἐψυγμένην δείκνυσι τὴν θρυαλλίδα,
ἧς τῷ μαρασμῷ καὶ τὸ τοῦ φωτὸς σέλας,
65 ἀμυδρὰ φαῖνον, οὐκ ἔχει λαμπηδόνα·
συνασθενεῖ γὰρ καὶ λόγος τῷ σαρκίῳ
ὥσπερ παθούσῃ μουσικὸν μέλος λύρᾳ.
Τὸ φωτὸς οὖν μοι λείψανον τηρητέον,
μετ' ἀσφαλείας ἔνδον ἐγκλείσαντί που
70 καὶ τῶν ὑπαίθρων πνευμάτων ἀπωτάτω,
μὴ παντελῶς μοι σβεσθὲν ἐν βραχεῖ λάθοι.
Αὐτὸς δὲ λύχνον ἄλλον ἐν μέσῳ τίθει,
ὅστις κύκλῳ τοσοῦτον ἐκπέμψει σέλας
ὅσον σὺ βούλει, μὴ δεδοικὼς τὴν σβέσιν·
75 ἴσως κακὸν γὰρ φῶς τε συγκλείειν μέγα,
καὶ μικρὸν αὖθις εἰς ὕπαιθρον ἐξάγειν·
ἅλις γὰρ ἂν σύμμετρον αὐγάζοι τόπον,
ἅλις δὲ κἂν ζῇ, καὶ διαυγείας δίχα.

If now I am somewhat idle, don't hold this against me at all:
for I am dried up by the burning of this illness,
and feel estranged from active life just as I am from farming,
and therefore I spend my time immersed in my books,
wanting to be a student, not a teacher,   55
for I know that this is by far the easiest
and also in all other respects the safest."
"So you will hide your lamp in a corner?"
"Why do you say that, man? Why do you give the name of
      lamp
to someone who does not have the right light for a lamp?   60
I had a lamp once, I know, I cannot deny that,
but since it does not have enough oil to feed upon,
it has a wick that has cooled down
and the flame of its light has withered away
and only shines faintly, not possessing any brilliance.   65
For the word shares in the sickness of the body
like a musical melody of a defective lyre.
Hence, I have to keep the remnant of the light
and securely lock it somewhere inside,
far from the winds of the open air,   70
so that it is not all suddenly extinguished by mistake.
You should place another lamp in the middle,
which will emit all around as much light
as you want, without fear that it will go out.
It is equally bad to lock in a great light   75
as it is to bring a small light out to the open;
it would be enough if it illuminates a proportional place,
enough if it lives, even without splendor.

Ἴσως γὰρ εἰς ἔναυσμα συμβάλοι τόπου,

80 κἂν αὐτὸ μηδὲν πρὸς τὸ νῦν φαίνειν ἔχοι,

ὡς ἡ καθ' ἡμᾶς ἀδρανεστάτη φάσις."

"Πῶς οὖν σε δόξα πρὸς μέγιστον ἐξάροι,

οὐκ ἐνδιδόντα τῇ φορᾷ τῆς ἡμέρας;"

"Μέν', ὦ ταλαίπωρ', ἀτρέμας σοῖς ἐν τρόποις·

85 ὁρᾷς γὰρ οὐδὲν ὧν νομίζεις φασμάτων.

Οὕτω δὲ μοὶ σκόπησον, ὡς σαφῶς μάθοις.

Τί δόξαν εἶπας; Οὐχὶ τὴν πλήθους πλάνην,

ἣν καὶ πλανῶνται καὶ πλανῶσι ἐξ ἴσου;

Οὐδὲν πρὸς ἡμᾶς τοῦτο τοὺς ᾐσθημένους·

90 πάλαι γὰρ ἴσμεν τίς μὲν ἀκριβεστάτη,

τίς δ' αὖ ματαία δόξα καὶ ψευδεστάτη·

πρὸς οὖν ἐκείνην πάντα συντείνων πόθον,

ἥκιστα χαίρω τῇδε τῇ ψευδωνύμῳ.

Δίκαια ποιῶν· τίς γὰρ εἰδώλου λόγος,

95 ἐξὸν πρὸς αὐτὴν τὴν ἀλήθειαν βλέπειν;

Καθ' ἣν ἐγὼ μέγιστον εὑροίμην κλέος,

αἰωνίως τέρπον με καὶ πληρεστάτως·

τὸ νῦν δὲ μικρὸν τοῦτο καὶ πρὸς ἡμέραν

τοὺς ὡς μέγα στέργοντας αὐτὸ παιζέτω,

100 ἕως ἀποπτὰν πάντας ἀθρόον φύγοι,

πεισθέντας ὀψὲ ταῦτα κἀκείνους λέγειν."

"Εὖγε. Κρατοῦμεν. Οὐκέτι τρικυμία.

Ἐξημέρωται πόντος ἠγριωμένος,

ἐξ οὐρίας ὁ πλοῦς τε τῷ σκάφει πάλιν.

105 Θάρρει, λογισμέ· σὺν Θεῷ γὰρ ἐμπλέεις,

παρ' οὗ τὸ νικᾶν ἐν ζάλης καιροῖς ἔχεις."

For it could perhaps contribute a glimmer to the place,
even if it is not able to shine forth now,   80
just like our feeble utterances."
"How then can glory lift you up to the top,
if you don't yield to the rush of the day?"
"Stay, poor fellow, calmly with your ways;
for you see nothing of the mirages that you imagine.   85
Look at it in the following way, to learn clearly.
What do you mean by glory? Surely not the delusion of the
     masses,
by which they are equally deluded and delude?
To me, this is nothing, since I am more sensible;
for I have known for a long time which glory is right,   90
and which is vain and deceitful.
So I direct all my desires to that glory,
and I can't find joy in the false one.
And I do rightly so. What is the purpose of an idol,
when you can look at truth itself?   95
By this truth I hope to find great renown,
which may bring eternal and full joy to me;
but this kind of renown, small and ephemeral,
let it fool the people who crave after it,
until it flies away and suddenly escapes everyone,   100
so that even they are persuaded to think alike, if belatedly."
"Well done. We hold on. No storm anymore.
The turbulent waters have calmed down.
The voyage of our ship has a fair wind again.
Have courage, reason. You are voyaging with God,   105
from whom you have victory even in times of storms."

93

Παλινῳδία πρὸς ταῦτα, μετὰ τὴν χειροτονίαν

Οὐκ ἔστιν ἡμῖν ἀτρεκὴς οὗτος λόγος
(ποιητικῶς γὰρ λάζομαι μῦθον πάλιν),
οὐδ' ἐμπεδοῦμεν τὰ πρὸ τοῦ δεδογμένα,
ἐπεὶ βροτοῖς πᾶς εὐμετάβλητος λόγος.
5 Ἐρῶ δὲ μᾶλλον ὡς ὁ μὲν λόγος μένει,
ἡ πραγμάτων φύσις δὲ τὴν τροπὴν ἔχει.
Ἄνθρωπος ὤν, ἄνθρωπε, μηδὲν φῆς μέγα·
"οὐ πείσομαι γὰρ τοῦτο," λῆρος κομπάσαι,
ἕως τις ἐμπνεῖ καὶ τὸν ἥλιον βλέπει.
10 Μάρτυς δὲ τούτων αὐτὸς οὗτος ὁ γράφων,
παθών, μαθών τε καὶ παλιλλογῶν τάδε,
ὃς χθὲς μὲν ἄλλα καὶ φρονῶν ἦν καὶ γράφων,
ὄναρ θεωρῶν (ὡς ἔοικεν), οὐχ ὕπαρ.
Τὴν μέχρι παντὸς ἐκτροπὴν τῶν πραγμάτων,
15 καὶ τὴν παροῦσαν εὖ καθεστῶσαν βλέπων,
τὴν αὔριον μάταιος οὐκ ἐπεσκόπει·
μέσην τε τὴν θάλασσαν εἰσέτι πλέων,
ὡς ἐντὸς ὅρμων ἐθρασύνετο φθάσας.
Τοιοῦτον ἡ βλάπτουσα τὸν νοῦν κουφότης
20 πείθει νομίζειν ὡς ἑαυτοῦ τις κρατεῖ,
καὶ τὸν βίον τίθησιν ὡς αὐτῷ φίλον,

93

Recantation of the previous words, after his ordination

These words are not accurate anymore,
for, as the poet says, *I retract my words again.*
We cannot confirm the views that we professed before,
since all human words are so easily changed.
Or I would rather say that the words remain,   5
but that the nature of things changes.
Being a human, man, you shouldn't talk big.
It is nonsense to brag, "I won't suffer that,"
as long as you are still breathing and seeing the sun.
Witness to this is this very man who is writing here,   10
he has experienced, he has learned, and now he recants
        these words.
Yesterday he thought, and wrote, different things,
gazing at a dream (as it seems), not reality.
Seeing how all things had turned out in his life,
and how the present was well disposed,   15
being foolish, he did not look ahead to tomorrow.
While he was still sailing in the midst of the sea,
he was confident that he had already arrived in the port.
The levity that perturbs our mind
persuades us to think that we are in control of ourselves,   20
and arrange our life as we like,

τὸν πάντα δὲ στρέφοντα πανσόφοις λόγοις
καὶ πάντας εὐθύνοντα πρὸς τὸ συμφέρον
οὐκ ἐννοεῖν δίδωσιν ὡς οὐ φευκτέος,
25 ἕως λαθών τις ἐμπέσοι καὶ νοῦν λάβοι.

Ὃς κἀμὲ πάντα τὸν πρὸ τοῦ γλυκὺν βίον
ἀπραγμόνως ζήσαντα καὶ γαληνίως,
πάλαι τε χαίρειν πᾶσι τοῖσδ᾽ εἰρηκότα—
βαθμοῖς, προπομπαῖς, ἀξιώμασι, θρόνοις,
30 αὐτῇ κακῶν ζάλῃ τε καὶ τρικυμίᾳ,
ὧν ἐμπέπλησται πᾶσα δόξα τοῦ βίου—
ἤδη τε νικᾶν εἰς τέλος πεπεισμένον
(ὡς ἄν τις ἔνθεν οἷς προγέγραπται τότε,
μᾶλλον δ᾽ ἐκεῖθεν οἷς προπέπρακται μάθοι),
35 καὶ δὴ πρὸς ὕψος χεῖρας ἐξαίροντά με,
καὶ δὴ κροτοῦντα σύμβολον νίκης μέγα
φθάσας κραταιᾷ χειρὶ νῦν συλλαμβάνει,
καὶ τὴν ἄκαμπτον καρδίαν κάμψας βίᾳ,
ἄγει φέρει τε, καὶ τίθησιν εἰς μέσον
40 τὸν ἐκφυγεῖν δόξαντα πᾶν ἤδη μέσον.

Τῶν πρὶν δ᾽ ἐκείνων ἀστάτων ἐνυπνίων
καὶ τῶν λογισμῶν οἷς ἐμαυτὸν ἐκράτουν,
κατεσκέδασται σύγχυσίς τις καὶ ζόφος,
οὕτω Θεοῦ σφήλαντος αὐτοὺς ἀθρόον,
45 οὕτω Θεοῦ φύραντος ἀρρήτῳ τρόπῳ
καὶ πάντα συγχέαντος, ὡς ἀγνωσίᾳ
σέβοιμεν αὐτόν, ὥς τις εἶπε τῶν πάλαι—
ἀλλότριος μέν, πλὴν καλῶς δοκῶν φάναι.
Τοῦ θαύματος γὰρ ἔνθεν αὐτῷ τὸ πλέον,

but it does not allow us to realize that he is not avoidable,
he who directs everything with wise reason
and guides everyone to his best destiny,
until one unwittingly tumbles into an experience and gains   25
    understanding.
I too led a life that was sweet until now,
free from cares and free from troubles,
and long ago I had said farewell to all these things,
offices, processions, dignities, thrones,
all this turbulence and storm of woes,   30
with which all life's fame is filled.
I thought that I had defeated them once and for all
(as one could learn from what I wrote then,
and above all from what I did then),
yes, I stretched my hands out to the sky,   35
yes, I clapped them as a great sign of victory,
but now he grasps me with a firm hand,
he forcibly bends my heart that was unyielding,
he carries me and leads me and puts me in the middle,
while I had thought that I could flee every middle.   40
The confusion and darkness of those fleeting dreams of
    before,
and those thoughts by which I controlled myself,
are now dissipated.
So did God dislodge them suddenly,
so did God confound them in an ineffable way,   45
and confused them all, *so that we can
worship him in ignorance,* as an ancient said—
he was a pagan, but I think he said it well;
for him, the greatest part of the miracle originated

50 ἐκ τῆς ἀβύσσου τῶν ἀδήλων κριμάτων,
ὧν οἶδεν οὐδεὶς τοὺς ἀπορρήτους λόγους,
οἷς εἶξα κἀγώ. Καὶ τί γὰρ παθεῖν ἔδει,
εἰς τὸν δυνάστην ἐμπεσόντα τὸν μέγαν;
Οὐκοῦν ἐκάμφθην. Καὶ κρατηθεὶς εἰς ἅπαν,
55 ὑπῆλθον ἤδη τοῦ ζυγοῦ τὸ φορτίον,
καὶ μάρτυς εἰμὶ τοῦ πανισχύρου κράτους,
ὃ ῥᾷστα πᾶσαν ἐκβιάζεται φύσιν,
κἂν σκληρότης τις αὐτόχρημα τυγχάνοι.
Ἀλλ᾽ εἴ τις αὐχεῖ στερρὸς εἶναι τὰς φρένας
60 καὶ τοῖς λογισμοῖς ἀσφαλῶς βεβηκέναι,
ἐντεῦθεν ἂν παίδευσιν ἀρκοῦσαν λάβοι,
μὴ σφόδρα θαρρεῖν μηδὲ πιστεύειν ἄγαν,
ὡς τοῖς ἑαυτοῦ χρήσεται πάντως νόμοις·
ἄλλος γὰρ ἡμῖν ὃς τὸ πᾶν ἔχει κράτος,
65 παρ᾽ οὗ μόνου δεῖ προσφυὲς ζητεῖν πέρας
ἅπαντας ἡμᾶς παντὸς ἔργου καὶ λόγου,
παντὸς σκοποῦ τε καὶ λογισμοῦ καὶ δρόμου,
ἐπεὶ καθ᾽ αὑτὸν οἶδεν οὐδεὶς οὗ τρέχει,
πρὶν ἂν θανών τις πεῖραν ἔξοι τῶν ὅλων—
70 ἀρχῆς ὁμοῦ, τέλους τε καὶ τῶν ἐν μέσῳ—
ἃ χρὴ σκοποῦντας, εὐλαβεστέρως ἔχειν,
ἀεὶ τὸ μέλλον χρηστὸν ἐξαιτουμένους.

from the abyss of unclear judgments,   50
of which nobody knows the secret reasons,
and which also won me over. For what can one do
when one is confronted with the great master?
So I yielded. And so, won over in every field,
I already took upon me the burden of the yoke,   55
and I am witness of the omnipotent power
which can easily overwhelm all natures,
even if one is hardness itself.
But if someone boasts that his mind is firm
and that his thoughts have solid foundations,   60
he can learn an adequate lesson from this:
not to be overconfident, and not to have too much belief
that one can hold on to his own laws in all circumstances.
It is another one who has all power over us,
and it is from him alone that all of us should ask   65
for the fitting end of all deeds and words,
all aims and thoughts and journeys,
since nobody knows by himself where he is running,
until he dies and has experiences of everything,
the beginning, the end, and the middle.   70
We should keep this in mind, and relent rather,
always praying for a favorable future.

94

Εἰς τὴν τοῦ νομοφύλακος νεαράν

Αὐτὸς σκοπήσας πρᾶγμα κοινῇ συμφέρον,
αὐτὸς βασιλεῖ τὸ σκοπηθὲν γνωρίσας,
αὐτός τε πείσας, αὐτός ἐστιν ὁ γράφων.

95

Εἰς τὸν δεύτερον λόγον τῶν εἰς τὸν τροπαιοφόρον

Μιᾶς ὁ μικρὸς ἔργον ἑσπέρας λόγος,
ὅθεν βραχύς τε καὶ τὸ πρὸς τέλει νόθος,
εἴπερ δίκαιον λοιδόρως καλεῖν νόθον
τὸν ἐξ ἀδελφοῦ μοῖραν ἠρανισμένον·
5 ἑνὸς γὰρ ἄμφω πατρὸς ὄντες οἱ λόγοι
ἀδελφικῶς θαρροῦσι τὴν κοινωνίαν.

94

On the edict pertaining to the guardian of laws

The man who conceived a cause of benefit to all,
the man who conveyed his idea to the emperor,
the man who convinced him, this is the man now writing.

95

On the second oration for the trophy-bearing saint

This small discourse is the work of one single night.
Hence it is brief, and toward the end it is spurious,
at least if we can rightly use the insult "spurious"
for a discourse that borrows a part from its brother.
Both discourses are from one and the same father,   5
and so, as brothers, they take confidence from their
    common origin.

96

Ὅτε ἀπέστη τῆς συγγραφῆς τοῦ χρονογράφου

Ὁ συγγραφεὺς ψεῦδος μὲν οὐκ εἴρηκέ πω,
ψεύσαιτο μέντ' ἂν ἔν γε τοῖς λοιποῖς λόγοις,
οὕτω φιλούντων τῶν κελευόντων τάδε·
ὧν τοῖς ἐπαίνοις ἐντρυφῶν τὸ βιβλίον,
5   ὅμως ἔδοξεν ἐνδεέστερον λέγειν·
ἐξουσία κρότων γὰρ οὐκ οἶδεν κόρον.
Οὐκοῦν ἀφείσθω ταῦτα τοῖς ἐγκωμίοις,
ἡ συγγραφὴ δὲ μὴ προχωρείτω πλέον·
οὐκ εὐφυῶς γὰρ πρὸς τὰ τοῦ ψεύδους ἔχει,
10   νόμος τε ταύτην ἐκτροπῆς ἀποτρέπει.
Ἐνταῦθα τοίνυν τὸν δρόμον παύει τέως,
ἕως κατ' εὐθὺ δῷ τις αὐτῇ τὸ τρέχειν.

96

When he gave up writing his chronicle

This author has never told a lie,
but he would do so in the remainder of his work,
because the patrons like it that way.
Even if the book would indulge in their praises,
they would still think it falls short of them.   5
Power is always hungry for more applause.
Therefore, let these praises be assigned to panegyrics,
and let the chronicle not proceed any further;
it does not lend itself to lies,
and there is a law that averts it from deviation.   10
So it stops its course here
until somebody allows it to walk straight.

97

Εἰς τὰ δωρηθέντα μηναῖα εἰς Εὐχάϊτα

Ὕμνων ἐπελθὼν ἡμερησίων βίβλους,
πᾶσάν τε τούτων τὴν γραφὴν ἐπιξέσας,
καὶ χεῖρα καὶ νοῦν ὡς ἐνῆν καταρτίσας,
δῶρον φίλον δίδωμι καὶ μάλα πρέπον
5 τῷ προστατοῦντι τοῦ τόπου στεφηφόρῳ,
ὃς ἔνδον οἰκεῖ τῆσδε τῆς ἐκκλησίας·
δι' οὗ τύχοιμι τῆς ἀκηράτου βίβλου,
τῇ χειρὶ τοῦ Πλάσαντος ἐγγεγραμμένος.

98

Εἰς τὰ αὐτά

Οὐ πολλὰ μέν, κράτιστα πάντα δ' ἐνθάδε·
οὐκ ἂν γὰρ εὕροις ἀλλαχοῦ τὰ βελτίω.
Ἐβουλόμην δὲ ταῦτα μὲν τύπους μένειν,
ἀντιγράφων εἶναι δὲ τὴν ὑπουργίαν.

97

On the *menaia* donated in Euchaïta

Going through the books with daily hymns,
I executed the writing of all of them,
and applying my hand and mind as well as possible,
I now donate this as a dear and certainly fitting gift,
to the crown-bearing protector of this place,   5
who lives inside this church,
through whom may I find my place in the imperishable book,
registered by the hand of the Creator.

98

On the same

This is not much, but it is supreme.
You would not find anything better elsewhere.
I wanted these to remain as models,
and the service to consist of copies.

99

Εἰς τὰ διορθωθέντα βιβλία

Καλὴν δεδωκὼς ταῖς βίβλοις ὑπουργίαν,
αὐτὸς πονηρὰν ἀντιλαμβάνω χάριν·
τῶν μὲν γὰρ ἤδη τὰς νόσους ἰασάμην,
ἐγὼ δὲ συντέτηκα καὶ κακῶς ἔχω,
5 κόπων τὸ σῶμα συντριβεὶς ἀμετρίᾳ.
Ἀλλ' οἱ τρυφῶντες ἐν πόνοις ἀλλοτρίοις
καὶ ταῖς ἐμαῖς πλέοντες εὔδια ζάλαις,
πρὸς Κύριον μέμνησθε τοῦ κεκμηκότος.

99

On the corrected books

While I have done these books a good service,
I myself have received a sour reward in exchange.
For I may have cured now the illnesses in those books,
but I pine away and am in a deplorable state,
my body being worn out by excessive labor.   5
But you who take pleasure in the works of others
and who sail quietly through my storms,
remember before the Lord this wearied man.

Abbreviations

BMFD = John P. Thomas and Angela Constantinides Hero, eds., *Byzantine Monastic Foundation Documents. A Complete Translation of the Surviving Founders' Typika and Testaments* (Washington, D.C., 2001)

CPG = Ernst L. von Leutsch and Friedrich G. Schneidewin, eds., *Corpus Paroemiographorum Graecorum,* 2 vols. (Göttingen, 1889)

Janin, *EglisesCP* = Raymond Janin, *Géographie ecclésiastique de l'Empire byzantin. Première partie: Le siège de Constantinople et le patriarcat oecuménique. Tome III: Les églises et les monastères,* 2nd ed. (Paris, 1969)

LbG = Erich Trapp (with Wolfram Hörandner, Johannes Diethart, et al.), eds., *Lexikon zur byzantinischen Gräzität, besonders des 9.–12. Jahrhunderts* (Vienna, 1994–)

ODB = Alexander Kazhdan et al., eds., *The Oxford Dictionary of Byzantium,* 3 vols. (New York, 1991)

PBW = Michael Jeffreys et al., eds., *Prosopography of the Byzantine World* (2011), available at <http://pbw.kcl.ac.uk>

PmbZ = Ralph-Johannes Lilie et al., eds., *Prosopographie der mittelbyzantinischen Zeit,* 2 parts, 14 vols. (Berlin, 1998–2013)

Note on the Texts

For the Greek texts of the poems, we relied on two copyright free editions: the 1903 edition by Eduard Kurtz of Christopher's poems, and the 1882 edition of Johannes Bollig, eventually completed by Paul de Lagarde, for Mauropous's. Both editions have generally proved their worth over the years, although Kurtz's edition has now been superseded by the edition of Marc De Groote, and Lagarde's edition deserves to be replaced, if only because this edition is marred by Lagarde's references to his other publications, among the most vicious of philological scholarship.

The Greek text of Christopher's poetry is not without problems. As explained in the Introduction, many poems are transmitted in just one manuscript, which was heavily damaged. As a result, for long stretches, only some scraps of verses survived. Kurtz provided many conjectures for these gaps, most of which were adopted by De Groote. Some of these are minor, and cannot be contested. Others are more speculative: while they render correctly the meaning of the missing words, there is little support for the exact Greek wording. We have adopted most (but not all) of these editorial conjectures and indicated them in the Greek text with angle brackets < >. Every departure from Kurtz's text (including better alternatives found in De Groote) is indicated.

We have followed De Groote's system of accentuation of enclitics.

In the corresponding translations, we have not bracketed each conjecture, because this would make the textual image too cumbersome. Lacunas are indicated by an ellipsis (. . .) in both Greek and English. In a few cases, to help the reader to follow the train of thought, we have added in our translation words that must have been in the lacuna, but for which no exact Greek equivalent can be reconstructed. These additions are marked by angle brackets < >.

In Mauropous's case, we have indicated every significant departure from Lagarde's text, occasionally checking a reproduction of *Vaticanus graecus* 676, the most important manuscript. Punctuation (including quotation marks) has been tacitly modified.

Notes to the Texts

CHRISTOPHER OF MYTILENE

17.13   καματώδεος Crimi, "Recuperi," De Groote: καματώδεις Kurtz
22.1   τὸ πᾶν στένεις De Groote: τὸ πᾶ ... Kurtz
22.31   τέλος Crimi, "Recuperi," De Groote: γέλος Kurtz
27.title τὸν Συνάδων: τῶν Συνάδων Kurtz, De Groote
30.1   φίλτατον φίλων Kurtz: ... De Groote
33.2   *supplied by* De Groote
34   *verses 1, 3, and 5 supplied by* De Groote
38.3   ἄνευ πολέμοιο De Groote: ... υευ πολέμοιο Kurtz
39.1   ἐξερυγγάνεις De Groote: ... γάνεις Kurtz
40.49   οὖν δύνῃ De Groote: οὖ ... Kurtz
43.title τὸν Συνάδων: τῶν Συνάδων Kurtz, De Groote
44.22   *lacuna*: Λοκρόν ῥόδον Kurtz, De Groote
46.4   ἔμπνοε De Groote: λαμπρῆς Kurtz
49.6   *lacuna*: σὺ Kurtz, De Groote. *Perhaps* νῦν?
51.3   γε Kurtz: με De Groote
57   *We have chosen not to adopt the conjectures by de Stefani, "Notes," to this poem (all accepted by De Groote), because they are unfounded, however attractive they may be.*
58.7   εὐλογωτάτας Crimi, "Motivi epigrammatici," 47, *and* De Groote
64.title περὶ τοῦ Crimi, "Recuperi," *and* De Groote: τρίτου Kurtz
68.title πεμφθείσης ὑπὸ De Groote
70.1   ἐκπρολιποῦσα *conjectured by* Demoen, "Phrasis poikilê," *and* De Groote: ἐκ ... Kurtz
73.1   *supplied by* De Groote
75.25   ἤδε De Groote: ἴδε Kurtz
77.113   *lacuna*: <φιλοφρόνως τάττ᾽> ἔνθα Kurtz

78.4   <αὐ>τόχρημα Crimi, "Recuperi," *and* De Groote; <ἤ> . . . τὸ
χρῆμα Kurtz

81.title   μνηστευ De Groote: μνηστευ<ομένην> Kurtz

81.1   *Kurtz has supplied* <Μάνθανε> *before* μοι.

90.65   *lacuna*: τὸν πρῶτον δρόμον Kurtz, De Groote. *However, at this
point, there is only one lap* (δίαυλος) *finished, not the whole course*
(δρόμος).

93.6   ἐπεὶ De Groote: . . . τεὶ Kurtz

105.30   πλέγματος De Groote, Kurtz *in critical apparatus*; πλεύματος
Kurtz *in main text*

105.57   τοὺς σικύους Crimi, *Canzoniere,* 97, *and* De Groote: τῶν βοτρύων
conjectured by Kurtz

109.90   εἴπες De Groote: εἴπε . . . Kurtz

115.7   τὰ δ᾽ οὔατα Crimi, *Canzoniere,* 156, *and* De Groote

120   *lines 5 and 6 supplied by* Crimi, "Recuperi," *and* De Groote

124.4   χάρι<ν> Crimi, *Canzoniere,* 164, *and* De Groote: χάρι<ς> Kurtz

129.4   κ<ινημάτων> *conjectured by us*: κ<ελευσμάτων> Kurtz, De
Groote, *but the sense must be that the visual is guiding the acoustic*

135.3   ὕσκας De Groote: ἃς καὶ Kurtz

136.58   κοσμοῦντα<ς> . . . <οἰκίας> De Groote: κοσμοῦντα<ς λαμπρῶς
τὰς ἑαυτῶν οἰκίας> Kurtz *(but unmetrical, as pointed out by Maas,
review of Kurtz, in* Byzantinische Zeitschrift *15 [1906]: 640)*

136.62   τυγχάνουσας Kurtz: τυγχάνουσι De Groote

140.5   Τίς οὐ φοβεῖται *conjectured by* Kurtz, De Groote, *assuming an al-
lusion to Amos 3:8*

John Mauropous

21.8   εὐτυχὴς δὲ καὶ τέχνη: *perhaps* εὐτυχεῖς δὲ καὶ τέχνη

23.title   κηδείαν: κηδίαν *Vat. gr.* 676, Lagarde

47.26   ἔρεις: ἔρις *Vat. gr.* 676, Lagarde

48.18   στρέφοντος *Vat. gr.* 676: στέφοντος Lagarde

55.43   ἐκπερῶσαι *Vat. gr.* 676: ἐκπερᾶσαι Lagarde

56.title   ἔπεμψαν: ἔπεμψεν *Vat. gr.* 676, Lagarde *(but clearly Sergios and
Bacchos are meant)*

86.title   μοναχῷ Karpozilos, *Συμβολή,* 81; ἀρχιερεῖ Lagarde

92.5   σπεῦσον: σπεῖσον De Groote

96.10   ἐκτροπῆς: ἐκ τροπῆς Lagarde

Notes to the Translations

1. On the feast of Saint Thomas, in the presence
   of also the person who . . . the feast

The feast day of Saint Thomas fell on October 6. The celebration of this saint included a procession going from Hagia Sophia to the church of Saint Thomas *en tois Amantiou,* situated in the southern part of the city (see Janin, *EglisesCP,* 248–50).

23   John 20:27. Christopher refers here to the story of Doubting Thomas. The apostle questioned Jesus's resurrection until he could touch Jesus with his finger.

28   See Job 30:31.

29   A *pantheotes* was a minor official responsible for order in the palace; see Oikonomides, "L'évolution de l'organisation administrative," 129.

34–35 There is a pun here on two meanings of the word *melos:* "melody" and "bodily member."

2. On the archivist Solomon

A *chartoularios* is a keeper of the archives. The Old Testament king Solomon was renowned for his wisdom. His namesake derided here by Christopher is not otherwise known to us.

1–2   See Matthew 18:3.

3. On the Baptism of Christ; hexameters

This poem is based on the theological notion, commonly expressed since the Council of Chalcedon (451), that in Christ two natures are united without being commingled.

4. On the monk Mourzoul, who kept silent

Mourzoulin is the name for a species of fish, but it is not known which one (see *LbG,* under "μουρζοῦλιν"). "Being silent as a fish" was a common expression in Byzantium, and the reproach of silence occurs very frequently in Byzantine epistolography.

5. On Saint Symeon the Stylite

This is most likely Saint Symeon the Elder, a pillar saint who lived in Syria in the fifth century (there is also Saint Symeon the Younger, who was less famous). Symeon attempted to achieve the ascetic ideal by living on a pillar for years. He is celebrated on September 1, the beginning of the Byzantine calendar year.

1–2   Psalms 8:6(8:5).

6. On Jephtha the charioteer, who crashed in the Golden Hippodrome

title   The Golden Hippodrome was a special race on the Tuesday after Easter, when the new chariot racing season began.

2   The imperial organs, whose pipes were clad in gold, accompanied various ceremonial occasions in the Hippodrome. See Egon Wellesz, *A History of Byzantine Music and Hymnography* (Oxford, 1961), 105–7.

8   Orpheus was a mythological figure who attracted all humans and animals with his music.

16   Bellerophon was a mythological hero, who on the back of his winged horse Pegasus achieved many feats, but also unsuccessfully tried to attack Mount Olympus.

18   The proverbial expression "running on foot beside a Lydian chariot" means "to be thoroughly defeated." See Pindar, fragment 206, in *Pindari carmina cum fragmentis*. Pars II, ed. Herwig Maehler (Leipzig, 1975), 133.

7. On the cleansed well of the monastery of the Mother of God;
verses spoken to the Mother of God as if by the
person responsible for the cleansing

There were many monasteries in Constantinople dedicated to Mary the Mother of God. The well mentioned in this poem probably refers to the monastery of the Mother of God of the Spring *(Theotokos tes Peges)*, an important monastery located just outside the city walls, which had a famous healing spring. See Janin, *EglisesCP*, 223–28. This epigram was probably intended to be an inscription on that well.

2   Genesis 21:19, 26:19.

8. On the emperor Romanos: funeral verses, in hexameter

The death of the emperor Romanos III Argyros occurred on Holy Thursday of 1034 (April 11). Many Byzantine historiographers suggest that Romanos's wife, Zoe, together with her lover, the future emperor Michael IV, was involved in his death. Christopher's poem teems with Homeric formulas and quotations of Homeric verses.

4   κοίρανε λαῶν is a frequent Homeric formula.
6   Wearing crimson (or purple) sandals was a prerogative for the emperor. θαῦμα ἰδέσθαι is a frequent Homeric expression.
7   See *Odyssey* 4.180.
9   See *Odyssey* 9.365.
15   ὄσσε φαεινώ is a frequent Homeric formula.
18   See *Odyssey* 23.2.
22   See *Iliad* 10.15. The first four words are a direct quotation, but Christopher has supplied synonyms for the latter two.
27   *Iliad* 16.776. See also *Odyssey* 24.40.
30   The church of the Theotokos Peribleptos in Constantinople

was founded by Romanos and cherished by him. See Janin, *EglisesCP,* 218–22.

32   Michael IV, supposedly the lover of Zoe, was crowned emperor the day after the death of Romanos.

9. On the school of Saint Theodore in Sphorakiou

The school of Saint Theodore of Sphorakiou was one of the many independent schools in the city; see Lemerle, *Cinq études,* 228–29. The Sphorakiou quarter was situated to the north of Hagia Sophia. Christopher's poems 9 and 10 are our most extensive sources on the school. The teachers Stylianos and Leo are not mentioned anywhere else.

2   A *proximos* was a teacher of second rank.

3   There is wordplay here on the name of Stylianos, since the Greek word *stylos* means "pillar."

4   The *schedos,* or *schedography,* was a didactic method to learn grammar and orthography. In the most common form in this period, the pupils had to reconstruct the correct form of a riddle-like text, based on the many homophones in Greek. The *schedos* became popular from the eleventh century onward, and contests between schools were organized with the *schedos* as a subject. See *ODB* 3:1849.

5   A *maïstor* is a teacher of first rank, or director, of a school. See *LbG,* under "μαγίστωρ."

6   στομόω can mean "sharpening," "giving a mouth," and "training," which can all apply here.

12   The proverb "no deer should wage battle with a lion" is also known to us from paroemiographical collections; see, for example, *CPG* 2:527, Apostolius 11.46, and elsewhere. There is a pun here on the name of the teacher, Leo (lit., "lion").

10. On the same school; hexameters

For the school of Saint Theodore in Sphorakiou, see the notes to the previous poem.

1   This is an allusion to Proverbs 9:1.

5–6   Christopher uses the same wordplay on Stylianos as in poem 9.

18–20   Christopher repeats his wordplay on Leo from poem 9.

11. On the headmaster of the school in the quarter of the Bronze Shops

The school of the Theotokos in the neighborhood of Chalkoprateia was another independent school in Constantinople; see Lemerle, *Cinq études,* 227–28 (where a French translation of this poem can also be found). Chalkoprateia, literally, "neighborhood of the bronze shops," was situated to the west of the Hagia Sophia church; the church of the Theotokos in that neighborhood was one of the most famous in Constantinople. Christopher uses the name of the school, Chalkoprateion, to create the similarly-sounding neologism *schedoprateion* (lit., *"schedos* shop"). For the title of *maïstor,* see the note to 9.5.

3   Midas was a mythological king, known for his greed. The gods granted his wish that everything he touched would be turned into gold, but Midas had not considered that his food would also thus become inedible.

9   On the dictations (*schede*) see the note to 9.4.

12. On the church restored by the money-weigher Eustathios; hexameters

title   A money-weigher (*zygostates*) was an official responsible for the weighing of coins; see *ODB* 3:2332. This Eustathios is otherwise not known to us.

2   A *chartoularios* was originally a keeper of the archives. Eustathios was a *megas chartoularios,* an important official in the administration, but at this time probably without any proper archival duties. *Illoustrios* was an honorary title given to officials. For all these functions, see Oikonomides, "L'évolution de l'organisation administrative."

13. On the inequality of life

2–3   An allusion to the creation of Adam in Genesis 2:7.

24   An allusion to Matthew 15:27 and Mark 7:28.

31–32 An allusion to Genesis 9:11.

34   Atlas was a mythological hero, who carried the earth on his
       shoulders.

14. On "Hail, woman full of grace," and "Behold here the Lord's maidservant"; hexameters

The subject of the poem is two quotations from Luke 1:28 and 1:38, both
relating to the Annunciation. The poem is a dialogue between the arch-
angel Gabriel and the Mother of God.

15. On the patrician and *parathalassites* Melias

A *parathalassites* was a military commander responsible for safety on the
seas surrounding the capital. Patrician (*patrikios*) is a high honorary func-
tion. Melias is not otherwise known to us. Christopher puns on the resem-
blance of Melias's name to *meli*, the Greek word for "honey."

16. On the grave of the same Melias, being depicted there both as a layman and as a monk

8–9   Ecclesiastes 1:2.

11–12 *Anthypatos* (proconsul) and *patrikios* (patrician) were high honor-
       ary titles, surviving from ancient Roman times but having a
       different meaning in this period, given to officials. *Vestes* is also
       an honorary title, conferred on important individuals.

12   The "judge of the Hippodrome" was a lower category of judge;
       see *ODB* 3:2157–58.

22   Black clothes and a tonsured head were the two most distinc-
       tive traits of a new monk.

26–27   This refers to Melias's function of *parathalassites* (see note to previous poem).

17. On the four seasons of the year; hexameters

2   The Byzantine administrative year, or *indictio,* began in September and ended in August. Christopher's calendars also begin with the month of September.

18. On the emperor Michael and his three brothers

This family of four brothers (originally five) hailed from Paphlagonia. Of humble origins, they managed to gain influence in the palace during the reign of Romanos III (1028–1034). The key figure in the career of this family was John, known as Orphanotrophos. This monk and eunuch was an influential courtier under Romanos. After Romanos's death, Michael, one of the brothers, married Zoe, the legitimate descendant of the Macedonian dynasty (see poem 8). This marriage brought him to the throne as the emperor Michael IV (1034–1041), called "the Paphlagonian." Behind the scenes, John took effective command of the empire. After Michael's death, the power of the family was secured by the ascension to the throne of his nephew Michael V Kalaphates (1041–1042). Among the other brothers, Constantine was a monk, while George was a powerful figure in his own right.

12   Wearing black is a distinctive feature of Byzantine monks.

19   Christopher plays on the name of the Arcturus star, since *arktos* also means "north." The Arcturus star, of the constellation Boötes, is one of the brightest stars in the sky.

19. On the same; hexameters

This poem is also addressed to Michael IV the Paphlagonian.

14   Byzantines often evoked the curse of the 318 bishops who according to tradition had attended the First Council of Nicaea (325 CE).

20. On the *protospatharios* and judge Basil Xeros

Basil Xeros is known to us from other sources, notably some seals dated to the second quarter of the eleventh century (see Follieri, "Le poesie," 142). "Hellas" was at that time a province of the empire roughly encompassing east central and southern Greece. The function of judge *(krites)* implied not only juridical duties but also the effective governance of a province. The title of *protospatharios* at this time referred to a high-ranking court office.

Christopher puns on the name of Xeros, which in Greek literally means "dry."

1   "A sea of goods" is a proverbial expression to describe a multitude of good things (see, for example, *CPG* 1:3, Zenobius 1.9).

21. Riddle on the balance scale

Most balance scales in Byzantium were suspended from above and supported a pair of pans on which the loads were placed. The number six perhaps refers to a tripartite mechanism that supported each pan.

22. To Demetrios, the metropolitan of Kyzikos, on his gout

Demetrios of Kyzikos is not attested otherwise. Kyzikos was a city in northwest Asia Minor.

6   Job, in the eponymous Old Testament book, was subjected to many sufferings to test his faith.

11   An allusion to Ephesians 6:12.

23. To the grammarian George, who wrote a failed *boustrophedon*

The proverb βοῦν ἐπὶ γλώττης φέρειν (lit., "carry an ox on the tongue") means "to be silent, not be able to speak" (see *CPG* 1:51, for example, Zenobius 2.70). A *boustrophedon* means "as an ox turns" (while plowing the field), and refers to a way of writing in which the first line is written left to right, the second right to left, and so on. The name of the grammarian, "Georgios," means, literally, "farmer," thus adding another twist to the wordplay in this poem.

24. On the procession of the emperor Michael

The emperor praised in this poem is Michael IV (1034–1041); see poem 18.

25. On the Transfiguration

The Transfiguration is the name for the biblical episode in which Jesus Christ appeared on Mount Tabor, together with the prophets Moses and Elijah, to his disciples Peter, John, and James (Matthew 17:1–9; Mark 9:2–8; Luke 9:28–36). In the Byzantine Church, the feast of the Transfiguration was commemorated on August 6. Christopher here interprets the three disciples as a symbol of the Holy Trinity, proclaimed at the Council of Nicaea in 325, and the two prophets as a symbol of the two natures of Christ, one divine and one human. The poem was composed for an inscription on an image of the Transfiguration.

7   This verse is reminiscent of the exact formula used in the Council of Chalcedon (451) to clarify the relationship between the two natures in Christ.

26. On Hezekiah, about the lengthening of his life

This poem refers to the story of King Hezekiah's miraculous healing (2 Kings 20; Isaiah 38:1–8). Hezekiah, who was gravely ill, sought advice from the prophet Isaiah. The prophet reassured him that he would recover and live a long life, but the king asked for a miraculous sign from God. Thereupon, the Lord brought the shadow ten degrees backward, thus extending the length of the day.

27. On the monk Niketas of Synada

Niketas of Synada was a friend of Christopher, also appearing in poem 43 and (probably) in poem 100, but he is not known from any other source.

9   Orpheus was a mythological figure, who attracted all humans and animals with his music. In Byzantine rhetoric, eloquent orators are frequently compared with him.

14   Manna is the food that God sent down on the people of Israel during their journey through the desert; see Exodus 16:1–36.

19   In Christopher's time, there was still a senate in Constantinople, but its political power was limited.

39   Homeric phrase; see *Iliad* 6.182.

50   Croesus and Midas were legendary or mythological kings famous for their wealth.

51   Sardanapalus was an Assyrian king, whose opulence was legendary.

28. On the veil of the Mother of God; hexameters

An *encheirion* was a woven veil that would be placed over an icon, typically an icon of the Virgin Mary. *Encheiria* were sometimes inscribed with epigrams. This poem was intended to be inscribed on a veil dedicated by a certain Eirene. Christopher puns on the donor's name, since *eirene* is the Greek word for peace. On *encheiria,* see Valerie Nunn, "The Encheirion as adjunct to the Icon in the Middle Byzantine Period," *Byzantine and Modern Greek Studies* 10 (1986): 73–102, with reference to Christopher's poem on page 78 of the article.

29. On the poor man Leo

The Gospels frequently mention the frugal lifestyle of the apostles (see Matthew 10:9–10; Mark 6:8–9; Luke 9:3), which gave rise to the phrase "apostolic life" as a life detached from earthly wealth. The specific attributes of poverty mentioned by Christopher echo these biblical passages.

30. On the urban prefect John of Amouda

The urban prefect (eparch) was the governor of the city of Constantinople. He was the supreme judge in the capital, second only to the emperor, and was the chief of police responsible for order in the city. This poem is our most important source on the attire of the eparch. See *ODB* 1:704.

John of Amouda is not otherwise known to us; Amouda was a town in Cilicia, in present southeast Turkey.

6–11   This passage depicts the juridical duties of the eparch. It was customary that a black vote signified condemnation, while a white vote meant a positive judgment.

12   The *simikinthion* mentioned here probably refers to a long scarf worn by important dignitaries (see *ODB* 2:1000, under "Insignia").

17   An allusion to Isaiah 52:7 (quoted in Romans 10:15), where the expression is used for proclaimers of good tidings.

31. On \<Moschos\>

This poem puns on the name of the addressee: Moschos literally means "calf." The Greek word for "horns" also refers to a cuckolded husband (see also poem 84).

32. On the laurel leaves that are strewn around in the church on feast days

The laurel was in antiquity commonly associated with oracles; the Pythian seer in Delphi chewed on laurel leaves before delivering an oracle.

33. On the Savior

This poem and the next were intended as inscriptions on an icon of Christ.

1   See John 16:24.

34. More verses on the Savior

3   Matthew 11:30.

5   An allusion to Matthew 19:30; Mark 10:31; Luke 13:30.

35. Riddle on the Iris in the sky, that is, the rainbow

In the Greek text of the title, there are two words for rainbow, of which the first is more learned, while the second is more common.

36. On somebody who had spoken in defense of a friend because of
the . . . against him, but was still recognized

The textual damage in the title makes it difficult to establish the precise
occasion that led to this polemical poem, but it appears that two friends
had attacked Christopher in an anonymous pamphlet. The translation of
the title is tentative.

1–2   Two mythological pairs of friends. The severing of the Hydra's
heads was one of the labors of Hercules; Meleager and Theseus
participated in the hunt for the Caledonian boar.

12   Protasiou was Christopher's neighborhood in Constantinople,
to the northwest of Hagia Sophia; see also poem 114.131. See
Janin, *Constantinople byzantine,* 417–18.

20   See Psalms 63:8(64:7). "Of babies" occurs only in the Septuagint,
not in the original Hebrew.

22   The proverb is reported in *Die Sprichwörtersammlung des Maxi-
mus Planudes,* ed. Eduard Kurtz (Leipzig, 1886), 83.

27–28   Christopher uses here three different words for a boar.

37. On the rhetor Menas, who loves to drink

Menas is otherwise unknown to us. The literal sense of the Greek is that
he "likes to drink more than to persuade."

38. On the soldier John, who had stolen the belongings of his
comrades; hexameters

This John is not otherwise known to us. The point of this poem is that
John manages to gather spoils, not from war as a normal soldier would do,
but by robbing his comrades.

2   "Gory spoils" (ἔναρα βροτόεντα) is a common Homeric phrase,
occurring eight times in the *Iliad.*

39. On the beardless Eugenios

This poem puns on the names Eugenios, the real name of the beardless
man derided here, and Eugeneios, meaning "well-bearded." Eugenios, per-

haps a eunuch, claimed the latter name by adding a diphthong (that is, replacing *i* with *ei*), and thus claiming the "beard" that he did not have in reality. Christopher jokingly says that he will pronounce the desired name in speech, but this promise is useless, because in Byzantine pronunciation both names sounded the same; therefore it is an "empty favor" (see l. 6).

40. On the . . . of Pothos, who is an uneducated man and compares the works of the wise

The identity of the person addressed in the poem cannot be ascertained.

14	For the proverb, see *CPG* 1:195, Diogenianus 1.98, and elsewhere.
18	This might refer to Plato's characterization of the poet in *Ion,* 534b.
36	Jeremiah was an Old Testament prophet known for his laments over the sins of Israel.
40	See Jeremiah 9:1.
42	An allusion to Jeremiah 4:19.

41. On the Presentation in the Temple

The Hypapante (commonly called the "Presentation in the Temple" in Western tradition) is one of the Lord's Feasts. According to the New Testament (Luke 2:22–38), Christ's parents brought their infant child to the temple in Jerusalem. They met an old man named Symeon, of whom it was foretold by the Holy Spirit that he would see the Savior before dying. Upon seeing the infant, Symeon prophesied that he would be the Messiah. Christopher's poem is addressed to this Symeon. It probably accompanied an image of this biblical scene.

4	Paraclete is a traditional name for the Holy Spirit, derived from John 14:16–17.

42. . . . with dough the zodiac cycle, in a circle; to his cousin

This poem describes a cake made by the poet's female cousin, depicting the firmament. Christopher describes the signs of the zodiac, connecting them with traditional character traits, the planets, some notable constellations, and the four cardinal points.

There is an existing English translation and commentary in Paul Magdalino, "Cosmological Confectionery and Equal Opportunity in the Eleventh Century. An Ekphrasis by Christopher of Mytilene (Poem 42)," in *Byzantine Authors: Literary Activities and Preoccupations. Texts and Translations Dedicated to the Memory of Nicolas Oikonomides,* ed. John Nesbitt (Leiden, 2003), 1–6.

1   See Psalms 8:4(8:3). Christopher has changed the verb from future (ὄψομαι) to aorist (εἶδον).

3   See Psalms 103(104):2. Christopher has substituted πόλον for the biblical οὐρανὸν.

5–16 Christopher connects the signs of the zodiac with human character traits, which is quite rare for ancient or Byzantine astrology. The basis for the connections seems to be simple symbolism.

9   The connection with fornicators might be inspired by the signification "testicles" of the Greek word *didymoi* ("twins").

17   "House" is a technical astrological term. In astrology, each planet ("wandering star") has its "home" in one of the twelve zodiac signs, where it is privileged and makes its influence particularly felt.

20–24 In ancient and Byzantine astronomy, there were seven "planets," or "wandering stars," here enumerated.

28   According to Aratus, *Phaenomena* 634–46, the mythological hero Orion touched Artemis's robe when hunting. The goddess punished him by sending a scorpion to attack him. This explains the fact that when Scorpio appears in the firmament, Orion disappears, as if fleeing from him. There are other slightly different versions of this mythological story.

32–35 Christopher uses here the technical astronomical/astrological terms for the appearance, disappearance, zenith, and nadir of constellations in the firmament.

41   *Arktos* means "north."

45   The *Horai* were mythological goddesses of the seasons. Usually, they are said to be three in number.

46–47   An allusion to *Iliad* 5.749.

49–50   In the medieval conception, there was above the stars another "starless" sphere, not visible to humans.

58–63   Phidias and Polyclitus were famous ancient sculptors, while Zeuxis, Parrhasius, Polygnotus, and Aglaophon were renowned painters. All of them worked in Athens in the fifth century BCE. Christopher includes puns on the names of Polygnotus (lit., "well-known"), Polyclitus ("reputed"), and Aglaophon ("clear-voiced"). Daedalus was a mythological craftsman.

67–69   Christopher paraphrases Job 38:36, directly quoting part of the verse while reworking the rest in order to fit the meter and, perhaps, to display his own playful dexterity with biblical allusions.

79–80   Penelope and Helen are depicted in the Homeric poems as diligent in the art of weaving. Moreover, women from Lesbos are praised as skilled in domestic activities (see *Iliad* 9.128–31).

43. To the monk Niketas of Synada, about the foot wrappers

This poem probably refers to gout, a disease often mentioned in Byzantine epistolography. The Greek word *podopanion* is very rare, and instead of "foot wrappers" it may mean "socks."

44. On his brother John

23   This is a very common phrase in funeral poetry, but it may ultimately derive from Job 24:24.

75   See Psalms 7:9; the phrase literally means "scrutinize the kidneys and hearts."

45. On the jars with cooled aromatic drinks sent to his friend

5–6   This refers to the words of Christ that whoever gives a cup of water to one of his disciples will be rewarded (Matthew 10:42; Mark 9:41).

46. On Job; elegiac couplets

This refers to the story of Job, the protagonist of the eponymous biblical book. At first a fortunate man, he was tested by God, who took away all his wealth and happiness. Clinging to his faith, he was ultimately honored by God.

This is one of three poems in the volume in elegiac couplets (or elegiac distichs), an ancient Greek meter in which the first line is a hexameter and the second line a pentameter. See also poems 57 and 83.

2   The word for "judge" *(agonothetes)* refers to someone who sets a contest and distributes the prizes. It was a common idea in Byzantium that God presides over the contest of life.

3   This is a universal motif; see, for example, the lesson of the story of Solon and Croesus in Herodotus, *History* 1.32.

48. On the sparrows that are sitting on the . . . and chirping

8   Christopher enumerates here some technical musicological terms, referring to the length of strings and their corresponding tones.

49. On the emperor Michael, when he was tonsured

This poem refers to the tonsure of the emperor Michael IV the Paphlagonian (1034–1041), just before his death on December 10, 1041. Michael was afflicted by epilepsy during the last years of his reign. Tonsure (that is, becoming a monk) was in Byzantium an effective and humane way to remove an emperor from the throne.

50. On the bronze horse in the Hippodrome which has its forefoot raised

The bronze horse mentioned in this poem was probably one of the four extant famous statues that once adorned the Hippodrome in Constantinople and are now to be found in Venice. See Janin, *Constantinople byzantine*, 194.

6   This seems to be a popular expression; see Emmanouel Kriaras, *Λεξικό της Μεσαιωνικής Ελληνικής Δημώδους Γραμματείας 1100–1669* (Thessalonike, 1968), under "λαμβάνω."

51. On the image of Saint Thekla, carved from stone

Saint Thekla, a companion of Saint Paul, was one of the most venerated female saints in Byzantium. When she was being attacked by a band of men, she prayed to be delivered from them. The rocks nearby opened and she disappeared into them, never to be seen again. This epigram was intended for inscription on a relief carving with her image, made of stone, which gives Christopher the occasion to create a paradoxical antithesis to the way she died.

52. On the ex-emperor Michael Kalaphates, when he was arrested and blinded for having banished the empress Zoe from imperial rule; hexameters

This poem refers to the turbulent events of 1042. The emperor Michael V Kalaphates had obtained the throne because he was the adoptive son of his uncle Michael IV and Zoe. Zoe was, together with her sister, Theodora, the only direct descendant of the legitimate Macedonian dynasty, and she was in theory co-ruler with Michael. On April 19, it was announced that Michael had exiled her from the palace to a monastery. This created an uproar among the populace of Constantinople. In a bloody battle, the crowd succeeded in subduing the palace guards. They seized Michael and his uncle Constantine, who had sought refuge in the Stoudios monastery. They were blinded, and Michael died shortly thereafter.

    Christopher's poem teems with expressions and phrases taken from the Homeric poems.

1   Byzas is a legendary figure, believed to have founded the ancient Megarian colony of Byzantion, later Constantinople.

2   Michael's father was a ship caulker by profession, hence his sobriquet "Kalaphates" (caulker).

"Dreadful battle" (φύλοπιν αἰνήν) is a frequent Homeric expression; see *Iliad* 4.15 and elsewhere.

4   "Fair" (εἶδος ἀρίστης) is a frequent Homeric expression; see *Iliad* 2.715 and elsewhere.

5–6   Zoe, born around 978 to Constantine VIII, while he was coemperor with Basil II, was born in a purple room in the palace, reserved for members of the dynasty.

6–7   This refers to the emperor Romanos III Argyros or Argyropoulos (1028–1034), first husband of Zoe.

7   *Iliad* 7.392.

9   *Odyssey* 11.245.

12   *Iliad* 7.237.

13   "Painful deaths" (λευγαλέους θανάτους) is a frequent Homeric expression; see *Iliad* 21.281 and elsewhere.

"Sorrow and moaning" (ἄλγεά τε στοναχάς τε) is quoted from *Iliad* 2.39 and *Odyssey* 14.39.

16   See *Iliad* 5.319.

19   "Truthful oaths" (ὅρκια πιστά) is a frequent Homeric expression; see *Iliad* 2.124 and elsewhere.

54. On the emperor Constantine Monomachos

Constantine IX Monomachos was Byzantine emperor from 1042 to 1055.

55. To the same emperor, as if spoken by the *protospatharios* John Hypsinous

Christopher here lends his voice to that of someone else: an official named John Hypsinous, who asks for a promotion. The title of *protospatharios* at this time referred to a high-ranking court office. The emperor Constantine Monomachos (see previous poem) was known for his generosity.

1   The Pactolus is a river in western Asia Minor that flowed through ancient Sardis. The mythological king Midas had washed himself in this river, thus turning it into gold.

4   Christopher coins here the neologism τιμορρόας, "streaming with honors," on the basis of the existing χρυσορρόας, "streaming with gold."

11 There is a pun here on the name of the applicant, Hypsinous, that literally means "with lofty mind." The verb ὑψόω, "raise up," has the same root.

57. On his mother Zoe who has died; elegiac couplets

20–25 Christopher refers to Proverbs 31:10–31, where the ideal woman is described. More particularly, line 24 echoes the wording of Proverbs 31:15, and line 25 that of Proverbs 31:27. The Proverbs were thought to have been written by Solomon.

37 *Iliad* 13.458.

58. To his father who is distressed and grieving

5 Christopher might be referring to the mythological figure of Echo, a nymph doomed to merely repeat the sounds she hears (see also l. 14).

59. . . . iambs; some of them to his mother . . . with another voice, as if from his mother . . . marvelously, through the echo . . . his father . . . distress, and as if consoled . . . spoken by the son

Christopher alternatively addresses one line to his deceased mother, who answers with an echo, and one line to his bereaved father. This poem is part of a tradition in which the dead were made to speak by answering with an echo; several funeral epigrams in the *Anthologia Palatina* (for example, IX 177) use this device.

At several points in this translation, the words between quotation marks do not correspond with those in the Greek, because English word order would make it otherwise impossible to preserve the echo effect.

61. To the patriarch Michael on the day after his installation

This poem was written on the occasion of the installation of Michael Keroularios as patriarch in 1043. This happened on March 25, the feast day of the Annunciation to the Virgin.

62. On the ironmonger Leo . . . standing before the emperor
and . . . while many were announced . . .

Due to the heavily damaged state of this poem, it is very difficult to establish what it is about, except that Christopher mocks an ironmonger who had come into contact with the emperor.

10   There might be a pun here on the later Greek expression εἰς σίδηρα ("to irons"), which means "in irons," "into jail."

63. On the . . . priests and deacons, who are of infinite numbers

Christopher mocks here the fact that laymen were ascending the clerical hierarchy to a greater degree than previously.

2   See Matthew 21:13.

4   An allusion to John 2:16.

12   A *sticharion* is a long tunic worn by clerics higher than or equal in rank to a deacon. See *ODB* 3:1956.

17   Cherubim were thought to have numerous eyes; see Ezekiel 10:12.

22   An *orarion* is a stole worn by deacons. See *ODB* 3:1531.

24   The choir pronounces this phrase during the "little entrance" (the procession of the clergy to the sanctuary). This phrase and the following ones that are quoted (at ll. 34 and 38) all occur in the Liturgy "of Chrysostom," which was by the eleventh century the most common text for the celebration of mass in the Byzantine rite.

34   The celebrant pronounces this phrase during the invitation to partake of the Eucharist.

38   The celebrant pronounces this phrase just before the Creed, when the doors of the church were closed.

64. To the head priest John and the . . . about the book
and the gold of the . . .

title   A *protopapas* is a priest who had precedence over other priests (but his exact authority in this time is not entirely clear). This *protopapas* John is not otherwise known to us.

65. Inscription in hexameters on the grave of Maniakes

George Maniakes (d. 1043) was a famous and successful Byzantine army commander. In 1042, he revolted against Constantine IX Monomachos. In the decisive battle against the imperial army, he was killed and his army defeated.

66. To Eudokia, about the golden apple that was sent to her . . . ,
as if spoken by a friend

This poem alludes to the golden apple that Eris, goddess of strife, threw on the table at a banquet of the gods. This apple bore the inscription "for the most beautiful," leading to the quarrel between Athena, Hera, and Aphrodite, and hence the judgment of Paris. Poems 66 and 67 may refer to the story of an apple given to Eudokia, wife of Theodosius II (r. 408–450), or might refer to the empress Eudokia Makrembolitissa (1021–1096).

3   The reconstruction of the sense of this lost verse is based on Crimi, *Canzoniere*, 109.

67. . . .

This epigram refers to the same golden apple for Eudokia mentioned in the previous poem. It is probable that poem 67 was the inscription on the apple, while poem 66 accompanied the gift in some way.

68. To the *synkellos* . . . of Argyropolos about the icon of
Saint Kyros in the . . . opposite the icon of Saint Panteleemon,
that was sent . . . by Saint Hermolaos to the same *synkellos* with
the present verses. . . . This icon of Saint Kyros was removed
from the house in Strategion . . . by Lykoleon . . . , and was
shortly thereafter transferred to . . . the house of Argyropolos

The occasion for this heavily damaged poem can be reconstructed along the following lines, although many details remain unclear. A certain Lykoleon had removed the icon of Saint Kyros from its original location in Strategion, a neighborhood northwest of Hagia Sophia, to somewhere in

Kynegion, a quarter on the Golden Horn in the northwest region of the city, where it came to occupy a place next to an icon of Saint Panteleemon. In this way the icon of Saint Panteleemon was separated from that of Saint Hermolaos, the saint who had converted Panteleemon to Christianity. The three saints now beg a *synkellos* (a title for a high-ranking cleric) to restore the original state of affairs.

This *synkellos* is named Argyropolos (or connected with him), but we cannot identify him further. Nor is Lykoleon known to us. Saints Kyros, Panteleemon, and Hermolaos are all healer saints (for Panteleemon, see also poem 89). The attribution of the words to the various speakers is our tentative reconstruction, and has no basis in the manuscript.

1	Saint Kyros was martyred together with John in Egypt under the emperor Diocletian; they were venerated at a healing shrine in Menouthis on the Mediterranean coast of Egypt. Kyros's feast day is celebrated on January 31.
9–10	There is a pun here on the name of the neighborhood of Kynegion, literally, "place for hunting with dogs."
15	There is a pun here on the name of the neighborhood of Strategion and the Greek word for "general," *strategos.*
20–21	The woolen cloak and the box with medical implements were typical attributes of healer saints, also seen in their depictions.
24	Crimi, *Canzoniere,* and De Groote, *Christophori Mitylenaii Versuum variorum collectio,* have Panteleemon's speech begin here. Instead, we think that the question at line 23 is rhetorical, answered by the poet himself. See the notes to lines 40 and 51.
26	There is a pun here on the name of Kyros and the Greek word for "lord," *Kyrios.*
40	This cannot refer to Panteleemon, since he was mostly portrayed as a young man.
51	We think Panteleemon's speech begins only here. Christopher introduces his speech with πρόσσχωμεν ("let us pay attention") at line 49.
63	Since the word for "envoys" is feminine in Greek, it refers to things, not to persons; one of the two is probably a book (see next verse).

71   Panteleemon, a convert to Christianity, was martyred under Diocletian around 305.

76–79   This refers to the fact that Hermolaos had converted Panteleemon to Christianity.

92   Hermolaos, a Christian priest, was martyred at Nikomedeia.

103   Christopher mentions here two healing saints, Sampson (who lived in Constantinople during the reign of Justinian) and Kosmas, the colleague of Damian.

126   This refers to Lykoleon, the man who had removed the icon of Saint Kyros. His name contains the Greek words for "wolf" and "lion."

69. Epigram on the verses on the icon of Saint Kyros

Christopher refers to the number 153: this is the number of fish that the apostles caught after Christ's appearance on the lake of Tiberias (see John 21:11), and also the number of lines in the previous poem.

70. On the *sebaste* Maria, when she died; hexameters

The subject of this poem is probably Maria Skleraina, mistress of Constantine IX Monomachos. She received the title of *sebaste,* the usual Greek translation of the Latin *augusta.* She died around 1045.

72. On Konstas, census taker and notary of . . .

The *kensoualios* was responsible for drawing up census lists (*LbG,* under "κηνσουάλιος"). This Konstas is not otherwise known.

73. On the tables game

The title of the poem refers to the so-called tables game (*tabula* in Latin, *tavli* in modern Greek). This board game, resembling backgammon, has been popular in the Mediterranean since antiquity. Palamedes is a mythological hero, credited with the invention of the game of dice.

74. To Herod, about the honorable head of John the Forerunner

Herod, king of Judaea in the time of Christ, was enamored of Salome, and promised her anything if she would dance for him. Mark's gospel specifies that Herod promised to give her up to half of his empire. At the instigation of her mother Herodias, the girl demanded the head of John the Baptist (Mark 6:22–28). John the Baptist was known in Byzantium as the Forerunner.

75. On his sister Anastaso, who has died and is
still laid out for burial; in anacreontics

This poem is the first of a cycle in which Christopher describes the funeral of his sister Anastaso. After being laid out (poem 75: the *prothesis*), she is carried in a procession (poem 76: the *ekphora*) to her grave (poem 77: funeral epigram).

This is the only poem in Christopher's collection that uses the anacreontic meter. This meter evolved from the ancient anacreontic and was in Byzantine times enriched with rhythmical features. It was often used for lament in Byzantium.

21   The *kinnor* (harp) is a Hebrew string instrument, known from the Septuagint.

77. Funeral verses on the same woman

19   The Heliades were the daughters of Helios, god of the sun. When Phaethon, their brother, died, they mourned so compassionately that the gods turned them into poplar trees, and their tears into amber.

31   Christopher's mother was already dead: see poem 57 (in the knowledge that the collection was ordered chronographically).

45   An allusion to Psalms 22(23):2.

46   See Psalms 112(113):9.

57–61   Christopher alludes to Odysseus summoning the dead; see *Odyssey* 11.25–43. "Hellene" here means above all "pagan."

112   Psalms 22(23):2. Christopher here quotes the words of the Psalms (εἰς χλόης τόπον) that he had alluded to in line 45 (τόπῳ χλοηφόρῳ).

78. On the grammarian Peter, who had asked for Christopher's funeral lament in iambs for his sister, and who kept it a long time and has not yet managed to give it back

This poem refers to poem 77, which Christopher apparently had loaned out to a grammarian named Peter.

1   In ancient mythology, the lotus flower was an intoxicating plant; see *Odyssey* 9.94–95.

79. More verses for the same person, who had sent back the verses and . . .

This poem continues the story of the previous poem, where a certain Peter had asked for a poem of Christopher (poem 77 in his collection).

80. On Saint Lazarus, friend of Christ, because he remained reticent about the other world

Lazarus was a close friend of Christ. After his death, Christ brought him back to life (John 11:1–44). While Lazarus remains silent in the Gospel, it is not explicitly stated that he refused to talk about the life after death.

81. . . . Theodora who is betrothed . . . and character

3   This echoes the compliment of Odysseus to Nausicaä in *Odyssey* 6.163.

13   "Glorious boons" (ἀγλαὰ δῶρα) is a fixed formula in the Homeric poems; see *Iliad* 1.213 and elsewhere.

82. On the gravediggers, who robbed the garments of the
dead when the cemetery at Saint Luke's was ablaze

The cemetery of Saint Luke was situated near the eponymous church in the western part of Constantinople and was reserved for the poor; see Janin, *EglisesCP,* 311.

83. Epigram in elegiac couplets about the saints of the whole year

This poem is an epigram on one of the four calendars that Christopher wrote, each of them in a different meter (see Introduction).

84. For Basil, surnamed "Porky," who had often
asked for some of Christopher's writings

The poem abounds with wordplay at various levels. The surname (or perhaps family name) of the addressee Basil is Choirinos, which means "porky," hence the comparison with a pig. The word κεράτιον, the diminutive of κέρας, means "carob" or "St. John's bread," a typical food for pigs, but it also refers to the proverbial "horns" of a cuckolded husband. Βάλανος (acorn) also possibly carries a double entendre, namely the glans penis, implying that Basil had sex with men.

85. On a conceited doctor

1   There is a pun on τῦφον, which means "fever," but also "delusion" or "affectation."

86. On Saint Dionysios because of ...

Saint Dionysios the Areopagite was a martyr saint from the first century. Under his name circulated a group of famous theological writings from a later date. This poem seems to refer to the *Celestial Hierarchy,* which explains the nature of the angels; Christopher's epigram also circulated as a poetic paratext in manuscripts with that work (see *Database of Byzantine Book Epigrams*, www.dbbe.ugent.be/typ/1238).

87. For a friend who had sent grapes from the countryside

The poem's argument is based on Genesis 3:7, for Adam covering his nakedness with a fig leaf, and Genesis 9:20–21, for the story of Noah, who exposed his nakedness when drunk.

88. For the same friend, who had sent figs

In contrast with the previous poem, Christopher shifts his biblical references from the Old Testament to the New.

10	An allusion to Matthew 21:19; Mark 11:14; Luke 13:6–9.
12	An allusion to John 15:1.
14	An allusion to Matthew 26:28–29; Mark 14:24–25.

89. On the honorable relic of Saint Panteleemon that dripped with sacred liquid

This poem was probably an inscription on a reliquary. Saint Panteleemon is venerated as a healer saint. It is believed that when he was beheaded, milk instead of blood gushed from his wound. The *hagiasma* mentioned here is the usual Greek term for a liquid to which miraculous powers were attributed, especially if it was identified with or came into contact with a relic; it most likely refers to a bone that exuded drops of blood or a reliquary in which water was poured over the bone relic to produce holy water. Many relics of Panteleemon were to be found in the churches of Constantinople.

1–2	This refers to Moses, who drew water from a rock when the Israelites were passing through the desert (Numbers 20:11).

90. To his friends who were out of town in the countryside,
and, having missed the horse race that had been
held, asked to be told about it

The chariot races, a Roman heritage, were enduringly popular in Byzantium (see also poem 6). They took place in the Hippodrome in Constantinople. Four chariot drivers competed with each other, each wearing the color of one of the four popular factions: green, blue, red, or white. A course consisted of seven laps around the track.

There exists an English translation of the beginning of the poem in Alice-Mary Talbot, "The Lure of the Hippodrome in the Middle Byzantine Era," in *Hippodrom/Atmeydanı: İstanbul'un tarih sahnesi/Hippodrome/Atmeydanı: A Stage for Istanbul's History,* ed. Brigitte Pitarakis (Istanbul, 2010), 65–68.

11	The chariots started from starting boxes, which had a mechanism to hold the horses before the beginning of the race. The assignment of these starting boxes was drawn by lot.
17	There were twelve starting boxes, so some were empty at the start of each race.
19	The supporters of the different colors (sometimes called "circus factions") performed various acclamations and chants in honor of the emperor before the beginning of the races.
54	The organs in the Hippodrome accompanied the chanting. See also notes to poem 6.
79–82	The so-called Masonry Obelisk is an obelisk, still extant, built by Constantine the Great or perhaps later. The monument was situated at the center of the *spina* (the central axis of the Hippodrome). The obelisk was once clad with plates of bronze.
92	The *Sphendone* (lit., "sling") is the curved part of the Hippodrome at the southern end, opposite to the starting gates.

91. . . . and John, his brother

John is known as the brother of Christopher; see poem 44.

6   The saying is recorded in *Die Sprichwörtersammlung des Maximus Planudes,* ed. Eduard Kurtz (Leipzig, 1886), 14. It means that you know how to do something because the fool shows how not to do it.

93. On the hymnographers John, Kosmas, and Theophanes, painted together

The subject of the poem (and the image it once accompanied) is three saints and hymnographers: John of Damascus, Kosmas Maioumas (also called Kosmas the Melode), and Theophanes Graptos. John of Damascus and Kosmas Maioumas lived in the eighth century, Theophanes slightly later. All three saints were associated with Jerusalem. John and Theophanes were also revered as famous iconodules, a point which seems to be taken up here. The hymns written by, or attributed to, John and Kosmas were frequently sung in Byzantine liturgy. John and Kosmas were sometimes depicted together, but we do not know of any image of the three hymnographers as a group.

94. ... the foodstuff that was sent

title   It is not known what foodstuff exactly is meant by the extremely rare Greek word *mesisklion* (see *LbG,* under "μεσίσκλιον"). We also have no clue as to the identity of Leo (l. 4).

6   See Psalms 19:4 (20:3).

95. On the church of Saint George in Mangana

The church of Saint George in Mangana was founded by Constantine IX Monomachos and was part of a larger complex, including a monastery, a library, and a law school. It was situated in the neighborhood of Kynegion, close to the Bosporos. Monomachos was later buried in the church. See Janin, *EglisesCP,* 70–76.

13–14   This is an allusion to Genesis 28:17, which Christopher has partially quoted while substituting synonyms or circumlocutions for some of the words. See the note to poem 42, lines 67–69 above.

96. ...

This poem is an epigram on a stone-inlaid floor, possibly in the church of Saint George, which is the subject of the preceding poem. We know from later travel reports that this church had a remarkable floor, inlaid with plaques of jasper and porphyry. See Janin, *EglisesCP,* 74.

97. ...

This poem is one of those thanking a friend for the words he had sent to Christopher.

3   Christopher alludes here to the girdle of Aphrodite, which gave irresistible charm to anyone who put it on (see *Iliad* 14.214).

98. On the Savior in the middle of the ceiling of the Oaton hall, who is looking down

The *Oaton,* or *Troullos,* was a hall in the imperial palace of Constantinople, so called because it had an egg-like shape. This poem is the only description of the image of Christ there. See Janin, *Constantinople byzantine,* 112.

99. On the cloak called *thalassa* that was worn by Stenites ...

This satirical poem is based on a pun on the word *thalassa,* which means "sea," but in Byzantine Greek could also refer to a purple garment (see *LbG*). Apparently, Stenites had worn his garment inside out, which reminded Christopher of a biblical passage (Psalms 113[114]:3). In this passage, it is said that the sea flees away, while the Jordan turns around; Byzantines associated this with the Baptism of Christ (see poem 3). The name Stenites may refer to someone living close to the Stenon, another name for the Bosporos, perhaps adding another pun to the poem.

100. On the monk Niketas the philosopher

This friend of Christopher is probably the same person as the monk Niketas of Synada addressed in poems 27 and 43.

101. On the image of the holy Elijah

It was believed that the prophet Elijah never died on earth; see 2 Kings 2:11.

4   This refers to the Transfiguration. Christ climbed Mount Tabor and was seen there together with Elijah and Moses (see also poem 25).

102. On the week before Lent

The week before Lent (*apokreos* in Byzantine Greek, see *LbG*) was an occasion for merrymaking and celebrations.

104. On the grave of Konstans, *protospatharios* and having the second rank among the . . . ; hexameters

The *protospatharios* Konstans mentioned here may be the same as the person addressed in poem 72. For the function, see poem 20.

105. On the cucumber bed in the vineyard of the monastery of the Spring . . .

The monastery where this vineyard and cucumber bed was situated was most likely the monastery of the Mother of God of the Spring (*Theotokos tes Peges*); see notes to poem 7.

106. On the Holy Forty Martyrs, with one lamp hanging in front of them

The Forty Martyrs of Sebasteia were frozen to death by being forced to stand naked in an icy lake. This scene was popular in Byzantine art; see poem 133 and *ODB* 2:799–800. This epigram was apparently intended for an icon of the martyrs lit by a single lamp. The fire may refer to their bodies being burned after their deaths, or to the divine fire they longed for; it stands in contrast with the icy lake, perhaps alluded to in the third line.

107. On . . .

The name John, mentioned at line 5, suggests that this poem is addressed to Christopher's deceased brother John (see poem 44).

108. On the embrace and kiss that people give each other at Easter

In the Orthodox liturgy of Easter, people exchange a kiss at the end of the Matins service, while "Christ has risen" is being chanted.

109. . . . those berating people who fear the sea

44	Job 32:19.
45	Job came from the land of Ausis; see Job 1:1.
73	Thales was a sixth-century BCE Greek philosopher, mathematician, and astronomer from Miletos.
92–94	Christopher probably refers here to the story of Arion, the ancient musician who, according to legend, was thrown out of his boat into the sea by pirates and was then rescued by dolphins. However, Arion played the lute *(kithara)* instead of the flute.
98	Christopher probably refers to the story of Jonah and the whale; see also line 123.
102	Christopher refers to the legend of Polycrates, tyrant of Samos in the sixth century BCE, who threw away his ring, only to get it back when fishermen caught a fish and found the ring inside.
104	An allusion to Matthew 17:27. On the advice of Christ, Peter found a *stater* (a valuable Roman coin) in the mouth of a fish.
110–14	See Psalms 68(69):14–16. Verse 111 may read "from those who hate me," as in the Psalms text.
123–36	This passage narrates the story of Jonah and the whale (Jonah 1). Jonah was sailing to Tarsus, when a storm hit the ship. At his own instigation, Jonah was thrown overboard, whereupon the

sea calmed down and the sailors started to believe in the Lord. Christopher's wording closely echoes the biblical text.

130   The word *sknips* refers to an insect living in trees, but it is not known exactly which species.

185   The "thin wooden board" refers to the ship's deck. The idea is from the philosopher Anacharsis, as related in Diogenes Laertius, 1.8.103.

204–5   An allusion to Job 38:8 and 10.

111. Riddle on the organ; in hexameters

The Byzantines used pneumatic organs, which worked with a system of bellows and pipes. Perhaps the "three souls" here refer to three blast-bags or bellows. See Egon Wellesz, *A History of Byzantine Music and Hymnography* (Oxford, 1961), 105–7.

112. On the painter Myron, painting the icon of Michael

The epigram probably accompanied an icon of the archangel Michael, but it is not excluded that a man named Michael (the emperor Michael VII?) is being praised here.

An English translation of the poem can be found in Mango, *Art of the Byzantine Empire*, 220.

113. On the birth of the venerable John the Forerunner

This poem refers to the story of Elizabeth, who in her old age, and believed to be sterile, gave birth to John the Baptist (Luke 1:57–58).

5–6   An allusion to Matthew 3:9; Luke 3:8.

114. To the monk Andrew, who buys up the bones of ordinary people as the relics of saints . . . and accepts them . . . and innumerable body parts as those of one and the same saint

This poem refers to the popular practice of venerating relics in Byzantium. It explicitly takes issue with the dubious collecting and selling of false relics.

The poem has many instances of the word *pistis,* which in Greek may mean "faith," but also "trust." It is not always possible here to distinguish between the two senses.

22   Hydra was a mythological monster having many heads.

27   The Byzantines considered the octopus as a fish.

29   Briareus was a mythological figure with one hundred hands, who was related to the Cyclops.

32   Christopher intends to say that it is quite impossible that John the Baptist had white hair: he was born around the same time as Christ and died before him. See also line 44.

34–35   This refers to the Massacre of the Innocents (Matthew 2:16–18); see notes to poem 139.

39   The Maccabees were the leaders of the Jewish rebellion against the Seleucid kings, as recounted in the biblical books called Maccabees. They became a symbol of heroic martyrdom and ardent faith.

83   There is a pun here on the name of Saint Probos and *probaton,* the Greek word for sheep.

90–91   An allusion to Matthew 17:20. Compare also Mark 11:23; Luke 13:19.

96–97   Enoch was one of the patriarchs. According to Genesis 5:24, he disappeared because God took him away from the earth. Thus his body was not found.

98–99   According to 4 Kings 2:11, the prophet Elijah ascended to heaven. Therefore, he did not die on earth and no remains of him could possibly be found.

102   Chonai was a town in Phrygia devoted to the archangel Michael, with a shrine in commemoration of the miracle he had performed.

116   The Cherubim are guardians of Paradise, holding a flaming sword; see Genesis 3:24.

131–32   The church of the Theotokos in Protasiou was situated in the Strategion neighborhood, to the northwest of the city center. Christopher also refers to Protasiou as his neighborhood in poem 36.12.

115. To his friend Nikephoros, who had sent him cakes around the time of the Broumalia

The Broumalia was an ancient Roman feast in honor of Dionysus held at the end of November. Although officially condemned, it remained popular throughout the Byzantine period. See *ODB* 1:327–28.

117. About the rose perfume he had sent to the monk Athanasios

The acquisition of the "fragrance of the fathers," both literally and figuratively, was commonly referred to as one of the goals of spiritual discipline in the Byzantine Church.

119. On the grave of the priest Theophilos

6   An allusion to Genesis 1:26.

8   The motif of inescapable death is a common one on grave epigrams, ancient and Byzantine.

120. To the monks of the monastery of Manuel

The monastery of Manuel was founded in the ninth century. It was situated in Constantinople, but it is not known exactly where. See Janin, *EglisesCP,* 320–22.

121. On Saint James the Persian

James the Persian, or James the Mutilated, was a saint who lived in Persia in the fifth century. He suffered a particularly grisly martyrdom: he was gradually dismembered and then decapitated. See *Bibliotheca Sanctorum* VI (Rome, 1961–1970), 356–65, under "Giacomo l'Interciso."

122. On the spider

2   Adonai is a Hebrew name for God.

82   Euclid was an ancient Greek mathematician, living around 300

BCE in Alexandria. His work was hugely influential for Byzantine mathematics.

83   Mamertius is likely a mistake (by Christopher or by later scribes) for Mamurius Veturius, a blacksmith under the Roman king Numa Pompilius, who sculpted shields of Mars. He is mentioned by Plutarch, *Life of Numa Pompilius,* §13.

89   Archimedes and Archytas were ancient Greek mathematicians and pioneers of geometry. Archytas lived in the fourth century BCE, Archimedes in the third, both in Sicily.

94   In Exodus 31:1–11 and 35:30–36:1, it is related that Oholiab and Bezaleel, the most skilled artisans of Israel, built the Tabernacle.

97   There is a pun here, because the word *mitous* and the phrase *moi tous* sound the same in Byzantine pronunciation.

100   See note on line 94.

109   Sabaoth is a divine name in Hebrew, meaning "Lord of hosts."

123. On the Nativity of Christ

Christopher plays here with the double meaning of humility as a condition (the lowest level of existence, personified by the humble shepherds) and as a virtue (the highest quality of Christ incarnate).

124. . . . friends . . . on the first day of the month

The *kalandai* or calends (referred to in l. 10) were the first day of the Roman year (that is, the beginning of January), and were an occasion for celebrations and exchanges of gifts. See *ODB* 1:367–68.

126. On the Ascension

This appears to be an epigram on an image of the Ascension of Christ, depicting an enthroned Christ in a mandorla, rising to Heaven.

127. On the casts of the fishing net that he bought

1   The Propontis is the ancient name for the Sea of Marmara, the enclosed body of water between Thrace and Asia Minor, connected to the Aegean Sea through the Hellespont and the Black Sea through the Bosporos. Some Byzantine texts, however, use the term for the Bosporos itself, and this could also apply here.

128. On the . . . in the . . . on the feast of the Holy Apostles

This poem is written on the occasion of the banquet traditionally given on the feast day of the Holy Twelve Apostles (June 30).

3–6   Christopher refers here to the Feeding of the Five Thousand (Matthew 14:13–21; Mark 6:30–44; Luke 9:10–17; John 6:1–14). Christ breaks off pieces from five loaves of bread and two fish and distributes them to his disciples. They give them in turn to a hungry throng of people, who are all fed.

130. On the hospitals and the sick people there; hexameters

Byzantine hospitals *(xenones)* were not only places for healing the sick but also shelters for the poor.

6   Hippocrates and Galen were two medical authorities from antiquity who remained hugely influential in Byzantine times.

131. On the owl, hooting . . . and keeping him awake

25   The "Third Odes" refer to a portion of the *orthros* (matins), the liturgical service in the early morning.

132. On the imperial notary Constantine, who had said that he loathed the mud and for that reason did not leave his house

6   Genesis 2:7 states that God made Adam from dust.

133. On the Holy Forty Martyrs, painted in
various postures; hexameters

The Forty Martyrs of Sebasteia were put to death by being forced to stand all night in an icy lake. See also poem 106.

134. On the rich man who buried his gold

1   See, for example, *CPG* 1:230, Diogenianus 3.83.

135. To the monks of the Proedros monastery about the sturgeons

The monastery of the Proedros is known only from two seals; see Eric McGeer, John Nesbitt, and Nicolas Oikonomides, eds., *Catalogue of Byzantine Seals at Dumbarton Oaks and in the Fogg Museum of Art,* vol. 5 (Washington, D.C., 2005), nos. 89.1–2.

136. . . . of the procession, the notaries

This poem was written for the occasion of a festive procession of notary students, held on October 25, the feast day of their patron saints, the martyrs Markianos and Martyrios, two secretaries *(notarioi)* of Saint Paul I, bishop of Constantinople (d. ca. 351). According to Byzantine sources, Markianos and Martyrios died in Constantinople around 342 (see also l. 4). The twelfth-century canon-law specialist Theodore Balsamon reports that this yearly parade was forbidden by the patriarch Loukas Chrysoberges (1156–1169), especially because of its subversive and carnivalesque elements. The poem is itself one of the most important sources about this festival, describing how the students and teachers dressed up for a colorful and role-subverting parade. Christopher appears to chide them for playing roles and contrasts the one-day event with the normal state of affairs during the rest of the year.

The term *"notarios"* refers to a common and rather low bureaucratic function, mostly in the imperial chancellery; the translation "notary" is thus slightly anachronistic.

4 The festive procession led to the church of Markianos and Martyrios, situated in an unknown location close to the western walls of Constantinople; see Janin, *EglisesCP,* 377–78.

49 Common proverb; see Plato, *Phaedrus,* 241b.

108 This refers to *The Vain Jackdaw,* one of Aesop's fables (Perry, *Aesopica,* 101). A jackdaw put on feathers of other birds in order to look more beautiful than he really was.

139. On the Holy Innocents massacred by Herod

The Holy Innocents were the infants massacred in Bethlehem by the Jewish king Herod upon hearing that a newborn would topple his reign (Matthew 2:16–18).

140. On the wife of the general Leo

The identity of this Leo is not known.

141. On the book of Saint John Chrysostom, the so-called *Pearls*

The *Pearls* of John Chrysostom are a selection of homilies of this fourth-century Church Father. See Karin Krause, *Die illustrierten Homilien des Johannes Chrysostomos in Byzanz* (Wiesbaden, 2004), 81 and 171.

142. To the *protospatharios* Niketas, about his eye disease

The title of *protospatharios* referred to a high-ranking court office.

10 The "disciples of Asklepios" is a term for physicians.

143. On the statue of Hercules that stands in the palace of Aretai

The palace of Aretai was built (or restored) by Romanos IV Diogenes (1068–1071). It may have been located at the southern end of the land walls.

See Janin, *Constantinople byzantine,* 406, and Henry Maguire, "Gardens and Parks in Constantinople," *Dumbarton Oaks Papers* 54 (2000): 254–56.

144. On Saint Bonifatios because of his laughter after his beheading

Saint Bonifatios (feast day December 18; not to be confused with a saint of the same name, Boniface, better known in Western Christianity) was martyred at Tarsus under Diocletian, after undergoing a sudden conversion from debaucher to Christian. An early saint's life indeed states that after the beheading Bonifatios's head laughed, when shown to his erstwhile companions; see Thierry Ruinart, ed., *Acta martyrum sincera et selecta* (Verona, 1731), 254, §15.

JOHN MAUROPOUS

1. Preface to the entire book

This poem is meant as a preface to Mauropous's collected works (poems, letters, orations), selected and assembled by the author himself in the manuscript now known as *Vaticanus graecus* 676.

Throughout this poem, Mauropous plays with the different meanings of some Greek words that have a rich tradition of ambiguity. Thus, the word *logos* can mean "words" (discourse, both written and spoken), "Word" (Son of God), and "reason" (see esp. ll. 5, and 35–37). It is impossible to convey all these meanings at once in the English translation. The word *metron* can mean "meter" (in a poetical sense), but also "moderation" in a moral sense (see ll. 1–2); our translation "measure" is meant to convey both meanings.

1   This aphorism is attributed to Cleobulus of Lindus, one of the
           Seven Sages of ancient Greece. Mauropous probably knew it
           from the funeral oration on Basil of Caesarea by Gregory of
           Nazianzos (or. 43, ch. 60.1.4).
10   Ecclesiastes 1:3.
37–39   An allusion to 1 Corinthians 3:12–15.

2. On the holy Nativity of Christ

In the manuscript, there is a general title above poem 2, "On large paintings of the Feasts: in the manner of an *ekphrasis*," that applies to poems 2 to 11. All these poems were on the Lord's Feasts, the events of Christ's life, as narrated by the New Testament, that were central to Byzantine Orthodox liturgy and iconography. The poems are here arranged according to the chronology of Jesus's life. See also *ODB* 2:868–69. An *ekphrasis* was a literary composition, in either prose or verse, that described works of art and architecture, feast days, gardens, and the like.

5	See Luke 2:14. Mauropous has rewritten the angels' doxology to include explicit reference to the Incarnation.
6–7	As often, Mauropous inserts here the words of an assumed viewer of the image.
17	An allusion to Matthew 2:9.
24	An allusion to 2 Corinthians 8:9.
26	Ἄνανδρος literally means "without a man." It normally means "unwed" when applied to women and "cowardly" when applied to men. Mary was married to Joseph when she gave birth but not when she conceived.
30	This old man is Joseph. In Matthew 1:19–20, it is said that Joseph was disturbed by Mary's pregnancy.

3. On the Baptism

The poem mirrors the Byzantine iconography of the Baptism, based on the relevant passages from the Gospels (Matthew 3:1–17; Mark 1:1–11; Luke 3:1–22; and John 1:19–34). The long-haired prophet is John the Baptist, the dove is a symbol of the Holy Spirit, and the river is the Jordan.

2	See Matthew 3:4 and Mark 1:6.
5	An allusion to John 1:15 and 30.
23	The pronoun "it" is used because the Greek word for spirit, *pneuma,* is grammatically neuter, but this in no way implies that the Spirit is any less a person than the Father and the Son.

25–27 Although not found in the canonical Gospels, some traditions
     hold that the Jordan stopped flowing at the Baptism of Christ,
     an idea inspired by Psalms 113(114):3. See, for instance, Roma-
     nos the Melode, *Second Hymn on the Epiphany,* prooimion,
     ed. and trans. José Grosdidier de Matons, *Romanos le Mélode.*
     Hymnes 2 (Paris, 1965), 270–71.

36   "This," that is, the Baptism of Christ.

4. On the Transfiguration

In Byzantine iconography of the Transfiguration, the three disciples of
Christ lie down or kneel because they cannot bear the light emitted by
Christ. Moses and Elijah flank Christ and converse with him. For the
Transfiguration, see also the notes to Christopher, poem 25.

5   Paul was struck by heavenly light on his way to Damascus, the
     event that made him convert to belief in Christ. See Acts 9:3.

5. On Lazarus

The Raising of Lazarus, reported in John 11, is commemorated on the day
before Palm Sunday. Middle Byzantine iconography of the scene depicted
Lazarus's sisters Mary and Martha supplicating Christ, who gestures to-
ward the shrouded figure of Lazarus, shown standing in a tomb or the
mouth of a cave. See also Christopher, poem 80.

6. On Palm Sunday

The Feast of Palm Sunday recalls the triumphal entry of Christ into Jeru-
salem (Sion). Many elements in Mauropous's poem (the garments spread
on the road, the palm branches, the donkey) are based on the relevant pas-
sages in the four gospels (Matthew 21:1–11; Mark 11:1–11; Luke 19:28–44;
and John 12:12–19) and are also present in middle Byzantine iconography
of the scene.

2   In Psalms 86(87):2, it is said that God loves the gates of Sion.

3–5   The wording here alludes to Matthew 21:5.

9–10   This refers to the raising of Lazarus, which happened the day before. For the crowd remembering this, see also John 12:17.

23–24   The word *pathos* (and the verb *pascho*) can mean both "passion" and "suffering," an ambiguity that can be only partly conveyed here by referring to the Passion of Christ (see also l. 28).

26   For these exclamations, see John 12:13.

7. On the Crucifixion

6   For the curse on anyone hanged on a tree, see Deuteronomy 21:23.

8   Christ's "beloved disciple" is John the Theologian.

14   This refers to Christ's exclamation "Father, why have you forsaken me?" (Matthew 27:46).

15   An allusion to John 8:29.

8. On the Resurrection

The Byzantine iconography of the Resurrection is based both on the canonical gospels and on apocryphal stories. Christ descended to hell, trampling its gates to pull out first Adam, the first ancestor, then the "old saints" (from the Old Testament), and finally the rest of humankind. Sometimes devilish figures, servants of Hades, are depicted (see ll. 24–25).

9   Τριέσπερον may be an allusion to Herakles Trihesperos (lit., "of three evenings"), so-called because his birth lasted three nights, and well known to the Byzantines because he had a conspicuous statue in Constantinople. According to the Bible, Christ died in the afternoon and was resurrected by the morning of the third day, so he was only dead during two nights.

10   This refers to the awakening of Lazarus, which happened four days after the latter's death. See John 11:39.

12   At Christ's Resurrection, the tombs of the old saints broke up and they awakened again; see Matthew 27:52. The term "forefathers" refers to Adam and Eve, dragged up from Hades by Christ.

9. On the Appearance to the Disciples

The "Touching" is the Byzantine term for this Feast of the Lord, which in English is commonly called the Appearance to the Disciples or the Doubting of Thomas. The disciples had gathered behind closed doors after Christ's death, when suddenly, to their amazement, Christ appeared in their midst. Thomas doubted Christ's resurrection until he could touch his side (John 20:19–29).

4   The disciples had shut themselves behind closed doors; see John 20:19.

8   The disciple Thomas is meant here. With the phrase "eloquent speaker," Mauropous perhaps refers to Thomas's defiant statements in John 20:25.

10. On the Ascension

Christ's Ascension, forty days after his death, is described in Acts 1:9–11. Most Byzantine representations of the Ascension include Christ ascending in a cloud, with his disciples and his mother, the Virgin Mary, looking upward at him.

11. On Pentecost

The story of Pentecost is related in Acts 2. The Holy Spirit descended upon the apostles in a rush of wind and tongues of fire. In the Byzantine iconography of the Pentecost, usually the apostles are gathered together, while fiery tongues descend upon them; sometimes the assembled masses are visible as well.

9–16   The Holy Spirit made the apostles preach in different languages; see Acts 2:4–11.

12. On Elijah being fed by the ravens

In 3 Kings 17:1–6, it is told that during a period of drought the Lord advised the prophet Elijah to go to a certain ravine, where he found water and where ravens fed him.

2   This refers to 4 Kings 1, where Elijah destroys the messengers of
         Ahaziah with fire from heaven.

13. On the picture of Saint Paul and Saint Chrysostom

Saint John Chrysostom (340/50–407), bishop of Constantinople from 398
to 404, was the most important Byzantine commentator on Paul's epistles
(see also notes to poem 14). Legend has it that when John was working on
his commentaries, Paul repeatedly came to him in a vision and whispered
wisdom in his ear. John's secretary, Proklos, was secretly witness to these
nightly visits. For the sources and illustrations of this scene in Byzantium,
see Karin Krause, *Die illustrierten Homilien des Johannes Chrysostomos in Byz-
anz* (Wiesbaden, 2004), 185–98. See also Margaret M. Mitchell, *The Heav-
enly Trumpet: John Chrysostom and the Art of Pauline Interpretation* (Louisville,
2002), 439, where an English translation of this poem can be found.

4–5   This is a reference to a vision of Paul described in 2 Corinthians
         12:2.
8   This refers to John's secretary, Proklos.

14. On Saint Chrysostom

This is an epigram on an image of John Chrysostom. It refers to Chrysos-
tom's "admonitions" *(paraineseis)* to live a sober and ascetic life, a theme in
many of the exegetical homilies on the Old and the New Testaments writ-
ten by or ascribed to Chrysostom. These often bore the title of λόγος
παραινετικός, "admonitory speech," and were widely read in Byzantium.

3   The image of fire builds further on the fire-breathing mouths
         (l. 1), a beloved image to describe overwhelming eloquence.

15. On Saint Gregory the Theologian

This is an epigram for an image of Saint Gregory of Nazianzos (329/30–ca.
390), called "the Theologian" by the Byzantines, a Cappadocian Church
father and bishop of Constantinople (380–381). He was author of many
orations, letters, and poems, all of them widely quoted, copied, and imi-
tated in Byzantium.

16. On Basil the Great

This is an epigram for an image of Saint Basil of Caesarea (ca. 329–379), called "the Great," a Cappadocian Church father. He wrote sets of rules for monks, and many other works that shaped Byzantine theology and religion.

17. On the three together

This is an epigram for an image of John Chrysostom, Gregory of Nazianzos, and Basil of Caesarea, the three subjects of poems 14 to 16. These three Church fathers are an extremely influential source for Byzantine theology and are venerated in the Orthodox Church as the Three Holy Hierarchs. Mauropous shows throughout his life and works a great attachment to these "teachers," which he expresses also in this poem, mentioning his own name (ll. 7–8). He wrote two encomia for them, and Byzantine sources mention that he initiated the Feast of the Three Holy Hierarchs, celebrated to this day on January 30. The first known joint depictions of the Three Holy Hierarchs date to Mauropous's lifetime. See Karpozilos, Συμβολή, 49–50 and 162–66.

7   This refers to John Mauropous himself.

18. On Saint Nicholas

This is an epigram on an image of Saint Nicholas, bishop of Myra, a very popular saint in Byzantium, revered for his miracles. He is always depicted as a bearded old man.

19. On Saint Constantine in Kamilas

The subject of this poem cannot be Constantine the Great or Constantine the Jew, but is apparently an unknown Saint Constantine, whose holiness was recognized only posthumously as a result of his miracles. The word καμηλῷ in the title does not refer to a camel, but to the place-name Kamilas (Καμιλᾶς). This was a building belonging to the Great Imperial Palace (see Janin, *Constantinople byzantine*, 114). This seems corroborated by the text of the poem, which clearly points to imperial veneration of the saint (see l. 6).

20. On the weeping Mother of God

In Byzantine iconography of the middle Byzantine period, a mourning Mother of God is portrayed in scenes of the Crucifixion and Deposition (the latter somewhat later than Mauropous's lifetime). The depiction of tears, however, is rare in middle Byzantine art. See Henry Maguire, "The Depiction of Sorrow in Middle Byzantine Art," *Dumbarton Oaks Papers* 31 (1977): 123–74.

21. On the Holy Anargyroi

This is an epigram on an image of the Holy Anargyroi (lit., "penniless ones"), saints venerated as healers and physicians who did not ask for payment, such as Kyros and John, Sampson, and Panteleemon. The allusion here is most likely to the saints Kosmas and Damian, who in the most common version of their legend were brothers.

22. On Saint Paul dictating, and Luke and Timothy standing by him and writing

Not much is known about the Byzantine iconography of Paul dictating to secretaries, although there are some images of Paul dictating to Luke. Timothy is mentioned as an aide in Romans 16:21.

23. On the funeral of Chrysostom and the picture of Adelphios

This epigram is related to an episode from the life of Saint John Chrysostom (see also poems 13–14), presented in some hagiographical texts. When the saint was sent into exile, he was received by Adelphios, the bishop of Koukoussos in Armenia. When news of John's death later reached Adelphios, he was greatly saddened, until in a vision he saw John standing next to the throne of God. See the encomium by Kosmas Vestitor, ed. Konstantinos I. Dyobouniotis, "Κοσμᾶ Βεστίτορος ἀνέκδοτα ἐγκώμια εἰς

Χρυσόστομον," Ἐπετηρὶς Ἑταιρείας Βυζαντινῶν Σπουδῶν 2 (1925): 50–83, esp. 61–62.

24. On the archangel Michael

Byzantine epigrams on images of the archangel Michael frequently exploit the idea that, as an angel, Michael was immaterial; see also Christopher, poem 112.

25. On the embrace of Peter and Paul

Paul persecuted Christians in his earlier years as the Pharisee Saul. Three years after his dramatic conversion to Christianity on the road to Damascus, he went to Jerusalem to visit Peter (Galatians 1:18–20). The embrace of Paul and Peter on this occasion is a common theme in Byzantine iconography, and the two are often depicted together.

9   Acts 9:1.

12   Paul was considered the apostle to the Gentiles, and Peter the apostle to the Jews.

26. On the Savior

4   George was the brother of Michael IV the Paphlagonian, the emperor who reigned from 1034 to 1041. See also Christopher, poem 18. George evidently commissioned a depiction of Christ as Pantokrator. The verb "to tend," *georgein*, puns on George's name.

27. Preface to the oration on the Dormition of the Virgin

This poem served as prologue to Mauropous's oration on the Dormition of the Virgin (or. 183).

1–2   These lines, with very minor adjustments, quote Euripides, *Hippolytus* 73–74, a favorite passage for Byzantine poets.

30   This line suggests that Mauropous lived close to a church dedicated to the Holy Virgin. Note that poem 28.18–20 indicates

that he also lived near a church of the Archangels. There are so
many churches in Constantinople dedicated to the Holy Vir-
gin and the Archangels that any hypothesis as to the location
of Mauropous's house must remain inconclusive.

28. Preface to the Oration on the Angels

This poem is a prologue to Mauropous's Oration on the Angels (or. 177).

18–20   See the note to poem 27.30.

29. On the orations of the Theologian that are not read aloud

Among the discourses of Gregory of Nazianzos, called "the Theologian" in
Byzantium, sixteen were regularly read on fixed feast days during the ec-
clesiastical year. The other twenty-six were not regularly read aloud during
services, and in some manuscripts we indeed find the title "orations that
are not read (aloud)." See Karpozilos, Συμβολή, 83–84, and Justin Mossay,
"La collection des discours «non-lus-à-date-fixe» dans le Ms. de New York
Gordan Goodhart Gr. 44," in *II. Symposium Nazianzenum,* ed. Justin Mos-
say (Paderborn, 1983), 15–21. This poem seems to be an epigram for a man-
uscript containing this group of orations.

9–10   An allusion to Matthew 5:15–16.

30. Preface to the laws

This poem perhaps served as a preface for a new edition of a law book.

31. On an illuminated gospel book in uncials

This poem is a book epigram for a gospel book sponsored by the emperor
Constantine IX Monomachos (mentioned at ll. 38–39).

16   This refers to the so-called liturgical majuscule (uncial), a script
       imitating older majuscule scripts, which was often used in lux-
       urious middle Byzantine gospel books.

22   The publican Zacchaeus was so short that he had to climb up a
       tree to see Jesus, who asked him for hospitality (Luke 19:1–10).

23   In Matthew 8:20 and Luke 9:58, Jesus says that foxes have their holes, while he himself has no place to rest his head.

39   This likely refers to Monomachos's earlier exile under the emperor Michael IV.

59–60   This refers to Saint George, the personal patron saint of Monomachos. George is commonly called the "victorious."

32. On a golden Crucifixion

This is an epigram designed to be inscribed on or near a depiction of the Crucifixion of Christ that was made of gold.

3   The gold refers to the betrayal of Christ by Judas (although, strictly speaking, Christ was betrayed for silver).

         "In his image" is an allusion to Genesis 1:26.

33. Against the man who criticized the verse "sold for gold," because the preposition is not rightly construed

This poem revolves around a grammatical issue in the foregoing poem (32). Apparently, a reader observed that the verb "sell" (πιπράσκω/πέρνημι) should govern a plain genitive case, and should not be followed by the preposition ἀντί, as Mauropous had written (see, indeed, l. 3 of poem 32). In poem 33, Mauropous addresses his critic and defends his choice in using the preposition ἀντί to represent the betrayal of Christ as a sale. Since Greek grammar is the subject of the poem, we have chosen not to translate some Greek terms, since the English cannot express the distinction between a plain genitive of price and a construction with a preposition.

1   This is Judas, the disciple who betrayed Jesus.

8   This was a proverbial expression: the Greek speaks about a "trough."

15–16   *Anti chrysou* means "for gold," while *chrysou* is the genitive of "gold."

18   Thales, the pre-Socratic philosopher from Miletus, was known for being obscure.

21   This is the preposition ἀντί that Mauropous has used.

25   *prathenai chrysiou* means "to sell for a piece of gold."

31   For the phenomenon of *schedos* (pl. *schede*) and *schedographia,* a grammatical school exercise, see notes to Christopher, poem 9. *Schede* gained a reputation for being riddle-like.

32   Mauropous puns on the adverb *scheden,* which means "slowly," and resembles the word *schedos*. He uses it again at line 34.

45   That is, the argument of clarity and the argument of being attested.

49–50 Mauropous uses here the word *logos* and its cognates/derivatives in different meanings.

34. Against those who versify in an inappropriate manner

This entire poem plays on the two different meanings of the word *metron:* on the one hand, it can mean "moderation," in an ethical sense; on the other hand, "meter," in a poetical sense (and for intellectuals like Mauropous, limited to prosodical meter). We have tried to reflect this ambiguity by translating *metron* with "measure." The person who is addressed here had apparently written a poem that did not have any moderation: either it was inappropriate in length or content (which seems implied by the title of the poem), or it contained metrical shortcomings, or both. One can also see in verse 5 a reference to an "unmeasured meter," by which Byzantines often referred to political verse, because this meter is not based on prosody, but purely on accentual rhythm.

1   This aphorism is attributed to Cleobulus of Lindus, one of the Seven Sages of ancient Greece. See also notes to Mauropous 1.1.

6   See Pindar, fragment 105a, in *Pindari carmina cum fragmentis,* Pars II, ed. Herwig Maehler (Leipzig, 1975), 95.

9   In this verse, *logos* is first used in its sense "word," then in its sense "reason."

35. Funeral verses for his friend Michael the deacon

Michael was deacon of the Hagia Sophia church in Constantinople, often called the Great Church (see l. 1). Several seals are preserved from the period of Mauropous's lifetime that belonged to deacons of this church named Michael.

11–12   See James 1:17, a phrase repeated in the Byzantine liturgy.

36. Funeral verses for Proteuon

The designation *proteuon* is problematic. Appearing first as an office for provincial commanders, it might have become a family name in the eleventh century; see Jean-Claude Cheynet, "Official and Non-Official Power," in *Fifty Years of Prosopography: The Later Roman Empire, Byzantium and Beyond,* ed. Averil Cameron (Oxford, 2013), 137–51, esp. 141. A Theodore calling himself "Proteuon" or "*proteuon,*" living during Mauropous's lifetime and having some higher offices, is known from several seals (see *PBW,* Theodore 20127, with further bibliography). In the titles of the other, adjacent funerary poems in Mauropous's highly uniform collection (poems 35, 37, 38), the office of the deceased is always mentioned, which suggests that in this poem "*proteuon*" likewise designates an office. However, the vocabulary in line 39 seems to hint at the name (κλῆσις) Proteuon. We are here following the interpretation that Proteuon is a family name.

7   We can infer from this verse that the first name of the deceased was Theodore ("gift of God").

38   The Greek for "prevailing" is *proteuon,* a pun on Theodore's surname or title.

40   "A shadow's dream" is a quotation from Pindar, *Pythia* 8.94. It is often used in Byzantine funerary literature.

41   This echoes "vanity of vanities," a familiar motif in Byzantine funerary literature, taken from Ecclesiastes 1:2.

46   An allusion to Genesis 3:19.

37. Funeral verses for the master of archives

From lines 4 and 40 we can infer that the name of the deceased was John, just like Mauropous. A *chartophylax* was an ecclesiastical official who served as head of the archives in the patriarchate or in a monastery. He also held other important responsibilities.

12   See 2 Corinthians 12:2.

47   See Zechariah 11:2. "The cedar has fallen" is a direct quotation. For "the pine must grieve," Mauropous has rewritten the biblical verse, changing ὀλολυξάτω πίτυς to πίτυς στεναζέτω.

38. Funeral verses for the *vestarches* Andronikos

The poems refer to a funerary image at the grave of the *vestarches* Andronikos, eulogized in this poem and the following one.

This Andronikos is not known otherwise. *Vestarches* was an honorific title conferred on some generals and judges; see *ODB* 3:2162. The reference to "laws" in line 2 of this poem and in line 11 of poem 39 suggests that he was a judge.

3   In Greek, there is a pun on the word *kosmos,* which means both "world" and "jewel."

42. On a common graveyard

1   With this "mother," probably a personification of the Earth (female *ge* in Greek) is meant.

43. Epigram on Plato and Plutarch

This celebrated epigram is often quoted to illustrate the approach of Byzantine learned men to the ancient pagan heritage.

2   This may refer to Matthew 23:33.

8   An allusion to 1 Timothy 2:4.

44. On the daily liturgy of the Hagia Sophia

For the reinstatement of a daily liturgy in the church of Hagia Sophia by Constantine IX Monomachos, see John Skylitzes, *A Synopsis of Byzantine History, 811–1057,* trans. John Wortley (Cambridge/New York, 2010), 444.

1–2   This refers to the continuous worship of the Ark of the Cove-

3   nant established by David (1 Chronicles 16:4–36). The "shadow of the law" refers to the Old Testament in general.
"The truth," that is, the Christian church of Holy Wisdom.

45. More verses

1–2   This can refer to several passages in Psalms, for example, 70(71):8; 144(145):2.

46. On the golden bull of the Lavra

A chrysobull *(chrysoboullon)* was a document signed by the emperor (as l. 12 implies) and sealed with a gold seal at the bottom (see l. 9); hence its name. Here Lavra most likely refers to the Great Lavra on Mount Athos, founded in 963 by Athanasios of Athos. It is possible that this poem was designed to accompany Constantine IX's chrysobull of 1052 for the Great Lavra, placing the monastery under the guardianship and protection of John, the keeper of the inkwell; see *ODB* 2:1190.

47. On his own home, when he sold and left it

This poem and the following may be connected to Mauropous's appointment as a metropolitan in Euchaïta (see Introduction), and his return to Constantinople much later (probably after 1075). The nostalgia for a life in seclusion (l. 53) corresponds with the other autobiographical texts (poems 91 to 93, and several letters) that Mauropous wrote at this pivotal moment in his life. But for doubts, see Karpozilos, *Letters,* 18–19.

48. When he recovered his house

4   If the hypothesis is correct that this poem along with the previous one was written on the occasion of Mauropous's return to Constantinople after his tenure as a metropolitan in Euchaïta, this can refer to Michael VII Doukas, but the exact chronology of events is unclear.

49. On a depiction of the holy fathers,
among whom was also Theodoret

The subject of this poem is Theodoret of Cyrrhus, an important theologian living in the fifth century. Theodoret held an ambiguous status: he was criticized by his antagonists (chiefly Cyril of Alexandria) for not doing enough to condemn the heretical teachings imputed to Nestorios. Therefore, his writings were condemned as heretical at the second council of Ephesus (449). At the same time, his writings and exegetical commentaries were highly influential.

This poem most probably describes an image of the Church fathers. Theodoret was only rarely included, but there are some contemporary miniatures (mostly in manuscripts with commentaries on Paul's letters) where he is depicted alongside other Church fathers. See for instance the manuscript *Parisinus graecus* 224, fol. 7 (tenth or eleventh century), where a lemma identifies Theodoret.

The verbs for "depicting" in this poem need not be taken literally: instead of doing the painting himself, the poet rather refers to the commissioning of an image.

9   This refers to Cyril of Alexandria, Theodoret's most important antagonist.

50. On the *typikon* of the Lavra

A *typikon* is a foundation document of a monastery, stipulating the regulations by which the monastery should function. There is indeed evidence that Mauropous founded a monastery of Saint Theodore in Paphlagonia and wrote the *typikon* for it (see Karpozilos, Συμβολή, 88), for which this poem would be the preface. It is also possible that the poem alludes to a *typikon* for the Great Lavra on Mount Athos (see poem 46). The *typikon* for that monastery was written, however, by its founder, Athanasios the Athonite, in the tenth century. Constantine IX Monomachos had a *typikon* prepared for the entire monastic community of Athos in 1045; see *BMFD*, vol. 1, no. 15.

51. On the man who ripped apart his own manuscript

It is impossible to ascertain the identity of the person attacked in this and the following poem.

4   The expression "wolves of Arabia" is to be found in the Septuagint: Habbakuk 1:8 and Zephaniah 3:3. It is a mistranslation from the Hebrew.

53. On the written insults against the emperor and the patriarch

It was common in Byzantium to attack enemies with defamatory pamphlets (often poems). The emperor and the patriarch mentioned here are probably Constantine IX Monomachos (1042–1055) and Michael Keroularios (1043–1058).

6   An allusion to Psalms 104(105):15.

13   Momus was the Greek god who personified satire, censure, and blame.

19–20   Compare, for example, the proverb in *CPG* 2:763, ὁ τρώσας ἰάσεται.

54. When he made his first acquaintance with the ruling family

This poem describes the introduction of Mauropous to the court of Constantine IX Monomachos, his purple-born wife Zoe, and her sister Theodora, oldest descendant of the dynasty.

28–33   This refers to Exodus 34:29–35. The face of Moses was radiant because he had seen the Lord, and not wanting to show this glory to the people of Israel, he put a veil over his face whenever he reported his conversations with God to them.

48   This refers to Genesis 1:26.

88–104   This seems to refer to courtiers controlling access to the emperor.

90   A Gorgon was a mythological creature, depicted as a woman with hair of living snakes.

92   Cerberus was the three-headed mythological dog guarding the underworld.

93   Brimo is an epithet applied to goddesses connected with the underworld.

97   The strange wording is due to the allusion to Hebrews 1:14 (λειτουργικὰ πνεύματα).

106   An allusion to Genesis 3:24.

117–18   This refers to the story of the three men who were thrown into the blazing furnace by King Nebuchadnezzar (Daniel 3). A fourth man miraculously appeared, saving the three men. Mauropous alludes to the fact that there were three rulers at this moment: Constantine IX Monomachos together with his wife (Zoe) and her sister (Theodora).

124   This refers to Zoe, who in contemporary court rhetoric is often represented as the moon.

127   Zoe means "life" in Greek.

128–29   This refers to Theodora, who in contemporary court rhetoric is often represented as a star.

55. For the empresses

This poem is addressed to Zoe and Theodora, the two daughters of the deceased emperor Constantine VIII and the only two legitimate ("purple-born") descendants of the Macedonian dynasty. After Constantine IX Monomachos gained the throne by marrying Zoe, she and Theodora were considered coempresses. This poem compares Constantine Monomachos to the sun, Zoe to the moon, and Theodora to a star, as is often done in imperial rhetoric of the period. Mauropous addresses Theodora at the beginning, and then Zoe from verse 10.

1–2   These two lines are in fact an epigram on the poem, which only begins at verse 3. This is made clear by the visually distinctive script of the first two lines and the bigger initial at the beginning of verse 3 in Mauropous's manuscript.

21   Mauropous alludes here to Zoe's name, which means "life."

27   The idea of "another self" (originally an Aristotelian notion) is
      often used in Byzantine rhetoric for close bonds between hu-
      mans.

56. On the commemoration day of Saints Sergios and Bacchos, when they also sent gifts

The church of Saints Sergios and Bacchos (the modern Küçükayasofya)
was situated close to the imperial palace. Every year, on the feast of the
saints, October 7, a solemn procession was held. This probably provided
the occasion for this poem, which seems to have accompanied a gift sent
by the church to the emperors as part of an invitation to join the celebra-
tion of the feast day (see ll. 25–28 and 31–36). Sergios and Bacchos were
popular warrior saints. See Janin, *EglisesCP*, 451–54.

8   The church was founded by Justinian I.

57. On the image of the emperor in Euchaïta

Euchaïta was a city in Pontus (present day northern Turkey) where Mauro-
pous became a metropolitan around 1050 (see also the Introduction). This
poem celebrates a gift from the emperor Constantine IX Monomachos to
the city, made through an imperial edict.

An English translation of the poem can be found in Mango, *Art of the
Byzantine Empire*, 220. The poem is also discussed in Karpozilos, "Biogra-
phy," 51–52, which reprints Mango's translation.

6   "The golden pillar" is an allusion to Pindar, *Olympian Odes* 6.1–2.
      It was a very familiar image for Byzantine authors. Here, it re-
      fers to the chrysobull.

7   A chrysobull (*chrysoboullos logos,* or "golden bull" in Western par-
      lance) was an imperial document; see also notes to Mauropous,
      poem 46.

10   The patron saint of Euchaïta was Saint Theodore Teron.

58. On the emperor's reliquary of the wood of the True Cross

This poem was an epigram on a reliquary containing a relic of the True Cross, belonging to the emperor Constantine IX Monomachos. Numerous pieces of wood were in circulation that were said to belong to the cross on which Christ died. The poem also refers to Constantine Monomachos's namesake, Constantine I the Great, who saw the sign of the cross on the eve of the decisive battle against his opponents at the Milvian Bridge, in 312.

59. On Saint Theophylact

Saint Theophylact of Nikomedeia (d. ca. 840; feast day, March 8) was a saint who opposed iconoclasm and performed many charitable deeds. His name literally means "guarded by God."

60. Riddle on the ship, as if said by someone else

The addition "as if said by someone else" in the title likely refers to the polemic in poem 61 (see notes to that poem).

61. To the person who presented the same riddle in other words and as another riddle

This poem accuses someone of plagiarizing Mauropous's poem 60.

6   This line was traditionally thought to be the first iambic verse, uttered by a woman named Iambe when someone overthrew her tub (*skaphe*), a word that can also mean "skiff," here of course referring to the subject of Mauropous's poem 60.

10   The Pythia was the priestess prophesying at the oracle of Delphi.

11   There is a pun here on the words for "original" (*kainos*) and "arid" (*kenos*), which were pronounced the same way in Byzantine Greek.

12   There is a pun here on the words for "hero" *(heros)* and "idle talk" *(leros)*.

62. On the blood of the Lord

This poem is an epigram on a relic of the blood of Christ. Relics with the Holy Blood were to be found in several places in Constantinople. Perhaps this one was kept in a church devoted to the Archangels.

63. On the Mother of God, when she revealed herself during sleep

This poem, and the next one, imply that the Virgin appeared to some people (the emperor?) in a dream or vision. Given the more exact references provided by poem 64, the historical events alluded to here may have taken place in 1043, during the reign of Constantine IX Monomachos: the rebellion of George Maniakes in the West and the attack of the Rus' on Constantinople immediately thereafter (see the references to "west" and "east" here in l. 5). See the notes to poem 64.

64. On the same

This poem gives more information about the historical events also alluded to in poem 63. These events took place in 1043. The "murderer" who was killed in the West (l. 2) can be identified with George Maniakes, who rebelled with a part of the army of the West and was killed near Thessalonike. After this victory, Constantine IX Monomachos immediately had to deal with a direct attack on Constantinople by a fleet of the Rus', which was defeated. This concurs with the references in lines 3 and 4 to barbarians defeated near the capital. For an account that also stresses the close connection between these two events, see Michael Attaleiates, *The History*, trans. Anthony Kaldellis and Dimitris Krallis (Cambridge, Mass., 2012), 33.

The reference to a painting here in line 6 suggests that the Holy Virgin appeared as an icon, or that the epigrams are primarily meant to celebrate an icon of the Virgin. Icons of the Holy Virgin (especially the so-called Blachernitissa) were carried on military campaigns to secure imperial victory and played an important role in imperial ideology and the personal devotions of the emperor.

65. On the two saints Theodore

There were two saints called Theodore: Theodore Teron and Theodore Stratelates. Both were warrior saints. They were frequently portrayed together; most likely they grew out of one original saint (see Nicolas Oikonomides, "Le dédoublement de Saint Théodore," *Analecta Bollandiana* 104 [1986]: 327–35). Theodore Teron was venerated in Euchaïta, the city where Mauropous was metropolitan.

66. On someone who was suddenly promoted

Many contemporary sources cite the suddenly increasing opportunities for social promotion during the reign of Constantine IX Monomachos.

11	This refers to Gregory of Nazianzos, *Oration* 19.4.
12	Perhaps an allusion to the famous saying of Heraclitus (see Plato, *Cratylus,* 402a).

67. On a grave

The first verse suggests that this grave was meant for three relatives or three close friends.

68. On a dictation exercise

For the *schedos,* see the notes to Christopher, poem 9. Mauropous's poem refers to a *schedos* contest between schools. This poem was written for the school of the Forty Martyrs, situated in Constantinople, and known otherwise for its zeal in *schedos* contests (see Lemerle, *Cinq études,* 229). On the Forty Martyrs, see the notes to Christopher, poem 106.

5	In this verse, there is a rare Greek word *(schideutes)* that only occurs in polemical poems, often connected with the *schedos.* We

have rendered it "dictation botcher"; however, its translation is uncertain.

69. On the bathhouse of Blachernai

The bathhouse of Blachernai was situated next to the famous church of the Theotokos of Blachernai, in the northwestern part of the city, where there was a spring. Emperors sometimes had a ceremonial bath in this bathhouse (*ODB* 1:293; Janin, *EglisesCP,* 161–71).

1   When the people of Israel were in the wilderness, Moses obtained water by striking a rock; see Exodus 17:1–7.

2   In 1 Corinthians 10:4, Paul refers to the above passage from Exodus, explaining that the rock giving water was Christ.

70. On the cinnabar writing of the dictations

This poem was written for an edition of *schede* made by the emperor Constantine IX Monomachos, an edition also mentioned in a letter of Michael Psellos (see Bernard, *Writing and Reading,* 264–65). Purple was the exclusive color of emperors. Cinnabar was used as a red pigment.

71. On the book for the liturgical services in the church of the victorious martyr

This poem and the following are epigrams for a book (likely a gospel book) offered to the church of Saint George of Mangana (see notes to Christopher, poem 95). As verse 6 suggests (but the wording is not unambiguous), an image representing the benefactors offering the book may have served as frontispiece to the manuscript. *Sinaiticus Graecus* 364 is an example of such a book depicting Monomachos and his coempresses as patrons.

4   Saint George, a warrior saint, was commonly represented as a victor.

8   This again refers to Zoe and Theodora (see notes to Mauropous, poem 55).

73. Dialogue verses on the Incorporeal One

The terms "incorporeal" and "archgeneral" (l. 7) refer to the archangel Michael, so this poem was meant as an epigram on an icon (or another representation) of the archangel Michael, donated by the empress Theodora. For the empress Theodora, see the notes to Mauropous, poem 54. The form of a dialogue is encountered frequently in Byzantine epigrams.

75. On an entreaty scene in which the emperor is lying prostrate at Christ's feet, as if spoken by the emperor

This type of entreaty scene, called a *deesis,* is an iconographical composition in which the Virgin Mary and Saint John the Baptist intercede with Christ. This scheme is sometimes supplemented with a supplicant donor, portrayed as kneeling, or lying prostrate, at Christ's feet.

This poem is the first in a series of four where an emperor (usually identified with Constantine IX Monomachos) entreats Christ, through the Virgin Mary and Saint John the Baptist. Each of the four actors is made to speak. Epigrams often consist of dialogues between the figures represented (see also poem 73).

An English translation of the poem can be found in Mango, *Art of the Byzantine Empire,* 220.

78. As if spoken by Christ

4   Matthew 25:23. Mauropous has changed the word order, presumably to fit the meter.

79. More verses to the Savior, as if spoken by the emperor

1   There may be a parallel here with 3 Kings 3:11, where God praises Solomon because he had not asked for any riches or for a long life.

80. On the icon in the monastery of Sosthenion

The monastery of the archangel Michael in Sosthenion was famous during the eleventh century. Sosthenion (mod. Istinye) is located on the western shore of the Bosporus (Janin, *EglisesCP*, 346–50). This poem is an epigram accompanying an icon that represents Christ crowning the ruling emperors, offered as a gift by the monks of the monastery. See also Georgios Tsantilas, "Ο Ιωάννης Μαυρόπους και η απεικόνιση των αυτοκρατόρων στο ναό του Αρχαγγέλου Μιχαήλ στο Σωσθένιο τον 11° αιώνα," in *Δελτίον της Χριστιανικής Αρχαιολογικής Εταιρείας* 26 (2005), 327–38, who argues that Michael VII Doukas is the emperor mentioned here (English synopsis on p. 338).

An English translation of the poem can be found in Mango, *Art of the Byzantine Empire*, 221.

81. Funeral verses on the grave of the emperor

It is not certain to which emperor these funeral verses refer, but Constantine IX Monomachos seems the most logical possibility. In any case, poems 81 to 85 seem to constitute one cycle, with the death of the same emperor as its subject.

13   This is a quotation from Gregory of Nazianzos, *Poem* 1.2.19, l. 9.

82. More verses, as if spoken by the emperor

3–4 An allusion to Matthew 16:26.
19   See Proverbs 10:16.
20   Mauropous juxtaposes life on earth with life in heaven.

83. More verses

9   An allusion to Psalms 118(119):73.

85. More verses

9–10 A repetition of lines 9 and 10 from poem 83.

86. On the icon of the three saints that he gave to the monk Gregory

Throughout his life and works, Mauropous showed a great concern and personal attachment to his "teachers" (l. 1), that is, the Three Hierarchs (Gregory of Nazianzos, John Chrysostom, and Basil of Caesarea). See also the notes to poem 17. We have no other information about the identity of the monk Gregory.

6   This namesake is Gregory of Nazianzos.

87. On the icon of the emperor and the patriarch

The poem most probably accompanied an icon depicting the emperor (probably Constantine IX Monomachos) and the patriarch (probably Michael Keroularios), together with representations of divine or saintly persons in a gesture of protection.

88. On the prophet Daniel

In the biblical book of Daniel, it is told that the eponymous prophet was thrown into a lion's den by the king of Babylon. Daniel miraculously survived. The poem puns on Leo's name, which is identical to the Greek word for "lion." This Leo (otherwise unknown) addresses a prayer (or makes a donation) to the prophet Daniel.

89. In defense of himself, addressed to Christ

This is the first in a series of poems with autobiographical (or apologetic) themes. While poems 89 and 90 generally deal with the opposition between a tranquil and an active life, from poem 91 (and especially 92) on, Mauropous's appointment as a metropolitan becomes the focus.

Throughout these poems, the concept *logoi* (here mostly just translated as "words") stands for learning and eloquence, as the hallmarks of the intellectual.

1–2   These verses recur throughout poems 89 and 90.

32   This metaphor echoes Basil of Caesarea's famous statement in his *Address to Young Men,* §4.

33   This idea has ancient roots, see Hesiod, *Shield of Heracles,* l. 395.

90. More verses about himself, addressed to Christ

This poem is similar to the following autobiographical poems in the collection, but there is no real dialogue, since "reason" speaks throughout, refuting suggestions allegedly coming from the opponent. See notes to poem 91, where the dialogic character is more clear.

91. To himself

This poem and the two following ones are constructed as inner dialogues between the rational and irrational part of the self. These parts are not named in Mauropous (only *logismos* in poem 92.7, which is here used in a positive sense). Mauropous's model, Gregory of Nazianzos, constructed poems "to himself" as dialogues between the soul *(psyche)* or emotions *(thymos)* and reason *(logos),* in a concept of the self that has Platonic roots. Reason speaks throughout most of this poem, with some interjections from soul or the emotions.

22–26   This refers to *The Vain Jackdaw,* one of Aesop's fables (Perry, *Aesopica,* 101). A jackdaw had put on feathers of other birds in order to look more beautiful than he was.

92. To himself

For the dialogic character of the poem, see notes to poem 91. Mauropous discusses the dangers of a successful life in human society; probably he alludes to his ordination as a metropolitan of Euchaïta (see also next poem). The division of speakers in the first lines is not entirely clear, but the bulk of the poem (starting from l. 10) is spoken by reason, with some interjections by the soul or the emotions. We tentatively attribute lines 1a, 2a, 3, 5a, 7, and 9 to *thymos* (emotions) and 1b, 2b, 4, 5b–6, 8 and 10f. to *logos* (reason)/the steersman.

58   This refers to a metaphor used in Matthew 5:15.

84–85 These two verses adapt a well-known phrase in Euripides, *Orestes*, 258–59.

93. Recantation of the previous words, after his ordination

This poem recants poem 92 (referred to by "these words" in l. 1). The poem implies that it was written after Mauropous's appointment as metropolitan of Euchaïta, while poem 92 was written before.

1   Mauropous adapts a phrase attributed to Stesichorus, transmitted in Plato, *Phaedrus*, 243a.

2   See *Iliad* 4.357 and *Odyssey* 13.254.

46–47 An allusion to Euripides, *Hecuba,* 958–60, with an adapted quotation of lines 959–60.

94. On the edict pertaining to the guardian of laws

This poem refers to the so-called *Neara* (lit., "new law"), written by Mauropous (no. 187 in Lagarde's edition). This was the foundation document of the law school of Saint George at Mangana, founded by Constantine IX Monomachos around 1047. With the *Neara,* the emperor appointed John Xiphilinos as *nomophylax,* the "guardian of laws," to preside over the newly founded law school.

95. On the second oration for the trophy-bearing saint

This poem refers to the two orations that Mauropous wrote for the inauguration of the church of Saint George of Mangana, founded by Constantine IX Monomachos. These orations for Saint George (known as the victorious saint), are numbered 181 and 182 in Lagarde's edition. Mauropous wrote 182 first, but at the last moment he replaced it with 181, and it is this version that was used for the feast of Saint George in 1047, which at the same time celebrated the recent Byzantine victory over the Pechenegs. As the poem indicates, oration 181 indeed takes over many elements from oration 182, especially toward the end.

96. When he gave up writing his chronicle

No other sources report that Mauropous wrote a historiographical work. Therefore, all conjectures about the exact circumstances of this poem are bound to remain speculative.

97. On the *menaia* donated in Euchaïta

A *menaion* is a liturgical book in the Orthodox rite, following day by day the fixed liturgical calendar, and containing the liturgical texts (primarily hymns) relating to the saints celebrated on that day.

5   This refers to Saint Theodore Teron, a soldier saint, patron of Euchaïta.

7   The book that in Christian tradition is thought to contain the names of the saved, based on Revelations 5:1 and 20:12.

98. On the same

4   The meaning of this verse is not entirely clear; perhaps Mauropous means that for the actual service they should make use of copies instead of the original.

99. On the corrected books

This poem perhaps refers to this very manuscript containing the complete works of Mauropous himself.

Bibliography

EDITIONS AND TRANSLATIONS

Anastasi, Rosario, trans. *Giovanni Mauropode, metropolita di Euchaita. Canzoniere.* Catania, 1984.

Bollig, Johannes, and Paul de Lagarde, eds. *Iohannis Euchaitorum Metropolitae quae in codice Vaticano graeco 676 supersunt.* Göttingen, 1882.

Crimi, Carmelo et al., trans. *Cristoforo di Mitilene. Canzoniere.* Catania, 1983.

De Groote, Marc, ed. *Christophori Mitylenaii Versuum variorum collectio Cryptensis.* Turnhout, 2012.

Kurtz, Eduard, ed. *Die Gedichte des Christophoros Mitylenaios.* Leipzig, 1903.

Mango, Cyril, trans. *Art of the Byzantine Empire 312–1453. Sources and Documents.* Pages 220–21. Toronto, 1986. [Christopher, poem 112; Mauropous, poems 57, 77, 80.]

SECONDARY LITERATURE

Bernard, Floris. *Writing and Reading Byzantine Secular Poetry (1025–1081).* Oxford, 2014.

Bernard, Floris, and Kristoffel Demoen, eds. *Poetry and Its Contexts in Eleventh-Century Byzantium.* Farnham, 2012.

Bianconi, Daniele. "'Piccolo assaggio di abbondante fragranza.' Giovanni Mauropode e il Vat. gr. 676." *Jahrbuch der Österreichischen Byzantinistik* 61 (2011): 89–103.

Crimi, Carmelo. "Motivi epigrammatici nei carmi sull' eco di Cristoforo di Mitelene." In *Graeca et Byzantina,* edited by Carmelo Crimi, 45–50. Catania, 1983.

———. "Recuperi cristoforei." *Bollettino della Badia Greca di Grottaferrata* 39 (1985): 231–42.

Demoen, Kristoffel. "Phrasis poikilê. Imitatio and Variatio in the Poetry

Book of Christophoros Mitylenaios." In *Imitatio - Aemulatio - Variatio. Akten des internationalen wissenschaftlichen Symposions zur byzantinischen Sprache und Literatur,* edited by Andreas Rhoby and Elizabeth Fischer, 103–18. Vienna, 2010.

de Stefani, Claudio. "Notes on Christophoros of Mytilene and Konstantinos Stilbes." *Jahrbuch der Österreichischen Byzantinistik* 58 (2008):45–52, at 45–48.

Follieri, Enrica. *I calendari in metro innografico di Cristoforo Mitileneo.* Brussels, 1980.

———. "Le poesie di Cristoforo Mitileneo come fonte storica." *Zbornik radova Vizantološkog instituta* 8 (1964): 133–48.

Janin, Raymond. *Constantinople byzantine: développement urbain et répertoire topographique.* 2nd ed. Paris, 1964.

Karpozilos, Apostolos. Συμβολή στη μελέτη του βίου και του έργου του Ιωάννη Μαυρόποδος. Ioannina, 1982.

———. "The Biography of Ioannes Mauropous Again." *Hellenika* 44 (1994): 51–60.

———. *The Letters of Ioannes Mauropus. Metropolitan of Euchaita.* Thessalonike, 1990.

Kazhdan, Alexander. "Some Problems in the Biography of John Mauropous." *Jahrbuch der Österreichischen Byzantinistik* 43 (1993): 87–111.

———. "Some Problems in the Biography of John Mauropous. II," *Byzantion* 65 (1995): 362–87.

Lauxtermann, Marc. "The Intertwined Lives of Michael Psellos and John Mauropous." In *The Letters of Psellos. Cultural Networks and Historical Realities,* edited by Marc Lauxtermann and Michael Jeffreys, 89–127. Oxford, 2017.

Lemerle, Paul. *Cinq études sur le XIe siècle byzantin.* Paris, 1977.

Livanos, Christopher. "Exile and Return in John Mauropous, Poem 47." *Byzantine and Modern Greek Studies* 32 (2008): 38–49.

———. "Justice, Equality and Dirt in the Poems of Christopher of Mytilene." *Jahrbuch der Österreichischen Byzantinistik* 57 (2007): 49–74.

Oikonomides, Nicolas. "L'évolution de l'organisation administrative de l'empire byzantin au XIe siècle." *Travaux et mémoires* 6 (1976): 126–52.

Perry, Ben Edwin. *Aesopica: A Series of Texts Relating to Aesop or Ascribed to Him or Closely Connected with the Literary Tradition That Bears His Name: Volume I: Greek and Latin Texts.* Urbana, Ill., 1952.

Index

Poems of Christopher of Mytilene are indicated with *C,* and those of John Mauropous with *M.*